Uncle John's BATHROOM READER® PLUNGES INTO HISTORY

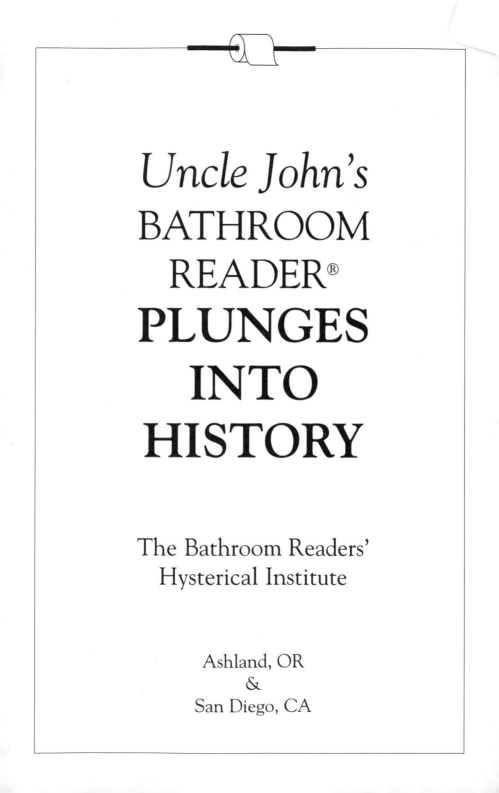

Uncle John's
BATHROOM
READER®
PLUNGES
INTO
HISTORY

The Bathroom Readers'
Hysterical Institute

Ashland, OR
&
San Diego, CA

For information, write
The Bathroom Readers' Hysterical Institute
5880 Oberlin Drive, San Diego, CA 92121

email: unclejohn@advmkt.com

Cover design by Michael Brunsfeld
San Rafael, CA (brunsfeldo@attbi.com)

ISBN: 1-57145-697-X

Library of Congress Catalog Card Number: 2001118782

Printed in the United States of America
First printing: September 2001
Second Printing: October 2001
Third Printing: December 2001
Fourth Printing: April 2002

10 9 8 7 6 5 4 02 03 04 05

v

Project Team:

Allen Orso, Publisher
JoAnn Padgett, Director, Editorial & Production
Allison Bocksruker, Project Manager
Elizabeth McNulty, Staff Editor
Cindy Tillinghast, Staff Editor
Georgine Lidell, Inventory Manager
Stephanie Spadaccini, Senior Project Editor
Susan Steiner, Project Editor

THANK YOU!

The Bathroom Readers' Hysterical Institute
sincerely thanks the people whose
advice and assistance made this book possible.

Jeff Altemus

Rudy Babauta

Bernadette Baillie

Victoria Bullman

Michael Brunsfeld

Dale Cornelius

Bruce Derkash

John Dollison

John Fritzenkotter

Laurel Graziano

John "J-Ho" Hogan

Gordon Javna

Jack Jennings

Paddy Laidley

Paula Leith

Dan Mansfield

Kathy Missell

Mana Monzavi

Pam Lopez-Morlett

Janet Nelson

Mike Nicita

Ellen O'Brien

Ken and Kelly Padgett

John Rowinski

Arnold Schmidt

Annette Sobel

Sydney Stanley

Kent Steigerwald

Charlie Tillinghast

Marty Vrabel

Cheri White

CONTENTS

A MOVING EXPERIENCE

It's a Gas 130

The Quest for Longitude 183

Life Insurance with Your Latte? . . .281

They Called Her "Lady Lindy" 319

ARTSY-FARTSY

When Readers Moved Their Lips . .31

Digitized History 32

Immanuel Kant Tries Comedy 165

Bad History! Bad! 214

Van Gogh: An Ear for Trouble 260

Unmasking Mona Lisa 383

AS THE WORLD TURNS

A Pox On Your House 5

Canada's Red Baron 8

The Mongol Horde 56

How Mosquitoes Changed History .176

History's Greatest Travel Bargain . .223

The Great Leap Backward 228

Anagrams 272

The Ancient City of King
Solomon? 273

Why Do They Call It the
Dark Ages? 278

When Childhood Was Born 297

With a Little Help from Barbarians 420

BOUDOIR, BATH & BEYOND

Dirty Secrets in the History of Hygiene
(Part I): Man on the Can 89

Dirty Secrets in the History of Hygiene
(Part II): Rub-a-Dub-Dub 153

Dirty Secrets in the History of Hygiene
(Part III): Smile 219

Class of the Head 285

CRUSADES & CRUSADERS

I Love a Crusade 21

The Crusade to End All Crusades .142

The Crusader Follies 239

Death of a Revolutionary 256

My Heroes! 276

Crusade of the Stars 286

The Crusade That Wasn't 409

Finally, the Last Crusades 467

DEAD ENDS

A Taste for the Unusual 148

What a Way to Go! Immortal, But
Dead .169

The Real Body Snatchers 220

Tombstone Territory 267

Here Lies 389

Grave Matters 417

Deathless Prose 447

Dear Departed: Burial Customs
and Curiosities 473

Goodbye Cruel World 484

DON'T QUOTE ME ON THAT

Proven Wrong by History: Part I . . .74

Proven Wrong by History: Part II .175

Historical Hindsights 227

Proven Wrong by History: Part III .296

FASHION VICTIMS

A Hair Piece 66

Makeup to Die For 120

Men in Skirts 186

Tie One On 232

Uncovering Underwear 324

Abe Lincoln, Harbinger of
Fashion? 399

These Boots Aren't Made
for Walking 427

FIGHTING WORDS

Them's Fightin' Words:
   Colonialism 18
Them's Fightin' Words:
   In the Trenches 101
Them's Fightin' Words: At Sea . . .253
Them's Fightin' Words: Korea 336

GIRLS JUST WANT TO HAVE FUN

Lady Killer 3
Buccaneer Babes 51
She Was Only a Pharaoh's
   Daughter... 108
Mata Hari, the Spy Who Wasn't . .200
Ladies First 401

HOAXES

World's Greatest Hoaxes,
   Plus One 39
An 1844 Flight Over the Atlantic?
   Who Said So! 99
Grey Owl 460

IT'S ALL ANCIENT HISTORY

7 Wonders of the Ancient World . .27
Port-a-Fortress 78
It's All Greek to Me 166
Stomped to Death by "Little
   Boots" 225
"Vandal-ized" 387
Rome at the Fall of the Empire . . .445

LAW & ORDER

The Code of Hammurabi 62
The Dreyfus Affair, and No, It's Not a
   Sex Scandal 116
Ye Olde Crime and Punishment . . .316
History's Hannibal Lecter 432
From Italy to Little Italy, the Mafia
   Comes to America 480

LET'S EAT

Food a Millennium Ago 191
Coffee Klatch 242
My Dinner With Attila 313
The Rich History of Chocolate . . .327
Fiesta! 358
Want Fries With That? 412
Don't Hold the Mayo! 426

MEDICINE

Pardon Me, Fritz—Is That My Leg
   Doing the Polka? 204
Breaking the Mold: The Discovery
   of Penicillin 206
Hippocrates, M.D. 311
Mr. Jenner and the Milkmaid 347
Nurse Nightingale 373
Dammit, Jim, I'm a Doctor! And a
   Medical Hobbyist! 440
Milk, Microbes, & Mad Dogs 450

MIXED BAG

How Short Was Napoleon? 59
The Hamilton Affair 114
Cowboys? We Call 'Em Sissies! . . .181
Hey, What About
   Those Freemasons? 197
The Ambling Room 244
Best List of Bests 325
Handicap? What Handicap? 368

MUSIC TO MY EARS

White Guys with Small Heads Didn't
   Invent the Banjo 13
What's So Big About Wagner? 87
Hitting the High Notes 124
Paganini Has Left the Building . . .146
Taking Note: Musical Notation . . .189
History's Hit Makers 374

PEOPLE-POURRI

Mother Goosed 46
Anna & the King: Fact or
  Fiction 138
Carousing Charisma 251
Gypsies: Tramps and Thieves? 330
Mister Sam, the Whiskey Man . . .333
Talking 'bout the Titanic 342
The Invasion of America 371
The Strange Constitution of
  Stonewall Jackson 390
Pop Was A Pope and I'm a
  Poisoner. Who Am I? 403
Listen, My Children. 405
Pocahontas: The Non-Disney
  Version 455

ROYAL FLUSH

Best Hideously Inbred Royal Family:
  The Hapsburgs 134
8 1/2 Not-so-Victorian Things About
  Queen Victoria 248
The Swan King's Castles 302
The Hunchback of Northern Fame:
  The Story of Richard III 352
Her Majesty's a Pretty Nice Girl . .359
The Adultery Awards 422

SAINTS & SINNERS

Pope-Pourri 43
The Pope was a Lady 202
Best Crackpot Religious Leader:
  Rasputin 339
Heavy Mettle 407
Saint 'Hood 437
Three Wise Men 462

SCIENCE

Hear About the Big Bang? 1
Better Living Through Alchemy . . .34
Breaking the Code: Cryptanalysis . .70
The Sticky Historian 258

Don't Let Your Daughters Grow
  Up to be Poets 290
Darwin's Cousin and the Apes 365

SPORTS

The Making of a Marathon 15
Nazi Olympics 127
The Olympics Exposed 194
The Game 459

STRANGE BUT TRUE

The Fish that Beat Napoleon 17
Without a Leg to Stand On 23
Peddling Pricey Petals 80
Deadly as Molasses in January 85
Waste of a Good Basketball Team .156
This Side Up 305
The King Who Stole the Congo . .344
Would it Kill You to Become
  Emperor of Mexico! 380
Before They Were Nazis 471

THE REAL WORLD

The Real Count Dracula 111
The Real Jekyll & Hyde 161
The Real Braveheart 209
The Real Robinson Crusoe 264
The Real Lady Godiva 348
Will the Real Shakespeare
  Please Take a Bow? 384
The Real Spartacus 413
The Real Captain Bligh 442

WAR—WHAT ARE WE
   FIGHTING FOR?

Shoot on a Shingle 38
Catcher, Lawyer, Linguist, Spy 75
The Longbow: Not For Sissies 96
Is This the Smell of Progress? 104
Hitler the Bum 122
I Ain't Giving Back That Medal . .140
Double-Crossed by a Dead Man . . .150

Monumental Waste of Effort:
  The Maginot Line 171
Most Lopsided War: Spanish-
  American War 237
The 100 Years' War 269
A Snowball's Chance 283
What Were the Wars of the Roses? 294
The Phantom Army 350
The Original Dogfights 452
The Battle of Trafalgar 477

WHAT A FIND!

Poles Apart 68
Cortès and the Feathered
  Serpent 132
It's Not Easy Being Marco Polo . . .178
The Real Legacy of Christopher
  Columbus 230
New World Order 279
Henry the Navigator 300
Who Conquered the North Pole? .356
Which Way Did They Go? 396

WHAT A GREAT IDEA!

Wear Computers Came From 11
Off With Their Heads! 82
The Monster That Philo Made . . .157
More Bounce to the Ounce 163
The Tooth About Dentures 212
To Hill and Gone 262
Magnificent Failure 292

WHEREWORDS: A QUIZ

WhereWords: A Quiz
  (His Closet) 60
WhereWords: A Quiz
  (The Bathroom) 94
WhereWords: A Quiz
  (Knight Life) 159
WhereWords: A Quiz
  (Countries of the World) 235
WhereWords: A Quiz
  (Cities of the World) 322

WhereWords: A Quiz
  (Her Closet) 394
WhereWords: A Quiz
  (The Kitchen Table) 435
WhereWords: A Quiz
  (Miscellaneous) 457

WORDPLAY

Being a Nosey Parker 92
Mesmerized 106
Riddles: A Serious Subject 308
Burning with Good Intentions 392
Spooner: The Man and
  His "Isms" 448

INTRODUCTION

Made it! We've finally reached the introduction, which is always the last stop on the Uncle John's Express before press time. And as always, it's been one heck of a ride.

As you probably know, we've put out one new *Bathroom Reader* each year since 1988. **Uncle John's All Purpose Extra-Strength** was our lucky thirteenth edition last year, and we're currently busting our hump to bring you the latest and greatest fourteenth edition this holiday season (t'anks, Santa).

After almost fourteen years of doing what we do best here at the BRI (and we're still doing it, don't you worry!), we decided that maybe it was time to flush out our system...a decision that brings us to our first Number Two in history.

For years, we've heard all you history buffs out there who kept bugging us for "bigger, better, more history, now!" So this year, in addition to our annual fall compendium of "All the Poop That's Fit to Print," we've busted our hump (our second hump?) to give you yet *another* (whew!) authoritative Uncle John's devoted entirely to...you guessed it...History.

In twenty-nine sections ranging all over the map, we've plumbed the depths of two millennia to bring you history at its best, funniest, and most interesting. Like the History Channel, but without the cheesy actors, **Uncle John's Plunges into History** shows you knights and ladies and the pots they peed in; saints and sinners and the bloody battles they fought; kings, queens, and in-betweens, in fact, the entire Royal Flush is represented; as are the real people and events that make up the most bizarre episodes you've never heard of. From the grueling tales of the food our ancestors ate, to the dirty secrets of historical hygiene (there's a whole 'nother meaning to "wrong end of the stick," friends), we think we've got it wiped.

We know that nobody, history buff or not, wants to lug a crusty old history tome to the throne, so we've selected all the best bits—sanitized for your protection—for your reading pleasure, with plenty of full-length articles for longer sittings. So here it is—our first attempt at packing 500-plus pages of the same great stuff, only all about one (well, one pretty big) category: history.

And now it's up to you, our loyal readers, to let us know what you think. This is a new thing for us, and we count on you to share your opinions with us. If there's one thing we've learned in all our years at the BRI, it's that our readers know what they like and they like to let us know too. Keep those letters and email a-comin'. We aim to please.

Now, join us, won't you, as Uncle John's makes history.

Your pal,

Uncle Al and the Out-House Staff, a.k.a.

the Bathroom Readers'
Hysterical Institute

P.S. Check out our website at www.bathroomreader.com. And email us at unclejohn@advmkt.com. We'd love to hear from you.

HEAR ABOUT THE BIG BANG?

Believe it or not.

According to most scientists, our universe started out as this eensy-weensy piece of matter and metamorphosed into an ever-expanding universe. For SUV owners and people of great girth, this is welcome news. Creation scientists, on the other hand, don't believe it happened. And you generally can't convince them that maybe God set off the explosion.

HUH?
Explanations of the Big Bang usually cause headaches among people who can't program VCRs. That's because the theory states, in essence, "A really long time ago there was nothing, and suddenly there was a whole lot of nothing, which was actually something, but nobody could really see it, even if there was somebody there, which there wasn't." Ouch!

The theory depends chiefly on the early theoretical work of Albert Einstein, the man who invented the "Bad Hair Day."

THE MAN WHO HEARD THE BANG
Russian-American physicist George Gamow announced the Big Bang Theory in 1948. It was based on Einstein's Theory of Relativity and Cosmological Principle. (Liberal Arts majors: You may want to reach for the aspirin.)

HERE'S WHAT IT SAYS
Some 12 to 14 billion years ago, maybe longer, the portion of the universe we can see today was only a few millimeters across (that's a little smaller than a gnat) and extremely hot (that's HOT). The bang in question is the expansion of this small, hot, dense state into the vastly expanding and much cooler cosmos we currently inhabit. The universe is still expanding, gradually increasing the distance between our galaxy and other galaxies. Astronomers have actually observed this, and it fits very nicely with the theory. For a theory to be taken seriously on its way to becoming accepted as fact, it has to undergo rigorous testing. Since 1948, when Gamow

---

The first ever income tax was levied in Great Britain, to fund the wars against Napoleon.

first mentioned it, scientists have found the Big Bang Theory consistent with a number of important observations:

- Astronomers can observe the expansion of the universe.

- There is an observed abundance of helium, deuterium, and lithium in the universe—three elements that scientists think were synthesized primarily in the first three minutes (wow!) of the universe.

- The existence of significant amounts of cosmic microwave background radiation.

This last, the cosmic microwave background radiation, is an important observation because radiation appears hotter in distant clouds of gas. Since light travels at a finite speed, we see these distant clouds at an earlier time in the history of the universe, when it was denser and, therefore, hotter.

WILL THE UNIVERSE GO AWAY?
One of the questions that keeps paranoiacs awake most nights is whether the currently expanding universe will continue to expand or whether it will ultimately contract and implode. This last is a definite possibility, but it won't happen tomorrow. We promise.

THE GRAVITY OF THE SITUATION
There's lots more to it, all about how space and time are altered by gravity (yes, Space Rangers, in some models of space-time morphing, you may actually be your own grandfather!), and the possible shape of the universe—ball-shaped, saddle-shaped, flat, or maybe even doughnut-shaped. Which brings up the question of whether the universe is open or closed, that is, infinite or not.

THAT DOUGHNUT'S NOT FOR DUNKIN'
In a closed universe like the doughnut-shaped model, you could start off in one direction and, if allowed enough time, ultimately return to your starting point. In an infinite universe, you would never return. Which means that if Kirk and Spock were working in an infinitely expanding universe, they would never have returned to the *Enterprise* from Pralax V and we would have missed all those great syndicated reruns! And that would have been a shame.

Lev Bronstein stole his jailer's passport and was thereafter known as Leon Trotsky.

LADY KILLER

While American kids are learning about that nice Betsy Ross and her pretty flag, English schoolchildren are thrilling to the blood-and-guts saga of Queen Boudicca, one of Britain's most revered heroines—despite the fact that she slaughtered tens of thousands of her countrymen.

BACK IN THE SIXTIES
In the first century A.D., when the Romans pretty much ruled the world, they regarded their subjects as barbarians. This included the people of Britain, which of course is much the way, later in history, that the British Empire felt about many of its subjects in nations they tried to colonize. But that's another story.

THE KING IS DEAD
During the Roman occupation of Britain, a Celtic tribe, the Iceni, was ruled by King Prasutagus and Queen Boudicca. When the king was dying, he wrote a will that he hoped would placate the Romans. In it, he divided his possessions between his daughters and the Roman emperor Nero. When the king died in A.D. 61, the local Roman authorities swooped in and started gathering up everything that belonged to the royal family. Boudicca protested, so they flogged her and, as they say in English textbooks, "ravished" her daughters.

LONG LIVE THE QUEEN
Boudicca was determined to have her revenge. She pow-wowed with some of the neighboring tribes, who hadn't been treated any better by the Romans. She incited rebellion; the tribes greeted the idea with enthusiasm. They prepared for war.

The man they'd have to go up against was Suetonius, the commander-in-chief of the Roman troops in Britain. At the moment, he was otherwise engaged, leading an attack on the island of Mona, where other British rebels had sought refuge among the Druids, priests of the Celtic religion. When news reached the mainland that the Romans had slaughtered the Druids and destroyed all the sacred shrines and altars, the rest of Britain gladly fell into step behind Boudicca.

Before he reunited Italy, Garibaldi lived briefly on Staten Island, working as a candle maker.

WITH A VENGEANCE

The queen climbed into her chariot—yes, she really rode a chariot—and stormed through the province, leading tens of thousands of warriors. Her first stop was the local Roman fortress. Boudicca's troops burned it to the ground and sacrificed the Roman prisoners to Andrasta, the Iceni's warrior goddess. The Romans sent the Ninth Legion against her, but her army mopped up the floor with their infantry. Only the cavalry escaped.

Figuring that Boudicca would make London her next target, Suetonius finished his job at Druid headquarters and made his way to the city. But instead of making a stand there, he abandoned London, leaving behind only the Britons who couldn't or wouldn't fight on the Roman side. When Boudicca and her army got there, they burned London to the ground and took no prisoners.

THE EMPIRE STRIKES BACK

Suetonius had only 10,000 men to Boudicca's 100,000, but he knew an unruly mob when he saw one. He laid a trap outside the city and waited for them to follow him. By now, the Britons were confident they could wipe out their Roman oppressors. So confident, in fact, that they brought their families to watch them do it. They threw themselves at the Roman troops again and again. When they realized they were outmatched and outsmarted, the British warriors turned and ran. Their families watched from the hillsides as the Romans mercilessly cut them down.

Boudicca and her daughters managed to escape. They knew very well that if they were captured, they'd be brought to Rome and marched through the city as defeated warriors. Rather than suffer that indignity, they poisoned themselves. The queen's loyal guards took her body and buried it where the Romans wouldn't find it. And where no one else has been able to either. But...

QUAINT BRITISH POSTSCRIPT

There is a rumor that Boudicca's final resting place lies beneath Platform 10 at King's Cross Station. It's built on the former village of Battle Bridge, which is said to be the site of Boudicca's last battle with Suetonius. Others say that "Battle Bridge" is a corruption of "Broad Ford Bridge" and insist she's buried on Parliament Hill, Hampstead, or in Suffolk.

A POX ON YOUR HOUSE

*After the bubonic plague had come and gone, the Europeans
who were left alive had to rethink a lot of things,
and they came up with some good ideas.*

As the middle of the 14th century approached, Europeans heard rumors of widespread death and disease on the Asian continent. But it all seemed very far away.

GERM WARFARE

Some Asians thought that Genoese sailors who traded along the coast of the Black Sea had brought the disease. They (either the Mongols or the Tatars, depending on who you talk to) laid siege to Kaffa, a Crimean city inhabited by Genoese, and used catapults to lob the decaying corpses of plague victims over the city walls. This early form of germ warfare killed just about everyone inside (but nobody at the time could figure out why). A few Genoese merchants escaped and sailed for home. They took the plague along.

SHIP OF DEATH

In 1347, a ship from Kaffa docked at Messina, Sicily. Most of the crew was dead; the rest were dying. The men had strange black egg-sized swellings called "buboes" (hence "bubonic") in their armpits and groins. Soon, boils and dark blotches spread over their bodies. Next thing you know, the locals had the same symptoms. Their deaths were painful and quick, usually in a matter of days.

A PLAGUE IN EVERY PORT

Messina started to turn away ships from the East, so those ships went to Genoa or other European ports instead, bringing the plague with them. Off the Italian coast, entire ships full of dead men floated by.

NOT A VERY GOOD YEAR

In 1348, the plague killed between 45,000 and 65,000 people in Florence, Italy alone. The plague raged through France that same year. When it reached Germany, thousands of Jews were accused of poisoning wells and were killed. In London, the plague killed half the population. By the spring of 1349, it moved on to Ireland.

THE TOLL
The Black Death wiped out one-fourth to one-half of Europe's population, from 20 million to 75 million people. Survivors might have gained immunity by genetic chance, or by a lucky exposure to a milder form of the disease. No one knew what brought on such a horror or what would make it go away. People blamed earthquakes, stagnant lakes, the stars, the devil, but mostly the wrath of God. Many believed this was the end of the world.

YOU DIRTY RATS!
The bubonic plague had been around for a long time and had killed people before (but not as many in one swell foop). The bacteria was carried by rats, but it didn't bother them. The fleas that fed on rats preferred the blood of small mammals to humans. As the world's population grew, rats and their fleas came into more frequent contact with humans. Now, a fleabite could mean death.

AIRBORNE GERMS
After the disease reached an infected person's lungs, it took on a form that could be transmitted through the air, propelled by coughs and sneezes. It could also be passed from person to person by direct contact. The various forms caused symptoms, ranging from rashes to buboes to vomiting blood to an overpowering stench that emanated from every breath and drop of sweat. Believe it or not, the bubonic plague still turns up occasionally. Now we can treat it with antibiotics, which work well if used early. It's even been suggested that the plague gave future generations an important gift—those who are immune to the human immuno-deficiency virus (HIV) might have inherited a genetic mutation from ancestors who survived the Black Death.

ABSOLUTE CHAOS
The Black Death was a nightmare, and the world that awoke from it was changed forever. By 1350, the worst was over. At first, chaos reigned. Law and order was a thing of the past. Schools and universities closed. Churches lacked priests to hear confessions. Debtors died, so creditors had no one to collect from. Construction projects stopped, and few craftsmen were available to make or repair anything. Morality? A thing of the past—people who weren't dead had good reason to think they soon might be, so they decided to have a good time before the plague got them.

THE PERKS: THERE WERE QUITE A FEW
Survivors had a lot to think about. Everything was different now.

- Landlords tried to get the peasants back to work, but there weren't as many peasants around. For the first time, workers could demand better treatment and lighter work. There were rebellions in the countryside, unheard of in more stable times. A lot of peasants moved into towns to find better jobs.

- There weren't a lot of working people in the cities, either. Wages rose. There were lots of goods to go around, so prices dropped. As a result, the standard of living improved. For the first time, working people began to think of themselves as individuals who mattered.

- Land values dropped because there was so much property available. People who couldn't have dreamed about becoming landowners now had a chance to buy property.

- Five years after the plague, England created three new colleges at Cambridge. Universities sprang up all over Europe. Many teachers had died, so new ones had to be found. A lot of them brought fresh ideas, and they taught classes in whatever the local language was, not Latin or Greek. For the first time, common people could get an education (probably the major contributing factor to bringing on the Renaissance).

- People started asking new questions. Most survivors couldn't imagine the plague being God's work. But if it wasn't, then who or what was responsible? Questions like these hadn't even been thought of before the plague.

THE PLAGUE RETURNS
The Black Death wasn't the end of the bubonic plague. It came back, but was limited to smaller areas. The last big outbreak in England was in London in 1665. By then, people knew enough to get out of town when the plague struck—if they had any place to go. One of them, a young professor named Isaac Newton, had not had time to develop some ideas he'd been mulling over. When the plague returned, Newton fled London to his country estate, where he worked out the math for his theory of gravity.

Josef Stalin was studying to become a Russian Orthodox priest when he found Communism.

CANADA'S RED BARON

Billy Bishop was more than an ordinary guy in an extraordinary time; he was a true Canadian hero.

World War I's daring young men in their flying machines have mostly slipped into the yellowed pages of military histories (or their own unread memoirs). Take Baron Manfred Von Richthofen, the Red Baron, for example. He's more often recognized as Snoopy's arch foe than as Germany's leading flying ace of his day.

SNOOPY'S FOREBEARS

During the war years, the "bloody Red Baron" had lots more to think about than Charlie Brown's family dog. In early 1917, just across the trenches from the Red Baron, was a Royal Flying Corps pilot who was to become the British Empire's top ace before the war ended 18 months later. The pilot was a Canadian named Billy Bishop, a most improbable hero.

BORN TO FLY

Lucky for the Baron, this was Billy's first assignment since he got his wings. His flight training had amounted to only four hours of solo flying time, but it sounds as if he didn't need much more than that. In that war, promotions came faster than planes could fly. Nice for Billy, but not so nice for the luckless German pilots who got caught in his gunsight. By the end of the war, Billy was credited with 72 kills, 11 more than the next best ace, another Canadian, Raymond Collishaw.

LIFE WITH FATHER

Billy Bishop grew up in the shadow of his father's great expectations: that he would marry well, and settle down to a conservative law practice and a proper, conformist family. From early on Billy was a bit of a maverick.

All the same, Billy showed a flair for enterprise. He dated his sister's girlfriends—as long as his sister paid him to do it. The story goes that he charged $5 to date a young lady named Margaret Burden. It was only later that he succumbed to her charms and married her. It turned out that she was the granddaughter of Timothy Eaton, whose department stores were as famous in Canada as

Macy's or Sears are in the United States. Eaton's annual mail order catalog could be found in more Canadian outhouses than every other catalog put together.

SAVED BY THE KAISER

So before he went to war, Billy managed to satisfy the "marry well" expectation. The "law" expectation didn't go as well, so his father enrolled him in Canada's Royal Military College. Billy failed his first year, managed to get his act together the second year, and was successfully grinding it out the third year until he (uh-oh) inadvertently handed in his "crib sheets" with his final exam. Luckily, that was in 1914, and the Kaiser came along to save him from being expelled. Off to war went Billy.

FROM COWBOY TO FLYBOY

By 1915 Billy was in England as part of a Canadian cavalry unit. Even before he saw action he tumbled to the fact that charging around on horses wasn't all that sensible in a trench war involving machine guns, tanks, and other monstrous devices. Our hero harkened to the freedom of the skies and the daring individuality of piloting a flying fighting machine. The only problem was that Canada didn't have an air force.

Billy used social connections to get into Britain's Royal Flying Corps as an observer and artillery spotter. The planes were slow and seriously outgunned. A truck accident, an abscessed tooth, a banged-up knee, and a piece of a plane falling on his head kept him on the ground and out of harm's way. He was sent back to Canada for a year to recover his health. He returned to England in late 1916, and started his pilot training. In February 1917 he shipped to France, and within five weeks of landing there he had gunned down 17 German aircraft.

BILLY'S BEST

In June 1917, Billy carried out his most audacious raid—single-handed, he attacked the Germans' Estourmel Aerodrome. He shot two planes from the air, a third crashed into a tree in its haste to attack him, and he destroyed a fourth on the ground. This foray earned him Britain's highest military honor, the Victoria Cross. It also earned him the disdain of some colleagues who thought him overly ambitious. The British citizenry lionized Billy Bishop, but it took more than that to make Canadian officials notice him. In

Russia's February Revolution was in March; the October Revolution was in November.

May 1918—wanting to keep their hero alive—Canada ordered him home. On the last day of his war, Billy celebrated by shooting down three planes and causing two others to collide.

Back home, Billy made some lecture tours, but eventually found it boring. After all, this had been the war to end all wars; prosperity and peace were no longer just around the corner, they were front and center. Goldfish swallowing, dance marathons, and high-wire walking over Niagara Falls were the news of the day. But Billy Bishop wanted to fly again.

BILLY LAYS A BOMB

Billy went into business with a fellow wartime ace: a charter air service, that ferried well-to-do people from Toronto to their summer lodges about 200 miles north, but the business bombed. It would have to wait for development of the executive jet. Billy and his partner thought stunt flying might be fun, so booked themselves into the air show at the Canadian National Exhibition, Canada's premier summer fair. Their daredevil routine, which included diving at the crowds and buzzing the stands, thrilled the audience all right, it caused a panic, and supposedly caused a pregnant woman spectator to miscarry. The partners moved on. Along the way, Billy discovered he was as much a born salesman as a pilot. And a good thing it was, because the market crash of 1929 wiped out the value of his wife's stock portfolio.

BILLY GETS HIMSELF ANOTHER WAR

His now-proven salesmanship and his cachet as a much-decorated flying ace made him a natural for the job of Canada's Air Marshall in Charge of Recruitment. He even got a role as a recruiting officer in the James Cagney movie, *Captains of the Clouds* (1942).

BILLY UP TO THE BAR

Make no mistake, Billy Bishop is a true Canadian hero. His hometown of Owen Sound, Ontario, has a Billy Bishop museum. He's such a legend that an Ottawa bartender recently created a shooter, the Billy Bishop Bullet, to be served only to veterans and served only on Canada's Remembrance Day, November 11. Its ingredients? For the English and French components, half gin and half cointreau respectively, for the Canadians a splash of rye whiskey on top, and for the Americans (who came on board later in the war), orange juice to taste.

The first child born on the *Mayflower* was named Oceanus Hopkins.

WEAR COMPUTERS CAME FROM

What do your clothes and your computer have in common?
Lots of history—and apparently a future, too.

About 7,000 years go, somebody invented the loom system, which makes cloth using threads attached to bars. About 5,000 years ago, someone in Asia developed the abacus system, which allows someone to perform calculations by sliding beads along wires attached to a frame. In the 19th century these two simple machines for weaving and counting were combined …and that changed the world.

A WARPED CHILDHOOD
Joseph Marie Jacquard grew up in France in the mid-19th century. At the age of ten, he was put to work in the weaving trade. His job was to lift certain warp threads on a weaving loom. Watching the loom, he could see that to weave fabrics, when some of the warp threads strung on the loom were raised, others stayed down. A shuttle pulled a weft thread through the space in between. Then different warp threads were raised, and the process was repeated. The order of raised threads created a pattern in the fabric. With fancy fabrics, the order got complicated.

PROGRESS LOOMS ON THE HORIZON
The process was too complicated and boring for young Jacquard. There had to be a way to make cloth more easily. When Jacquard was grown, he introduced a loom that did the job automatically, with punched cards that gave his loom instructions. Each warp thread was connected to a separate metal needle. With a punched card in place, only the needles corresponding to the holes could move—meaning only certain warp threads were raised. A different card controlled each group of threads to be raised, and the cards came around in a continuous loop, repeating the pattern again and again. Apparently a lot of people were as bored by manual weaving as Jacquard. By 1812, he had a medal and a pension from Napoleon, and the automatic loom was in widespread use.

Before he died, Lenin attacked the despotism and bureaucracy of Communism.

MATHEMATICAL DUMMKOPFS
Enter an English mathematician named Charles Babbage. In the 1830s, Babbage was annoyed by errors he saw in astronomical tables used for navigation. Mechanical calculators using combinations of wheels and gears had been invented, but none had a memory, so none could do complicated calculations. People did the complicated calculations, and people made mistakes. Mistakes in astronomical tables could mean lost ships and lost lives.

A CALCULATED EFFORT
Babbage tried to build a machine to produce those tables automatically and accurately, without human mistakes. After 20 years he abandoned his prototype for a better idea—the Analytical Engine. The Analytical Engine used Jacquard's punch-card system. If a mathematician could create the cards, Babbage realized that anyone could put them into the machine. With simple commands from the operator, the machine would do whatever job was programmed into the card. The cards had a kind of memory and could be used again and again. However, after waiting 20 years for action on the prototype, nobody paid much attention to Babbage's new machine. It would be another century before his ideas were rediscovered and understood. Too bad, because his designs led the way to the modern computer.

A HOLE NEW WAY TO COUNT HEADS
Punch-card computing got practical in 1889 when American inventor Herman Hollerith used the cards to record and store data from the United States census. The original estimate for compiling census results was ten years. With his punches, Hollerith speeded up the process to six weeks. In 1896, Hollerith founded the Tabulating Machine Company, which later became International Business Machines (IBM). The rest, as they say, is history.

WHAT LOOMS AHEAD?
Appropriately enough, today's commercial looms are run by computers. There's even futuristic talk about "wearable computers"—miniature screens in glasses or contact lenses, and even clothing with woven-in sensors designed to process information with your every move. Soon you'll be able to wear your computer and you can work while walking, jogging, and driving... Too bad we can't go back and burn Jacquard's first automatic loom.

WHITE GUYS WITH SMALL HEADS DIDN'T INVENT THE BANJO

Carry a banjo into a public place and no doubt someone will say "Saw you in Deliverance! *My, my, you're all growed up now!" What most people don't know is that the banjo was invented at least 400 years ago on the other side of the world.*

Most banjo players lament the best-known image of their musical calling—that strange-looking gnome plucking away at a 5-string banjo in the movie *Deliverance*.

BAD PRESS FOR THE BANJO

Unlike a violin or guitar, the mere sight of a banjo triggers spontaneous derision in many otherwise kindly citizens. This is probably due to the banjo's early history in American entertainment as a universal prop for stage comics playing the witless "rube" for all it was worth while strumming the old "banjar." But in spite of such unpleasant associations, the banjo was not born in America. Nor did white guys of any nationality—or I.Q.—have anything to do with its creation.

PINHEADS NEED NOT APPLY

Drums with strings stretched over them (which is what a banjo is) can be traced throughout western Africa as well as the Far East and Middle East almost from the beginning of recorded history. These primitive instruments can be played like the banjo, with a bow like a violin, or plucked like a harp depending on the style of music.

AFRICAN ROOTS

The banjo as we know it today most likely began in southwestern Africa. The original instrument is believed to have been called an "akonting," but scholars have found countless entries in diaries of 17th century British explorers that refer to instruments with names surprisingly close to the modern word "banjo": banjar, banza, and banshaw among them.

Founded in 1923 in Vienna, Interpol was absorbed into the Gestapo during the Nazi era.

WITH STRINGS ATTACHED

The earliest African version was a gourd sliced in half, with an animal skin membrane stretched tightly across the opening to which a wooden neck and twine or animal gut for strings were attached. It may have had as few as two and as many as ten strings, depending on local custom. Westerners were first exposed to the banjo through the slave trades beginning in the 1600s.

CLAWHAMMER STYLE

The Europeans' playing style was to pluck stringed instruments like the guitar. Evidence from African-American communities in the United States' Appalachian Mountains in the 19th and early 20th centuries suggests that African slaves played instruments much differently: They used their fingernails in a downward "rapping" motion, hitting the strings percussively. This style of banjo playing has survived to this day and is called "clawhammer" style. Enter Southern peanut planter Joel Sweeney, who claimed that he learned to play the 4-string "banjar" from slaves on his family's Virginia plantation when he was growing up early in the 19th century. In 1835, he added what most historians believe to be the fifth string, creating for posterity the 5-string banjo as it is known today. Sweeney took what he'd learned to the stage, playing as an "Ethiopian"-style banjoist in minstrel shows, using that percussive "clawhammer" style of playing he learned from the slaves.

THE MINSTREL SHOW

In the 1830s, minstrel shows featured banjo-playing whites in blackface. The minstrel show first developed as a way for whites to explore what they perceived to be the "mystery" of African-American culture. In the early days they weren't the mean-spirited, racist parodies they became by the 1890s and early 1900s. Billed as "Ethiopian [African] characterizations," these performances of music, dance, and comedy were based more on whites' perceptions of Africans than on the reality of African-American slave life. The minstrel show's comic descendants continued the tradition of the witless banjoist into the 20th century. We cite *Hee-Haw* comics Stringbean and Grandpa Jones popping out of the cornfield, pluckin' away on the old banjo. And did anybody happen to notice that arrow sticking out of Steve Martin's head while he was strummin' on the old ban-jo? Banjo case closed.

THE MAKING OF A MARATHON

...in which a runner named Pheidippides ran his heart out.

Marathon was a place before it was a race: ten square miles of open land just northeast of Athens. During the summer of 490 B.C., it was a battlefield where the soldiers of the Greek army fought the Persians. The odds weren't good for the home team. The Greek army, at 10,000 strong, was outnumbered by more than two to one.

ADVANTAGE, PERSIA

Miltiades, the Greek general, noted the disadvantage. What he needed was some Spartans, Greece's fiercest soldiers. The army had a stable of messengers, runners who were the elite athletes of the day, trained to cross difficult terrain in a short amount of time. The general sent his strongest messenger, Pheidippides (whose name was pronounced "fi-DIP-uh-dees"), to fetch some Spartans.

OVER HILL, OVER DALE

Pheidippides ran nearly 100 miles, up and down hills in summer heat, through enemy territory to the Spartan camp, only to find them in the middle of a religious ceremony. The Greek army would have to wait a few days for reinforcements. Pheidippides ran back to camp to give Miltiades the bad news. He'd run about 200 miles in two days.

FOUR-STAR GENERAL

Undaunted, Miltiades waged a brilliant attack on the Persians by using smaller, faster, lighter units of troops to surround the slower, more numerous Persians. In all, the Greeks lost 192 men. The Persians lost over 6,000 and retreated back to their ships. Ironically, the Spartans arrived later that same day.

THE THRILL OF VICTORY

Pleased with his victory, Miltiades once again dispatched his best runner to bring the good news to Athens, a distance of only 26 miles. Pheidippides raced to Athens, entered the city, exclaimed

Until 1709, Sweden was a major European military power.

"Nike!" (which means "victory"—thus the name of the sneaker company) and then collapsed and died.

MODERN MARATHON SCANDALS

The modern marathon was established in Pheidippides' honor. The exact distance is 26.2 miles, and the participants, while encouraged to run with as much heart and effort as Pheidippides, are strongly discouraged from dying as they cross the finish line.

- The first Olympic marathon was held in 1896 and followed Pheidippides' original route. It was won by Spiridon Louis, a Greek, in a time of 2 hours, 58 minutes, and 50 seconds. The second-place finisher was also a Greek, Spiridon Belocas. However, the fourth-place finisher, the Hungarian Gyula Kellner, didn't remember Belocas passing him. It turned out that Belocas completed the marathon with the assistance of a horse-drawn cart. He was later disqualified and Kellner was awarded second place.

- In 1909, Howard Pearce, competing in the Boston Marathon, ran the first eight miles and then hopped in a car to "run" the remainder of the race. Officials tried to stop him, but encouraged by the cheers of the crowd, he pressed on to the finish. Pearce was later disqualified.

- In 1980, Rosie Ruiz, also competing in the Boston Marathon, took the subway for most of the race. One mile from the finish line, she joined a pack of passing runners to finish before the legitimate female winner, Jacqueline Gareau. Ruiz was later disqualified.

* * *

AND THE WINNER IS...DEAD?

The Ancient Greeks took their competition seriously. Dead seriously. In 564 B.C., Arrachion of Phigalia became an Olympic champion and died in the process. His downfall was the pankration event, a mix of boxing and wrestling where virtually anything was permitted. After a very tough fight, his opponent conceded the bout as Arrachion lay on the ground. Unbeknownst to his rival, Arrachion had expired from the duel, becoming the only dead person to win an Olympic event.

Persian king Xerxes I punished stormy water by having it whipped 300 times.

THE FISH THAT BEAT NAPOLEON

How a turbot was the secret weapon in the battle of Copenhagen.

In 1800, the British Navy was blockading France, boarding neutral ships, and even confiscating cargoes to prevent supplies getting through to the enemy. This angered the Russians, who allied with the Scandinavian countries to break the blockade.

HYDE HIDES FROM NELSON
Admiral Horatio Nelson, the hero of the Navy for his victories against Napoleon, was eager to attack before much damage was done. But the Admiral in charge, sixty-two-year-old Sir Hyde Parker, had recently taken an 18-year-old bride and was reluctant to go to sea. When he finally did, he insisted on negotiating with the alliance, and wouldn't even speak to Nelson.

NELSON FINDS SOMETHING FISHY
However, Nelson understood that Sir Hyde's voluptuous young wife (known as "The Batter Pudding") was not his boss's only indulgence. Hyde was also a noted gourmand. On a dark and stormy night, Nelson sent his crew out searching for a turbot, which he then sent, with his compliments, to Sir Hyde.

HYDE STOPS HIDING
Pleased with the tasty gift, Sir Hyde relented, invited Nelson to the next meeting, and listened to the younger admiral's suggestions. Nelson got his way—and a stunning victory for the English.

THE (FISH) SCALES TILT AGAINST THE FRENCH
Napoleon threw a temper tantrum when he heard about the defeat of the Russians and Scandinavians. The alliance was disbanded. The blockade against Napoleon was successfully resumed, eventually contributing to his final defeat at Waterloo.

NO ONE KNEW THE NEWS
Actually Czar Paul I of Russia, instigator of the alliance, had been assassinated. Had the British gotten the news, the battle need never have taken place. But then we wouldn't have this fish story.

Karl Marx was once a correspondent for Horace Greeley's *New York Daily Tribune*.

THEM'S FIGHTIN' WORDS: COLONIALISM

As if they were dividing up what was left in the world, the European nations—beginning about 1870—stepped up the pace of acquiring new colonies, mostly in Africa and Asia.

By 1905 nearly all of the choicest territories in Africa were gobbled up by the Belgians, British, and French, who maintained their hold for the next half-century. By the late 1950s, numerous African colonies sought independence, sometimes by peaceful means (like Ghana and Nigeria) and sometimes by violence, as in the Congo and in the Mau-Mau rebellion.

trek
The acquisition wasn't a universally peaceful process. One area of periodic clashes was South Africa, which saw conflict between the British and the Boers (descendants of the early Dutch settlers) from the time the British took Cape Province from the Dutch (1806). The Boers found life unbearable alongside the British, and in 1835 they began a mass migration to the north and east, away from British rule. This movement was known as the Great Trek, **trek** being Dutch for a journey by ox wagon and today used for any difficult journey. This meaning also appears in *Star Trek*, the popular television and motion picture series about space travel.

commando
In their inevitable difficulties with hostile native tribes, the Boers organized small military units or **kommandos**, capable of making quick raids against native villages. During World War II, the British anglicized the term to **commando** and applied it to small elite units trained to engage in some especially hazardous undertaking. In perhaps the first commando raid, on March 7, 1941, the commandos destroyed a plant in occupied Norway that was making glycerine for the Germans. Americans also used the word as an adjective to describe military actions involving surprise and shock, as in "commando tactics."

Kaiser Wilhelm II, Czar Nicholas II, and George V were all grandchildren of Queen Victoria.

commandeer

Another term adopted from the Boers' Afrikaans language was to **commandeer**, originally meaning to conscript or appropriate for military use. The latter is now used more broadly to mean taking over something arbitrarily, as in "the director **commandeered** Main Street for shooting the last scene."

fed up

The Boers eventually set up the republics of Transvaal, Natal, and the Orange Free State, but in succeeding decades the British took over Natal and moved into the other two states. Hostile relations continued until 1899, when Transvaal and the Orange Free State finally declared war on Britain. This Boer War proved to be a long struggle. At first the British suffered serious setbacks, but in 1900 reinforcements arrived in large numbers. Along them were Australian troops, who, at least one authority believes, expressed their exasperation by saying they were **fed up**, a phrase that continues to be a synonym for "disgusted" or "having had enough."

khaki

It was during this conflict that the British army adopted **khaki** as the proper color for active-service uniforms. The name for this greenish shade of brown comes from the Urdu word for dust or dust-colored and was adopted in English in the mid-1800s by British troops serving in India. But it was not generally used until the Boer War, during which "khaki" also was a slang name for a volunteer. That usage has died out, but the color and its name survive, not only in British and American soldiers' summer uniforms (also called **khakis**), but in all kinds of nonmilitary clothing.

washout

A term that came from the British rifle range during this period was **washout**. If a shot landed completely wide of the target, it was called a washout, because on old iron targets the space they landed on was covered with some kind of paint or "wash." At first, washout simply meant a bad shot, but it soon was broadened to mean any kind of failure, and it's still used that way.

concentration camps

In time both the Transvaal and Orange Free State were occupied by the British. Their commander-in-chief, F. S. Roberts, then returned to England and left the final mopping-up to his assistant, Horatio Kitchener. To counter the Boers' strong guerrilla resistance, Kitchener decided to move systematically through Boer territory and round up not only enemy soldiers but also their wives and children. All captives were thrown into improvised **concentration camps**—the first use of this term (although probably not of the practice). There, under appalling living conditions, many of them died from disease.

apartheid
After more than a year the Boers surrendered, and in 1902 a peace treaty was signed that encouraged self-government within the British Commonwealth. In 1910, the Union of South Africa was formed, but for much of the remainder of the 20th century the legacy of the Boer War survived in tensions between Boer and Britisher. Once in control of the government, the Boers enacted a rigid policy of segregation against all nonwhites. The name of the policy, **apartheid**, also has entered our language, where it refers to any practice that separates people on the basis of race or caste.

> Christine Ammer's book, *Fighting Words*, explores the linguistic legacy of armed conflicts over the centuries, from biblical times to the present.

* * *

MORE FALLOUT FROM COLONIALISM

The English language gained more than just military terms when the British took India. **Calico**, a type of cotton cloth, is named for the Indian city of Calicut. **Cashmere**, a soft fabric made from the hair of a certain kind of goat, came from the Indian province of Kashmir. **Pariah**, meaning a social outcast, comes from the Tamil word "paraiyan," the low social caste who played the traditional drum (the "parai") at festivals. And **curry,** a spiced stew or sauce, comes from the Tamil "kari" which means much the same.

Ho Chi Minh based the opening of Vietnam's Declaration of Independence on America's.

I LOVE A CRUSADE

The era of the Crusades lasted from 1095 to 1291; that's over 200 years of holy war. Here are some highlights from the first—an unofficial, misbegotten venture also known as the "People's Crusade."

THE GUY WHO STARTED IT

When Odo de Lagery—Pope Urban II to you—spoke to a church council in France in November 1095, he delivered what may have been the single most effective speech in all of human history. According to His Holiness, the infidel Turks who occupied the Holy Land were defiling the Christian holy places and molesting Christian pilgrims. He called for a holy war to recapture these lands for Christendom.

HEY, DID YOU BRING THE MAP?

The average Joe had a swift and feverish reaction. Before the French knights and princes could gather their forces, peasant mobs from cities all over France set out in the general direction of Jerusalem. Poorly armed and poorly trained, they knew nothing about fighting Turks, and even less about the geography of Asia Minor. They believed they could overcome the infidels by faith alone. So began the first campaign to win the Holy Land—the People's Crusade.

THE PEOPLE'S CHOICE

About 100,000 souls, ragtag armies of men, women, and children, were led by popular preachers such as Peter the Hermit. Peter was a kind of Gandhi figure, a small, ugly man who walked barefoot and cared nothing for possessions. His zealous followers sang the latest hymns from the Holy Hit Parade as they marched along. Each of them wore an X-shaped strip of cloth on one shoulder in memory of the heavy cross that Christ carried to Calvary.

THOSE DARN CRUSADERS

The first big battle of the Crusades was fought not in the Holy Land, but in Hungary, against fellow Christians. It seems that some Crusaders felt entitled to all the Hungarian crops and sundries they could lay their hands on. So began a pitched battle with the Hungarians, who had only recently been converted to Chris-

---

Although Frederick the Great doubled Germany's territory, he spoke German poorly.

tianity by St. Stephen. About 4,000 Hungarians were killed to the Crusaders' 100 or so.

BACK TO YOU, PETER

Meanwhile, Peter was having the same trouble. In a battle against fellow Christians from the Byzantine army, over 10,000 of Peter's people were killed or captured. Just as he was beginning to think that maybe this Crusade wasn't such a good idea, things took a temporary turn for the better. When his army finally arrived at the gates of Constantinople on August 1, 1096, Peter managed to make peace with the Byzantine emperor himself. The emperor took one look at Peter's sorry-looking troops and told him to wait for the real army—the gentlemen knights and princes—to show up. But would Peter listen? As if.

A MAJOR DISASTER IN ASIA MINOR

Peter appointed a deputy to lead his army into enemy territory and very wisely waited behind in Constantinople. With banners flying and trumpets blaring, the Crusaders marched on the well-fortified and well-defended Turkish fortress of Nicaea. By coincidence, the Turks had decided on that very day to attack the Christians. And when they left their fortress, what did they see, marching toward them like lambs to the slaughter?

A (SORT OF) HAPPY ENDING

After the first Turkish assault, the Christian army panicked and ran for their lives. Three thousand Crusaders escaped and hid out in an ancient seaside fortress. The Turks followed and attacked, killing most of them. They would have finished the job if that nice Byzantine emperor hadn't ordered part of his fleet to go to their rescue. So Peter's followers weren't completely wiped out, but they were defeated. And with that, the disaster known as the "People's Crusade" was finally over.

* * *

APOCALYPSE 968

As the year 1000 loomed, Christendom got nervous that the world would end. In 968, when Holy Roman Emperor Otto I sent troops against the Saracens of Calabria, a solar eclipse sent his soldiers diving headfirst into barrels and under carts in abject fear. They were sure it was a sign from heaven. Or perhaps the other place.

There really was a King Macbeth. He ruled Scotland from 1040 to 1057.

WITHOUT A LEG TO STAND ON

Mexican leader Santa Anna was the world's greatest comeback king. He had more than his share of ups and downs, but his leg—the real star of this story—had a life of its own.

Antonio Lopez de Santa Anna was president of Mexico in the early 19th century. Actually, he was president more than once. Actually, he was president 11 times between 1833 and 1855. He was even dictator for a while. Between most of his presidencies, he was the most despised man in Mexico.

REMEMBER THE ALAMO?

Yes, we mean that Santa Anna, the one who led the charge on the Alamo and took no prisoners. Back then, Texas wasn't a U.S. state—it was still part of Mexico. In 1836, partly because Santa Anna had abolished the Mexican constitution, the citizens of Texas declared their independence. So General Santa Anna led his sizeable army across the Rio Grande, where he met with surprising resistance from a tiny contingent of Texas soldiers at the Alamo, an old Spanish mission. The general took the Alamo and massacred everyone in sight, so he probably deserved what happened to his leg—both the real one and the fake one.

EL PRESIDENTE

The first time Santa Anna was elected president of Mexico, he didn't even bother—ho-hum—to attend his own inauguration. He left the work of running the government to his vice-president, but when nobody liked the vice-president's reforms, Santa Anna and a group of conspirators pulled off a coup against his own government. Santa Anna took power again, this time, as supreme dictator of Mexico, a position he held from 1834–1836.

SIESTA TIME

Being supreme dictator gave Santa Anna supreme confidence, so during an ensuing battle at San Jacinto, he decided to take a siesta without bothering to post guards. This pretty much guaranteed a victory to Texas hero Sam Houston and his troops (whose war cry, by the way, was "Remember the Alamo!"). Santa Anna was taken prisoner and delivered to President Andrew Jackson in Washington, where he signed a treaty agreeing to independence for Texas. But when Santa Anna went back home, Mexico repudiated the treaty he'd signed. Santa Anna was branded a traitor and fell into disgrace. But only for a while.

THE FRENCH PASTRY WAR

His next big chance to regain the favor of his people came in 1838, when a French baker in Mexico City sued the Mexican government for damages, claiming that some Mexican soldiers had looted his shop. This small incident led to the "Pastry War," in which Mexico took on the French army. They needed a general, so guess who was elected?

ENTER THE LEG

Santa Anna was only too happy to lead his troops against the French. At Vera Cruz, the general was so badly wounded that his leg had to be amputated from the knee down. Santa Anna milked this wound for every last drop of good press he could squeeze. He organized ceremonies, speeches, and even held a hero's funeral for the severed limb. The leg was buried with high military honors.

FIESTA TIME

Now sporting an artificial leg made out of cork and covered in leather, Santa Anna became president again. But he gave so many parties—mostly in honor of himself—and spent so much money outfitting his own private army that by 1842, he'd run through every peso in the Mexican treasury. He couldn't pay his troops, so they rose up against him. El Presidente headed for the hills—so far into the hills, in fact, that the Mexican people couldn't find him.

ATTACK ... ON THE LEG

Since they couldn't take out their frustration on Santa Anna himself, they dug up his leg and tossed it around, then finally chopped it up into little pieces and scattered it to the four winds.

GOOD RIDDANCE!

When the Mexican government caught up with Santa Anna a couple of years later, the country was still peeved enough to exile him to Cuba. In 1846, when the Mexican-American War was about to break out, Santa Anna sensed an opportunity for another

---

The longest serving monarch ever was Pepi II, who ruled Egypt for 90 years.

comeback. He wrote to U.S. president James Polk, promising to settle things without any further bloodshed. Polk fell for it. And as soon as Santa Anna hit Mexico, he went back on his promise. The general was back in business.

ON THE FRONT LINES

The war was underway. U.S. federal forces led by Captain Robert E. Lee (yes, the same Robert E. Lee who led Confederate forces in the Civil War) were closing in on Santa Anna. While they attacked the Mexican defense from the front, a volunteer force from the state of Illinois circled around to strike from behind.

SANTA ANNA LOSES HIS LEG—AGAIN

Meanwhile, Santa Anna was kicking back. He'd taken off his artificial leg and was about to enjoy a roast chicken dinner when the Illinois Volunteers came charging out of the woods, shouting and shooting. A Mexican cavalry soldier picked up the general and carried him to safety. But in his rush to get away, Santa Anna left his cork leg behind. The Illinois Volunteers ate the chicken and took the leg home as a war souvenir.

"THE LEG I LEFT BEHIND ME"

The American troops made up a song about Santa Anna's leg. (The words can be found among documents at the University of Kansas.) It goes to the tune of "The Girl I Left Behind Me." Here are a couple of verses:

I am stumpless quite since from
    the shot
Of Cerro Gordo peggin',
I left behind, to pay Gen. Scott,
My grub, and gave my leg in.
I dare not turn to view the place
Lest Yankee foes should find me,
And mocking shake before my face
The Leg I Left Behind Me.

Should Gen. Taylor of my track
    get scent,
Or Gen. Scott beat up my quarters,
I may as well just be content
To go across the waters.
But should that my fortune be,
Fate has not quite resigned me
For in the museum I will see
The Leg I Left Behind Me.

THE REST OF SANTA ANNA

Santa Anna was given one more chance to rule Mexico, this time as military dictator. But after he sold some property to the American government—30,000 square miles, now part of southern

---

Louis XIV of France was an avid ballet dancer in his youth.

Arizona and New Mexico—a furious group of Mexican politicians drove him out of office and into exile again. He kept trying to get back into Mexico, but it wasn't until 1874, when he was considered too old to cause trouble, that he was allowed to return. He immediately demanded a government pension for his past services to the nation. The pension was refused, and Santa Anna died at the age of 84—poor, nearly blind, and still one-legged.

WHERE IS SANTA ANNA'S LEG?

The wooden leg would seem to be a very valuable commodity. At various times, the Mexican government, Santa Anna himself, and the state of Texas tried to get it back from Illinois. In 1942, the leg became a political issue in the United States. Chicago Democrats introduced a bill to return it as a sign of friendship to Mexico. Republicans refused, insisting that "the Democrats don't have a leg to stand on." You can see the famous leg—if you want to—today in the Illinois State Military Museum's collection at Camp Lincoln, in Springfield, Illinois.

*　*　*

STAIRWAYS TO HEAVEN

Santa Anna had some bad luck, but you shouldn't have to. Get the facts on walking under ladders. From Egyptian times, ladders were used to help spirits climb to heaven. Walking under a ladder might disturb and anger a spirit who was using it. In the Middle Ages, walking under a ladder was unlucky because leaning a ladder against a wall formed a triangle. This symbol of the divine trinity, Father Son and Holy Ghost, was broken when someone walked through it. But there was another powerful reason for staying away from ladders. Before gallows were invented, criminals were hung from the top rungs of ladders, and their angry ghosts might still be "hanging around." Not to worry. If you fear bad luck while walking under a ladder, the historic solution is to spit three times through the rungs. This probably disgusts the evil spirits into leaving you alone.

The United Kingdom originally offered Kenya to the Zionists as a Jewish homeland.

7 WONDERS OF THE ANCIENT WORLD

We were wondering what was so wonderful about the ancient wonders of the world, so we did a little excavating. Here are the wonders, presented in order of appearance.

1. THE GREAT PYRAMID AT GIZA
Where: The greater metropolitan area of Cairo, Egypt
Who Built It and Why: Pharaoh Khufu built it for his tomb.
When: Around 2500 B.C.
Particulars: The oldest of the seven ancient wonders and the only one still standing. Each of the pyramid's four sides is perfectly oriented to north, south, east, and west. Its base covers 13 acres. The Great Pyramid was the tallest structure on earth for more than 4,000 years, until the Eiffel Tower—actually a tall, skinny pyramid itself—was completed in 1889.
What's Left: Originally 481 feet high, time and nature have worn the pyramid down to about 450 feet. It's still one of the most popular tourist attractions in the world.

2. THE HANGING GARDENS OF BABYLON
Where: Ancient Babylon, near present-day Baghdad, Iraq
Who Built It and Why: Babylon was very flat, so King Nebuchadnezzar built it for his wife, Amyitis, who was homesick for the mountains of her native land.
When: About 600 B.C.
Particulars: Picture a terraced garden, built on higher and higher levels, covered with trees, flowers, fountains, and waterfalls. Estimates say it probably covered 100 by 150 feet. Now picture the whole thing supported by columns 75 feet high. Reports say that slaves worked around the clock to irrigate the garden with water from the nearby Euphrates River.
What happened: While there is no concrete proof of their exitence, if they were real, time eroded them.
What's Left: Virtually nothing, but stay tuned; archaeologists are still digging.

Lady Nancy Astor, the first woman in the British House of Commons, was born in Virginia.

3. THE TEMPLE OF ARTEMIS AT EPHESUS

Where: The ancient city of Ephesus, near modern Selcuk, Turkey
Who Built It and Why: King Croesus, the man from whom we get the term "rich as Croesus," was the heaviest contributor to the shrine to Artemis, the Greek goddess of the hunt and wild nature.
When: About 550 B.C.
Particulars: Except for the roof, the temple was made entirely of marble. Writers called it the most beautiful structure on earth, with pillars of gold, glorious frescoes on the walls, and its most famous feature: four bronze statues of Amazons, the women warriors who were Artemis's most faithful followers. The temple was a bustling tourist center, where everyone was expected to leave gifts for the goddess. Outside the temple, souvenir stands sold little statues of her. In one of her forms, Artemis was the goddess of the moon. Her father, Zeus, and her brother, the sun god, Helios, were honored with wonders of their own (read on).
What Happened: A fire set by a pre-Christian publicity seeker destroyed the temple in 356 B.C. It was rebuilt, then burned down by invading Goths. Early Christians demolished what remained.
What's Left: Excavations have uncovered the foundation and one column. You can see other columns that were excavated and shipped to the British Museum in London.

4. THE STATUE OF ZEUS

Where: Olympia, Greece, the site of the ancient Olympic Games
Who Built It and Why: The Greeks wanted visitors to the ancient Olympics to be impressed, so what was originally a simple temple to Zeus was turned into the home of an enormous statue of Greece's most powerful god.
When: Around 450 B.C.
Particulars: The 40-foot-high statue of Zeus sitting on a throne made the temple look like a playhouse. Zeus's head was just below the ceiling, giving the impression that if he stood up, he'd go right through the roof. His body was made of ivory, and his beard, robe, and sandals were made of gold. His throne, also made of gold, was encrusted with precious stones.
What happened: A fire in A.D. 462
What's Left: Nothing is left of the statue. The temple is one of those picturesque ruins you can visit on vacation.

The castle of Bavaria's King Ludwig II was the model for Cinderella's castle at Disney World.

5. THE MAUSOLEUM AT HALICARNASSUS

Where: Southwestern Turkey
Who Built It and Why: Queen Artemisia built it as a tribute to her husband, King Mausolus.
When: About 353 B.C.
Particulars: Except for the fact that Artemisia was King Mausolus's sister as well as his wife, the only interesting thing about him was his death: The word for a large above-ground tomb, "mausoleum," comes from his name.
What's Left: Some of the foundation. Once again, the British Museum scores big, with statues taken from the tomb.

6. THE COLOSSUS OF RHODES

Where: Overlooking the harbor of Rhodes, a Greek island in the Aegean Sea
Who Built It and Why: The people of Rhodes built it in honor of Helios, the sun god, to celebrate a military victory.
When: 282 B.C.
Particulars: The Colossus was a colossal statue of Artemis's brother, Helios. No one knows exactly what it looked like, but most artists' reconstructions show him naked, or at least scantily clad, which must have been quite a sight at 120 feet high from his toes to his sunburst-shaped crown. In fact, Frenchman Fréderic Bartholdi used the statue for inspiration when he designed the "New Colossus," America's Statue of Liberty, who wears the same pointy headdress.
What Happened: An earthquake hit around 226 B.C. and the statue broke off at its weakest point—the knee.
What's Left: Nothing.

7. THE LIGHTHOUSE OF ALEXANDRIA

Where: The ancient island of Pharos, in Alexandria harbor, Egypt
Who Built It and Why: Finally, a wonder that actually served a purpose. Designed to guide ships into the harbor, it was completed during the reign of King Ptolemy II.
When: About 270 B.C.
Particulars: This wasn't some puny little wooden lighthouse. We're talking magnificence: Covered in marble and close to 400 feet high (the height of a 40-story skyscraper), the lighthouse was

---

Twenty-eight U.S. states and 4 Canadian provinces have names with Native American origins.

famous enough to be pictured on Roman coins minted in Alexandria in the second century A.D. During the day, an enormous mirror reflected the sun; at night, a fire at the top did the job. It was apparently also a tourist attraction, selling food on the first level, with a balcony above for climbers who wanted the scenic view. After 1,500 years as a working lighthouse, it became the last of the six lost wonders to disappear.

What Happened: Another earthquake, this one in the 14th century A.D.

What's Left: Deep-sea divers may have found the ruins in 1996. There are plans to turn it into a tourist attraction again, though visitors may have to snorkel to see the best stuff.

AND THE WINNERS ARE:

We were so impressed with the people who built the wonders that we held an awards dinner—hosted by Mother Nature and Father Time. A round of applause for:

Best Builders: Egyptians
Most Ostentatious Display of God-Worshipping: Greeks
Most Romantic: Babylonians
Most Far-Sighted Accumulators of Other People's Ruins: British
Best Adapters (Copiers) of the Ancient Style: French

*   *   *

OTHER WONDERS

The U.N. World Heritage has compiled a list of the natural wonders of the world. They include: Angel Falls in Venezuela; the Bay of Fundy in Nova Scotia; the Grand Canyon in Arizona; the Great Barrier Reef in Australia; Iguassu Falls in Brazil/Argentina; Krakatoa Island in Indonesia; Mount Everest in Nepal; Mount Fuji in Japan; Mount Kilimanjaro in Tanzania; Niagara Falls in Ontario and New York; Paricutin Volcano in Mexico; and Victoria Falls in Zambia/Zimbabwe. Yes, there are 12! No one could agree on just seven when faced with the glory of Mother Nature.

When the Civil War started, Robert E. Lee owned no slaves, but Ulysses S. Grant did.

WHEN READERS MOVED THEIR LIPS

When people first started learning to read, most couldn't understand the words unless they said them out loud. You might be surprised at how recently that's changed.

For most of human history, storytellers passed everything there was to know from one generation to the next—out loud. Rhyme and rhythm made things easier to remember, so the stories were usually told in poems or songs.

STORY TIME

Singing storytellers were the keepers of information during Europe's Middle Ages. In 13th century Ireland, they called them "bards." The really good ones got to sit next to the king in court. Then there were the troubadors, singers who wandered around the countryside, telling stories in the form of ballads. And of course, that's how your everyday news was passed along, too.

So it's not surprising that when people started reading, it was generally out loud and to each other—just like stories had always been told. Readers needed to hear the words as well as to see them. It wasn't until the 15th century that people got the hang of reading silently.

DIRTY BOOKS

Once silent reading caught on, a person didn't have to let everybody else know what he or she was reading, and therefore, thinking. Silent reading allowed for private thoughts. And it created a demand for different kinds of books—including nonreligious and erotic stories.

By the time the printing press started turning out books in the 16th century, lots of people had libraries of handwritten books. More and more of them had already learned the pleasures of retreating into a private place and reading—just like you're probably doing now.

Women in Switzerland didn't get the vote until 1971.

DIGITIZED HISTORY

Who says you can't change history?
Some of our favorite (good) video games with historical themes.

A s you might expect, video games aren't typically a very good way to learn about history. Even the ones with strong historical themes tend to put the player in the action in order to influence outcomes, so that a smart person playing as the Confederates in a Civil War simulation might actually win the Battle of Gettysburg (so much for that address, Abe). Be that as it may, there are lots of interesting games that use history as a backdrop or use historical data to accurately capture a moment in time. Here are five mostly recent games that make the grade, all available for the PC.

Age of Empires II: Age of Kings
Help! Rome has fallen and it can't get up! Thus begins the Age of Feudalism on the European continent, and players take on one of 13 different civilizations, ranging from the Turks to the Vikings, to rule all the land. The game features innovations and cultural advantages consistent to each of these emerging civilizations' strengths, and also uses lessons from history to advance the player in the game—for example, the tutorial for the game has a player re-creating the battles of William "Braveheart" Wallace. And if that wasn't enough, the game ships with actual, accurate historical information about each civilization represented.

Railroad Tycoon II
Dust off your top hat and wax your Snidely Whiplash moustache, it's time to play railroad baron. Players aim to lay track across any of the seven continents, squaring off against historically modeled opponents in an effort to rule the rails. But it's not all blowing the whistle on the choo-choo, players have to master the stock market as well to bury their competitors. (Watch out for J.P. Morgan—he'll sell you short.) Players lay track, manage their railroads, deal with "real-world" events like wars or disasters and try to take over the world one whistle stop at a time.

Rowan's Battle of Britain
Someone's got to stop those pesky Nazis from pummeling Britain

Japan's Emperor Akihito is 125th in an unbroken line that goes back to first century B.C.

into submission at the start of the Second World War, and that person is you. The game allows players to command the entire RAF effort against the Germans (or the other way around, if you've got a soft spot for the Luftwaffe), but the real action here is in the flight simulator mode, which fairly accurately re-creates what it was like to fly a Supermarine Spitfire or a Messerschmidt Me-109 in dogfight situations (i.e., don't expect to be an Ace your first time out). As you dogfight, you'll see dozens of other planes fighting in the skies as well, which will give you an idea of the scope of these battles as they happened in the real world.

Shogun: Total War

If there's one shortcoming in historical video games, it's that they tend to be centered on the Western hemisphere, re-creating events in European or American history. "Shogun" redresses this, offering game play steeped in Japanese history and culture. Shogun units and their movements are modeled on real 16th century Japanese troops, and the story line re-creates some of the historical milieu of the times (for example, Buddhist Shoguns are fighting with Christian Shoguns). And in case everything you ever learned about Japanese history came from Godzilla movies, the game also has a primer on 16th Japanese history.

Sid Meier's Gettysburg!

Yes, yes, the exclamation point in the title is a little much (it makes it seem like a bad Broadway musical, with Robert E. Lee played by Nathan Lane), but this is one of the very best examples of the historical genre. Creator Meier (who was already a legend to historical game buffs via his "Civilization" series), has painstakingly re-created the circumstances of this pivotal battle in the American Civil War. Players can take either side to seize the high ground and hold it, re-creating select battles or the entire Gettysburg campaign. (If you play as the Rebs, mind you, additional and fictional storylines open up if you win.) Can't get enough? There's a sequel that takes on Antietam.

* * *

"Man is a gaming animal.
He must always be trying to
get the better in something or other."
Charles Lamb

Polish king Augustus the Strong had more than 300 kids, but only had one legitimate son.

BETTER LIVING THROUGH ALCHEMY

The history of alchemy is the history of massive, unceasing, never-ending, total, and complete failure.

For two thousand years (at least!), alchemists strove mightily towards two goals: transmuting base metals into gold, and discovering the Elixir of Life, which would grant immortality to those who drank of it. In all that time, not one alchemist changed lead (or any other metal) into gold. And everyone who drank various elixirs has since died—a significant number of whom died from the elixirs themselves. In all, it's a remarkable history of failure that only a few today have the capacity to fully appreciate.

PREMISES, PREMISES
How could so many have failed so often and for so long? The reasons are numerous, but sooner or later they can all be boiled down to this: alchemists—all of them—simply had no clue as to how the universe actually functions. Although they were diligent experimenters and fervent researchers (and occasional grifters as well), alchemists invariably started from bad premises. In science, and in alchemy (which are not the same things), bad premises get you bad results.

HERE'S HOW IT'S DONE
For example, let's take the whole "making gold" concept. The alchemists weren't wrong on one important idea: You can make gold from other elements. Here's how you do it: start with a huge cloud of hydrogen floating around in the universe. Collapse it into a supergiant star. Let that star run through its natural life, fusing hydrogen into helium, and then helium into carbon, then oxygen, silicon, and iron, and so on through the process of thermonuclear fusion in its core. Soon (relatively speaking) the star will totally collapse and explode in a supernova, shooting out millions of tons of gold and other heavy elements in its final dying outburst. There you have it: gold from hydrogen. Really, it couldn't be simpler.

King Alfonso XIII of Spain was so tone deaf, he couldn't recognize Spain's national anthem.

WHAT DID THEY KNOW?

Sadly for our alchemists, they had no convenient access to stellar cores. Not that they'd know what to do with them, anyway. Alchemists were to a man woefully ignorant of atomic theory, the periodic table, and stellar physics. (It wasn't entirely their fault, mind you—everyone was ignorant of these subjects until the 18th and 19th centuries at the earliest.)

WEREN'T THEY A ROCK GROUP?

Instead, they had some practical knowledge of metals and ores, gleaned from the experience of metallurgists and other metal workers, and a belief that everything in the universe is comprised of varying amounts of four "elements"—earth, fire, air, and water. If one presumes everything is made from these four things, then changing one metal to another is simply a matter of rejiggering the proportions—typically through the use of acidic solvents and alloys. It makes perfect sense, provided all matter is actually comprised of these four "elements." Which it is not.

WHEN THE MOON IS IN THE SEVENTH HOUSE

Compounded to this misapprehension of matter was the belief (in Western alchemy, at least) that the seven known metals (gold, silver, copper, tin, lead, iron, and mercury) were in some way aligned with the seven major "planets" in the sky (the Sun, the Moon, Venus, Jupiter, Saturn, Mars, and Mercury). Astrology touched on alchemy, making it as much a mystical art as a practical endeavor. Alchemy was known to ancient Greeks, Chinese, and Indians as "the Art." The word "alchemy" doesn't show up until the Middle Ages. With these as the guiding principles of alchemy, it's no wonder alchemists didn't get much done in terms of making gold.

WHAT A LOT OF BOLOS

Which is not to say alchemists didn't put on a good show, or didn't claim to make gold. In the 3rd century B.C., Bolos of Mende, writing under the name of Democritus (and not to be confused with the real Democritus, who was, interestingly, a philosopher who believed in the existence of atoms), claimed in his treatise, *Physica et Mystica*, to have made gold. Unfortunately for would-be transmuters, the directions for changing other metals into gold were maddeningly vague, with heaps of astrological mumbo-jumbo thrown in to further muddy the waters.

The Finnish capital of Helsinki was founded in 1550 by a Swedish king.

MONEY ISN'T EVERYTHING
Further up the timeline, a 14th century alchemist named
Raymond Lully was rumored to have created gold for England's
Edward II. Of course, this is not verifiable, and in any event,
didn't seem to do Edward any good, even if it were true. (He was
overthrown by his wife, and skewered on a red-hot poker. Ow.)

SOME OF OUR BEST MINDS
Not everyone who dabbled in alchemy was an out-and-out fraud:
English philosopher Roger Bacon, Dutch astronomer Tycho Brahe,
and Isaac Newton are examples of real scientists who tried their
hand at alchemy. Whatever their other accomplishments, however, as alchemists, these guys were flops just like the rest of them.

SOLID GOLD FEVER
Using alchemy to create gold was a Western obsession. It started
with the Greeks, continued with the Arabs and Muslims (who, as
with so many other subjects, preserved and generously added to
previously existing Greek and European alchemic knowledge,
while Europe festered in what some people call the Dark Ages),
and re-emerged in Europe in the 12th century. Over in China,
which had developed its own alchemic tradition, the emphasis
was far less on transmuting gold than it was on finding an Elixir of
Life, which would grant immortality.

IT'S NOW OR NEVER
Why? One suggestion is that pre-Buddhist Chinese theological
thinking left open a lot of questions about immortality after death,
unlike Western religions, which describe the afterlife in exhaus-
tive and sometimes sadistic detail. The Chinese were hedging
their bets by trying to stay alive in this world. It could be that the
Europeans weren't as interested in the immortality angle because
medieval Europe was largely an unlivable cesspool. So why would
anybody want to prolong living in it?

NOBODY LIVES FOREVER
Whatever the reason for the emphasis on immortality, Chinese
alchemists had as little luck in developing an Elixir of Life as
European alchemists had in making gold. In fact, there's a great
deal of evidence that suggests Chinese alchemists killed off a number of China's principal citizens with their dodgy "elixirs"—so

---

Peter the Great died after rescuing people from a foundering ship.

much evidence that British historian Joseph Needham once compiled a list of Chinese emperors who were likely poisoned to death by their alchemists. Oops. The Chinese emperors eventually wised up and Chinese alchemy died out.

BETTER LIVING THROUGH CHEMISTRY

Western alchemy also petered out by the 18th century. The growing science of chemistry took some of the practical aspects of alchemic thought, discarded the obsession with gold and the mystical aspects, and used them to begin uncovering the true chemical nature of the world. What was left over for alchemy was distilled into a quasi-religious discipline known as Hermetism (named for Hermes Trismegistus, the Greek god associated with chemical knowledge).

THINKING JUNG

The last gasp of alchemy was heard in the 1920s from none other than Carl Jung, who declared that alchemical literature, particularly this mystical stuff, was a manifestation of the "collective unconsciousness." Whatever you say, Carl.

DUMB AND DUMBER

To this date, this is still no practical way either to create gold or to live forever. You have to figure this is a small, bitter comfort for the alchemists. Yes, they were barking up the wrong tree, monumental failures for all time. But we, for all our knowledge of how the universe really works, have yet to do any better.

* * *

NERO FIDDLES AS ROME BURNS, RIGHT? WRONG.

Legend has it that it was the power-crazed Emperor himself who put Rome to the torch in A.D. 64—and then stood atop a tower in the middle of the city and blissfully plucked away at his fiddle as the city went up in flames. History, however, tells quite a different story. According to 1st century historian Tacitus, Nero was 50 miles away at his villa in Antium when the fire started. And when he got the news, rather than reaching for his fiddle, he rushed back to Rome and desperately tried to contain the blaze. His anger over the fire, in fact, brought a massive wave of persecution upon an easy scapegoat—the Christians.

SHOOT ON A SHINGLE

*American G.I.'s had to do something to make their chow
palatable. Can you match the various food and drink items
(1-14) with the slang terms (a-n) that World War II soldiers
invented for them? The answers follow.*

1. Beans
2. Bread
3. Canned milk
4. Coffee
5. Crackers
6. Grape Nuts
7. Hash
8. Ketchup
9. Maple syrup
10. Meatloaf
11. Pancakes
12. Powdered milk
13. Salt and pepper
14. Soup

a. Ammunition
b. Armored cow
c. Chalk
d. Dog biscuits
e. Gun wadding
f. Hot water
g. Machine oil
h. Mystery plate
i. Battery acid
j. Ptomaine steak
k. Rubber Patches
l. Sand and dirt
m. Shrapnel
n. Transfusion

Answers:
1-a; 2-e; 3-b; 4-i; 5-d; 6-m; 7-h;
8-n; 9-g; 10-j; 11-k; 12-c; 13-l; 14-f.

* * *

THE TITANIC WAS ADVERTISED AS UNSINKABLE?

The story of the ship that was billed as unsinkable going down on
her maiden voyage is not quite accurate. The White Star Line
never advertised the fact that *Titanic* or her sister ship *Olympia*
were unsinkable. Instead, their promotion focused on the claim
that the two ships were the "largest and finest steamers in the
world." The supposed advertising of the ship as unsinkable was the
invention of a reporter after the *Titanic* sank. The irony of it made
for copy.

From 1918 to 1944, Norway's Christian X was also king of Iceland.

WORLD'S GREATEST HOAXES, PLUS ONE

*Uncle John loves hoaxes so much that he's decided to
put one over on you.*

Four of the following are real hoaxes, that is, they really happened. One didn't. The challenge is to figure out which one is a hoax that Uncle John's playing on you. Look for the answer at the end. No peeking.

THE COTTINGLEY FAIRIES
The Set-Up: In 1917, two young girls, Elsie Wright and her cousin Frances Griffiths, claimed that they'd played with fairies in the garden of their home in Cottingley, England. They even produced photographs of the fairies to prove it.
The Impact: The pictures made headlines around the world and the story was believed by many, including Sherlock Holmes creator Sir Arthur Conan Doyle, who became an ardent supporter of the girls' story.
It Was All a Hoax: But 55 years later the girls, now old women, admitted that it had all been a hoax and that they had cut pictures of fairies out of a book and attached them with paper clips to branches and shrubs before taking the photographs. Frances Griffiths expressed her amazement that anyone believed the story, saying, "How on earth anyone could be so gullible as to believe that they were real has always been a mystery to me."

THE CARDIFF GIANT
The Set-Up: In 1869, at an upstate New York farm just outside the town of Cardiff, well diggers found what seemed to be the petrified body of a man, but more than a man, a 10-foot-tall giant. The diggers had been hired by New York cigar maker George Hull, a relative of the farm's owner.
The Impact: News of the amazing discovery spread quickly around the world. Hull charged people 50 cents to take a peek at the giant. Experts cried fraud, but the fundamentalists ate it up. So did the civic boosters in whatever town it was exhibited in. The sign

that accompanied the giant claimed that P. T. Barnum had offered $150,00 to buy it. The figure may have been lower, but an offer was made. Hull refused to sell, so Barnum made his own replica of the giant and sued Hull, declaring the original to be a fake.

It Was All a Hoax: Under cross-examination during the ensuing trial, Hull admitted that the giant was nothing more than an elaborate hoax, carved from gypsum and washed with sulfuric acid to make it look old. He had thought up the idea after an argument with a fundamentalist preacher. He wondered if he could convince the preacher that the "giants in the earth" mentioned in the Bible were real. Of course, there was the money-making angle, too. Hull came out of the deal some $30,000 ahead.

P.T. BARNUM'S "FEEJEE" MERMAID
The Set-Up: In August 1842, an Englishman named Dr. J. Griffin arrived in New York bearing a most unusual artifact—what he said was a real mermaid. Or at least the remains of one. Griffin claimed that the mermaid (not a beautiful blonde like in *Splash,* but an ugly creature with the withered body of a monkey and the dried tail of a fish) had been caught in the Fiji Islands.

The Impact: Griffin exhibited the mermaid for one week before taking it to London. The exhibit was a sensation; the story was picked up by newspapers around the world. The mermaid was exhibited for one more month before it was taken on a nationwide tour. The little creature was a tremendous boost in establishing Barnum's reputation as the master purveyor of freak shows.

It Was All a Hoax: The public soon realized that the mermaid was, in fact, the brainchild of promoter extraordinaire P. T. Barnum, and that Dr. Griffin was actually one of Barnum's employees. Griffin's Feejee mermaid was nothing more than a handicraft made by Southeast Asian fishermen who mass-produced the items and sold them as "mermaids." Although the original Feejee mermaid was probably lost when Barnum's exhibition hall burned down in the 1860s, similar specimens show that it was probably made of papier-mâché molded to represent the creature's limbs and combined with the jaw, teeth, spine, and fins of a carp.

WILLARD, THE "TALKING" DONKEY

The Set-Up: An ad in the *Cleveland Plain Dealer* invited the curious to a local auditorium on September 15th, 1873, where they could see what Ohio farmer George Hampton called "an ass that had the uncanny ability to communicate with human beings." Farmer Hampton billed the animal as "proof positive that we came from the lower orders."

The Impact: On the date in question, a crowd of 2,000 people—at 50 cents per head—packed into a Cleveland auditorium. Of course, Willard didn't actually speak. Instead, he tapped his front right hoof on the floor in response to questions. In addition to simple math problems, Willard could answer yes-or-no questions and get them right every time. Willard's fame and Hampton's bank account ballooned. Months later, as Willard was leaving to perform in London for England's Queen Victoria at the Palladium, Willard collapsed of a massive heart attack. He was dead.

It Was All a Hoax: The ensuing autopsy revealed that Willard's heart attack was caused by continual exposure to electric shock treatment. Hampton's assistant, an off-stage operator, triggered the wire to give the donkey a jolt each time he was required to pound his hoof. This continued shock treatment eventually proved too much for the "talking donkey," but not before the world had, once again, been taken for a ride.

THE GIRL WHO BORE RABBITS

The Set-Up: In 1726, an English maid, Mary Toft, claimed to have been assaulted by an exceptionally amorous (and very tall) six-foot rabbit. People actually believed her and the local towns-people went to great lengths to keep their wives and daughters from suffering likewise. Five months later Mary collapsed in a field. A local doctor declared that Mary was pregnant. Four weeks later she gave birth to a dead rabbit, then another. Over the next few days, Howard helped Mary deliver seven more dead rabbits.

The Impact: The news spread quickly. King George I sent two of England's finest physicians to investigate. Mary was still producing rabbits—all dead. The doctors performed tests on the animals. In one, a portion of the lung of one of the rabbits was placed in water. The fact that it floated should have told the doctors that the rabbit had breathed before its "birth." They found digested food in the rabbits' intestines as well as dung in their rectums. They pronounced the births genuine.

It Was All a Hoax: Another third expert arranged for Mary to be moved to a London hospital where she was put under constant surveillance. The rabbits stopped coming. Then a gardener stepped forward, claiming that he'd been supplying Mary with baby rabbits. Mary broke down and confessed. She'd made the whole thing up, inserting the dead rabbits in her womb, then pretending to give birth to them. The motive? Her husband had lost his job and they thought that the publicity might get them a pension from the king. All that Mary got out of it, however, was a prison sentence for fraud.

*　　*　　*

SIR WALTER RALEIGH LAYS DOWN HIS COAT—NOT!

Queen Elizabeth I is leading a procession through the streets of London. She stops in front of a puddle of mud and looks expectantly at her entourage. Suddenly a gallant seaman emerges from the crowd, whips off his cloak and, with a flourish, lays it on top of the offending puddle. The day is saved and two of the great figures of 16th century history come face to face. It's a cute story but it never happened. This tale is the invention of 17th century historian named Thomas Fuller, who's histories are filled with such anecdotal flavorings to enliven otherwise boring stories. Sir Walter Scott picked up on the story in his 1821 novel *Kenilworth*, adding a short exchange between the two famous figures. Raleigh beams that he will never clean the coat, whereupon the Queen instructs him to her wardrobe keeper with orders for a new suit. It's a cute story, but it never happened.

Which is our hoax?
Willard the Talking Donkey was our hoax. All the others are real. By the way, the word "hoax" is a shortening of "hocus-pocus," a synonym for trickery that in turn comes from the Latin "hoc corpus est," — "This is my body,"—the phrase spoken during the Catholic mass when bread is supposedly transformed into the body of Christ.

Canada's 1880 Indian Act defined "person" as "an individual other than an Indian."

POPE-POURRI

Some lesser known tales about some more than human popes.

AND THEN THERE WERE THREE
Traditionally the center of papal life was situated in Rome, but in 1309, Pope Clement V moved the papacy to the French city of Avignon, where it remained until 1377, when Pope Gregory XI returned to Rome. France wasn't pleased by this shift of papal power, so in turn, they elected their own pope. This started what is known as the Great Schism.

Now there were two recognized popes with countries scrambling to align with one or the other. The situation climaxed in 1409, when the Council of Pisa was called to fix the problem. The council simply elected a whole new Pope, Alexander V, and tried to dissolve the papacies of the current Italian Pope, Gregory XII, and the Avignon Pope, Benedict XIII. Of course, neither pope wanted to surrender his seat of wealth and power, thus making a grand total of three popes.

Eventually, the Italian pope resigned and the Avignon pope was deposed (rumor has it, he was defenestrated—literally "thrown out the window" of the palace), finally ending the Great Schism in 1417 after 39 years of papal confusion.

DAMNED IF YOU DO
Pope Gregory IX was hell-bent on purging heretics from the church so he established the Inquisition in 1232. The most popular choice of heretic removal was burning at the stake. After Gregory's death in 1241, the use of torture was employed by Pope Innocent IV, but not without guidelines.

According to the *Book of the Dead* (a guideline for inquisitors), heretics were found guilty if they confessed, had a witness confess against them, or denied their guilt (because anyone who denied their guilt was surely a servant of the devil).

WELCOME TO MY CAVE
It's not easy to decide on a pope. After the death of Pope Nicholas IV in 1292, the two leading families of Rome (the Orsinis and the Colonnas) lobbied hard to have their man elected. Neither family could arrive at a satisfactory nomination until one cardinal, as a

---

Frankenstein author Mary Shelley was the daughter of feminist author Mary Wollstonecraft.

joke, suggested they elect Peter of Morone, an illiterate peasant farmer who lived as a hermit in a mountain cave. The idea caught on. The cardinals arrived at Peter's cave and told the overwhelmed hermit that he had been elected in his absence. He took the name of Celestine V, and the public took him to their hearts. Clearly out of his political element from the start, he resigned after five months. He was later imprisoned by the new elected Pope Boniface VIII (one of the least favorite popes in history), who feared the public's loyalty to Peter. The saintly hermit died months later in a filthy prison cell amid rumors that he'd been starved to death.

NOTABLE PAPAL DEATHS
• Saint Peter, the first pope, was crucified upside-down by the Emperor Nero in A.D. 67.
• John VIII, after surviving a poisoning attempt, was beaten to death with a hammer in 882.
• John XXI was crushed to death while sleeping when a piece of the papal palace at Viterbo fell on him in 1277.
• Pope Martin IV, immortalized as a glutton in Dante's *Inferno* (which he was to an incredible degree), died of indigestion in 1285.
• Alexander VI, the Borgia pope, received a secret message from Caterina Sforza, whom he had imprisoned in Rome. The message was rolled up inside a bamboo cane that had been rubbed with the clothing of a plague victim. They say he died in extreme pain.

RANDOM PAPAL FACTS
• Adrian IV (1154–1159) was the only English pope.
• Boniface VIII (1294–1303) lived in terror of being poisoned. He had a collection of poison-detectors, including a series of "magic knives" that could supposedly detect the presence of poison.
• Pope Leo X was a Medici, the son of the extremely powerful Lorenzo the Magnificent. He was elected pope at age 37 in 1513, even though he'd never even been a priest. He had been a cardinal since he was 13, which made him electable. When the cynical people of Rome heard the news they cried, "Palle! Palle!" Literally, this means "Balls! Balls!" Figuratively, it means "Bulls—t!"
• Before Cardinal Fregnese became Pope Paul III in the sixteenth century, they called him "Cardinal Fregnese the Skirt-Chaser." He sired many children, they say, but only acknowledged three.

It wasn't until 1980 that a country, Iceland, had a democratically elected female head of state.

- When Napoleon conquered Italy, he forced Pius VI (1775–1799) to take a long march from Siena through Italy and into France. A tavern in Siena commemorates the event; it's named "La Pisciata del Papa" — "The Pope's Piss."
- Pope Pius IX (1846–1878) supposedly had the "evil eye"—the ability to cause harm to others just by looking at them—but didn't know he had it. When he rode through towns and villages in Italy, parents would hide their children, and no one would dare look him in the eye.
- Angelo Roncalli (the very popular John XXIII) chose his papal name because "John" was his father's name. There hadn't been a Pope John in more than 500 years, and in fact, the previous one was an anti-pope. Since anti-popes didn't count in Vatican City, Roncalli became the (second) Pope John XXIII.

*   *   *

A NEIGHBOR'S HERBAL TEA

In England in 1775, Dr. William Withering treated an elderly woman for dropsy, a severe swelling of the lower limbs. This would now be diagnosed as caused by congestive heart failure, a condition where the heart pumps so weakly that there is not an adequate circulation of blood. Dr. Withering had nothing to prescribe for the woman and was sure that she would soon die. But a few weeks later he learned that she had recovered from her illness, and that she owed her recovery to a neighbor's herbal tea! Withering asked for the herbal tea recipe, and the doctor realized that the recipe included an old remedy for dropsy that dated back to the Middle Ages—the foxglove plant. Dr. Withering began to experiment, and his results surprised him. The extracts helped cure the swelling of the lower limbs in patients with dropsy. They stimulated the heart rate and improved circulation. Today, the drug digitalis is widely prescribed for congestive heart failure, and the foxglove plant, along with related plant species, is still the basic source of digitalis.

Joan of Arc was actually captured by the French, not the English.

MOTHER GOOSED

Keep her away from the kiddies!
Her rhymes aren't what they appear to be.

WANTED!! A sweet-faced granny riding on a goose. Armed with rhymes and considered dangerous. Goes by the alias Mother Goose. Fills innocent children's heads with verses of violence that slander the kings, queens, and religious leaders of previous centuries. Mother Goose contains some rhymes that were never meant for children. Among the innocent counting verses and tips for learning the ABCs are old songs from the taverns and the streets: war songs, romantic ballads, and political satires based on scandals among the ruling classes.

MURDER AND MAYHEM

Inside every Mother Goose book are "sweet" rhymes about broken heads (Jack and Jill), starving dogs (Mother Hubbard), slashers (Three Blind Mice), and babies crashing out of trees (Rock-a-bye-baby). Who was this violent granny goose?

SHE WAS FRENCH?

The first known Mother Goose book was Charles Perrault's *Contes de Ma Mere L'Oye*, or *Tales of My Mother Goose*, published in 1697 in France. Perrault's book was a collection of fairy tales including *Sleeping Beauty* and *Little Red Riding Hood*.

Mother Goose "rhymes" first appeared in 1765 in England in a book called *Mother Goose's Melody*, or *Sonnets for the Cradle*. The book was published by John Newbery, the same Newbery (one "R" in is his name is correct) that the Newbery Medal, the modern award for the best children's books, is named for. Around 1785, a pirated edition of the book was reprinted in the United States.

THE GOOSE DEBATE

Though most people know the rhymes, they don't know that folklorists still debate the origin of Mother Goose's verses. What did Mother Goose know about crime and death and taxes? Was Jack going up the hill in England or in Scandinavia? Is there a Mother Goose graveyard in Massachusetts? If you think all this arguing is only about some nonsense for kids, take a gander at the history of these rhymes.

Mata Hari was actually a Dutch woman named Margarete Gertrude Zelle.

Little Jack Horner: Turns out that Little Jack wasn't a very good boy. He was really a bureaucrat who proved that crime does pay.

> Little Jack Horner sat in the a corner
> Eating his Christmas pie.
> He stuck in a thumb
> And pulled out a plum.
> And said, "What a good boy am I."

Around 1540, Jack Horner was a steward who was sent to deliver deeds of church properties to King Henry VIII. The deeds were hidden inside a Christmas pie to foil highway robbers. According to the legend, one property never made it to the king. Horner stole a deed out of the pie and kept it for himself. This "plum" that Horner pulled from the pie was the deed to the estate of Mells Manor. Horner's descendants lived on the property for generations. They claimed the verses were false and that Mells Manor was purchased legitimately.

Baa Baa, Black Sheep: This verse can be traced to the Middle Ages. It's a bitter complaint about an export tax, not about sheep.

> Baa baa,
> Black Sheep,
> Have you any wool?
> Yes, marry, have I. Three bags full:
> One for my master,
> One for my dame,
> And one for the little boy
> That lives in the lane!

The hard-working peasant in this rhyme gave a third of his income to the king, called "my master" and another third to the nobility, sneeringly labeled "my dame." That left only a third of his income for the "the little boy," who was the peasant himself.

Ring-Around-the-Rosie: Many sources will tell you that this rhyme is about Black Death in England and Scotland.

> Ring-around-the-rosie
> Pocket full of posies
> Ashes, ashes
> We all fall down.

They think that "rosie" refers to the rash that was a symptom of the plague, and interpret the other lines as representing other aspects of the illness, with death at the last line. But this idea has been debunked—for one thing, the rhyme is from a period 450 years after the Black Death. Folklorists now believe that this rhyme came out of the Protestant ban on dancing in the 19th century. In the United States, young people would have "play-parties" with rhymes and games that were basically square dances without the music. "Ring Around the Rosie" was one of these.

Georgie Porgie: A rhyme that may have mocked a royal scandal.

> Georgie Porgie pudding and pie,
> Kissed the girls and made them cry.
> When the boys came out to play,
> Georgie Porgie ran away.

When King George IV of England was the Prince of Wales, he was notorious for his drinking, gambling, and womanizing. In 1780, at age 18, "Georgie" had an affair with an actress, a Mrs. Perdita Robinson. This was followed by a relationship with a Lady Melbourne. Soon George's string of mistresses was legendary. Lots of people believed he was the Georgie Porgie in the rhyme.

Humpty Dumpty: This rhyme is an "eggsellent" example of the controversies surrounding Mother Goose. There is no consensus yet on Humpty's true identity.

> Humpty Dumpty sat on a wall,
> Humpty Dumpty had a great fall;
> All the king's horses and all the king's men
> Couldn't put Humpty together again.

In 1930, Katherine Thomas's book, *The Real Personages of Mother Goose*, explained that Humpty Dumpty was about King Richard III of England. At the Battle of Bosworth in 1485, Richard commanded a hilltop (the wall in the rhyme). In spite of all the efforts of his horses and men, Richard fell from his horse (he's the Shakespearean character who cried, "My kingdom for a horse!"), and after this "great fall," was killed.

Other folklorists think Humpty dates back to the English Civil War in 1648, and that Humpty Dumpty refers to King Charles I's huge cannon mounted on the wall of a church tower. When the wall was blown up, the cannon tumbled to the ground, where it lay, broken and useless; the king's men couldn't fix it.

Then there's the camp that believes Humpty Dumpty was

Woodrow Wilson couldn't read until he was 9, but became the only president with a Ph.D.

Charles himself. When he lost the war, that was his "great fall." He was beheaded by his enemies and—obviously—his men couldn't put him back together. Scholars continue to debate the identity of a sadly scrambled egg.

Jack and Jill: Probably the most controversial of all the rhymes: the tiny village of Kilmersdon, England, takes first claim, but others say that the village's ideas are just plain "cracked."

> Jack and Jill went up the hill
> To fetch a pail of water.
> Jack fell down and broke his crown,
> And Jill came tumbling after.

Kilmersdon, 200 miles west of London, formed a Jack and Jill committee to renovate the hill where they claim Jack broke his crown in the 15th century. Some say that Jack and Jill went up the hill, not to get water, but to…uh, well…be alone. Jill supposedly died of a broken heart after she gave birth to their son. Many people living nearby have the last name Gilson (Jill's son, get it?).

But the Scandinavians cite a myth that dates back to the 13th century. Two children went to steal a bucket of dew from the moon god. The moon captured them, and the images of the children with a bucket suspended between them can be viewed on the surface of a full moon. Some folklorists say that this myth, and not an accident in Kilmersdon, is the origin of the rhyme. In another interpretation, there was never any female Jill and the rhyme mocks Jack and Gill, two boys, who were actually Cardinal Wolsey and Bishop Tarbes, who were hated for trying to raise an unpopular war tax. Other folklorists are sure that Jack and Jill aren't even human. A "jack and a gill" were liquid measurements, and drinking was taxed by jacks and gills. According to some historians, Charles I (the same Charles who was beheaded) tried to increase taxes by making the actual measurement of jacks and gills smaller while taxing them at the same rate. As explained in Humpty Dumpty, Charles lost his crown…and his head.

Hey, Diddle, Diddle: The 17th and 18th centuries had their share of sex and scandal. Nosy Mother Goose put some of those scandals into verse.

> Hey diddle, diddle
> The cat and fiddle.
> The cow jumped over the moon.

The little dog laughed to see such sport.
And the dish ran away with the spoon.

Queen Elizabeth I may have been known as the Virgin Queen, but according to some interpretations of this rhyme it was an honorary title. In her court, she was known as "the cat," and some believe that the rhyme refers to the way Elizabeth "diddled" with her lovers. It's also said that the "little dog" refers to the Earl of Leicester, who was the Queen's favorite for a time. The dish running away with the spoon may refer to a young couple in her court who married secretly. The marriage, by the way, enraged Elizabeth and she shut the pair up in the Tower of London.

WAS THERE A REAL MOTHER GOOSE?
Even the legend of Mother Goose herself has its controversies.

Old Mother Goose
When she wanted to wander
Would ride through the air,
On a very fine gander.

HUNTING THE GOOSE
Some folklorists trace Mother Goose to an 8th-century French noblewoman, Bertrada II of Loan. Queen Bertrada was the mother of Emperor Charlemagne, who united much of Europe. The empress-mum may have been pigeon-toed, and was apparently known by the unflattering title of Queen Goosefoot. Eight centuries later, a French poem of 1650 includes a line about a "tale from Mother Goose." By the time Charles Perrault's *Le Conte de Ma Mere L'Oye* appeared, the French legend of an old woman who entertained children with fascinating stories was well established.

THE GOOSE MIGRATES
Eventually Mother Goose became well known to American children as a rhyme-reciting granny riding a goose. In Boston, Massachusetts, tourists still flock to the Tremont Street grave of Mistress Elizabeth Foster VerGoose. Tourists are told that this widow entertained her grandchildren with rhymes and that her son-in-law, Thomas Fleet, published the rhymes as *Songs for the Nursery* or *Mother Goose's Melodies* in 1719. But no such book has ever been found. Like many other celebrities, Mother Goose may have had to deal with impostors who took advantage of her celebrity.

BUCCANEER BABES

*If pirating separated the men from the boys,
how come the best pirates were women?*

I f ever there was an old boys' club it was under the Jolly Roger. Pirating was a man's world, and most buccaneers wouldn't let women on board unless they were captives. Some ladies managed to become pirates and beat the men at the plundering game.

ANNE BONNY

Pirate Benjamin: The woman pirate most famous for her fierceness and temper was Anne Bonny. Born Anne O'Malley, she was the heiress to a fortune. She could have lived a spoiled, genteel life as the belle of a Southern plantation, but she threw it all away for a cutlass and a pair of breeches (that's pants, to you).

Who She Was: She was born in Ireland, the illegitimate daughter of a lawyer and his serving maid. Her father pretended that she was a child of one of his relatives. Eventually he left his wife for Anne's mother and took the new family to South Carolina. Daddy got rich in America and Anne found herself living a life of luxury. Everything changed when her father made the mistake of objecting to her choice of husband. James Bonny was a seafaring man who was later described as "not worth a groat," old-fashioned talk for saying he was pretty much worthless. Rather than submit to her father's wishes, Anne eloped with James to the Bahamas.

From Lady to Pirate: Most stories depict James Bonny as spinelessly unworthy of Anne. Whatever the reason, Anne soon rebelled and left home again, this time with a handsome, free-spending man, a pirate named Calico Jack Rackham.

Where and When She Sailed: Anne and Calico Jack were part of the early eighteenth-century Caribbean piracy boom.

A Legend in Her Time: Anne's temper and courage were legendary. A man had once tried to rape her, and she "beat him so, that he lay ill of it a considerable time."

Pirate Fashions: Anne "wore men's cloaths" into battle, but most other times she wore "women's cloaths." Her battle outfit was a man's jacket, long "trouzers," a handkerchief tied around her head, a pistol in one hand and a machete in the other.

Elizabeth Blackwell was the first woman doctor in both the U.S. and the U.K.

Anne Shows Her Stuff: In 1720, the British, determined to put an end to piracy in their Caribbean colonies, chased down Calico Jack. When the British boarded the ship, only three pirates stayed on deck and fought. One of them was Anne. The rest of the pirates, including Calico Jack, holed up belowdecks. The British captured Calico Jack and his crew and took them to prison. Just before he was to be hanged, Calico Jack was granted leave to visit Anne in prison. If he hoped for any last-minute tenderness, he was disappointed. Anne told him bluntly that she was sorry, "but if he had fought like a man he need not have been hang'd like a dog." Anne had proved her mettle in her last days at sea.

Her Last Days: Anne would have swung beside her lover, but she "pleaded her belly," old-fashioned talk for "I'm pregnant." She didn't hang, and there's no record of what did happen to her. Some say her wealthy father secretly arranged her release. Others are sure that clever, feisty Anne saved herself somehow.

MARY READ

Cross-Dresser Extraordinaire: Mary spent a lot of her life impersonating a fighting man. Some historians think she favored women in the romance department, including Anne Bonny. However she spent her shore leave, her biography portrays her as courageous and loyal, a great friend and terrible enemy.

Who She Was: Mary Read was born near London. Like Anne Bonny, Mary was an illegitimate child. Her mother was married, but not to Mary's father. When her father died, her mother started dressing Mary as a boy and pretended that Mary was her husband's child, a son who had recently died. By the time Mary was 16, she was a sailor on a "man-of-war," an English navy ship. Next, she tried the army for awhile. She fought with great distinction until she fell in love with a comrade-in-arms and neglected her fighting duties, not to mention her efforts at male impersonation. Mary got her man, and they gave up soldiering to become innkeepers.

From Innkeeper to Pirate: Mary might have spent her life slinging ale instead of slicing up cabin boys, but her husband died, and Mary started to feel the pinch of poverty. She tried soldiering again, and at the end of her service, sailed to the West Indies. On the way, she was captured by pirates. Before you know it, she was one of the boldest "men" who ever sailed under a pirate flag.

France's Charles VI had iron rods put into his clothes to keep his "glass body" from breaking.

Where and When She Sailed: Small world. Captain Calico Jack Rackham and his crew were the pirates who boarded Mary's ship. Mary joined them and sailed on the *Revenge* until 1720.

A Legend in Her Time: Mary was famous for her fearlessness and loyalty. She still had a romantic side. While on the *Revenge*, she fell in love again. This time with a fellow pirate who was in trouble because he'd pledged to fight a duel with another mean, tough pirate. Mary's sweetheart was sure to lose. To protect him, Mary picked a fight with the guy. When her terrified boyfriend showed up for the duel, his opponent was dead. Mary had killed him.

Mary Shows Her Stuff: In 1720, when the British boarded the *Revenge* to take its captain and crew to prison, Mary stayed on deck with Anne Bonny and fought the enemy off. When she saw other pirates retreating with the captain into the hold, Mary fired on them in anger and disgust. When captured, like Anne, she told the court that she was pregnant. Yet she believed in hanging. If it wasn't for hanging, "every cowardly fellow would turn pyrate and so infest the seas, that men of courage must starve."

Her Last Days: Mary Read died in prison of fever.

CHENG I SAO

The Pirate Godmother: History's most successful pirate wasn't Blackbeard or Red Beard. It was Cheng I Sao, a Chinese woman.

Who She Was: Born around 1775, Cheng I Sao lived on the banks of the South China Sea, where families lived on sail-powered houseboats called junks. Women on these junks fished, traded, and pirated alongside their men. In her youth, Cheng I Sao was a prostitute, on the low rung of poverty's ladder.

From Hooker to Pirate: She was lucky to marry well; her husband owned a fleet of pirate junks, so they went into business. Pirating was an entrepreneurial opportunity, and she grabbed it.

Where and When She Sailed: The newlyweds were among the many pirates on the coasts and inland waterways of Kwangtung province in China during the early 19th century.

A Legend in Her Time: Most Chinese pirates operated in quarrelsome gangs. Cheng I Sao and her husband operated a family business. They realized that if the pirates stopped quarreling, they could become a true power. Cheng I unified the pirates into a confederation. When he died in 1807, Cheng I Sao took over.

She made her husband's adopted son, Cheng Pao, her lover and trusted lieutenant. Then she built up six fleets of junks that carried cannons and up to 400 men each. Plunder was shared, and warehouses were filled to keep the pirates well supplied and well armed. The first time pirates stole booty they were flogged, the second time they were executed. Deserters lost their ears. Fornicators could lose their heads. But thanks to discipline, the confederation of pirates became a fighting force and a moneymaking machine that not only robbed ships, but also sold "protection" to fishermen and merchants and even entire villages.

Cheng I Sao Shows Her Stuff: When the Chinese government tried to tame her organization, Cheng I Sao sent her pirates (who ate their enemies' hearts with rice for fortitude) to terrorize the nation and its rulers. Government fleets, sent to destroy the pirates, were themselves destroyed. A captured government officer was nailed to a deck and beaten horribly before he was killed.

Her Last Days: After negotiating a deal with the government so she wouldn't be prosecuted, Cheng I Sao retired in 1810. She married Cheng Pao, and kept her nose clean until he died. Then she went back to a life of crime, running illegal businesses that involved gambling and possible smuggling. For ambitious Cheng I Sao, this was a quiet life. She died of natural causes in 1844.

GRACE O'MALLEY

Rebel With a Cause: If ever a woman was a pirate-queen, it was 16th century Irishwoman Gráinne, a.k.a. Grania or Grace O'Malley. The English considered her a dangerous rebel. Those who depended on her viewed her as a fearless, shrewd leader who put food on their table and defended their Gaelic way of life.

Who She Was: Around 1530, in Ireland's Mayo County, Grace was born into the Gaelic aristocracy. Her wealthy father, Owen O'Malley was the elected chief of the O'Malley clan and captain of a fleet of ships. Grace loved the sea, but girls were not supposed to be sailors. As legend has it, she cut off her hair and dressed in boy's clothes so she could go to sea. The family laughingly nicknamed her "Gráinne Mhaol" meaning "bald Grace," and allowed her to travel with her father. It was a life-saving decision. When Owen O'Malley's ship was attacked and a pirate came up behind him with a dagger, little Grace jumped down from the rigging to go after the pirate. This distraction saved Owen, and his men defeated the pirates.

Where and When She Sailed: At 16, Grace was given in a political marriage to Donal O'Flaherty, the heir to the leadership of the O'Flaherty clan. The united clans controlled the waters off the west coast of Ireland. The couple lived in castles when not at sea.

Pirate Queen: After 19 years of marriage, Donal died defending Cork's Castle from a rival clan. Grace, now the widowed mother of three children, stormed and regained the castle. Her bravery led to Cork's Castle being renamed Hen's Castle—the name it has today. Grace returned to O'Malley territory and went back to sea. She charged money for safe passage along the west coast and plundered any ship that didn't pay tribute. Eventually, she married again, and moved into her new husband's home, Rockfleet Castle. She dominated her second husband, Richard Burke, while controlling the seas from Clew Island to Galway.

A Legend in Her Time: Legend says that Grace gave birth to her fourth child onboard ship, one day before Turkish pirates attacked. When a crewman told her that the Turks were winning, she said "May you be seven times worse this day twelve months, who cannot do without me for one day." She rushed into battle wrapped in a blanket, defeated the pirates, and added their ship to her fleet.

The Pirate Queen Meets the Virgin Queen: In 1586, Gráinne was captured by a hated enemy, Sir Richard Bingham. He confiscated her cattle and horses, tied her up, and built a special gallows to hang her. She escaped hanging and was sent home. Bingham had destroyed her livelihood on the land, and she feared he would keep her from the sea too. The wily pirate petitioned Queen Elizabeth I for justice and went to London to plead her case—risking death since Elizabeth showed no mercy to rebellious Irish chiefs.

No one knows what passed between the two queens at the meeting, but in September 1593, Queen Elizabeth ordered Bingham to pardon Grace and her family. In addition the Queen demanded that the governor give "the old woman" a stipend to live on. Elizabeth wrote that she considered the Irish leader an ally who would "fight in our quarrel with all the world."

Her Last Days: Gráinne controlled a fleet of ships into her seventies. It's believed she died in 1603, at home in Rockfleet Castle.

Jean-Paul Marat and Agamemnon were both slain in their bathtubs by women.

THE MONGOL HORDE

*The difference between the Mongols and everyone else
was the personal touch they provided each and every
town, hamlet, and village they visited.*

Other notable invading armies didn't really give a damn about your pathetic little hole-in-the-wall burg. It was just another bump on the road to, oh, let's say, Russia. You could just feed 'em lunch and send them on their way, and still get the harvest in on time. Everyone was happy, at least until the army froze itself to death outside of St. Petersburg later that winter. But hey, like that's *your* problem.

THE DIFFERENCE

Not so the Mongols. Sure, they were gonna kick the stuffing out of China, sooner or later. But they weren't in that much of a rush. China wasn't going anywhere—heck, it's just over that wall they built. Handy marker, that. In the meantime, they were happy to devote their full and undivided attention to *you*. But at least they made it simple. You had two choices: Resist, and die a totally horrible death, what with the screaming and the stabbing and the horse trampling with the clop clop *clop*, or surrender, and have your villagers serve as the shock troops to invade the pathetic little hole-in-the-wall burg two miles down the road. Unless they decided to kill you anyway, for tactical reasons. Nothing personal.

WHOSE VERSION OF HISTORY?

Historians typified the Mongols as a "horde." While admittedly this would appear an apt description, as tens of thousands of yowling Asiatic warriors bore down on you with spears, atop a sea of fiery steeds, the fact is that the Mongols were both amazingly well disciplined and utterly loyal to the aims of their maximum leader. He's a fellow we call Genghis Khan, but who, to his friends and family, was known as Temüjin.

GONE WITH THE YAK'S MILK

You can't tell the story of the Mongols without telling the story of Genghis, a story that reads like the script pitch of a desperate hack screenwriter to a development minion for a third-rate director. Genghis, pampered son of a clan leader, found his life shattered

---

David Livingstone wasn't exactly lost. He just wasn't interested in being found.

when his noble father, Yesügei, was poisoned by the evil Tartars.
(It was in the yak's milk!). Abandoned by his clan, Genghis'
family was reduced to eating roots and fish. Genghis swore, with
God as his witness, that he would never be hungry again!

HIS START IN THE INVADING BUSINESS

Genghis's father had prepared for his son's future by finding him a
fiancée when he was just a little boy. When Genghis went to
claim the woman he was betrothed to, he found that she had been
kidnapped and ravished by the nefarious Merkit people! Enraged,
Genghis allied himself with an old blood brother of his father,
gathered an army together, and crushed those nasty Merkits like
the fiancée-ravishing worms they were! While he was away, the
Jürkins, supposedly his allies, plundered his lands! Those Jürks! He
squashed them too, and killed every member of the clan taller
than a wagon axle, leaving only children alive.

MURDER, PILLAGE, AND MORE

Thus Genghis began his conquering ways. It wasn't all murder and
pillage, mind you. Genghis actually had a plan. It had been the
old clan system that contributed to his father's death and that
kept the Mongol people set against themselves; Genghis changed
all that by scattering the members of conquered clans among his
troops, and by arranging those troops into divisions that were
arranged numerically rather than by clan. Advancement in the
army was thus tied to a soldier's loyalty to Genghis, not to his former clan; soon enough, everyone was sucking up to Genghis, and
of course he liked that just fine.

THE BABY-EATING RUMOR

By 1206, Genghis and his highly regimented not-at-all-a-horde
horde was ready to kick some serious non-Mongol booty, and off
they went. They were almost all on horseback, which gave them
exceptional mobility and range, since all the horses needed to eat
was the grass they found on the way to clobbering some poor foes.
The Mongols also made use of whatever technology they found;
they were extremely happy to use a nation's own knowledge
against it.

Genghis himself, despite his current reputation for crazed,
baby-eating dictatorship, actually took advice rather well. For
example, he had planned to turn the whole of northern China

Abel Tasman discovered Tasmania, New Zealand, and Fiji, but never noticed Australia.

into a horse pasture, until it was pointed out to him that it might be better to raise food there and then profit from the taxes and trade. Only *after* he made that decision did he eat any babies (no, not *really*).

WHAT MADE THEM SO GOOD

It was in fact this combination of ruthlessness and adaptability that made the Mongols the invaders to beat—literally—throughout all of history. They were smarter, they were meaner, and they could rides circles around you on their little horses. Their empire ultimately reached from China to the Russian steppes. And they would have gotten Japan, too, were it not for a fortuitous typhoon that sunk their attacking ships—the fabled *kamikaze*, or "divine wind," which would serve as a motivation for Japanese fighter pilots to ram explosives-laden fighter planes into American battleships in WWII.

WHAT THEY WEREN'T SO GOOD AT

The Mongols' problem was that they were better at conquering than they were at actual empire ruling; after the death of Genghis's grandkid Kublai Khan in 1294, it all sort of fell apart. But who cares? When they knocked on the door, and said "Hi! We're the Mongol Horde!" you just *knew* they weren't selling magazine subscriptions to work their way through college. It was trouble with a capital "T," and that rhymed with "G," and that stood for "Genghis." That's what it took to be the best invaders in history, and the Mongols had it, with plenty to spare.

* * *

HANG 'EM HIGH

Lynching didn't start in the old West but during the American Revolution. A justice of the peace and farmer in prewar days, Colonel Charles Lynch led a bunch of vigilantes to dispense their own brand of justice on British supporters and outlaws. Thus, hanging someone without a trial became known as "lynching," and bands of vigilantes bent on hanging their quarry were called "lynch mobs."

Although John Cabot sailed for the British, he was really an Italian named Giovanni Caboto.

HOW SHORT WAS NAPOLEON?

*Everybody knows at least two things about Napoleon Bonaparte.
First, that he met his Waterloo, and second, that he was short.
But exactly how short was he?*

Napoleon Bonaparte, emperor of France, stood 5 feet, 6½ inches in his stocking feet; short by today's standards— but not by the standards of his time or his countrymen.

NOT YOUR AVERAGE PARISIAN

The average height of a Parisian man circa 1800 was about 5 feet, 6 inches. Which makes Napoleon a teensy bit *above* average in height. So why does the world think of him as short?

THE SHORT MAN ON THE TEAM

The men he was most often seen with—the grenadiers of his Imperial Guard—were very tall men. That might have started the first inkling of a rumor, and might be why the English political cartoons of the day depicted him as short. But that's not the answer. Napoleon's height didn't become carved in the stone of history until he died.

WHERE IT ALL STARTED

During his autopsy, Napoleon's body was measured using the old French system called "pieds de roi," which translates to "feet of the king." The French 5 feet, 2 inches translates to 5 feet, 6½ inches in English measurements.

P.S. THE HAND INSIDE THE SHIRT

Most depictions of Napoleon show him with his hand inside his vest. While some historians believe that he suffered from ulcers and was pressing his hand against the painful spot, it's also true that the hand-in-the-vest pose was often used for gentlemen's portraits in that period. So we'll never know for certain—unless someone builds a time machine and goes back to ask, "Pardonnez-moi, Your Imperial Highness—does the stress of running the Empire give you tummy troubles?"

The British Empire started in Newfoundland, where England founded its first overseas colony.

WHEREWORDS: A QUIZ
(His Closet)

There's just no telling what you'll find when you start snooping around some old closet, even if it's your own! Where did all this stuff come from? Choose the best answer, then check it against our answers on the next page.

1. SOCK
a. The first were woven from fine Egyptian linen called "sax."
b. Named for Sir William Soxbury, who first wore them in public.
c. The Latin word "soccus," a shoe made of thin leather.

2. TUXEDO
a. Its resemblance to Aptenodytes tuxidoa, the tuxedo penguin.
b. Mark Twain, who ridiculed formalwear as "tailored & tucksied."
c. It made its 1886 debut at a country club in Tuxedo Park, NY.

3. STETSON
a. In prairie pidgin, to "stet" means to "stay," and this hat "stay's on."
b. Alteration of "State Son," honoring Texans who died at Alamo.
c. Named for its creator, Philadelphia haberdasher John Stetson.

4. UMBRELLA
a. It was patterned after the Alaskan "umbriak," a round canoe.
b. From the Latin "umbra," which means "shade.'
c. For Londoner Ed Umbrell, its inventor.

5. PAJAMAS
a. Their Central American town of origin, Pajama (near Panama.)
b. The Farsi "pae" for "leg," and "jamah" meaning "garment" because they started out as pants.
c. It was developed and marketed by flannel baron Sanjib Pajima.

6. GLOVE
a. From the Anglo-Saxon "glof," meaning the palm of the hand.
b. Named after Sir Gloveston, a knight of the Round Table.
c. The oldest pair came from King Tut's Gluvrii Chamber.

7. TROUSERS
a. The Gaelic "trews" for "leg covers."
b. Leather garments first seen on Nordic fishermen, on River Trow.
c. After French prelate Henri Trouseur, who wore them under his robe.

8. SHOE
a. From the practice of hurling footwear at undesirable critters while yelling "shoo!"
b. The Anglo-Saxon "sceo," pluralized to "schewis," meaning "to cover."
c. It was popularized by Japanese leather merchant Shu' Ze.

Magellan was not the first person to sail around the world. He was killed partway through.

1-c. The ancient Greeks wore them first; they were made of a light leather and called "sykhos." Roman soldiers used them as boot liners and wore them to Britain, where the name "soccus" was clipped to "socks."

2-c. Heir to the tobacco fortune, Pierre Lorillard IV, a blueblood New Yorker set the fashion world on its collective ear in 1886. His family commissioned and wore the first of the future prom rentals to the Autumn Ball at his exclusive country club in the village Tuxedo Park.

3-c. John Stetson worked in his family's Philadelphia hat business as a boy. He traveled out west in the 1860s to improve his health. When he returned to Philly, he started making hats that were suited to the needs of the Western cowboy. The hats soon became the most popular cowboy headgear in the west. Buffalo Bill, General George Custer, Annie Oakley, and Calamity Jane all wore 'em.

4-b. In 1750s London, a British merchant named John Hanway popularized the umbrella. Before that, anything more than a casual attempt to avoid the rain was considered unmanly; the humble umbrella was for women to escape the sun.

5-b. From late in the sixteenth century, both men and women wore nightgowns (true!) Two hundred years later, as women's nightgowns got filmier, men's got shorter, and turned into nightshirts. The loose pants called "pajamas" were worn on the bottom. The two didn't match, of course. But eventually they did, and—voila!—the pajamas that we know today.

6-a. Men have been wearing gloves for 10,000 years. Women didn't get in on the digital fun until 1550, when France's Catherine de Medici stunned the fashion world with hers: lavishly embroidered and richly jeweled.

7-a. Anyone can wear the pants in your family, but only men can wear trousers; when women wear them, they're "slacks" (from Latin, "laxus," for "loose.")

8-b. Egyptian sandals of woven papyrus were the first footwear, worn as early as 2000 B.C. Greeks fashioned fitted footwear from leather by 600 B.C., followed by the Romans who added rights and lefts around 200 B.C. But our word for shoe comes from the Anglo-Saxons.

Saint Augustine, Jamestown, and Quebec City were all founded before Plymouth.

THE CODE OF HAMMURABI

Hammurabi was the king of Babylon, a city synonymous with decadence and moral depravity—a sort of Sodom and Gomorrah all rolled into one. We thought it was our duty to look into it. For purely historical reasons, of course.

LAYING DOWN THE LAW

Sometime around 1780 B.C., King Hammurabi of Babylon decided to have his favorite 281 laws carved into an eight-foot-high stone column. At the top, the royal artists carved a picture of the great king on his throne. Below that is the text, which begins with a rambling message from Hammurabi, in which he calls himself "the exalted prince" and vows to "destroy the wicked and the evil-doers." On the rest of the column is carved a list of laws, from #1 to #282, called the Code of Hammurabi. It's believed that the code was displayed in a conspicuous place, probably the town square or something. This way, it's assumed, nobody had an excuse for breaking the law.

The laws are arranged in orderly groups: a cluster of laws governing slaves here, laws concerning marriage and inheritance there. And so on. Some of the laws you already know about: an eye for an eye, for instance. It's specified in Law #196 this way: "If a man put out the eye of another man, his eye shall be put out." Pretty basic. A tooth for a tooth is covered under law #200. There's no mention of prison. The only alternatives were fines, a death sentence, or, as in the case of the eye and tooth mentioned above, the occasional "pound of flesh."

LET THE PUNISHMENT FIT THE CRIMINAL

Crimes and their punishment had a direct correlation to social status. Unless the crime was serious, the higher you were on the social ladder, the less severely you were punished. The poor slobs clustered around the bottom of the ladder paid dearly—often with their lives. Law #8 is a perfect example. It covers the theft of livestock. Say someone steals a goat. If the goat "belonged to a god,"

i.e., was stolen from a temple—the tippy-top of the social scale—
the thief had to pay 30 times the worth of the goat. If the goat
belonged to a "free man"—someone a step up from a regular
citizen—the thief had to pay less, just 10 times the amount. If the
thief was too poor to pay the fine, he was put to death.

OFF WITH THEIR HEADS!

There were plenty of other opportunities for the average Babylonian to be sentenced to death. Here's a list of crimes that called for
capital punishment. You would be put to death for:

- Accusing someone of a crime without proof
- Falsely accusing someone of a crime
- Stealing the property of a temple or a court
- Receiving the stolen property of a temple or a court
- Stealing a slave
- Helping a slave escape
- Hiding a slave
- Breaking and entering
- Committing a robbery
- Allowing conspirators to meet in your tavern
- Violating a virgin who is promised in marriage to another

Even an innocent bystander could be included in the death
sentence. Take Law #229, for example, which states that a house
builder will be put to death if the house he built falls in and kills
the owner. The next law, #230, adds a nuance: "If it kill the son of
the owner, the son of that builder shall be put to death."

WHICH WAY DID THEY GO?

In most cases, the exact manner of death is left to the imagination, but in some cases it's well-defined. For example:

- If a wife and her lover have their mates (her husband and the
other man's wife) murdered, "both of them shall be impaled."
- If a robbery is committed during a fire, the criminal will be
thrown into that "self-same fire." Which doesn't leave much time
for a trial.
- If you're a priestess and you own or enter a tavern, you'll be
burned to death.

Lady Jane Grey was England's first queen in nearly 400 years, but lasted just nine days.

MINOR OFFENSES
You could have your hands cut off:

- If you're a surgeon who kills someone during surgery
- If you hit your father
- If you steal corn or plants from a farm owner you work for

You could have your ear cut off:

- If you're a slave who says to his master, "You are not my master."

TRY AND PROVE IT!
Apparently the Babylonians had no idea there was such a thing as swimming. If a crime couldn't be proven, the accused would be thrown into the water. If she (and it was usually a she) floated, she was innocent. If she didn't, she drowned.

You would be thrown into the water:
- If your husband accused you of being unfaithful, but couldn't catch you in the act
- If you quarreled with your husband for no reason, then left him or neglected him

Then there were the occasions when you wouldn't be given the option of trying to stay afloat. For instance, you would be tied up and thrown into the water:

- If your husband surprised you with another man. Or if you were the other man with the wife when the husband surprised her.

Perhaps by now you're thinking, ho-hum, what's so decadent? The Babylonians didn't do anything we don't do every day in our society. We were beginning to think the same thing, until we came across a mention of the goddess Ishtar, a.k.a. "The Great Whore of Babylon."

THEY DON'T CALL IT BABYLON FOR NOTHING
Ishtar was the goddess of war and sexual love, and the most powerful goddess in the Mesopotamian religion. If you wanted to be part of her cult (and everyone did) you had to participate.

Every female citizen was expected to go at least once in her life to the temple of Ishtar and offer herself to any male worshipper who paid the required contribution. There was no shame attached to being one of Ishtar's prostitutes, in fact, it was considered a sacred means of attaining divine union between man and goddess. Oh, yeah. The English writer Sir James Frazer, in *The Golden Bough*, mentions the girls who didn't make the cut:

> The sacred precinct (Ishtar's temple) was crowded with women waiting to observe the custom. Some of them had to wait there for years.

We assume they were the less attractive of Ishtar's temporary prostitutes. Poor wallflowers, waiting all their lives in the temple for some poor schmo to ask them for a date.

HOW WE KNOW ALL THIS

In A.D. 1901, a team of archeologists led by a French scholar found the fairly well-preserved column we call the Code of Hammurabi in Persia. Besides its importance as a historical curiosity, we think it's given us a pretty good look into the customs and mores of ancient Mesopotamia. You can see it for yourself the next time you're in Paris, where it's on display at the Louvre Museum. Just saunter over to it and impress your friends with everything you know about the Code of Hammurabi. Including the fact that there is no Law #13. The Babylonians were as superstitious as us.

* * *

THE EVIL KIMONO

Modern man has little respect for evil spirits. But as Japanese legend tells it, a priest in Tokyo was able to tell when they were present. In February 1867, the priest knew he had to remove evil spirits from a kimono that he believed to be cursed. Three teenaged girls had owned the innocent-looking garment, and all three had fallen ill and died. As the fathers of the young victims watched, the priest solemnly set a torch to the kimono. But just as the cloth caught fire, a fierce wind came up. The evil wind swept the flames out of control until they ignited the wooden dwellings of the city. Before it was extinguished, the infamous "long-sleeved kimono" fire killed more than 100,000 people and left three-quarters of Tokyo burned to the ground.

After William the Conqueror died, someone stole every bone in his body but his thighbone.

A HAIR PIECE

Shaved, snipped, or braided, hair has gone through a bewildering variety of fashions throughout history. Here are some of the high points in hair fashions for men.

Who says guys aren't into fashion? Their sideburns and dreadlocks have gone through as many changes as feminine hemlines. Geography and historical time period clue you in to the way hairs sit atop a guy's head. A crew cut would have been as laughable to the fashionable hunks of the Sun King's court as their powdered wigs are to us, today.

LOOK MUMMY, NO HAIR!
The ancient Egyptians removed all body hair by shaving, tweezing, or "waxing" it off with a paste made of honey and turpentine. Archaeologists found jeweled wigs in lots of tombs. Those fancy, long beards worn by the Pharaohs were glued-on fakes as well.

HEY, SHORTY!
In the time of Saint Paul, cropped hair was the style, especially after Paul called long hair, "a shame unto a man." In the mid-12th century, King Louis VII of France followed Paul's advice and cut off his long hair. Unfortunately, his queen, Eleanor of Aquitaine, took one look at Louis' shorn head and flew the coop, taking her vast land-holdings with her.

WIGGING OUT
Short hair was the rage for a century or two. Around the time of the Renaissance, cool dudes supplemented the hair God gave them with wigs. Louis XIII of France was the trendsetter. Doomed to male pattern baldness at a relatively young age, the king hid his skimpy hairs under a wig. Louis XIII passed both his baldness and his wig preference along to Louis XIV. (You could say Louis gave his hair to his heir.) Actually, Louis XIV, the Sun King, was so disgusted by his baldness that only his barber saw his naked head. To prevent anyone from glimpsing his royal pate, Louis made servants pass him his wig through his closed bed curtains before he would leave his bed.

England's Queen Anne became so heavy that she needed to be moved with pulleys.

WHEN FASHION WAS IN FLOUR
During the reign of the Sun King, men, women, and even children all wore large white wigs. "Everyone wants to be so old as to appear wise," commented a lady-in-waiting. The wealthy built closets for their headgear. In the 1700s, British soldiers got a weekly pound of flour—just so they could powder their wigs.

AU NATURAL
The French Revolution put an end to powdered wigs. Who wanted their hair to look like a king's if that king was about to lose his hair...and his head? The Brits also cooled the hot wig trend by enacting a 1795 tax of one guinea on wig powder. After the tax was passed, blokes who wore powdered wigs were called "Guinea Pigs." Soon, Lord Byron became the new model for males, with long, tax-free, natural locks.

HAIR TO DIE FOR
Meanwhile, men of the American colonies suffered through their own hair fashions. The Puritans in the 1600s championed short bowl cuts. They were laughed at as "Roundheads." (Actually, those Puritans were pretty square.)

But by 1776, and the American Revolution, longer hair was back in vogue. Men wanted to look like that gorgeous hunk... Ben Franklin. Franklin was the U.S. diplomat to France. He tried to wear a wig to his court appearance, but it didn't fit. He showed up with his long hair covered by a simple beaver cap, and high society decided that his natural appearance befitted a revolutionary warrior. (Guess they thought old Ben had hair to die for.) Today Americans celebrate Ben's straggly locks on the hundred-dollar bill—though not every American guy wants long green hair.

* * *

"Money is the root of all evil."   **—The Apostle Paul**
Perhaps the most misquoted passage of scripture actually says, "The love of money is the root of all evil." Thus Paul was focusing not on the possession of wealth but rather the heart condition that goes along with it.

Winston Churchill's mother was American and his father was a famous political failure.

POLES APART

Norwegian explorer Roald Amundsen hadn't wanted to go to the South Pole in the first place, but that's the way the iceberg crumbles.

In 1909, when Norwegian explorer Roald Amundsen found out that Robert Peary had reached the North Pole, he was crushed. He'd wanted to get there first. Because he was a true explorer, he wasn't about to sit around feeling sorry for himself. He'd already been the first man to sail through the Northwest Passage. He immediately switched his focus to the other end of the world. He'd be the first man to reach the South Pole.

GOIN' SOUTH
He only told his brother where he and his crew were headed. The Norwegian Antarctic Expedition, consisting of the 39-year-old Captain Amundsen and four compatriots, sailed south from Norway in June 1910. They established a base camp, and by October they were ready. They set out from their winter quarters with 52 dogs and four sleds loaded with food and equipment. Traveling at a pace of 15 miles per day, the five Norwegians soon came to appreciate just what a frozen waste they'd chosen to take on. On the coldest day, the temperature dropped to a staggering negative 140 degrees Fahrenheit.

RALLY 'ROUND THE FLAG, BOYS
By December 8, they reached the spot where, in 1909, Englishman Ernest Shackleton had given up in an earlier attempt to reach the Pole. The journey had taken the Norwegians 10,000 feet up into a mountain stretch, an area that Amundsen named for the queen of Norway, the Queen Maud Mountains. When they finally reached the Pole on December 14, the five exhausted explorers gathered around their national flag and, with frostbitten hands, grabbed hold of the flag and planted it in the snow.

GREAT SCOTT!
But the Amundsen team wasn't alone out there. They had some competition, in the person of English explorer Captain Robert Falcon Scott, who was heading up the British Antarctic Terra Nova Expedition. It was Scott's second Antarctic expedition. But

he'd established his base camp 60 miles behind Amundsen's; the added distance allowed Amundsen to beat Scott by over a month.

TRAGIC ENDING

When the British explorers finally reached their destination on January 17th, 1912, they were bitterly disappointed to find the Norwegian flag already there. On the way back, insufficient food and a blizzard took the lives of all five men. Scott's diary detailed the expedition's last days. It was found by a search party the following November.

SNAIL MAIL

It took the hardy Norwegians 53 days to reach the South Pole. News of their feat, on December 14th, 1911, took three and a half months to reach England, longer than the expedition itself.

*   *   *

DO YOU BELIEVE IN LUCKY UNDERWEAR?

In South Texas, underwear made its most courageous stand. In August 1840, Juliet Watts had been married for less than a month to Hugh, the customs collector at the port town of Linnville. One morning in August a large war party of Comanches surprised the town, galloping in on horseback, burning, looting, and murdering. Most of the citizens fled to the water on boats, but the Watts rushed to their house to save Hugh's gold watch.

Rampaging Comanches killed Hugh and kidnapped his wife. According to some accounts, they attempted to rape her. They tore off her dress, but were stopped cold by her corset! Frustrated by the labyrinth of hooks and laces, the warriors went back to robbing the town, loading their plunder onto mules. As they left the burning town the Indians took captives with them, including Mrs. Watts.

A posse went after the Comanches, defeating them at the Battle of Plum Creek. The retreating Indians killed many of their captives but though they'd shot an arrow at Mrs. Watts' breast, the weapon did not pierce her fully because of her corset! Tightly bound corsets have been criticized for harming the circulation and even the internal organs of their wearers, but cruel fashion saved Mrs. Watts. She lived to remarry—thanks to her secret weapon, her underwear.

Thomas More, who coined the word "utopia," was executed by Henry VIII.

BREAKING THE CODE: CRYPTANALYSIS

It's harder than it looks, and it looks damned difficult.

U p until the advent of the Internet, the only people who used codes were armies and bankers and spies. Now they've got 128-bit algorithms that encode your purchase of the latest bestselling book or video game, so no one knows what you're buying. Crack an encoded message sent by spies, and trust me, you were on to something. The Nazis were not purchasing music CDs with their encrypted messages, you know.

Cryptanalysis is nearly as difficult as cryptology (putting the information into code to begin with). People have been coding information as long as there's been a reason to hide news from someone, though early methods were almost charmingly simplistic.

A REALLY SERIOUS HISTORY OF THE SUBJECT

The Greeks did it by writing messages on a piece of cloth spiraled down a stick of a certain thickness; unraveled, the cloth strip was gibberish (it was all Greek to them). The Romans used letter transposition, shifting all the letters by a certain amount, not unlike you would do for your Lucky Charms Secret Decoder Ring. Although, it would be Julius Caesar and not some fey leprechaun telling you how many letters to click over, and the secret message would be to take Masada rather than to eat more sugary cereal.

ARABIAN KNOW-HOW

Serious coding had to wait until the 15th century. The Arabs (who had been caretaking and expanding on Western knowledge while Europe festered in that unfortunate dark age it had going) codified the fundamentals of both cryptology and cryptanalysis. They were the first people to figure out that certain letters (such as vowels) appear with more frequency than others, and that you could crack a simple code based principally on frequency counts of certain letters. I know, you're thinking, "Duh, who doesn't know about letter frequency distributions in cryptanalysis?" But remember, this was a simpler time.

The Marquis de Lafayette was labeled a traitor during the French Revolution.

YANKEE INGENUITY

Cryptology in itself probably never won any wars, but cryptanalysis certainly helped to win them, and it was enough of a priority that combatants would often go to desperate measures to crack the enemy's codes. Take the Confederate army. The Confederate army had such a difficult time cracking the Union's codes that they actually published encoded Union messages in newspapers to encourage the folks at home to play along. Sort of like a Word Jumble, where the unjumbled message would be Sherman's request for torches, the better to burn his way from Atlanta to the sea. The Union had no problem cracking Confederate codes, incidentally; the Rebs were using a relatively unsophisticated cipher.

ULTRA-COOL

Probably the most famous example of the importance of cryptanalysis comes from the Second World War, and the vaunted British "Ultra" program to crack the German encryption code, known as "Enigma."

Spearheaded by the famous mathematician Alan Turing, the Ultra project gave the Allies an immense advantage in terms of knowing what the Germans were up to—even if they couldn't take advantage of all the information. If Allied forces just happened to show up where the Germans were, the Germans would figure out their code had been broken, you see.

WHAT BOMBS?

This made for some torturous maneuverings: The Brits would decrypt the location of a German convoy, for example, and then send out a plane that would "discover" the convoy, after which they would blow it up right pretty. Be that as it may, sometimes sacrifices were made: the British once discovered that the town of Coventry was going to be bombed, and rather than evacuate the town—and risk exposing their knowledge—the bombing was allowed to happen.

NOT A POLISH JOKE

A little-known secret about the British Ultra project is that much of the heavy lifting in that effort came not from the British but from the Poles. During the 1930s the Polish government, who had a justifiably dim view of the Germans, assigned Marian Rejewski,

Jerzy Rózycki, and Henryk Zygalski to crack the Enigma code. They did it the old-fashioned way: first they procured expired Enigma codes and a booklet that explained how to set up an Enigma ("So You Want To Send Secret Messages: A Beginner's Guide"). Then they built a replica of the Enigma machine. Then they whacked away at the codes and the rewired the Enigma machine until they got actual deciphered messages.

HOW TERRIBLY BRITISH

In 1939, realizing Poland was about to be carved up (they had the Germans' messages, after all), the Poles set up a secret meeting with the Brits and handed over all their research on Enigma up to that point. The Brits were dumbfounded, to put it mildly. Did they let Rejewski, Rózycki, and Zygalski in on the Ultra project? Of course not. They were foreigners, you see. They had enough problems sharing information with the Americans. (Who, incidentally, were busy cracking a code of their own: "Purple," an Enigma-like code used by the Japanese. It was no small task—the lead researcher on Purple suffered a total nervous breakdown—but it yielded very positive results. Thanks to cracking Purple, American fighter planes "just happened" to shoot down a plane carrying Isoroku Yamamoto, commander-in-chief of Japan's naval forces. He was the guy who suggested attacking Pearl Harbor, you know, so there were probably very few tears shed over what was, in fact, a bald-faced assassination by airplane.)

DO THE MATH

It's not an exaggeration to say that the need to crack the Enigma code expanded human knowledge considerably. Much of this expansion took place in the rarified field of mathematics—by the time of WWII, cryptanalysis was indistinguishable from higher-order math, and today it's even more so—but other fields also got their share.

BEATEN TO THE PUNCHCARD

The first programmable computer was not constructed in the United States after the war as is generally presumed, but in Bletchley Park, home of the Ultra project. The computer, called "Colossus" (because it was), was designed to crack codes quicker than any human could. When you're at your computer, you're reading on the spiritual descendent of Colossus— "spiritual" because the machine, secret during the war, was destroyed just as secretly afterward—the Brits were nothing if not paranoid, and by extension, thorough in covering their sneaky little tracks. The world didn't find out about Enigma or Ultra until the 1970s. At which time, the Argentine air was filled with the sound of former Nazis smacking their foreheads in aggravation.

THE REAL SECRET

As mighty an intellectual feat as cracking the Enigma and Purple codes were, the tale is also an example of how when it comes down to it, people with big brains often have to rely on people with teeny brains making really dumb mistakes.

The Enigma code was broken partially because German army soldiers were so confident the code was invincible, that they got sloppy and used simple "initial" codes—a three-letter code at the beginning of a transmission that allowed the guy at the other end to "tune" his machine to receive the message. That's what allowed the Brits their window of opportunity (The German navy was more circumspect with codes and who sent messages—as a result, the naval codes were cracked years later than the army codes). It's proof that the biggest problem with any perfect system is the imperfect humans that use it.

*   *   *

IT'S A SMALL WORLD

Like a lot of writers before and since, Geoffrey Chaucer had a day job. While working as a clerk in England's royal household, he came into contact with Philippa, the granddaughter of King Edward III and the daughter of Prince John of Gaunt. Philippa found out that one of Chaucer's interests was navigation. She was fascinated by the subject and Chaucer taught her everything he knew about it. Later, when she became queen of Portugal, she passed it all on to her son, Henry the Navigator.

In 1892, Italy raised the minimum age for marriage for girls to 12.

PROVEN WRONG BY HISTORY: PART I

A collection of ill-conceived comments on the march of technology by people who watched from the sidelines— and should have known better.

"I think there is a world market for maybe five computers."

—**Thomas Watson, chairman of IBM, 1943**

"Computers in the future may weigh no more than 1.5 tons."

—*Popular Mechanics,* 1949

"But what ... is it good for?"

—**Engineer at the Advanced Computing Systems Division of IBM, 1968, commenting on the microchip**

"There is no reason anyone would want a computer in their home."

—**Ken Olson, president, chairman, and founder of Digital Equipment Corporation, 1977**

"So we went to Atari and said, 'Hey, we've got this amazing thing, even built with some of your parts, and what do you think about funding us? Or we'll give it to you. We just want to do it. Pay our salary, we'll come work for you.' And they said, 'No.' So then we went to Hewlett-Packard, and they said, 'Hey, we don't need you. You haven't got through college yet.'"

—**Apple Computer, Inc., founder Steve Jobs on attempts to get Atari and Hewlett-Packard interested in the personal computer that he and Steve Wozniak created**

"640K ought to be enough for anybody."

—**Bill Gates, 1981**

In 1787 the official U.S. currency was established as the dollar.

CATCHER, LAWYER, LINGUIST, SPY

Moe Berg was a man of many talents—and many quirks. By all accounts, he was a much better spy than he was a baseball player.

Morris "Moe" Berg was born in New York City in 1902, the son of Russian immigrants. He graduated from high school with honors and was accepted at Princeton. His father wanted him to be a lawyer, so he eventually got a law degree. But Berg found other professions—such as baseball player, linguist, and spy—much more interesting than law. As a spy, he was sent on an assignment with very high stakes—the outcome of World War II.

THE SHORTSTOP WHO SPOKE LATIN

Berg played shortstop for the Princeton baseball team. That's where it became obvious that he was a different sort of ballplayer: instead of the usual hand signals, Berg communicated with his second baseman in Latin. Moe studied languages at Princeton, including ancient Indian Sanskrit and Egyptian hieroglyphics, as well as the everyday ones. After he graduated in 1923—to his father's horror—Berg joined the Brooklyn Robins (the team that later became the Brooklyn Dodgers) as a backup catcher. His baseball salary paid for linguistics study at the Sorbonne in Paris and put him through the law program at Columbia University.

STRIKING OUT IN ANY LANGUAGE

Moe Berg played for five different major league teams during his 16-year baseball career. When he played for the Washington Senators, he broke an American League record in the 1932–1933 seasons by playing 117 consecutive full games without an error. But his hitting record was so deplorable (his lifetime average was .243) that it inspired the line: "Moe Berg can speak 12 languages, and he can't hit in any of them."

ALL-STAR SPY

In 1934, an American League all-star team was put together for a tour of Japan. On it were such outstanding players as Babe Ruth and Lou Gehrig—and the definitely less skillful Moe Berg. Some say Berg was put on the team because he spoke Japanese. He also understood Japan's culture better than the average American did, which made him very popular with the Japanese.

JAPANESE MOVIES

He took advantage of the opportunity to make movies of Tokyo from the rooftop of a hospital building—including the harbor and shipyards, industrial sites, and military installations. Some sources say that Berg was working for U.S. intelligence even then. Others insist that Berg did the filming on his own. There's a similar disagreement over the value of Berg's home movies. According to an often-told story, they were used in 1942 to help plan General Jimmy Doolittle's bombing raids on Japan. Other historians say the pictures were probably of little use.

THE SPY WHO CAME IN FROM LEFT FIELD

Either way, making those movies steered Berg toward a new career. The Office of Strategic Services (OSS, the forerunner of the CIA) was run by William J. "Wild Bill" Donovan, and he thought Moe Berg would make a good spy. After all, Berg spoke a number of languages, he was exceptionally intelligent, and he had a knack for getting people to talk to him. All good spy qualities.

DROP THAT GUN!

So when his baseball career was over in 1939, the OSS offered Moe Berg a job. He was somewhat inept at first—he couldn't even figure out where to carry his gun. He tried to tuck it into his jacket, his belt, and his sock—but it kept falling out. One time, he just had a friend hold it for him. He traveled the world—to Casablanca, Algiers, Rome, Yugoslavia, and Norway—always wearing that traditional spy-wear: the trench coat.

ASSIGNMENT TO KILL

In 1944, U.S. scientists were hard at work on the Manhattan Project, the effort to build an atomic bomb before the Germans did. That December, Berg was sent to Zurich, Switzerland, to attend a conference of scientists. His job was to find out how far along the Germans were in building their bomb. And if they were close, to kill Werner Heisenberg, Germany's leading atomic physicist, right then and there.

COOL AS AN ICE-BERG
Posing as a Swiss physics student and carrying his trusty gun (which he'd finally learned how to carry) and a suicide pill (a cyanide tablet, just in case), Berg listened as Heisenberg gave a lecture on basic physics. Ho-hum: Berg would have to do more digging. Right after the lecture an opportunity presented itself.

At a dinner party that night, Berg had a chance to chat with Heisenberg. The physicist spilled the beans: he complained that the German project was lagging behind the Allies. He supposedly told Berg, "It's a shame, Germany has already lost the war." (Yes!)

WHEW!
So Berg didn't have to use his gun or his suicide pill. He cabled the good news to the OSS in Washington; they passed it on to President Roosevelt, who responded with, "My regards to the catcher."

THANKS, BUT NO THANKS
Moe Berg probably did other espionage work for the OSS, and maybe even for the FBI. (It's top secret, so how are we supposed to know?) He was awarded the Medal of Freedom. But he refused the award, although he said he respected "the spirit in which it was offered."

STILL A FAN
Berg had always had the habit of disappearing without warning and suddenly turning up again. After the war, he apparently became something of a vagabond, but he still went to baseball games as often as he could. He was an entertaining storyteller who sometimes expanded on the facts, which has made it hard for historians to sort out the actual events of his life. When he died in 1972, he left no estate—only the remarkable legend of a man of many abilities and many mysteries.

*   *   *

JUST PLAIN LEONARDO
Leonardo da Vinci got his last name from the Italian town he was born—Vinci, in Tuscany. "Da" means "from" in Italian, so his full name was "Leonardo from Vinci." That's why when you look him up in books, he's always under the L's.

Charles Curtis, who became U.S. vice-president in 1929, was part Kaw Indian.

PORT-A-FORTRESS

It seems like an impossible feat to build an entire fortress in just a few hours, but no one ever told the Romans that. At the end of every day, they literally took out their portable fortress and rebuilt it!

At the end of a long day's march, the Roman infantry soldier had to put off thoughts about a warm fire and good food—first, he had a fortress to build. Once his legion arrived at the site picked out by a scouting party, the soldier shucked his pack, took out his shovel, and his piece of wall (yes, that's right), and started digging.

A WELL-OILED MACHINE
Every soldier knew his job. And since it was the whip or worse for anyone who dared disobey his commander, each soldier hopped to it. First, the soldiers built a large, square-shaped wall of dirt that left behind a moat-shaped hole around the whole thing. Then each man attached his personal piece of wall—lengths of wood lashed together—to the dirt wall. And presto, a fortress, complete with moat (albeit a not very deep one, but it served the purpose).

INSTANT CITY
Once the fortress was complete, the soldiers trooped inside to raise a city of tents. But a city can't be complete without streets. In this case, they were sketched out along a precise military grid. The principal street was called—well, Principal Street (Via Principalis). And all along it were the most important tents, such as headquarters and the supply tents.

Tucked away on the rear streets you'd find the hospital and the reserves, also called the "extraordinarii," which was made up of the general's bodyguards and hostages from cities that Rome had conquered. Camp followers (including the officers' servants and slaves, doctors, and even merchants who ran a kind of traveling market) had their places, too. It was just like being in the same fortress every night, except for the daily change in scenery.

CAMP SWEET CAMP
Before the infantry soldier put up his own tent he had to raise the tents of all the commanders and support personnel, which included carpenters, engineers to operate the catapults and other

siege engines, sappers (the guys who had to dig under walls during sieges—hey, somebody had to do it), and various other laborers.

DON'T GET YOUR HOPES UP

Once that was done, the work was still far from complete. Some of the soldiers could hit the hay, but there was always guard duty, not to mention chores like foraging for food, gathering wood, and hauling water—that still had to be done at all hours of the day and night. And the lowly infantry were just the guys to do it.

SOUP'S ON!

Trumpets signaled when it was time to get up, time to go to bed, time to change the guard-watch—you get the idea. Oh, and time to eat. Luckily most of them were used to their normal fare, which consisted of bread and sour wine. That's it.

UP THROUGH THE RANKS, AND DOWN

Every morning, all the solders reported to their centurion, all the centurions reported to their tribunes, and all the tribunes reported to the consuls, who doled out the orders. Then, the entire process reversed itself. Nothing was done unless someone in charge commanded it. There was a procedure for everything, and it was followed to the letter, every time.

ON THE ROAD AGAIN

When it was time to break camp, the trumpet sounded with yet another signal. The troops scurried to fold away the tents and pack everything up. At a second signal, they loaded the tents, wall sections, and baggage onto themselves and the horses and mules. Then, in strict military fashion, they set fire to what was left of the camp. The last thing that they wanted was someone else using a camp they'd so effectively built. At a third signal, they lined up into formation, unit by unit. After a rallying cry to boost morale, they marched away, only to repeat the entire process that night.

WORTH THE TROUBLE?

Conquering the world was a Roman talent second only to their ability to organize. When they combined the two with their portable fortress, they were ready for anything. Add to this their practice of always seizing the initiative, and they became well nigh invincible.

Winston Churchill wrote much of Edward VIII's famous abdication speech.

PEDDLING PRICEY PETALS

When the tulip took on the sweet smell of success.

Think the Internet stock rally of the late 90s was unique? Though it may have seemed odd when investors paid high prices for stock in companies that never turned a profit, the Dot-Com craze was only the latest in the history of risky speculative investments. The Dutch could have told new investors a thing or two about stock market crashes.

WORTH THEIR WEIGHT IN GOLD

Colorful tulips are available in just about any garden store for around $2 a bulb, with rarer varieties selling for perhaps $10 apiece. It's hard to believe that this common flower was once valued more highly than gold. Or that 17th century Dutch stock traders indulged in tulip trading and caused a market crash.

POTTED SHOW-OFFS

The tulip craze began in the early 1600s, when tulips, particularly rare ones, became a status symbol in Holland. Moneyed society types showed off their rare Admiral Leifken or Semper Augustus varieties to dinner guests as a way of flaunting wealth. Imitating the wealthy, middle-class tulip fanciers snatched up tulip bulbs.

DIM BULBS TRADE IN LONDON

What started out as price inflation due to ravenous demand for a short supply, soon turned to stock trading. Tulip bulbs were listed on stock exchanges in Amsterdam, Rotterdam, Haarlem, Leyden, and eventually Paris and London. At first, the traders were Dutch citizens going after valuable bulbs; later foreigners joined in the game. Investors speculated wildly on the rarest varieties of tulips. The valuation of tulip bulbs soared. Crop "futures" were bought and sold, and merchants abandoned their businesses to grow tulips. In 1635, a man offered 12 acres of downtown property for a single tulip bulb of the rare Semper Augustus variety. Speculators mortgaged homes and businesses to buy bulbs to resell, while others offered up to $20,000 for rare varieties. A rare tulip bulb was said to be a suitable dowry for a bride.

Benjamin Harrison, who left office in 1893, was the last bearded U.S. president.

GETTING BACK TO THEIR ROOTS

But the bottom dropped out of the market in 1637, when a consortium of bulb merchants couldn't sell their bulbs for the usual inflated prices. Stock prices slid down, since the tulips were worth only what someone would pay for them. Thousands of Dutch merchants, many of whom had spent their life savings on the bulbs, were reduced to begging in less than two months. The Dutch love affair with tulips continued on undiminished, but the whole debacle left scars on the Dutch economy for decades.

THE VAST VASELAND

As Internet stock traders watch their profits evaporate, you might do well to remember the lowly tulip. Then if someone gives you a hot stock tip on an unproven business you can tell them you're not a blooming idiot.

*   *   *

THE DEVIL WITH HORSESHOES

Step on a rusty horseshoe nail and your reward is a tetanus shot. So why are horseshoes lucky? The pagans found horseshoes lucky because they were made of iron, a sacred metal of great power. The Norse god of war, Thor, wielded an iron hammer. The Greeks thought the horseshoe had a lucky shape because it resembled a new moon, a sign of fertility. The shape was considered lucky in the Middle Ages, too. Medieval church doors were sometimes shaped like a crescent moon. But it was the tenth century legend of blacksmith Dunstan that sealed the lucky fate of horseshoes. When a man came in asking to be shod in horseshoes, quick-witted Dunstan realized that the request was unusual. Then he saw that his customer had a cloven foot—he was shoeing the devil himself! Dunstan, who later became archbishop of Canterbury, tortured the devil with hot irons and nails until the devil promised that neither he nor any of his demons would enter a building protected by a horseshoe. The horseshoe must be nailed upside down on the building so that its luck doesn't run out.

Diana was the first British subject to marry an heir to the throne since 1659.

OFF WITH THEIR HEADS!

How a really nice man came to be associated with a deadly machine, and whose name is even more famous worldwide than TV commercial pioneer Ron Popeil and his Popeil Chop-O-Matic.

D r. Joseph Ignace Guillotin was a kindly man. That's why, when he rose to make a speech before the French Constituent Assembly in October 1789, he proposed that all executions of criminals be performed by a beheading device—a machine that would chop off a head as quickly as you could say, "lickety-split."

THE MAN

Guillotin had taken this one issue as his life's work; that people convicted of a capital offense should have the right to a quick and painless form of execution. Up to this point, French commoners were dispatched by hanging. The nobility, of course, died a nobler death—by sword.

THE MACHINE

The kinder, gentler beheading machine that Guillotin had in mind was already being used in Italy, England, and Germany. Okay, said the French government, let's try it. They asked a German piano maker, Tobias Schmidt, to build the prototype, which he did, and which was successfully tested on dead bodies supplied by local French hospitals. The guillotine was ensconced just in time to become the symbol of the French Revolution.

HIS 'N' HERS EXECUTIONS

His: King Louis XVI

The French masses were in revolt; their target the nobility. After Louis XVI attempted to escape from France with the rest of the royal family in 1791, he was branded a traitor. So his trial in 1793 was just a formality: the guilty verdict was never in doubt. Because the proceedings (which dragged on for 72 hours) therefore lacked the element of suspense, bored spectators in the gallery ate little snacks and passed the wine and the brandy. Outside, at the local cafes, the rest of the rabble took bets on the outcome of the trial.

Cats first domesticated humanity around 8000 B.C.

Louis' Big Day

A light rain began to fall in Paris as the portly Louis XVI walked from his prison cell to a large green carriage. A procession that included 1,200 guards made its way to a huge square packed with spectators. His chubbiness, the king, was guided to the guillotine, where stood one Charles Sanson, the city executioner, and a consummate professional whose father had preceded him in the office and whose son was to follow him.

A Royal Pain in the Neck

As the heavy blade rushed down between the upright posts, the king's attendant screamed a terrible scream. The king—have we mentioned his weight problem?—had had one too many French pastries over the years and, as a result, his neck was so fat that his head "did not fall at the first stroke." The crowd stood in hushed silence, then suddenly rushed forward to dip their handkerchiefs or pieces of paper in Louis' royal blood. (The perfect souvenir of a very important day.)

Hers: Marie Antoinette

Even before the French Revolution, Marie Antoinette was the most hated person in France. In songs, poems, and cartoons, her political enemies portrayed the Austrian-born queen as a person with perverse, despicable habits. These included plotting to starve the poor, sending money to Austria (France's hated arch-rival), and indulging her voracious sexual appetite for both men and women. The failed attempt to flee the country with the king in 1791 only served to fuel the people's hatred and suspicion of their queen. Whether any of the charges leveled against her were true, it didn't matter. The fix was in. Her trial in the fall of 1793 was speeded up; she was found guilty and condemned to death.

The Queen's Last Outfit

On a morning in 1793, nine months after Louis' death, Marie Antoinette dressed herself for the last time. Ever the fashion plate, the queen decked herself out in a white dress, white bonnet, black stockings, and plum-colored high heels. Henri Sanson, the son of the man who had pulled the rope on the King's guillotine, entered her cell and brutally tied the queen's hands behind her back. Then, he removed her bonnet, cut off her hair, and stashed it in his pocket, perhaps to keep or sell as a souvenir. Outside, a tum-

---

Cleopatra wasn't even Egyptian. She was Greek.

bril—a small cart used to carry political prisoners to the guillo-tine—was waiting. At the sight of the tumbril, Marie began to tremble and had to have her hands untied so she could relieve herself in the corner of a courtyard wall. But once seated in the cart, she regained her composure. The cart proceeded slowly to the guillotine through a dense crowd. As she climbed to the top of the scaffold, she stumbled and stepped on the executioner's foot. "Monsieur," she apologized, "I beg your pardon. I did not do it on purpose." They were the last words she spoke.

EVERYONE ELSE'S EXECUTIONS

Nearly 3,000 men and women were guillotined in Paris during the fall and winter of 1793. Another 14,000 executions were carried out in the provinces. Most of the victims were designated "ene-mies of the people" because their politics didn't agree with whichever revolutionary party held the balance of power at the time. But in hundreds of other cases, innocent people were hauled off to the guillotine on the flimsiest of excuses, such as the denun-ciations of jealous or vindictive neighbors. In a few cases, people were guillotined because of clerical and administrative errors.

Postscripts:
After Dr. Guillotin's death in 1814, his children tried to get the guillotine's name legally changed. When their efforts failed, they changed their own name instead.

The last execution by guillotine took place not so long ago. Hamida Djandoubi, a Tunisian immigrant convicted of murder, was guillotined at Baumetes Prison in Marseilles, France, on Sep-tember 10, 1977.

* * *

"Thieves respect property. They merely wish the property to become their property that they may more perfectly respect it."

G.K. Chesterton

The airfield from which Charles Lindbergh began his famous trip is a shopping center.

DEADLY AS MOLASSES IN JANUARY

What was 15 feet high, moved at 35 miles per hour,
and killed 21 people in 1919?

The 50-foot high tank at the Purity Distilling Company of Boston, Massachusetts, was going full-bore. Filled to near-capacity, it contained two million gallons of steam-heated molasses, soon to be gallons of rum and industrial alcohol. Little did the Purity people and the citizens of Boston know the tragic and bizarre disaster in store for them that warm January day.

THE FIRST SIGNS

Witnesses later reported hearing a banging and tapping sound coming from the tank. The sounds they heard were the rivets that held the tank together popping free. Next thing anyone knew, the tank burst, sending—did we mention two million gallons?—warm, sticky molasses into the streets of Boston, moving at 35 miles an hour. Which might have been funny if it hadn't also been carrying huge, jagged sections of the tank with it.

MOLASSES IN JANUARY

In an irony only found in truth, this event really did take place during January. Too bad it had to be an unusually warm January day, 43 degrees, well above freezing. If the weather had been more typical, it might have given the soon-to-be victims time to notice the oncoming calamity, maybe pack their things, move their belongings, and get the hell out of there, before the brown wall of molasses reached them.

THE BLOB

Moving with a dull, muffled roar, the 15-foot-high wall of brown goo surged and rumbled into Boston's North End. It crushed trolley cars, swallowed trucks, horses, and carts, and knocked buildings off their foundations.

AMAZING RESCUE

The parts of the tank propelled by molasses tore into the supports

---

Charlemagne's parents were Pepin the Short and Bertha of the Big Foot.

holding up the Atlantic Avenue elevated train. The steel trestles twisted and snapped and the track collapsed to the ground, just as a train was approaching. A quick-witted motorman reacted with enviable cool. He walked to the rear of his train and reversed the engines. The train ground to a halt, saved from the still-surging molasses below.

STICKY DOOM
The greatest number of fatalities that day was at a Public Works building, where municipal employees were just having lunch. The molasses slammed into the building, shattering it and throwing fragments 150 feet in the air. Another city building was similarly torn from its foundations; the tenement apartments on the upper floors collapsed into kindling.

MOLASSES SWALLOWS PEOPLE
It was literally a tidal wave, swallowing dozens of people, rolling and crushing them under its brown mass. Dozens were critically injured by the debris picked up and carried by the sticky mess, while others were simply crushed to death by the heavy molasses.

THE RESCUE
Finally, the molasses began to cool and congeal. The tidal wave slowed, then stopped. The first group of rescuers arrived: sailors from the harbor patrol ship *Nantucket*. They plunged into the mess and started pulling survivors out. Right behind them were the local boys in blue, followed by soldiers from a nearby army base. The Red Cross arrived next, in their crisp white uniforms, but soon you couldn't tell them apart: everyone was covered with the same brown goo.

PUMPING IRONY
The final toll was 21 people dead, 150 injured. The clean-up crew pumped sea water from the harbor via hoses. But the molasses and saltwater didn't mix, and soon the whole area was buried under brown foam. It took months before the streets of Boston were their old familiar dirty gray again. How could anything as harmless—and sweet—as molasses cause such devastation?

The mummy of Ramses II, thought to be the pharaoh in Exodus, is in the British Museum.

WHAT'S SO BIG ABOUT WAGNER?

*Everything, actually. His operas. His influence.
His sins. His ego.*

His operas were huge in every way. We've all seen the schtick: the huge blonde lady with the braids, wearing breastplates and a helmet, squalling high Cs that could cause sonic booms in the next county. There's some truth to it.

HIS STYLE
Richard Wagner wanted his music to be big, loud, and long. And voices that can outshout a hundred-piece orchestra—and don't go hoarse after three or four hours—don't come from undersized lungs.

In Wagner's operas, music flows in an endless stream of melody; no separate musical numbers, no breaks for applause, just continuous "music drama."

HIS IMPACT
Wagner's fans found it thrilling; his enemies called it boring. Other composers hotly denied being influenced by him—and started writing their operas more and more like his anyway.

HIS OPUS
Wagner chose towering, epic stories for his operas. His biggest work was *The Ring of the Nibelung*, finished in 1874. It's a series of four operas, three of which last over four hours each. (Here's a hint: never take your seat at a Wagner opera without hitting the john first.)

HIS SHOWMANSHIP
Nowadays any Hollywood director with a fat special-effects budget could show you mermaids singing underwater, warrior women riding winged horses, or a magic helmet that could change a man into any kind of animal right before your eyes. Wagner packed all of these and much more into *The Ring of the Nibelung*, and he expected it to look realistic, live and on stage. Practical guy, huh?

Teddy Roosevelt's "cavalry charge" up San Juan Hill was done on foot.

HIS EXTRAVAGANCE

The story? Nothing much. Only a gargantuan power struggle between gods and men, a few giants, dwarfs, and fire-breathing dragons; all of them scheming to get their hands on a magic ring that gives its wearer the power to run the world. (If this reminds you of *Lord of the Rings*, it's because the two stories are based on a lot of the same Norse myths. Wagner was the J.R.R. Tolkien of his time—including the huge cult following.)

HIS SELF-INDULGENCE

Wagner may have written on noble themes, but in real life he was as selfish as they come. He'd flatter you to your face if he needed a favor, and then curse you to your friends as soon as you'd left the room. When he didn't have enough money to pay the rent, he'd borrow heavily from friends—and then blow it all on the fancy silk clothes he liked to wear. He'd run up huge bills and then skip town and cross the border to avoid debtor's prison. Then he'd do it all again in a new country.

HIS WIFE

His wife, the long-suffering Minna, stood by him through years of poverty and disgrace, and he rewarded her by constantly having affairs with other women. When the money finally began to roll in, he abandoned Minna to run off with Cosima von Bülow, who was the daughter of composer Franz Liszt and the wife of one of his best friends. (He eventually married her after Minna's death.)

HIS BIG BREAK

In 1864 Ludwig II became King of Bavaria at the ripe old age of 18. Ludwig was fabulously wealthy, something of a lunatic, and a huge fan of Wagner's music. Wagner, now in his fifties, sweet-talked Ludwig into paying off his creditors (the line stretched halfway across Europe) and bankrolling the construction of a new theater in Bayreuth, Germany, specially designed for—what else?—presenting Wagner's own operas.

As a result of Ludwig's patronage, Wagner lived on Easy Street for the rest of his life. Who says nice guys finish last? Because in this case, they're right.

DIRTY SECRETS IN THE HISTORY OF HYGIENE (Part I): <u>MAN ON THE CAN</u>

Over the centuries, man has experimented with different solutions to one of life's stickiest problems—the sanitary elimination of human waste. We've unearthed a few facts you won't find in most history books.

While excavating an early Egyptian house, archaeologists found a toilet seat that conformed perfectly to a pair of buttocks. The seat was made of limestone, providing cooling relief in the hot Egyptian climate. It sounded comfy—we wanted to know more.

"WHAT'S NEW, MAXIMUS?"
To the Romans, going to the bathroom was a social occasion. And they brought their customs to the far corners of their Empire. In North Africa, for example, a large privy dating from ancient Rome had 25 seats arranged around three sides of a room. There was no privacy: only a carved dolphin separated each seat.

MEANWHILE, BACK HOME
After using the public latrines, the citizen of Rome looked for the bucket, which held salt water and a long stick with a sponge attached to one end. The user rubbed his posterior with the sponge and then returned it to the water bucket for the next patron's use. Careless use of this device has been said to be the origin of the expression "getting the wrong end of the stick." (True!)

RENDER UNTO CAESAR...
Public urinals were a source of income for Emperor Vespasian, who had the the urine collected; the ammonia in it was used to make fabric dyes.

TAKE ME TO THE RIVER
Romans developed the art of plumbing and built their sewer system to last. The Cloaca Maxima ("big sewer"), which connected the Forum to the Tiber River, is still in use today, 2,500 years later.

Catherine the Great's court held transvestite balls to evade the prohibition on women drinking.

AFTER THE FALL

For a thousand years after the decline and fall of Rome, Europe was a sanitation disaster. The only indoor plumbing consisted of chamber pots, portable containers that were kept under beds or at least, hopefully, in the corner. Human waste was thrown from chamber pots directly onto the streets or into rivers. Diseases borne by fecal matter flourished.

GET THAT S— OUT OF HERE!

Things have got to be bad when even kings notice. England's Richard II issued a proclamation in 1388 that prohibited the throwing of waste matter into ditches, rivers, or waters of any kind. The perpetrator was either to remove the offending material or pay a fine of 20 English pounds. The practice continued, so by the 1500s, King Henry VIII, describing a trip to Cambridge, wrote that both the main roads and the lanes were lined with large mounds of filth. In London, the public latrines were built over the Thames, the same river that provided drinking water.

"HEADS UP," IN FRENCH

The British slang word for toilet, the "loo," comes from a French custom of the Middle Ages. When tossing the contents of their chamber pots into the streets, the French very considerately shouted a warning to any luckless passersby, "Gardez l'eau" (pronounced LOO) which meant "Watch out for the water!"

WHY NO ONE SWAM THE CASTLE MOAT

Castles had bathrooms, privies really, built into bays that jutted out from the castle walls. The more sophisticated kind drained into stone channels or underground pits. The primitive ones simply had holes in the bottoms of the bay, so the waste fell directly into the moat or river below. The more deluxe town houses also had privy bays that hung over the streets.

THEY LAUGHED WHEN I SAT DOWN

Sir John Harington invented the first flush toilet in 1596. Harington was a godson of Queen Elizabeth I and presented the queen with his invention for Her Majesty's personal use. The device was mocked and never caught on. The first patent for a flush toilet was taken out in 1755 by Alexander Cummings of London. But most people continued to use chamber pots.

The father of U.K. Prime Minister John Major was a trapeze artist.

CHAMBER POTS OF THE RICH AND FAMOUS

Henry VIII's privy chamber housed a "close stool," that is, a chair that enclosed the royal chamber pot. It was padded in black velvet trimmed with ribbons, fringes, and quilting, all tacked on with 2,000 gilt nails. His daughter, Elizabeth I, preferred red velvet, and even had a portable loo that she took with her on trips.

THOSE ZANY VICTORIANS!

Some Victorian chamber pots played a tune when a hidden drawer in the commode was opened. Others had portraits of political figures such as Napoleon or Benjamin Franklin painted in the center, so you could show them what you thought of them. One popular model had a large eye with the words, "Use me well and keep me clean and I'll not tell what I have seen."

THE AMERICAN SCENE

One of Thomas Jefferson's many inventions was an indoor privy. Using a system of pulleys, servants hauled away President Jefferson's chamber pots from an "earth closet," a seat with a hole over a wooden box that was lined with a pan of wood ashes.

The poet, Henry Wadsworth Longfellow, may have been the first American to have a flush toilet. He had it installed in 1840, and proudly showed it off to his guests.

ENTER THOMAS CRAPPER

Forever altering the family name, in 1872 Thomas Crapper developed a new type of flushing toilet. For his achievement, Crapper became the royal plumber to Queen Victoria's son Edward, Prince of Wales.

HAND ME THAT SEARS CATALOG!

By the way, that other modern essential, toilet paper, wasn't invented until 1857.

BEING A NOSY PARKER

The original Nosy Parker was a 16th century
Archbishop of Canterbury with a lengthy proboscis
both literally and otherwise.

I n 1504 Henry VII was king of a still firmly Catholic England. That same year, a man named William Parker, who worked as a "calenderer of stuffs" (he had to smooth out cotton and wool using a tool called a calender), was about to become a dad.

The child, once born—and you had be strong to survive your arrival in 1504—was destined for a more prominent, and some would say glamorous, profession than his pop.

HE-E-E-RE'S NOSY!

Matthew Parker turned out to be an exceptionally bright lad. He had a long thin face and a long pointed nose to match. No prizes for guessing what they called him at school. At St Mary's Hostel Cambridge and then at the famous Corpus Christi College, he was nicknamed "Nosy." In fact, the name stuck permanently. They called him Nosy Parker for the rest of his life and it didn't stop when he died. Whenever you or I wail, "You Nosy Parker" at someone we are remembering Matthew and his proboscis.

REGARDING HENRY VIII

Nosy lived through the reigns of no fewer than six monarchs: Henry VII, Henry VIII, Edward VI, Lady Jane Grey (who reigned for 9 days at age 15), Mary Tudor, and Elizabeth. But we're getting ahead of ourselves.

Nosy was ordained as a priest in 1527 and in 1537 was appointed chaplain to the hapless, and soon to be headless, Anne Boleyn, the second of Henry VIII's six wives. Once Anne was done away with, Nosy became Master of his alma mater, Corpus Christi College. Nosy loved Cambridge and fought like a dog when Henry VIII, having separated England from the Pope and the Catholic Church, tried to break up the old colleges mainly in the interest of smashing up a perceived power base and running away with the spoils.

Sherlock Holmes mystery writer Arthur Conan Doyle was an opthalmologist.

UNDER MARY, THEN ELIZABETH

Bloody Mary (who gave her name to the cocktail) was bad news for Nosy when she became the aggressively Catholic and angry queen in 1553. She quickly took away all of Nosy's privileges because he wasn't a Catholic. Not wanting to be thrown into the Tower to be tortured—or worse—Nosy wisely lived in hiding for the five years of Mary's reign.

But it was different once Mary was succeeded by the Virgin Queen (for whom the state of Virginia was named—a bit more dignified than being remembered for a drink made of vodka and tomato juice). She brought Protestantism and calm to the throne, at least on the surface. Old Nosy promptly came out of his hidey-hole and Elizabeth asked him to be her Archbishop of Canterbury.

LIVING UP TO HIS NAME

It was then that he had to get nosy by nature as well as by name. Elizabeth wanted him to build an Anglican party that would be a middle way between the fiercely Protestant killjoy Puritans on the one hand and the emotional, dangerous Catholics on the other.

Some task. Soon his agents were nosing into what he regarded as obnoxious Puritan practices. You could say he presided over a sort of Tudor anti-Puritan thought police. Corrupted by power, he unashamedly used it to get what he wanted.

Needless to say, he wasn't much loved. And 73 years after his death in 1575, when the Puritans under Oliver Cromwell were beginning to get the upper hand, poor old Nosy's remains were dug out of their resting place in the private chapel at Lambeth Palace and buried ignominiously and gleefully under a dung hill. That, presumably, was to show him just what they thought of him in case the old chap happened to be nosily looking down from heaven—or sneaking a peek up from the other place.

BUT NOSY LIVES ON

Nosy Parker left more to us than a convenient way to tell people to mind their own business. He also left lasting legacies in his beloved Cambridge. Besides his contributions to his alma mater and a road called University Street that he had built, there's a large, square, grassy area of common land near the city center known to this day as Parker's Piece.

We get the abbreviation "lb." from the Latin word for pound: "libra."

WHEREWORDS: A QUIZ (The Bathroom)

Let's take a quick trip down the hall and to the left.
Where did all these bathroom sundries come from? Choose the best
answer, then check it against our answers on the next page
And don't forget to wash your hands when you're done.

1. ASPIRIN:
a. It was originally taken to ease breathing or "aspiration."
b. From the willow tree, whose Latin genus is "spirea."
c. First box was labeled A. S. Pirin, for the chemist inventor.

2. LAXATIVE
a. A former trademarked brand name from "reLAX AcTIVE."
b. Transliteration of "luxative," a castor oil from Luxembourg.
c. From Latin "laxus," or "loose."

3. WITCH HAZEL
a. Made from witch hazel plant.
b. Named after a Salem witch.
c. It was the original trademark for a brand of astringent.

4. IBUPROFEN
a. From its chemical name, "isobutylphenylpropionic acid."
b. Developed for the International Ballet Union in Germany: it was "IBU-proven."
c. From Swedish "ibu profen" for "no profit," because the inventor forfeited the patent.

5. SOAP
a. The Middle English "sope," meaning "to trickle or run out."
b. After Cheops' sister Shoap, who bathed daily in 999 B.C.
c. A recipe: it stands for Salt, Oil, Alkali, and Potash.

6. SHAMPOO
a. Nonsense name of a brand of soap used to wash dogs.
b. From the Hindu "champo," meaning "to massage."
c. From the French "champ eau," meaning "water land."

7. COLOGNE
a. First extracted from orchid flowers of the genus Colognus.
b. Italian plural of "cologna," the word for "bouquet."
c. After the city of Cologne, Germany, where it was created.

8. COMB
a. The first were comb and brush "combinations."
b. After British dandy John Breck, the duke of Combs.
c. The ancient Indo-European word "gombhos" for "teeth."

Jungle Book author Rudyard Kipling would only write with black ink.

1-b. Aspirin (acetylsalicylic acid) is a man-made variation of an ancient remedy. It was rediscovered in 1893 by a German chemist who was looking for something to relieve his father's arthritis pain. Chemists at Bayer (yes, Bayer) in Dusseldorf knew a winner when they saw one, and took the "a" from "acetyl," the "spir" from "spirea," and tacked on the "in" for good measure. In 1921, in a court decision, it lost its trademarked status.

2-c. From the Latin, that simple. But one interesting story concerns a pharmacist named Max Kiss, who added chocolate to a chemical laxative and marketed it under the name Bo-Bo. Someone, thank goodness, told him it was too close to "poo-poo," so he changed the name to a contraction for "Excellent Laxative," or ExLax.

3-a. In the fall, long after it's lost every leaf and is presumed dead, this woody shrub produces yellow flowers; for this reason it was thought to be magic. In fact Native-American witch hazel twigs have long been used as divining rods for finding water. American Indian tribes taught the colonists how to use the plant to soothe cuts and abrasions.

4-a. The name is derived from an abbreviation of the chemical name.

5-a. Why its earliest derivation meant "to trickle," it's hard to say, except that soap and water have been best buds for as long as we can remember.

6-b. In 1870s England, Hindu fashions, art, and phrases were all the rage, so British hairdressers added the word to their vocabularies.

7-c. An Italian barber, Jean-Baptiste Farina, was living in Cologne, Germany, when he developed a concoction of lemon spirits, orange bitters, and bergamot oil. It was the first "eau de Cologne," or "water of Cologne," later shortened to just plain old "cologne."

8-c. The first combs were dried backbones and jawbones (or "gombhos") of fish, as depicted in 6,000-year-old cave art, and found in later Egyptian tombs.

Only four words in English begin with "dw": dweeb, dwarf, dwell, and dwindle.

THE LONGBOW: NOT FOR SISSIES

A longbow, properly used, is still a heck of a weapon.

THE DAWN OF THE EMPIRE

Back in its day, roughly the 13th to 16th centuries, it wasn't just a weapon, it was *the* weapon, the Über-tool of any serious arsenal. It made England a superpower in Europe, much to the surprise of the Continentals, especially the French. More on that in a minute.

THE LONG AND THE SHORT OF IT

Right now, let's concentrate on the actual longbow itself. Historians debate on the original length of the longbow, but it was generally considered to be no less than five feet. Ideally, the bow was as tall or maybe just a little taller than the person wielding it, and made from yew, a type of wood known for its elasticity.

A MANLY MAN'S WEAPON

The longbow was not an easy weapon to master. The "pull" of a longbow, the amount of force needed to stretch the bowstring back to where it needed to be, was between 80 and 110 pounds; it's a heck of an aerobic exercise, a fact which I'm sure generations of English longbowmen appreciated. Back in the 14th century, stair-stepping to the oldies was not considered manly.

ATTACHED AT THE HIP

You put your whole body into being a longbowman, and I don't mean this metaphorically. Skeletons of longbow archers show signs of deformation consistent with the use of the bow: A spine curved in the direction of the pull arm, arm bones thick with compression, and coarsened bones in the fingers used to yank back the bowstring. It wasn't just a weapon, it was a way of life.

THE LONGBOW IN ACTION

The good news was that all that work paid off in the long run. An experienced longbowman could hit a target with killing force 200 yards out. He could fire six to ten times in a minute, a rate of fire

---

Canada didn't become a completely independent country until 1982.

that no practical weapon would match well into the 19th century. A longbow arrow wouldn't just bounce off a knight's armor—it would go right through, spearing the knight inside like a crab impaled on a pick. Get a couple of thousand longbowmen together, point them at an equal or greater number of knights in armor, and what you've got, friends, is a massacre.

80 YEARS OF LESSONS...

This fact the French learned—or more to the point, didn't learn—in three major battles that defined the Hundred Years' War:

1. The Battle of Crécy

The first of these is the Battle of Crécy, in 1346. The English came to the party with 10,000 archers and 4,000 men-at-arms (or, in modern terminology, "grunts"). The French had 12,000 men-at-arms and backup from cavalry. In this battle, the French kept driving up the middle of the English forces with their horses and knights; the bad news was that the English longbowmen were on the sides, picking them off as they came. It was a slaughter. The French lost 1,500 knights and King Phillip VI himself was wounded. The lesson: Watch out for those longbowmen, they'll get you bad.

2. The Battle of Poitiers

Flash forward 20 years to the Battle of Poitiers. The French had the numbers, but the English had the archers and the terrain (thickets and marshes) on their side; when the dim-witted French lumbered in with horses and heavy armor, the longbowmen picked them off like wolves going after crippled sheep. This time the French king wasn't wounded, he was taken prisoner. Will they ever learn?

3. The Battle of Agincourt

Leap another 60 years or so to perhaps the greatest single example of the superiority of the English longbowmen and the incredible military incompetence of the French in dealing with them: the fabled Battle of Agincourt, October 25, 1415. King Henry V of England, with 5,000 sick and wounded troops, was desperately trying to drag his troops back to England, when he ran smack dab into 30,000 French, fresh and spoiling for a fight. He and his exhausted crew were in deep foie gras, and would have been—should have been—brutally defeated, had not the French made an

Only one divorced man has become president of the U.S.—Ronald Reagan.

amazing tactical blunder, namely, picking Agincourt as the locale.

3a. The Set-Up

The field was more or less a narrow channel between two stands of forest; in order for the French to get at the English, they'd basically have to funnel their vast forces into a bottleneck. They would thus lose both the advantage of their huge number of troops, who would be unable to perform any large-scale maneuvers, and of their cavalry, who would have to wade through throngs of their own men-at-arms. As an added bonus, long rains in the days before the battle made the field of Agincourt a mudpit—not optimal cavalry ground. The bottleneck served the English longbowmen admirably as well, however. By concentrating their forces, the French made them incredibly easy to hit with longbow fire.

3b. The Massacre

The French funneled into Agincourt and died by the thousands, pincushioned with arrows from 5,000 English longbows. And while the English losses were not so light as Shakespeare indicated in *Henry V* (in which the dead were tallied at 25, not counting the occasional nobleman), they were nevertheless spectacularly low—something on the order of 500 compared to the French tally of at least 6,000 (1,500 of whom were knights in armor). The reason they were so low, of course, is that the longbowmen did all the heavy lifting; by the time Henry ordered his men-at-arms into the fray, the French were already decimated and in chaos. Agincourt won the French crown for Henry, and rightfully so.

THE LONGBOW'S LAST FLING

As for the longbow, its military service came to an end at the end of the 16th century not because it was obsolete as a weapon—in the late 1500s there was still no weapon that could beat its combination of power, accuracy, and rate of fire—but because there were too few people taking up archery as a profession. The longbow didn't fail us, we failed it.

* * *

To be, or not to be: that is the question:
Whether 'tis nobler in the mind to suffer
The slings and arrows of outrageous fortune,
Or to take arms against a sea of troubles…(Hamlet III.i)

Before becoming leader of Solidarity, Lech Walesa was a shipyard electrician.

AN 1844 FLIGHT OVER THE ATLANTIC? WHO SAID SO!

An extraordinary ballooning story that demonstrates the truly amazing power of hot air.

On April 13, 1844, the *New York Sun* announced the first transatlantic balloon flight. Seems a Mr. Monck Mason, and his crew in Wales, tried to cross the English Channel, got caught in a strong wind, and landed in South Carolina! The story described the pioneering balloon in great detail, including a discussion of the use of ballast and even data on the amount of gas used.

THE SUN WAS HOT
When the balloon story appeared, an author named Edgar Allan Poe was anxious to buy a copy of the *Sun*, but he couldn't even get near the building where the paper was published, the crowds were so thick. People paid outrageous prices for a copy of the paper, and crooked newsboys made huge profits. The unlucky Mr. Poe couldn't get his hands on a single copy.

THE BALLOON BURSTS
On April 15, the *Sun* had to admit that the story was all hot air. Their mail came in without a single mention of the landing of a balloon. In fact, there would be no successful transatlantic balloon flight until 1919. All the same, the *Sun* story got a lot of details right in their story. A Mr. Monck Mason crossed the English Channel by balloon in 1837, and his craft was like the one described in the story. Even more surprising, when someone actually did make the transatlantic crossing, the return flight took exactly the length of time the *Sun* article had announced— "seventy-five hours from shore to shore!"

WHODUNNIT?
The author of the hoax knew newspapers like the *Sun* wanted to

---

In 1978, John Paul II became the first non-Italian pope since 1522.

be first with a story. Since there was no telephone or telegraph available to confirm the facts, the newspaper would print first and worry about mistakes later. The author was also someone who knew a lot about science and knew how to tell a convincing tale. He was Edgar Allan Poe.

WHY-DUNNIT?

Poe's total wealth amounted to less than $5 at the time. (Even in 1844 that was chump change.) He and his family had just moved to New York, and Poe had a sick wife and her mother to support. They'd found rooms in a house that the author described as "old and buggy." Aside from an obvious need for money, Poe also loved literary pranks. He'd been fascinated by a hoax about an astronomer with a powerful new telescope who had supposedly spotted human-like creatures (with fur and bat wings) living on the moon.

HE DUNNIT AGAIN

The "balloon hoax" wasn't Poe's last little joke. In 1845, he published another article entitled "The Facts in the Case of M. Valdemar," which convinced many readers that hypnotism enabled people to communicate with the dead. Poe may have been famous for stories about premature burials and noblemen walled up alive, but he was only writing what his readers liked best. Edgar wasn't nearly as gloomy as he's usually made out to be. He loved a good laugh—especially at someone else's expense.

* * *

ELEMENTARY, MY DEAR WATSON

Believe it or not, the world's most famous detective never spoke the line for which he is most remembered. In only two of Sir Arthur Conan Doyle's stories does he even come close. In 1893's "The Crooked Man," Holmes makes his usual array of deductive conclusions, to which his assistant Dr. Watson exclaims, "Excellent!" Holmes's one-word reply is "Elementary." In "A Case of Identity," Holmes says, "All this is amusing, though rather elementary, but I must go back to business, Watson."

It was Samuel Prescott, not Paul Revere, who finished the midnight ride.

THEM'S FIGHTIN' WORDS: IN THE TRENCHES

In World War I thousands of miles of trenches held thousands of troops in a four-year-long stalemate.

Of course, the use of trenches to conceal military forces predates 1914 by a long, long time, and in fact, they were called "trenches" from about 1500 on. But their use in World War I, where they far exceeded any prior deployment, gave our language a number of lasting terms.

in the trenches
During the war being **in the trenches** meant being in action. The same thing today is meant by the term, that is, actively working at something. Thus, "He spent years in the trenches before they made him president of the company."

digging in
After the trenches were dug, soldiers on both sides lived in them for months on end, with neither side advancing or retreating measurably. From this, **digging in** acquired the meaning of standing firm in one's position or views.

foxhole
In addition to very long trenches, soldiers occasionally used a small slit trench that housed one or a few men. Although it was used much more rarely, the name given it, **foxhole**, survived. It was to play a much larger role in subsequent wars.

trench coat
The trenches were frequently, if not always, wet. Consequently, the officers wore long waterproof coats, or **trench coats**, a noun later applied to and still used for similar civilian raincoats.

trench mouth
The long months in the trenches took a terrible toll on a soldier's health. One condition that afflicted many of them was **trench mouth** (formerly called Vincent's disease), characterized by painful, bleeding gums and bad breath. It was caused by poor oral

hygiene and nutrition, heavy smoking, and stress—all conditions endemic in the trenches. Today **trench mouth** is readily treated with dental care and antibiotics.

shell shock

In addition to physical ailments, soldiers frequently suffered from nervous conditions. One was an acute stress syndrome resulting from exposure to constant shelling by the enemy and therefore called **shell shock**. It was thought to be caused by both the noise of the artillery and the constant fear it engendered. Today this term is still loosely used to describe the after-effects of any traumatic experience, as in, "That series of lousy boyfriends gave her a bad case of shell shock."

screaming-meemies

A similar expression is **screaming meemies,** a term that was coined for German artillery shells that emitted an exceptionally high-pitched whine before exploding. The term was later used to describe a state of extreme nervousness, bordering on hysteria.

over the top

When ordered to advance, the soldiers climbed over the parapet of front-line trenches to attack the enemy's front line. The "top" referred both to the trench's top and to the open no-man's-land between them and the enemy. After the war, the term survived, assisted by Arthur Guy Empey's use of the term as the title for his popular World War I account. In civilian use it was extended to mean taking the final plunge and doing something dangerous or notable.

no-man's-land

Although **no-man's-land** dates from the 1300s, when it meant the waste ground between two kingdoms, it didn't take on its military meaning until World War I, when it was applied to the territory between the thousands of miles of Allied and German trenches. This area, a virtually stationary battle line for three years, was covered with barbed wire and pitted with shell holes made by the artillery of both sides. Since then, this term also has been used loosely to describe an indefinite situation where one is neither here nor there.

France has been ruled by Charles the Fat, the Bold, the Simple, and the Well-Served.

tripwire
Troops who advanced close to the German line often had to cut through a wire that had been strung to set off a trap or an alarm. The soldiers called it a **tripwire**, because it was meant literally to trip them up. Later the term was used to signify anything that might trip someone up, as in a *New York Times* headline on October 7, 1997, "Looking for Tripwires, Ickes Heads to the Witness Stand." (The term today is also employed for a small military force used as a first line of defense.)

various (now politically incorrect) names for the enemy
During this period the traditional offensive slang for a German was **kraut**, an abbreviation for what was regarded as a quintessential German food, sauerkraut. Another was **Heinie**, an abbreviation for the common German name Heinrich. A third was **Jerry**, either derived from the British nickname for chamber pots (which the German helmets resembled), or a shortening of "German." These terms survived, on a small scale, but again came into wider use during World War II, when Germany was again the enemy of the Allies.

Christine Ammer's book, *Fighting Words*, explores the linguistic legacy of armed conflicts over the centuries, from biblical times to the present.

* * *

GAS ATTACK
World War I originated more than vocabulary: gas warfare was first used in WWI with as many as 17 different kinds of gases tried out by both sides. There were three kinds of gases, of which only the lachrymator (tear gases, from the Latin *lachrima* "tear") were combatible by gas mask. The other two varieties included asphyxiant, or poisonous, gases such as chlorine, and the dreaded blistering gases, such as mustard gas which produced burns on contact.

A contemporary news report of the use of poison gas:
"[The] vapor settled to the ground like a swamp mist and drifted toward the French trenches on a brisk wind. Its effect on the French was a violent nausea and faintness, followed by an utter collapse. [The] Germans, who charged in behind the vapor, met no resistance at all...." *New York Tribune*, April 27, 1915

George Washington may have been Father of His Country, but he had no children himself.

IS THIS THE SMELL OF PROGRESS?

It's known as "nonlethal weapons development," but you could say that the U.S. military has been nosing around for the proper bomb since WWII. Here's the unsavory history behind the making of a stink bomb for the 21st century.

Patriotic pro-war songs and movies aside, the actual business of making war is dirty indeed, involving blood, guts, and variously nasty forms of death. So it may be a good sign when the military seeks weapons that can disarm enemies rather than kill them. But when it comes to the details—better hold your nose.

AROMAS TO DIE FOR

For decades the U.S. military has conducted tests on nonlethal weapons. They've tried the subsonic sound blasters that can make enemies too nauseous to fight, and an amazing variety of deterrent sprays that make the ground too slippery to drive on, or can obscure the windows on a tank. But some of the oddest weapons center on the good old nose. The Odorous Substances Project of the Joint Nonlethal Weapons Directorate has been hard at work creating a stink bomb for the 21st century nose.

A ROTTEN IDEA

A chemical that smells like a ripe corpse, rotten eggs, or human feces seems to deserve its place in weaponry—would you want to spend a lot of time by an open sewer? Chemical stinks were tried by the military during World War II, particularly a substance known as "Who Me" designed by the French Resistance. Who Me, a sulphurous compound reminiscent of rotting flesh, was loaded into a pocket-sized atomizer. The idea was for Who Me carriers to casually brush by one of the German officers occupying Paris, spray him with the substance and render him unfit for duty until the smell wore off, which could take days or even weeks of careful scrubbing.

Before the Boston Tea Party, the British actually lowered tea taxes, not raised them.

STINKS THAT BOMBED

Who Me, however, didn't provide much help to occupied Paris—
the atomized Who Me mist had a tendency to share the wealth,
dousing the sprayer with as liberal a dose of unholy stink as the
sprayee. The U.S. military was still intrigued enough to perform
experiments with Who Me, hoping to douse double agents. The
U.S. developed another chemical compound intended to make
Japanese soldiers reek of sweaty armpits to exploit the Japanese
repugnance for body odors, but they faced the same difficulties in
applying the substance accurately.

THREE STINKS, YOU'RE OUT!

Since the last World War the U.S. military has tried out various
stink bomb projects, generally rejecting them as just too difficult
to administer. Back in the 1970s, for instance, the army tried
draining chicken eggs, filling them with stinky chemicals and
lobbing them at enlisted men to test the effects. (Service above
and beyond the call of duty.) That project never really got off the
ground, but as warfare has advanced and public criticism about
limiting necessary force has grown, the military has began examining the science of stink anew.

NOSING OUT THE ENEMY

Just what smells are foul enough to convince an enemy to drop his
gun and run like hell? That's what scientist Pam Dalton at the
Monell Chemical Senses Center in Philadelphia intends to find
out, thanks to the U.S. military subsidy that funds her work.
Dalton has found that few odors are universally offensive. After
all, though the smell of manure might offend an American subur-
banite, a rural Japanese person used to the odors drifting over from
fertilized farms would be much less horrified.

POT SHOTS

Extensive testing has proved that the most universally reviled
substances are good old Who Me, and a substance known in the
fragrance/deodorizer industry as U.S. Government Bathroom
Malodor. Bathroom Malodor is the standard stinky scent used for
testing air-freshener products. Although the aromas are vile, they
aren't ready for the battlefield. The same old problem of creating
better delivery systems may take some time. Scientists may tell us
that stink bombs are coming soon—but don't hold your breath.

MESMERIZED

His name is linked with hypnotism, but in fact he never hypnotized anybody. What did Franz Anton Mesmer do to deserve such an honor?

Franz Mesmer was a kind of astrological psychotherapist and scientific faith healer all rolled into one. He was operating out of Vienna when he came to the notice of the Imperial Morality Police there (yes, there was such an organization). Someone had reported him after observing that young girls who entered his house didn't come out for a long time—like days and weeks! Mesmer claimed that the girls suffered from various nervous conditions and he'd moved them into his house for treatment, which involved him massaging them all over. Hmm. The cure that made him famous involved a blind girl who said she was cured after a few days of this rubbing stuff, but in the 1760s, just like today, this sort of thing was looked at askance. So when the medical profession of Vienna ganged up on him and denounced his treatments as quackery, he packed up and headed for Paris.

ANIMAL MAGNETISM 101

Mesmer claimed that illness was caused by blockages in the body—and he was one of the few people who knew how to remove them. The whole universe was full of an invisible energy, which he called "animal magnetism," and it was controlled by the movements of the stars and planets. By "magnetizing" his clients, that is, rubbing them, he could dislodge that nasty blockage and— voila!—the patient would be cured.

A MAGNETIC PERSONALITY

As he got more popular, more people wanted to see him. He didn't have enough time (or hands), so he started magnetizing whole crowds at once. He even invented a contraption, a wooden tub of water with metal rods attached, so that one group could gather around it holding onto the metal rods and transfer their magnetism to the water. Then he would spray the water over the rest of the onlookers with a hose and tell them they were cured. He "magnetized" trees, too. Then he'd hang ropes from them. His patients touched the ropes and the miracle energy would flood through them. Mesmer claimed that this channeling of energy also explained psychic phenomena like telepathy, clairvoyance, and the ability to see the future.

THE TOAST OF PARIS GETS BURNED

Eighteenth-century Paris went wild for Mesmer, and King Louis XVI was one of his biggest fans—for a while. The king offered Mesmer a pension for life, on one condition: Mesmer had to submit his work to scientific investigation. Mesmer said merci, but no thanks. The king, being a king, appointed a royal commission to investigate Mesmer's claims in 1784. The commission gathered the greatest scientists in Paris, among them Benjamin Franklin, as an expert on electricity (and then American ambassador to France); Antoine Lavoisier, the father of modern chemistry; and Dr. Joseph Guillotin, inventor of the guillotine. The commission concluded that Mesmer was a fraud. Some people seemed to have been cured, they admitted, but there was no truth in what Mesmer had to say about scientific astrology, trees, ropes, tubs of water, and the rest. Animal magnetism was nothing but a hoax.

Mesmer knew he was beaten. He left France and the mesmerizing business for good and settled in Austria. While he was enjoying a life of quiet retirement, the French were killing people left and right, including Mesmer's old friends and enemies: King Louis, Marie Antoinette, and Lavoisier all died by the guillotine.

GETTING "PUYSGURIZED"

In 1789, the year the revolution began, one of Mesmer's disciples, the Marquis de Puysgur, was applying the Mesmer method of "animal magnetism" to a young boy. The marquis discovered to his surprise that the boy was in a trance: he would stand, walk, and sit on command. And when he woke, he didn't remember anything about it. So it's de Puysgur who really discovered hypnotism. And who can remember him—much less pronounce his name?

"YOU'RE FEELING SLEEPY... "

Stage illusionists in Europe and America who claimed to be followers of Mesmer quickly added this amazing new trick to their acts. It was so impressive that animal magnetism was all but forgotten—and "mesmerism" and hypnosis became synonymous. Add an attractive female assistant, and you've got the forerunner of the classic stage hypnosis acts that are still popular today.

Until 1946, there was no such thing as a "Canadian citizen," just "British subjects."

SHE WAS ONLY A PHARAOH'S DAUGHTER

…but, boy, could she dazzle those hotshot Italian boys.

TEEN QUEEN

Cleopatra VII was born in 69 B.C. and died in 30 B.C. When she was 17 or 18, she and her younger brother, Ptolemy XIII, inherited the throne of Egypt on their father's death. According to custom, they would rule jointly as husband and wife. But in the third year of their reign, Ptolemy, age 15 or so, forced his sister into exile. Determined to regain her throne, Cleopatra gathered an army in Syria, just across Egypt's border.

LUST AT FIRST SIGHT

Debate rages over Cleopatra's looks: she was either short and ugly, or willowy and beautiful. Either way, she was apparently charming and seductive, and let's not forget smart. So when Julius Caesar and the Roman army captured Alexandria soon after, Cleopatra sneaked into the city rolled up in an Oriental rug. Once inside the palace, the rug was unrolled and out stepped this Egyptian cutie. Gossip has it that she and Caesar became lovers that very night. Naturally, that put her on his good side. And steamed the heck out of her brother, who had escaped with his army. The six-month Alexandrian War ensued, but nobody was a match for the Roman troops. Ptolemy drowned in the Nile while trying to flee them. It was 48 B.C.; Cleo was twenty-one.

CRUISIN'

Caesar restored Cleopatra to the throne, which she now had to share with an even younger brother, Ptolemy XIV. Meanwhile, Caesar and Cleopatra cruised the Nile for two months. After which, Caesar returned to Rome—and his wife, Calpurnia. But he must have missed Cleo, because a year later he invited her to come live in Rome. His fellow Romans were scandalized by their affair, even more so when she gave birth to their son, Caesarion.

At any rate, two years after that, when Caesar was assassinated in the Roman senate, Cleopatra grabbed the first train to Egypt. Once back at home, historians say she most likely poisoned her brother-pharaoh and appointed little Caesarion her coregent.

I FEEL LIKE A NEW MAN!
Caesar was replaced by a triumvirate, consisting of Marcus Lepidus, Gaius Octavian—and Marc Antony. Supposedly for diplomatic purposes, he arranged a meeting with Cleopatra at Tarsus in Asia Minor. Secretly, he wanted to rule Rome solo, and hoped she could fund his ambitions. The meeting gave her an opportunity to make one more dramatic entrance. This time she arrived floating down the river on a golden barge with purple sails. (A little over the top? Read on.) Her maids were dressed as sea nymphs and Cleopatra herself was dressed as Venus, the goddess of love. She reclined under a gold canopy, fanned by boys in Cupid costumes.

In a few days, she and Marc Antony were lovers. Enthralled, he forgot everything else and stayed the winter in Egypt.

WHEN IN ROME
But he had an empire to run and eventually he returned to Rome. Six months later, Cleopatra gave birth to twins, naming the girl Cleopatra Selene and the boy Alexander Helios. It was four years before she saw Antony again. And he'd married in the meantime. His new wife was Octavia, half-sister of Gaius Octavian—a politically advantageous match, but Antony's heart still belonged to the Egyptian queen.

A NEW RENDEZVOUS
In 37 B.C., Antony couldn't stand it anymore. He left his Roman wife, came back to Egypt to stay, and married Cleopatra. Soon they had another child—a son, Ptolemy Philadelphaos. Meanwhile, Antony's brother-in-law Octavian plotted against them. When Antony gave Cleopatra Cyprus, Crete, and Syria (what a lovely present, but how did he wrap it?), and gave their children huge tracts of land that used to belong to Alexander the Great, Octavian had proof that Antony was wrapped around Cleo's little finger and posed a threat to Rome. Rome declared war on Egypt and sent a fleet to fight Antony and Cleopatra's combined forces.

Canadian Indians couldn't vote in national elections until 1960.

CLEO WIMPS OUT

Antony's forces were no match for the Roman Navy. Cleo had 60 ships of her own, but she knew when she was outclassed militarily. So she fled the scene while Rome crushed Antony's forces at the Battle of Actium in 31 B.C. Antony only made it worse by abandoning his men to follow her. The Romans saw it as proof that he was enslaved by love. The plucky Cleopatra prepared for an invasion by Rome, while Antony sulked and brooded.

CLEO WIMPS OUT AGAIN

Maybe if he'd spent more time paying attention to his troops, his navy and his cavalry wouldn't have deserted him, which they did. When his infantry fell to Octavian's troops, Antony returned to Alexandria, looking for Cleopatra, shouting that she'd betrayed him. Terrified, the queen of Egypt hid out and ordered her servants to tell Antony she was dead.

ALL IS LOST

Even if you don't know how the story ends, you must be getting that "tragic ending" feeling. Okay, so here goes. Antony stabbed himself, but he didn't quite finish the job, so when the news arrived that Cleopatra was still alive, he had himself carried to see her. He died in her arms. Tragic enough? Wait.

Cleopatra knew that Octavian planned to drag her back to Rome so he could march her through the city in chains. No way would she let that happen. So she planned a feast, her last meal, and had an asp (a poisonous snake) smuggled into her quarters in a basket of figs.

Octavian found her later, dead.

THE LAST OF THE RED-HOT PHARAOHS

Her dazzling days were done. Cleopatra was Egypt's last pharaoh; after her death, Egypt became a Roman province. More tragedy: Because Caesarion was Julius Caesar's son and might pose a threat to Octavian's power, Octavian had the boy murdered. Cleopatra's surviving three children were sent to Rome to be raised by Octavia. Her daughter, Cleopatra Selene, married the king of Mauritania and had two children. But we don't know what happened to Cleopatra's other two sons, Alexander and Ptolemy.

Of the 17 million military casualties during World War II, 7.5 million were from the U.S.S.R.

THE REAL COUNT DRACULA

He was a prince, not a count. He didn't live in Transylvania, but he was born there. He didn't have to be home in his coffin at sundown, but he was still a pretty scary guy. They called him "Vlad the Impaler" because…well…he liked impaling people.

B ram Stoker was going to call his book *Wampyr*, which means "vampire" in Romanian, but while he was doing research he came across a 15th-century prince named Vlad the Impaler, who called himself "Dracula." First published in 1897, *Dracula* has never been out of print. But the book didn't achieve worldwide recognition until the release of the first movies about the count, especially *Dracula*, the 1931 version starring Bela Lugosi.

ENTER THE DRAGON
The real Dracula's ancestors were warlord princes of Wallachia, a principality in what is now Romania. Dracula's father, Basarab, was in line for the throne, but there were a lot of relatives in the way. So for the moment, Basarab had to settle for the post of governor of Transylvania. In 1431 he was inducted as a knight into the Royal Order of the Dragon. He started calling himself the Dragon, which in Romanian is Dracul. His second son, Vlad, was born a few months later, and the little tyke was nicknamed "Dracula," which means son of the dragon.

THE LITTLE PRINCE
Vlad was born into a world of nonstop intrigues, power struggles, and war. When he was about three years old, his father, the Dragon, seized the throne of Wallachia after defeating one of his cousins. Now little Vlad was a true prince. His father made pint-sized warriors of Dracula and his two brothers. The boys learned the medieval martial arts—archery, swordsmanship, and riding—while wearing little chain-mail suits just like their pop. Vlad might have grown into a Prince Charming, but his father made one fatal mistake that changed Vlad's life forever.

Indira Ghandi and her son Rajiv were both assassinated.

In those days, the Ottoman Turks were a force to be reckoned with, so when the sultan of Turkey summoned the Dragon, he jumped. Believing it to be a call under truce, he brought Vlad and his younger brother with him. The sultan seized the boys as hostages so that the Dragon would side with him against an ambitious political shark of the time, the White Knight.

TOUGH TURKEY

The boys were locked in a dungeon, denied food, and flogged daily. But it was what was going on *outside* their cell that would prove to be more important to Vlad's development as an evil-doer.

The dungeon window faced onto the yard where executions were held several times a week. Young Dracula watched as, depending on their crimes, the sultan's victims were hanged, shot with arrows or spears, beheaded, crushed under wheels, and even occasionally given to wild beasts of prey. Most of them, though, were impaled…a process somewhat like spitting a chicken.

ENTER THE WHITE KNIGHT

In most stories, it's the White Knight who rides in on his charger and saves the day. But this is real life. And this particular White Knight wanted more than anything to be the king of Hungary. He saw Wallachia as a stepping-stone, and the Dragon as an impediment. The White Knight killed Vlad's father, mother, and older brother, and took the throne of Wallachia. When Vlad found out what had happened, he vowed revenge. The sultan released him and gave him a contingent of troops to lead against the White Knight. This was in 1448. Vlad was 17 years old.

THE UPSTART

Vlad did pretty well for a kid. The Turks by his side, he routed the White Knight, and placed himself on the Wallachian throne. But it wasn't going to be that easy. He held the throne for two months before being forced out. Eight years later, while the White Knight was invading Turkish Serbia, Vlad finally secured his position as the ruler of all Wallachia. The White Knight was killed in the fight against the Turks, and his army was defeated. Denied his revenge, Vlad took it out on everyone else who crossed his path.

LOVELY DOWNTOWN WALLACHIA

Wallachia was about the size of New York State. Its populace, mostly peasants, stood at half a million. On Dracula's coronation, he declared martial law. His first act of revenge was directed at the boyars, or nobles, who had sided with the White Knight against the Dragon. He gathered up hundreds of them, including their families, at the cathedral on Easter Sunday. He impaled the oldest, then forced the others to march 50 miles to where they were put to work building a castle for him. They mixed mortar, carried rocks and lumber, dug a moat. So much for the upper classes.

AN EQUAL OPPORTUNITY IMPALER

Dracula didn't neglect the lower classes either. He had the poor and sick of Wallachia gathered up and treated them to a banquet at his castle. Needless to say, it was their last meal. He sometimes wiped out entire villages for no particular reason. but he didn't just kill his own people. Foreign dignitaries and traders, monks, priests, Turks—everyone was a likely candidate. Travelers started to go the long way around Wallachia. It was during this time that the Turks named him "Vlad the Impaler."

Virtually any crime was punishable by impalement. Sometimes Vlad killed just because he was bored. He tortured and mutilated people, hanged them, burned them at the stake, and boiled them alive, but impalement was his favorite. It's estimated that Vlad the Impaler was responsible for 100,000 deaths.

THE END...?

All this murder and mayhem made Tirgoviste, Wallachia's capital, the safest place on earth. To prove it, Vlad put a golden cup on display in the central square, supposedly for thirsty travelers to use. You can bet that cup stayed right where it was for the six years that Dracula was in charge.

Vlad was killed outside Bucharest in a skirmish against his oldest enemy, the Turks, but it's an historical toss-up as to whether he died in battle or was killed by his own men. The Turks decapitated him and sent his head to Constantinople, where it was put on display to prove that the man they had named "the Impaler" was really dead. His body was buried at a monastery near Bucharest, but disappeared. When archeologists in the 1930s removed the slab over Dracula's supposed grave, they found an empty pit. Think about it.

THE HAMILTON AFFAIR

Here's proof that politicians never change!

Americans today are sick and tired of sleazy politicians and their scandals. We long for the good old days of honorable leaders like our founding fathers. Well, not so fast...

THE GREAT PATRIOT

Alexander Hamilton was one of the greatest of America's founding fathers. He was a powerhouse of ideas and action who put his personal stamp on the creation of America through his hard work, tenacity, and sheer brilliance. He served as George Washington's trusted aide during the Revolutionary War. He was one of the primary architects of the Constitution, the first Secretary of the Treasury, and he created the National Bank. Quite a résumé.

THE GREAT PATRIOT AND THE OTHER WOMAN...

In 1791, at the height of his influence and power (and while he was happily married), Hamilton met Maria Reynolds. This captivating young woman asked him for money, saying her philandering husband had abandoned her. Hamilton later said he was touched by the poor woman's story. Evidently, touched enough to begin an affair. Several months later, Maria's husband appeared at Hamilton's door. (Uh-oh.)

...AND THE OTHER WOMAN'S HUSBAND

The nervous Hamilton expected the outraged husband to demand "satisfaction"—a duel to the death. But to Hamilton's relief, James Reynolds only demanded $1,000 as compensation for husbandly pain and suffering. Hamilton paid up, and James generously granted Hamilton leeway to continue the affair with Maria, in return for future payments.

THE GREAT PATRIOT AND A COUPLE OF SCAMMERS

Hamilton continued his relationship with the ever-more-clutching Maria until he could wriggle out of her grasp. He knew he'd been taken by a husband and wife con team. Hamilton breathed a sigh of relief. He considered himself lucky to be a few thousand dollars poorer as long as he was rid of Mr. and Mrs. Reynolds. (But it's not over yet.)

Louis XVI might have escaped France, but he was recognized from his portrait on currency.

THE GREAT PATRIOT WASN'T OUT OF IT AFTER ALL

In 1792, Hamilton received another disturbing visit, this time from three U.S. senators, including James Monroe. The senators told Hamilton about a rumor that he had given money and secret Treasury Department information to a petty grifter named James Reynolds. (James was currently residing in a Philadelphia prison.) Faced with these accusations, Hamilton came clean. He confessed the affair with Maria, but denied giving away secret information. The senators believed him and withdrew. Hamilton had squeaked by again. (Or had he?)

THE GREAT PATRIOT LEARNS THAT POLITICS AND SECRETS DON'T MIX

A few years later, Hamilton left the Treasury Department and returned to private law practice. His scandals remained hidden, and he was an influential figure in national politics. He even considered running for president in 1800. Then in 1797, a pamphlet dredged up the whole Reynolds Affair. The tale of sex and payoffs in high places created a sensation. Hamilton suspected that James Monroe (one of the senators who came to his office) had leaked the story. Monroe was an ally of Hamilton's competitor for the presidency, Thomas Jefferson (who may have had dirty laundry of his own with his slave Sally Hemings, but that's another story).

"I AM NOT A CROOK"

Hamilton decided to have it all out. He dashed off a fiery essay admitting he had sex with Maria, but he denied any wrongdoing at the Treasury Department. Hamilton wanted everyone to know that he might be a two-timing skunk, but he wasn't a crook. His public career survived, but just barely. His enemies continued to discuss the affair, and his friends were embarrassed by it. There was no chance that Hamilton could run for president. Thomas Jefferson won the election of 1800.

WHAT ABOUT BETSY?

The reaction of Hamilton's long-suffering wife, Betsy, to the public exposure of her husband's embarrassing behavior is unknown. After Hamilton's dramatic death in the famous 1804 duel with Aaron Burr, Betsy burned all her correspondence. By the way, Maria Reynolds later had an affair with Aaron Burr too.

When Julius Caesar said, "I came, I saw, I conquered," he came, saw, and conquered Turkey.

THE DREYFUS AFFAIR, AND NO, IT'S NOT A SEX SCANDAL

The French army may have surrendered to Germany more than once, but on some issues, they'll never give up.

It started, as so many of these sorts of things do, with someone digging through some trash. This particular can of trash was located in the office of a German military attaché, in France, in 1894. In it were some handwritten papers that made it clear that someone in the French War Ministry was providing the Germans with French military secrets. Clearly, this would not do. Clearly, someone would have to be blamed.

THE OBVIOUS CHOICE
And someone was: Alfred Dreyfus, a French captain who worked in the War Ministry and who was (this will become important rather quickly) a Jew—the only one in the War Ministry, in fact. On the surface, Dreyfus was a fine candidate to be the traitor. His work in the War Ministry allowed him access to the secrets in question. Moreover, his family had come from Alsace, a former French province that had been annexed by the Germans in 1871, shortly after the Germans had seriously kicked French butt in the deeply embarrassing Franco-German War. Also, Dreyfus was a Jew, and in the conservative and largely anti-Semitic French military of the time, that pretty much made him as good as guilty.

A ONE-WAY TRIP TO DEVIL'S ISLAND
Dreyfus was arrested on October 15, 1894 and charged with treason. With the handwritten papers attributed to him, he was found guilty on December 22 and sentenced to life imprisonment on the Devil's Island penal colony (yes, it really existed; it was located just off the coast of French Guiana in South America).

MERCI, I NEEDED THAT
The Dreyfus treason conviction was the slam-dunk, feel-good hit

of the French military's year; it gave the military and other conservative elements of French society the fuel they needed to take whacks at France's Third Republic, the government formed in 1870 as the result of a particularly numbskulled military failure at the Battle of Sedan. The anti-Semitic press of the day also had a field day with the conviction, using it as proof that French Jews were treacherous curs.

THE SPYING ISN'T DYING
There was just one tiny little problem, however. Alfred Dreyfus was convicted and shipped off across the drink to South America, yet French secrets were still somehow making their way to the Germans. Unless Dreyfus had heretofore unrecognized telekinetic gifts that worked across several time zones, someone else had to be slipping notes to the Germans.

WELL, EXCUSEZ-MOI!
Enter Lieutenant Colonel Georges Picquart, who became head of the French military's counterintelligence unit a couple of years after Dreyfus' conviction. Picquart was an anti-Semite himself, so he wasn't naturally sympathetic to Dreyfus, but after he'd examined the papers that had been used as evidence against Dreyfus, he realized a major error had been made.

A MAJOR PLAYER
The handwriting on the papers belonged not to Dreyfus but to a Major Ferdinand Walsin Esterhazy. Esterhazy, who was something of a piece of work even before his traitorous activities (he'd posed as nobility and served in the Austrian army in 1866, and had joined the French Foreign Legion before joining the French regulars in 1892), had gotten himself in debt and was selling French secrets to dig himself out of it. Picquart was not sympathetic to Esterhazy's financial woes and had him court-martialed in 1897.

A MAJOR UPSET
This is the point where conspiracy buffs can officially begin drooling. Despite clear evidence that Esterhazy was a greedy backstabbing traitor, he was acquitted of treason by his fellow officers. Picquart, for his pains, was eventually arrested and tossed into jail.

The Pilgrims first touched shore, not at Plymouth, but at nearby Provincetown.

Here, the conspiracy-minded will imagine the French military smugly sitting back and swilling their wine glasses, convinced that this whole irritating Dreyfus thing would now just go away.

OH, NO, YOU DON'T!

And they would have gotten away with it, too, if it weren't for those meddling intellectuals. In this case, novelist Émile Zola: on January 13, 1898, a few days after Esterhazy's acquittal at court-martial, Zola published his famous "J'Accuse!" letter in the newspaper. In it, Zola accused the French army of knowing that Dreyfus was innocent and conspiring to cover it up. French society, which had already suffered stress fractures over the case, instantly polarized, with the artists and intellectuals on the side of Dreyfus and the military and church on the other (funny how these groups always seem split this way). Anti-Semitic riots broke out in the provinces; and Zola himself was tried for libel and convicted. He fled to England.

DREYFUS WAS FRAMED!

Then, just when you thought this thing couldn't possibly get any more exciting, what with the riots and class divisions and fleeing novelists and innocent men rotting away in tropical island jails—it does! One Major Hubert Joseph Henry, the man who discovered the papers that started the whole thing, was found to have planted forged documents that implicated Dreyfus in treason. Major Henry confessed to his forgeries and then committed suicide in August of 1898. Esterhazy, the real traitor, suddenly remembered he had pressing business in Belgium and skipped town.

A pro-Dreyfus government was swept into office in June 1899; it brought back Dreyfus from Devil's Island, and provided him with another court-martial. And at this court-martial, in light of all the shocking revelations concerning Henry and Esterhazy and forged documents and mixed-up handwriting...

NO, HE WAS NOT'!

.... He was found guilty again by the French army, which was clearly not taking the hint. At this point, the French president stepped in and pardoned Dreyfus, who accepted the pardon on the condition that he could continue to press his case for an official verdict of innocence. Dreyfus finally got his chance, and in 1906,

---

Eleanor of Aquitaine was the only person to be queen of both England and France.

12 years after it all started, a civilian court of appeals cleared Dreyfus of wrongdoing and reversed his previous convictions. He was formally reinstated to the army on July 22, 1906, and for all his pains he was awarded the Legion of Honor.

AFTER THE AFFAIR

Dreyfus stayed with the institution that tried to ruin him, rising to the rank of lieutenant colonel, and serving in WWI as the commander of an ammunition column. He died in 1935.

Esterhazy, who eventually admitted he was a German spy, moved to England and worked as a translator and writer. He died in Hertfordshire (instead of Devil's Island, where by all rights he should have been) in 1923.

Picquart, who established Esterhazy's guilt and spent time in jail for his investigations, was made a general in 1906 after Dreyfus' innocence was established.

Émile Zola died in 1902 from asphyxiation as a result of a stuck chimney flue—which some believe was the work of anti-Dreyfusards bent on revenge. In 1908, Zola's remains were interred at the Pantheon; at the ceremony, a right-wing journalist tried to assassinate Dreyfus but only winged him. The journalist was put on trial for shooting Dreyfus...and (what else?) acquitted.

THE ARMY IS DEFEATED

The French army, whose position in French society was deeply damaged by the scandal (along with the positions of the church, the anti-Semitic movement, and the other conservative elements who ended up on the losing side of the Dreyfus affair), and which, as you'll recall, found Dreyfus guilty a second time, finally did get around to admitting that he actually was, you know, well, innocent and all that. They did it in 1995—101 years after the "incriminating" papers were found in the wastebasket—and then only after an army historical journal not so subtly suggested that the French army still thought Dreyfus was guilty.

Proving that if you can't be right, at least be consistent about being wrong.

*　　*　　*

The 1972 movie *Papillon* stars Steve McQueen as the real-life Henri Charrière, who attempted to escape the Devil's Island prison colony in French Guyana in the 1930s.

MAKEUP TO DIE FOR

*Today, courageous women everywhere scorn the perils of
bankruptcy to keep themselves supplied with the latest
clothes and makeup. But that's nothing compared to
the brave ladies of history who risked their lives
daily for the sake of beauty.*

Snow-white skin was a sign of nobility, wealth, and delicacy
to the fashionable women of the 16th century. Their eyes
had to be just as bright, and their cheeks and lips just as red,
as that forerunner of fashion, Queen Elizabeth herself. Few came
by the painted-doll look naturally. Here are a few favorite recipes
from that era (and their sometimes lethal side effects).

VENETIAN CERUSE
Ingredients: vinegar and white lead.
Desired effect: For that pale white skin. It was applied to the face,
neck, and bosom.
Side effect: Lead poisoning, which in adults can cause increased
blood pressure, digestive problems, kidney damage, nerve disor-
ders, sleep problems, muscle and joint pain, and mood changes—
not to mention turning the skin a sickly gray.

SOLIMAN'S WATER
Ingredient: sublimate of mercury.
Desired effect: To remove spots, freckles, and warts.
Side effect: Polishes off the outer layer of skin, but also corrodes
the skin underneath. Teeth fall out prematurely, gums recede, and
a buildup of mercury in the system will eventually cause insanity.
Bargain alternative: For Elizabethan women on a budget, there
was always a mixture of sulfur and borax.
Side effect: Borax causes a sloughing of the skin, but can also
cause blistering and facial twitches, and in large amounts can
induce fever, vomiting, and eventual coma.

BELLADONNA
Ingredient: Belladonna, also known as deadly nightshade. And
not for nothing.

In Ancient Egypt, killing a cat was often a capital offense.

Desired effect: Drops in the eyes for that bright sparkle. It was also used to redden lips and cheeks.
Side effect: Belladonna contains atropine, which in large doses causes delirium, convulsions, and coma. Extremely poisonous.

PERMANENT RED OF FUCUS, a.k.a. FACEPAINT
Ingredient: red mercuric sulfide.
Desired effect: To redden lips and cheeks.
Side effect: Also made of mercury, so the side effects are the same as Soliman's Water, above. Namely, teeth fall out prematurely, gums recede, and a buildup of mercury in the system will eventually cause insanity.
Bargain alternative: a mixture of hard-boiled egg-white, cochineal (made from a South American insect that is dried and crushed, producing a deep red dye), and gum arabic.
Side effect: This one is actually harmless. For once, real value for less!

* * *

DIRTY ROTTEN ROYALS

While the ladies were beautifying with deadly creams and potions, *everybody* was stinking in an era in which baths were often annual occasions. Some stunk more offensively than others, however.

Peter the Great of Russia seldom washed and, like an 18th century rock star, left a trail of trashed accommodations behind him. One British gentleman presented his government with a bill for £350 (about $47,000 U.S. today) after Peter and his henchman stayed at his house. The group had torn up the furniture, smeared vomit and excrement on the floors and walls, and used the paintings for target practice. This must have been particularly galling for his hosts, because Peter had a phobia about cockroaches and insisted that every room be sparkling clean and guaranteed free of critters before he would enter.

A Canadian pilot, Roy Brown, is credited with shooting down the Red Baron.

HITLER THE BUM

*Adolf Hitler, the penniless Austrian who wreaked havoc on the
Western world of the 1930s and '40s, began his career as a
tramp. For nine years, from age 16 to age 25, he was a bum.*

H itler's parents wanted him to go into the Austrian civil
service like his father, but young Adolf had other plans.
He would be a great artist, he decided, and he went off to
Vienna to make his fortune.

THE LOSER
He applied twice at the Academy of Art, but they wouldn't accept
him as a student. He liked drawing buildings, so they advised him
to try the school of architecture instead. But he hadn't graduated
from high school, and so he was refused entry there, too. The
money from home ran out, and Hitler was on the street. In his
autobiography, *Mein Kampf* ("my struggle"), he described his time
in Vienna as a period of study. The reality was different.

THE HOUSEPAINTER
Hitler did some house painting and other odd jobs occasionally,
but most of the time he was flat broke. He stayed in a hostel for
homeless men, and this was where he developed his skill at public
speaking.

THE ARTIST
An older tramp found out that Hitler knew how to draw pictures
of buildings and encouraged him to paint postcards of Viennese
street scenes, which the older man would then take out and sell.
They shared the profits from this sporadic business venture.

THE SPEECH MAKER
The two set up their workspace in the hostel's large dayroom. But
they didn't get a lot of work done because Hitler could never resist
an audience. So while his partner kept trying to persuade him to
sit down and concentrate on the postcards, Hitler kept jumping to
his feet to make passionate speeches against the Jews. His audience, the other bums who were sleeping off their hangovers or
sitting waiting for their free meals, would cheer him on as he

worked himself up into incoherent ecstasies of nationalism. As time went by, he became a kind of bum celebrity.

THE WAR HERO
He moved to Munich just before the outbreak of World War I. His life changed forever when he joined the German army, where he reached the rank of corporal and won an Iron Cross.

His success as leader of the Nazi movement in later life relied mainly on the unique and passionate style of public speaking he had developed during those long years as a bum in Vienna.

THE LITTLE TRAMP
Charlie Chaplin always maintained that Hitler's trademark moustache was copied from Chaplin's "Little Tramp" character, and that Hitler adopted it to make himself more popular with the masses.

THE MONSTER
However he managed it, Adolf Hitler had learned, more than any other political leader of the 20th century, how to get through to the people who lived on the bottom rungs of society. And that was where he found his first and best supporters.

* * *

WHY WAS IT CALLED THE 3RD REICH?
"Reich" is German for "empire." The Holy Roman Empire, which united much of present-day Germany and Italy, was the First Reich. The Second Reich was established by Otto Von Bismarck in 1871. Hitler's Third Reich, which was supposed to last 1,000 years, lasted only 12.

Did you know that Hitler...
- Banned Charlie Chaplin for being "Jewish" (he wasn't)?
- Had a half brother who ran a bar in Germany that was popular with high-ranking Nazi officers?
- Liked to show people how much his own hands resembled those of his hero Frederick the Great?
- Was voted *Time* magazine Man of the Year in 1938?

At its height in A.D. 117, the Roman Empire covered 2.5 million square miles.

HITTING THE
HIGH NOTES

The castrati were male singers who were emasculated for the sake
of music. How did this shocking practice originate? And why did
parents willingly volunteer their sons for such mutilation?

Choir singing has always played a prominent role in Roman
Catholic church services. And one of its mainstays has
always been the boy soprano. The problem is, a boy's voice
breaks in his early teens, then it deepens. All that time and trouble training a kid, then you have to start all over.

RENAISSANCE BOYS
Back in the late 16th century, though, some genius figured out
how to fix that. The obvious solution—to use female sopranos—
wasn't an option. Women and Catholic church choirs didn't mix
back then, but there was an alternative.

A CURE FOR PUBERTY
The church fathers may have led sheltered lives (okay, some of
them did), but they knew that if a boy was castrated, his voice
wouldn't break. This was because, whereas the chest and
diaphragm would grow normally, the post-castration vocal cords
would grow much more slowly. But it was unthinkable, right?
Who would contemplate such mutilation for the sake of music?

Why, the Roman Catholic church, of course. What did a boy
need with those darn things, anyway? They would only get him
into trouble.

THE PAPAL OKAY
Pope Sixtus V officially sanctioned the practice of castrating boys
for choirs in 1589. With the church backing it, castration became
all the rage. Famous composers like Handel and Rossini composed
music specifically for these little boys with high voices. Collec-
tively, they were called the "castrati." (And since the Italians have
a funny way of pluralizing things, the word for one of them was
"castrato." Just trust us on it.)

A flush toilet exists that dates back to 2000 B.C.

WHO'S NEXT?

In the cities, barbers performed castrations as a sideline: the signs in their shop windows read, "Boys castrated here." Out in the country, pig farmers, who had some experience in the field, picked up a little extra cash on the side for the same service.

There was no anesthetic available, of course. The most common practice was to compress the carotid arteries, which briefly interrupted circulation and put the boy into a comatose state during the operation. Sometimes he didn't wake up again. Hemorraghing and infection were universal, too, in the days before sterilization. It's estimated that three in ten boys died on the table. But it was worth it for the sake of art. Right?

JUNIOR HIGH IS TOUGH ENOUGH...

Most of the castrati were the children of poor parents. If a son showed musical aptitude, he would be sold to a musical institution. These were usually orphanages or charitable schools for the poor that saw the popularity of the castrati as a way to make money. They adapted to the times: they became musical schools that trained castrati as well as musicians and baritone singers who still had their equipment. Opera societies regularly toured these institutions in search of fresh talent.

Parents had high hopes for their little emasculated ones, that they'd become famous and provide for mama and papa in their old age. But that nasty operation didn't guarantee results. And of course, boys who had no musical aptitude before the operation were unlikely to suddenly become good singers afterward.

The castrated boys—even those who could sing—were taunted mercilessly for being "freaks." If they turned out to be inferior singers, the musical institutions kicked them out. And where could they go? Now they were an embarrassment to their parents and ostracized by the community.

THE END OF A TREND

All good things must come to an end, and so all of a sudden the castrato was as unfashionable as last season's bell-bottoms. Quite a few had been international celebrities. Now they were has-beens—and freaks. As of 1825, the year of the last operatic castrato performance, the newspapers were advising their readers to steer clear of those "travesties of nature." In 1903, after more

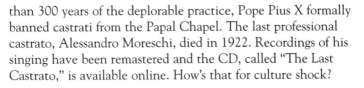

than 300 years of the deplorable practice, Pope Pius X formally banned castrati from the Papal Chapel. The last professional castrato, Alessandro Moreschi, died in 1922. Recordings of his singing have been remastered and the CD, called "The Last Castrato," is available online. How's that for culture shock?

FAMOUS CASTRATI

Carlos Broschi—Better known as "Farrinelli," he was the most famous of them all. Unlike most castrati, Farrinelli came from a well-to-do family (what were they thinking?). He was trained by the great composer Nicola Porpora. His arias sent the crowds into raptures. He famously accompanied world-class trumpet players in the trumpeter's "duel"—outperforming them every time.

Geatano Majoramo—Geatano performed under the name of "Cafferelli." He was a marvelous operatic singer but, by all accounts, not a very nice guy. He was famous for his violent mood swings (you'd be, too) and temper tantrums, and for his romantic carryings-on with the ladies—quite a feat considering his biological limitations.

Giovanni Battista Velluti—Velluti was never meant to be a castrato at all, but rather a military officer. As a child he was taken ill and rushed to a surgeon. However, the doctor thought little Giovanni was there to be castrated and proceeded as such. Velluti was more reknowned for his striking good looks than for his vocal abilities. There's one in every crowd, isn't there?

Giusto Tenducci—This famous castrato made his home in London after a wildly successful tour of Europe in the 1750s. He became a friend of the great composer Mozart, who wrote pieces especially for him. Tenducci's voice made him a star throughout England. In his fictional work *The Expedition of Humphrey Clinker*, 18th century author Tobias Smollet has one enchanted Tenducci listener proclaim, on hearing him for the first time, "The voice to be sure is neither man nor woman's but it is more melodious than either; and it warbled so divinely that while I listened I really thought myself in paradise."

*   *   *

Men who sing parts in these ranges today are called countertenors or sopranists. Their range is a result of genetics and training.

From the age of 30, humans gradually begin to shrink.

NAZI OLYMPICS

The 1936 Summer Olympics were meant to bring Germany back into the international fold after World War I. But Hitler had his own ideas. And so did an American athlete named Jesse Owens.

In 1931, the International Olympic Committee (IOC) awarded the 1936 Summer Olympic Games to the city of Berlin. This was meant to mark Germany's unofficial welcoming into the international arena after her discipline following World War I. But the IOC didn't foresee the rising tide of Nazism and the coming to power in 1933 of Chancellor Adolf Hitler, who saw the Games as a showcase of Aryan supremacy.

DER SHOW-OFF
The Games were an opportunity to show a skeptical world how he'd lifted his nation from the depths of despair and transformed it into a well-oiled machine that allowed the natural Germanic superiority to flourish. The Games were to be perfect, just like Germany.

CLEANING UP HIS ACT
First he had to clean up Berlin. The streets were cleared of the homeless, and anti-Jewish signs were removed. Hitler's architects designed four massive stadiums and a splendid Olympic village. In all, Germany spent $25 million getting ready—an enormous sum in those days. And of course, the German (amateur) athletes were supported while they trained full time in the years leading up to the games.

HELL NO, WE WON'T GO
Meanwhile, around the world there was a growing movement to boycott the Games because of the German government's anti-Semitic policies. An alternative, dubbed "The People's Games," was proposed, to be held in Barcelona. But the Spanish Civil War squashed that idea. In the end, the 1936 Olympic Games would see more participant countries (49) and more competitors (4,066) than any previous Olympics.

Until 1752, England rang in the new year on March 25.

GERMAN SUPREMACY

In fact, when the medals were tallied in the end, Germany easily won with 101 medals overall, including 41 golds. Its nearest rival was the United States (a country with three times its population) with 66 medals, 25 of which were gold. But all of Germany's achievements were cast into the shadows by the unbelievable performance of one American athlete—a man who most definitely bucked the Aryan superiority myth. His name, of course, was Jesse Owens.

JESSE JAMES OWENS

They called Owens the "Tan Cyclone" and he brilliantly lived up to that name by bagging four gold medals for his country: in the 100 meter dash, the 200 meter sprint (in world record time, mind you), the 400 meter relay, and the long jump.

SOME FRIENDLY ADVICE

Owens had started badly in the long jump, fouling on his first two jumps by overstepping the mark. He had just one last chance to get it right. As he psyched himself for his final jump, he was approached by his major rival, a stocky blond German who was a prototype of Hitler's ideal. The man's name was Luz Long and in one of the great acts of sporting comradeship he offered Owens some advice: he suggested that Owens draw a line a few inches in front of the take-off board and use that as his mark. It worked.

THE HITLER SNUB MYTH

Did Hitler really snub Jesse Owens because he was a black man? No, he did not. On the first day of the Games, Hitler formally shook hands with the medal winners from Germany and Finland. But that night, Hitler received a polite message from the President of the International Olympic Committee, Count Baillet-Latour, that informed him that it wasn't proper protocol for a national leader to congratulate the athletes: he was there merely as a spectator. Hitler took the advice graciously and, from then on, didn't congratulate the individual athletes. Therefore, Jesse Owens was not personally congratulated by Hitler. But neither were any of the other competitors.

Here's what Owens had to say when he was interviewed on the matter a few years later, "When I passed the Chancellor, he arose, waved his hand at me, and I waved back at him."

It wasn't until 1939 that a British monarch, George VI, visited either Canada or the U.S.

THE UNFORGIVABLE SNUB

The real snub came on Jesse's return to the United States. His own president, Franklin Roosevelt, refused a face-to-face meeting with him and did not congratulate him in any way, by letter or phone call, on his outstanding accomplishment. It's also interesting to note that, back in Hitler's Germany, Jesse could sit wherever he wanted to on a bus.

P.S. THE U.S. RELAY SCANDAL

Sports announcer Marty Glickman was at the Games that year—as a participant. He was, by all accounts, the fastest man on the U.S. relay team. The day before the big event, 18-year-old Marty and the other runners were called in for a team meeting. Their coach, Dean Cromwell, had an announcement: Marty wouldn't be running; his replacement was wonderboy Jesse Owens.

Glickman's fellow athlete Sam Stoller was also bumped, in favor of Frank Metcalfe. No reason was given for the unprecedented substitution. But everyone understood. Glickman and Stoller were Jewish. The U.S. Olympic Committee was afraid a loss to a couple of Jewish guys would compound the damage that Jesse and the other black athletes had already caused to Germany's Aryan image of itself.

Jesse Owens protested, "I've won the three gold medals I set out to win. I've had it. I'm tired. Let Marty and Sam run. They deserve it." Owens was informed that he would do as he was told. And so the relay event was run without Glickman and Stoller. The U.S. team won by 15 yards.

BITTER VICTORY

But no one on the U.S. team was celebrating. In the 100-year history of the modern Olympic Games no other fit American athlete has been pulled from an event. And until the day he died, Marty Glickman had a bitter taste in his mouth—a bitterness caused, not by Adolf Hitler or Germany, but by his own American Olympic Committee.

* * *

Themistocles was asked whether he would rather be Achilles or Homer, to which he responded, "Which would you rather be—a conqueror in the Olympic games, or the crier that proclaims who are conquerors?"—Plutarch

IT'S A GAS

Using a little ingenuity and a lot of hot air,
18th-century inventors really got off the ground.

In the 18th century inventors began to attach something heavy to a large amount of something lighter than normal air—hot air for example. Hot air balloons might have been invented as far back as 1709, by a Brazilian priest and inventor named Bartolomeu Lourenço de Gusmão. But it was closer to the end of that century before human beings began to fly, or at least to float through the air. In 1782, brothers Joseph and Étienne Montgolfier experimented with hot-air balloons in France. By 1783, they were ready to send up passengers—a rooster, a duck, and a sheep! Everything went well, except for a minor injury to the rooster when the sheep kicked it. Next, the Montgolfier brothers sent up a man in a balloon that was tethered—attached to a line that remained firmly anchored on the ground.

Then in November 1783, Jean Francois Piulatre de Rozier and the Marquis d'Arlandes went aloft, cut their balloon loose, and sailed over Paris at about 3,000 feet. Burning wool and straw to maintain a supply of hot air, they traveled for about 25 minutes and covered 5.5 miles. Delighted Parisians went into a frenzy over balloons. In fact, balloon mania spread quickly and, all over Europe, people stitched up balloons and flew into the air.

WHAT'S THE USE?

In December 1783, inventor J. A. C. Charles flew a gas-filled balloon for two hours, covering 27 miles. The aging American philosopher-statesman (and inventor) Benjamin Franklin was in Paris at the time and called the flight "a most beautiful spectacle." Not everybody understood what all the fuss was about. Someone asked Franklin what those floating things could possibly be used for. Franklin replied, "What use is a newborn baby?" But a use was soon found, in 1793 the first airmail letter was sent from London to Paris by balloon—the letter was addressed to B. Franklin.

Another American patriot, President Abraham Lincoln, got interested in balloons on June 17, 1861, when he received a tele-graph message from high up in the air. A balloon enthusiast named Thaddeus Lowe had taken several representatives of the

---

Henry VIII is credited with writing the song "Greensleeves."

American Telegraph Company up over Washington, D.C., in a tethered balloon. They ran a wire down the tether and sent the first air-to-land telegram. It was forwarded to Lincoln.

HIGH SPYS

That night Lowe's balloon was tethered on the White House lawn while Lincoln asked about military possibilities. During the war, Lowe gave valuable information to Union troops. Tethered balloons provided a high platform from which to spy on the enemy. As a psychological benefit, the balloons looked scary as they lurked above the battle zone. After trying unsuccessfully to shoot down Union balloons, the Confederacy decided they needed some of their own. They gave war that graceful Southern touch with silk balloon bags. This gave rise to the tale that Southern belles had donated their best dresses to the air-war effort.

GOT GAS?

Inventors kept working on balloons. Heated air could get a balloon up, but the air cooled when the fuel ran out—and the balloon came down wherever it happened to be. Keeping a fire going in the air was complicated and dangerous. Instead of warmed air, hydrogen gas—the lightest of the elements—worked well, though it was very flammable. Hydrogen was produced when a metal was dissolved in an acid. Sometimes other gases were used, such as the coal gas used for lighting in some towns.

FOR THE BIRDS

Unfortunately balloons still couldn't be steered. They could be made to go up by dropping ballast and down by letting out gas, but they had no controls for side-to-side motion or for speed. Off its tether, a balloon was at the mercy of the winds, and the "pilot" was just a passenger, which could quickly become an unhealthy situation. Inventors worked on devices to get the craft to go where the pilot wanted. They tried adding oars, sails, wings, parachutes, even propellers, but nothing worked. Someone suggested harnessing a team of vultures, but that didn't seem like a good idea. With limited success, the French tried a steam engine, human muscle power, and a small electric motor. In the late 1880s, Gottlieb Daimler's new lightweight gasoline engine changed everything. By the beginning of World War I, balloons were using motors, propellers and rudders, and venturing farther than ever before.

Cincinnati was named for a Roman dictator who quit the job after 16 days.

CORTÉS AND THE FEATHERED SERPENT

*The highly aggressive Hernan Cortés owes a huge debt to an
ancient Aztec god. Either that, or he was an Aztec god.*

THE FEATHERED SERPENT

In what is now Mexico, the Feathered Serpent god was widely worshipped from about 300 A.D. The Aztecs called him by the virtually unpronounceable "Quetzalcoatl." He was the god of self-sacrifice, wisdom, science, and the father of the human race. A pretty important deity, we'd say. He had a dark side, too, which makes what happened in this story not surprising, especially if you're an Aztec.

THE MAKING OF A LEGEND

The ancient stories about him said that he had light skin, red hair, and light eyes. According to legend, he was a kind and thoughtful ruler who forbade the ritual sacrifice of living things, human or animal. But he had to leave his people. Why? The stories differ: he either left in disgrace, or was forced out. But one thing the stories agree on is that Quetzalcoatl promised to return someday to reclaim his throne and help his people again.

A thousand years later, a fair-skinned man with red hair and light eyes landed in the Aztec world—coincidentally on their calendar day of Quetzalcoatl's birth. His name was Hernan Cortés, a young Spanish nobleman-turned-explorer. With him, he had 11 ships, about 600 men, and 16 horses. Plenty enough paraphernalia to impress anybody at the time.

OF KINGS AND SLAVES

Montezuma—you remember him—was the Aztecs' head honcho. He was sure that the Feathered Serpent had returned, just as the ancient prophecy had said. Montezuma greeted Cortés as a god. Cortés thought this was a pretty nice greeting and entered the Aztec capital peacefully.

Cortés had been given a slave in Tabasco. The Spanish called her Doña Marina (in fact, she'd been a princess before she became

---

Although she couldn't vote, feminist Victoria Woodhull ran for U.S. president in 1872.

a slave), and she acted as Cortés' handy-dandy interpreter, aide, and sometimes chief negotiator. She was also the mother of his son, who is thought of as the first Mexican. Her real name was Malinche; an inconvenient stepchild in her aristocratic family, she had been secretly sold to the Mayans. The Indians Cortés dealt with saw her as a traitor, and she is still seen that way in Mexico even though her negotiating skills probably saved Indian lives.

THEY CAN'T ALL BE GOLDEN

The amazing Tenochtitlan stood on an island in an artificial lake, with causeways connecting it to the other shore. The population was then more than 150,000 (some estimate 300,000) and the city was laid out on a grid that covered almost five sqare miles. At the center were temples, schools, priests' quarters, courts for ball games, sculptures, and Montezuma's palace. Luxury items included chocolate, gemstones, jaguar skins, and gold. Lots of gold.

It was either the chocolate or the gold, but Cortés was impressed enough to show his true hand: he took Montezuma hostage. This, unsurprisingly, led to a war. Cortés lost no time making use of potential advantages. For example, the ruling Aztec empire had serious internal problems, including a lot of unwilling subjects who resented being forced to pay tribute. Some volunteered to join Cortés right away. By the end, 200,000 Indians fought on his side.

ADVANTAGE, CONQUISTADORS

The Spaniards had some other important things in their favor. Although they didn't have many horses, the animals were new and frightening to the Aztecs. Cortés and his men also had European weapons such as crossbows, muskets, and steel swords. Even disease turned out to be an advantage for the Spaniards. During the years of battle, smallpox, measles, and other European diseases devastated the Indian population. The Aztecs, diminished by disease as well as warfare, were ultimately defeated.

SO?

Was Cortés the human personification of the dark side of the Feathered Serpent? If so, the ancient prophecy about the return of Quetzalcoatl, in fact, led to the destruction of the Aztec empire. Pretty creepy.

Because of harsh terrain and a lack of pack animals, no Indian nation used the wheel.

BEST HIDEOUSLY INBRED ROYAL FAMILY: THE HAPSBURGS

And here you thought inbreeding was just a low-rent sort of activity. In fact, it's the sport of kings.

All your royal families of Europe have participated in a program of inbreeding so unwise that it would disgust Jerry Springer's booker. They paid for it, of course (how many royal families are left any more?), but not before polluting their bloodlines to an intolerable degree. Any little girl who dreams of marrying a handsome prince on a white steed is advised to marry the horse instead. The horse probably has better DNA.

THE ROYAL TREATMENT
You'd think that the royal families of Europe would have figured out that marrying your cousin was not the way to go. At the very least, when you'd go to a royal function and everyone was married to a relative, you'd clue in that something was amiss. But royalty are different from you and me, and not just because all their children were still drooling well into the teenage years. Royalty wasn't just about kings and queens, it was about families and dynasties—single families ruling multiple countries. Or in the case of the Hapsburgs, most of the continent. You can't let just anyone marry into that sort of thing. There had to be standards, genetically haphazard as they might be.

ENTER THE HAPSBURGS
The Hapsburgs, based in Austria, carried this caution to the extreme, even for the royal families of Europe. Take the case of Archduke Franz Ferdinand. (You may remember him as the nominal cause of World War I, when the poor fellow was assassinated in Sarajevo by a Serbian nationalist. What, you don't? Ah, the glories of our educational system.)

THE DUKE AND THE DUCHESS

Long before his assassination, Franz fell in love with Sophia von Chotkowa und Wognin, who was a duchess of Hohenburg. For most men, linking up with a duchess of Hohenburg would probably be a step up in the grand scheme of things, certainly something to brag about at the family reunion at the municipal park. ("You married a doctor? How nice. I married nobility. Look, here come our dukelings now.")

WHAT HE DID FOR LOVE

Franz's family, on the other hand, was horrified. Franz was an heir to the Austrian-Hungarian empire! He couldn't marry any shameless duchess who just happened to bat her hereditary lands at him! It was a scandal! Franz eventually married Sophie, but he was made to renounce all claims of rank for their offspring (i.e., no little emperors for Franz and Sophie). As a final insult, Sophie, the hussy, was not allowed to ride in the same car as her husband during affairs of state.

In retrospect, this may not have been such a bad idea; Sophie was in the same car as Franz in Sarajevo (presumably not a state function) and she got assassinated right along with him. But at the time, it probably just came across as mean.

TOMORROW, THE WORLD

No, in the grand scheme of things, the Hapsburgs figured it was better to marry a Hapsburg when you could (and one of those degenerate French or Italian Bourbons if you couldn't). On a territorial level, this worked like a charm; at the height of the Hapsburg influence, the family ruled the Holy Roman Empire and the Iberian Peninsula (that's Portugal and Spain), and had good and serious claims on a large portion of what is now France.

THE SECRET OF THEIR SUCCESS

The family had initially achieved much of this, interestingly enough, by marrying people who were not blood relatives; after a particularly profitable spate of marriages arranged by the family in the late 15th century, it was said of the Hapsburgs, *Bella gerant alii, tu felix Austria nube* ("Let others wage wars: you, fortunate Austria, marry"). Once lands were assimilated, of course, it was first cousins all the way.

THOSE LIPS, THOSE... EARS?

In the short run, the interbreeding caused some noticeable but essentially minor physical distinctions: the famed "Hapsburg lip," in which a full lower lip jutted out in front of a somewhat less lavish upper lip. This distinction was on a par with other royal families, who had (and have) their own physical distinctions. The Bourbons, for one, had a distinctive nose (it was huge), while today, the English House of Windsor (i.e., the royal family) is known for its Dumbo-like ears. Proof that there were worse things than to have uneven lips.

MARRIED, CARRIED TO EXTREMES

Here's the thing, though. It's one thing to marry your cousin. Not the smartest thing you can do, but so long as you move to another state and don't talk much about your family, you can get away with it. But if you marry a cousin, who was him- or herself the product of cousins, who were themselves products of cousins, and so on and so forth—and you're all in the same family—well, you don't have to be a geneticist to see what's coming. Alas for the Hapsburgs, what was coming was Charles II, king of Spain from 1665 through 1700.

THE END OF THE LINE

With Charles, the question was not what was wrong with him, but what wasn't wrong. To begin with, thanks to all that cousin cuddling, the Hapsburg lip stopped being a distinctive facial characteristic and became a jaw deformity so profound that Chuck couldn't chew his own food. This might depress a person of normal intelligence, but alas! Charles was also mentally disabled. Anyway, it wasn't the most depressing deformity Charles had; let's just say that generations of inbreeding kept Charles from breeding new generations. It was bad enough to have a sick freak ruling Spain; it was even worse that there were no more sick freaks coming.

GOODBYE, CHARLIE

For lack of a better idea, Charles willed his possessions to a relative. Unfortunately, it was a relative who was also a Bourbon. Enter the War of Spanish Succession, at the end of which Spain would lose most of its European holdings (such as the Netherlands), and the Hapsburgs would begin their long decline, which would end with the first World War and a final dismemberment of the family's territorial holdings.

THE MORAL OF THE STORY

Clearly, this might never have happened had the Hapsburgs slipped in a commoner now and then, just to set a genetic Roto-Rooter to their chromosomes. Wouldn't that have been an irony—a few more serfs in the gene pool, and there might still be a Holy Roman Emperor. The Hapsburgs probably wouldn't think that was funny. But a sense of humor was probably not what they bred for, anyway.

* * *

NOW *THAT'S* A MOTTO!

The Hapsburgs may have had beans for brains when it came to breeding, but man, they knew a good will-to-power slogan when they saw one. Witness these gems of the Hapsburg "dynasty":

- *Österreich Über Alles*—literally means "Austria Over All" in German, the native language of the Austrian Hapsburgs. This credo has its origins from the Hapsburg Emperor Frederick III's cryptic device of "A.E.I.O.U." (see below).
- *A.E.I.O.U.*—usually interpreted to stand for *Austria Est Imperare Orbi Universo* or *Austria Erit In Orbe Ultima*. Translated from Latin, the first phrase roughly means "Austria is destined to rule the world" and the latter "Austria will be in existence until the end of the world."

Fun with Latin. The cool thing is, what with that snappy highly declined grammar, Latin is sometimes open to more than one interpretation. Thus, some might say a more far-seeing reading was that of Frederick II of Prussia: *Austria Erit In Orbe Ultima*, "Austria will one day be lowest in the world." Today, while certainly not the lowest in the world, Austria cannot be compared, either in physical size or political stature, to Austria under Hapsburg rule.

Indira Gandhi wasn't related to Mahatma Gandhi, but was the daughter of Nehru.

ANNA & THE KING: FACT OR FICTION?

Hollywood has presented her as a romantic heroine.
Was she really just a self-promoting prevaricator in a hoopskirt?

We didn't want to believe it at first. Was Anna Leonowens—the heroine of *The King and I*, the head-strong governess portrayed by the adorable Deborah Kerr and the feisty Jodie Foster, the Anna who tamed the king of Siam—a low-down dirty liar? The facts and fabrications follow.

Fabrication No. 1: Anna's autobiography says she was born Anna Crawford in 1834 in Wales.
The Truth: Her maiden name was Anna Edwards and she was born in India in 1831.

Fabrication No. 2: Her father was an army captain who died during a Sikh uprising in India when she was six years old.
The Truth: Her father was a cabinetmaker who died three months before she was born.

Fabrication No. 3: She married Major Thomas Leonowens when she was 17. He died of sunstroke during a tiger hunt in Singapore.
The Truth: She did, in fact, marry young—at age 18. Her husband's name was Thomas Leon Owens. Thomas had difficulty keeping a job and the couple moved around a lot. He died of apoplexy in Penang, Malaya in 1859.

Fabrication No. 4: She was a highly respected British governess.
The Truth: She was not a governess—a position with a broad range of duties in the royal household of Siam—but simply a teacher of English. It was in this capacity that King Mongkut employed her.

Fabrication No. 5: In her book *The Romance of the Harem*, she claimed that King Mongkut was a despot and threw his wives into underground dungeons if they failed to please him.
The Truth: There were no underground dungeons in Siam.

Fabrication No. 6: As famously depicted in Anna's story, King Mongkut ordered the public torture and beheading of of his concubines who had fallen in love with a monk.

The Truth: This whole episode appears to be nothing more than an invention. There were many foreign correspondents in Siam at the time and none of them mention such an incident.

Fabrication No. 7: Anna became very close to the king (the movie even hints at a romance).

The Truth: King Mongkut hardly knew Anna Leonowens. The king kept detailed diaries and, in the five years that she worked in the royal court, he mentions her only once and, then, only briefly.

Fabrication No. 8: Anna came to respect King Mongkut and praised him for his visionary outlook.

The Truth: In her writings Anna presented the king as a conservative, intolerant, reactionary bigot who was stuck in a time warp. She did not give him any credit for his modern policies and his embracing of Western knowledge.

Fabrication No. 9: Anna was opposed to the British imperialist attitude toward Siam and courageously stood up to the British hierarchy on behalf of her adopted people.

The Truth: Anna was, in fact, an imperialist apologist and a great supporter of the British colonial ventures in the Far East. She purposefully portrayed the people of Siam as childlike and backward to bolster public support for British intervention and "enlightenment."

Fabrication No. 10: Anna became known as an authority on all things Siamese and lived her later years in respected retirement.

The Truth: As soon as her first book was published, Anna was sued for plagiarism and the dissemination of false information. As her books kept coming, so did the court cases. The academic world refused to acknowledge her writings, and she was roundly condemned as a sensationalist writer of fiction.

THE FACT IS...

About the only part of the Anna legend that holds up is that she did serve for five years in the royal court of Siam. And the rest, as we at Uncle John's Hysterical Society say, is history.

I AIN'T GIVING BACK THAT MEDAL!

The story of Mary Edwards Walker, the only woman who has ever won the Medal of Honor, and the guys who wanted to take it away from her.

THAT'S DOCTOR WALKER TO YOU, BUDDY!
Mary Edwards Walker grew up in rural New York and graduated from Syracuse Medical College in 1855. Her father was one of those free-thinkers who was active in the reform movements that thrived in upstate New York in the mid-1800s. So no wonder his daughter became an early supporter of women's rights.

Mary was particularly drawn to the issue of dress reform. She declared, "Corsets are coffins." Instead of wearing the restrictive women's clothing of the day, she went around in "bloomers," the then-scandalous, completely nonrevealing, skirt-and-pants outfit designed by and named for feminist Amelia Bloomer. Later in life, Mary would lecture on women's rights wearing full men's evening dress, including top hat. She prided herself on the number of times she'd been arrested for wearing men's clothing.

DR. WALKER IN LOVE AND WAR

After med school, she married fellow medical student Albert Miller, but kept her own name (naturally). Mary and Albert set up a medical practice in Rome, New York, but the natives weren't ready to accept a woman physician, and their practice didn't do very well. The couple divorced 13 years later.

During the Civil War, Walker enlisted in the Union Army but was refused a commission as an army surgeon. So she bit the bullet, served as a nurse, and finally got promoted to field surgeon, a job she worked at for almost two years near the Union front lines. Finally, she was appointed assistant surgeon of the 52nd Ohio Infantry. It's during this assignment that she most likely also served as a spy. (But it's all very hush-hush and nobody wants to talk about it.)

Australian Prime Minister Harold Holt vanished while swimming in Port Phillip Bay.

DR. MARY "SPUNKY" WALKER

She crossed Confederate lines to treat civilians (or spy on the other side) as casually as we cross the street. That is, until a day in 1864, dressed in a slightly modified officer's uniform of her own design, she accidentally bumped into a group of rebel soldiers just south of the Georgia-Tennessee border. Their commanding officer sent the good doctor to a jail in Richmond, Virginia. Four months later, she was released during a prisoner exchange, and was greatly pleased that she'd been traded "man for man" for a Confederate officer. After her release, she served out the rest of the war practicing medicine at a women's prison in Kentucky and an orphan asylum in Tennessee.

GIVE 'EM HELL, DR. WALKER!

For her service during the Civil War, President Andrew Johnson awarded Mary Walker the Congressional Medal of Honor. But during what's known as "The Purge of 1917," the federal government acted on a congressional law revising the Medal of Honor standards to include only "actual combat with an enemy." Mary Walker's medal was revoked. Like heck, said the 85-year-old Mary. She refused to turn the medal back to the Army and according to her friends, she wore it proudly every day until her death two years later. In 1977, President Jimmy Carter reinstated the award, and Mary Edwards Walker remains the only woman to be so honored.

MORE HONORS FOR DR. WALKER

A 20¢ stamp honoring Mary Walker was issued in 1982. The stamp commemorates her as the first woman to have been awarded the CMH and the second woman to graduate from a U.S. medical school. She died just before the 19th amendment gave women the right to vote.

* * *

FAMOUS FEMALE MEDICAL FIRSTS

Elizabeth Blackwell—1849, 1st U.S. medical degree
Gerty Radnitz Cory—1947, Nobel Prize for Medicine
Louise Brown—Test tube baby
Elizabeth Oliver—Broadcast her child's birth on Internet
Mary Lund—1st female artificial heart recipient

THE CRUSADE TO END ALL CRUSADES

The People's Crusade of 1096 had been a well-meaning bust, so it was time for the real army to swing into action. And even though it was really the "second" crusade, it's called the "first."

K nights and princes—experienced, battle-hardened warriors—led a series of campaigns against the infidel Turks to conquer the Holy Land for the Christian cause. The first of these *official* campaigns was named, not surprisingly, the First Crusade (1096–1099).

THE BAD BOYS

Frenchmen and Normans made up the bulk of the Christian forces, which numbered between 25,000 and 30,000 (a relatively modest figure by modern standards but an immense number back then). The Normans were the bad boys of Europe in the 11th century, a daring, adventurous bunch that had conquered England in 1066 and taken most of southern Italy from the Byzantine Empire. They made their way slowly across Europe and into the Balkans, finally assembling at Constantinople (present-day Istanbul) in May of 1097.

THE BYZANTINES

Constantinople was a city of great wealth and culture. It was also the staging ground for the crusaders' attack on the Holy Land. But from the beginning there was friction between the crusaders and their allies, the Byzantines, who were Greek Orthodox Christians.

All the Byzantines wanted was to recapture the provinces in Asia Minor (present-day Turkey) that they'd lost to the infidels. The crusaders wanted nothing less than to conquer the Holy Land itself (a region that included Palestine and Syria), including Jerusalem, the most sacred city in all of Christendom.

LIKE OIL AND WATER

The friction between the Byzantines and the crusaders wasn't bad enough: there was almost constant tension and bickering between the leaders. Bohemond, a Norman and one of the greatest

---

John Adams made it a crime to publish anything scandalous about the U.S. government.

adventurers of the day, was a 40-year-old veteran warrior with a well-deserved reputation for being fearless, imaginative—and ruthless. He was in almost constant disagreement with another of the Crusade's great leaders, the Count of Toulouse. In stark contrast to Bohemond, the Count had a reputation for being courteous, honest, and deeply religious: he believed strongly in visions and miracles.

ASSIGNMENT: ANTIOCH

The crusaders moved southeastward from Constantinople toward Syria and the ancient city of Antioch. In the time of the Crusades it was the richest and most powerful city on the Palestinian coast. Four hundred towers had been built into the formidable walls, which snaked for miles around the perimeter. Given the sheer strength of the city's defenses, it was highly likely that Antioch could only be conquered by treachery from within. (Antioch was still a predominantly Christian city with a large population of Greeks and Armenians who were likely to go over to the enemy at the first opportunity.)

ROAST TURKEY

The crusaders spent months there, while their supplies steadily dwindled. After a cold, rainy winter, new supplies arrived and morale improved. Bohemond felt a lot better, too. He decided that too many Turkish spies were coming out of Antioch. He had the spies he'd captured killed, then ordered his cooks to roast them on a spit. That night, all the spies who hadn't been captured sneaked back into Antioch.

FRIENDS IN HIGH PLACES

Bohemond had some spies of his own. When he found out that a large Turkish relief column was making its way to Antioch, he knew it was time to act. He sent his spies into the city, where they devised a plan with an Armenian captain named Firouz who was secretly loyal to the Christian cause. Bohemond's men would climb up a leather ladder slung from one of the three towers controlled by Firouz.

OVER THE TOP, BOYS!

Sixty men climbed up the ladder, captured the three towers, and opened the first gate. Soon other gates were opened, and the rest of the crusaders streamed in and overwhelmed the defenders. Because the Turkish relief army was fast approaching, the crusaders had to act quickly. And they did: by the end of the day there was scarcely a single Turk left alive in Antioch.

FRIENDS IN EVEN HIGHER PLACES

Next day, the Turkish relief force arrived at Antioch and quickly encircled it. The besiegers were now the besieged. Panic started spreading among the knights and foot soldiers, many of whom began to desert. But the crusaders were men of faith who believed that miracles were real, that God spoke in signs and through visions. So right on cue, a miracle was conveniently produced in the form of the Holy Lance—the very same weapon that had pierced the side of the Savior during the Crucifixion. A poor French peasant named Peter Bartholemew, who claimed that he had seen many visions of Christ, found the Lance buried in the floor of Antioch's cathedral.

CHECKMATE

Inspired by this miraculous discovery, the crusaders marched out through the gates of Antioch early on the morning of June 28, 1098, to confront the Turks in battle. The Turkish commander, who was playing chess at the time, was so sure he could defeat the Christian forces that he let them to come out unchallenged. His lieutenants advised him to attack at once. Instead he continued his game of chess and waited.

As the crusaders continued their steady advance, a contingent crept around to the rear of the Turkish defenses and charged. The Turkish commander suddenly lost his nerve, and his army fled in disarray. Antioch was now securely in Christian hands.

THE SIEGE OF JERUSALEM

It was six months before the crusaders marched on Jerusalem. By early summer they'd arrived at the gates of the city. The besieging force—diminished by battle casualties at Antioch, exhaustion, starvation, and disease—consisted of 1,200 knights and 12,000 foot soldiers, perhaps half the strength of the original army.

THEY THOUGHT OF EVERYTHING

The Muslim commander of Jerusalem was more than ready for the crusaders. He had ample supplies of food and water for a long siege and a sizeable garrison of loyal soldiers. He'd made sure that all the wells around the city had been poisoned, and the sheep and goats on the neighboring hills were rounded up and brought into the city. The commander ordered that the towers along the city walls be filled with bales of cotton and hay to strengthen them against bombardment from the crusaders' catapults (used for hurling large rocks into and over the walls). As a final touch, the city's defenders chopped down all the trees around Jerusalem, depriving the crusaders of any shade from the blazing sun.

OR SO THEY THOUGHT
On the night of July 13, 1099, the crusaders launched their assault. Under cover of darkness, the siege engines—huge towers on wheels with covered bridges from which men could cross over to the tops of the walls—were moved ever closer to the city.

FULL FRONTAL ASSAULT
After a few days of vicious fighting, the crusaders managed to maneuver one of their siege engines into position. At first, only a few men succeeded in crossing over the tower's bridge and climbing to the top of the nearest wall. But soon the number increased from ones and twos to dozens. More ladders were placed against the walls, and large numbers of crusaders climbed up and steadily drove the defenders back. The attack was a complete success; Jerusalem was now in Christian hands.

CHRISTIANS: 1, EVERYBODY ELSE: DEAD
After three years of deprivation, disease, and death the Christian soldiers were ready to celebrate their great victory. They did so by plundering Jerusalem and slaughtering its Muslim inhabitants. The local Jews had all rushed to the synagogue, but the crusaders were determined to make Jerusalem a purely Christian city. They burned down the synagogue and everyone inside perished.

TUNE IN NEXT TIME
The goal of the First Crusade—retaking Jerusalem and most of the Holy Land for Christianity—had been achieved. No future crusade would enjoy as much success. (Oh, you thought it was over? No, there's lots more blood to be spilled.) During the next two centuries the original conquests in the Holy Land, including Jerusalem, were gradually lost.

The very last Egyptian king of ancient times was Ptolemy XV, son of Cleopatra.

PAGANINI HAS LEFT THE BUILDING

*Chicks dig violinists. At least they did when
Nicolò Paganini was the hottest ticket in music.*

Nicolò Paganini was a gifted virtuoso who may be the greatest violinist in history. Fans worshipped him. But Paganini fell victim to the darker side of fame—abuse, excess, and rumors of consorting with the devil.

THE YOUNG PHENOM
In the early 1800s, Nicolò Paganini was a superstar. Born in Genoa, Italy, in 1782, he was a violin prodigy who began touring at age 15. Soon he was famous for his extraordinary, almost supernatural, skill. Unlike famous predecessors such as Bach or Mozart, Paganini was never a court musician living off an archduke's patronage. He played the concert circuit and survived on ticket sales. In 1828, he began an epic six-year tour of Europe. The great capitals fell under his spell: Vienna, Berlin, London, and Paris.

A PASSION FOR PAGANINI
Despite outrageous ticket prices, Paganini's concerts could be life-altering experiences for fans. Ladies swooned, men cried, and the reviews were fabulous. The Paris papers exhorted their readers to "sell or pawn all their possessions to hear Paganini." And one reviewer wrote, "Woe to him who lets (Paganini) depart unheard."

As his legend grew, stories spread that Paganini had acquired his talent by selling his soul to the devil. His appearance played perfectly into this tale. Paganini suffered with poor health most of his life, making him deathly pale and gaunt. But his tortured appearance only made him a more devilishly romantic figure.

PAGANINI PRESLEY?
He sometimes wore a black cloak that swirled around him like wings, while his long, black hair flew wildly. When performing, his lean legs twirled him across the stage and his flexible hands fingered the frets in a way that no other violinist could duplicate.

For four days, Nazi Rudolf Hess became the last prisoner in the Tower of London.

REACHING THE BREAKING POINT

Paganini would sometimes play a game of breaking three strings on his violin, one after another, and finish a flawless concert using only one. Such theatrical foolishness enraged establishment critics who dismissed him as all style and no substance, a musician of mediocre talent and garish tricks.

Critics also derided Paganini as "an acrobat, a mountebank, a woman-hunter…and disgustingly rich." Rumors described a legion of women, young and old, common and aristocratic, that dallied with the maestro. Vast amounts of money rolled in from concerts.

THE DARK SIDE OF FAME

Yet Paganini often ran short of cash. He was a heavy gambler, and not a very good one. He also had to support a growing crew of hangers-on, including an agent and a biographer. Pressures took a toll on the violinist as the tour progressed. His health suffered, and he sometimes canceled concerts due to illness. Cancellations also sprang from the fact that sensitive Paganini was easily insulted—even by a minor slight. After he canceled a concert in Ireland, an angry mob gathered outside his hotel, forcing him to play as scheduled.

THE DARKER SIDE OF FAME

Turning away from touring, Paganini was drawn into a grandiose scheme to build a fabulous Casino Paganini in Paris. He sank a lot of money into the venture, but the Parisian casino was a colossal failure. After years in court suing his former partners, he never recovered one franc. He envisioned launching a stunning come-back tour in America, but before it could begin, his health failed catastrophically.

In 1840 in Nice on his deathbed, Paganini refused the last rites, believing he had longer to live. He guessed wrong. The archbishop issued an edict refusing him Christian burial, and even went so far as to notify the authorities in Paganini's hometown of Genoa. His son sued, but while waiting for the court's decision, the embalmed body was on display under glass. Thousands upon thousands are reported to have flocked to get a last glimpse of this first rock-'n'-roll style superstar. His body was not laid in hallowed ground until 1845.

Weighing 332 pounds, U.S. President William Howard Taft once trapped himself in a bathtub.

A TASTE FOR THE UNUSUAL

The crimes of Jeffrey Dahmer are well known, but there are other criminals with odd tastes that you may not have heard about.

BEANE'S CANNIBAL FAMILY
Some swear the tale of this Scottish cannibal clan is true. Others call it the ultimate urban legend, but the tales about Sawney Beane and his family refuse to die. According to the legend, Sawney Beane raised three inbred generations on the coast of Gallows in Scotland in the 15th century. He sustained his huge family by attacking, robbing, killing and eating travelers who passed by the family cave. At first Beane took only the odd traveler. But as the decades passed and his clan grew, the death toll began to rise.

When local villagers discovered odd, preserved bits of bodies washing up on the shore near the cave, they hunted for the murderer. Beane and his family were discovered, and publicly burned for their crimes on the order of King James of Scotland. The story may be hard to believe, but Scottish and British kids know all about it. Their mums used tales of the Beanes to scare their kids into being good.

LEWIS KESEBERG: DONNER PARTY DESPERADO
In the winter of 1846, when the Donner Party was trapped and starving in the Sierra Nevadas they turned, famously, to cannibalism. Most of those who survived were forgiven. Society understood the terrible desperation of starvation. But nobody ever forgave Lewis Keseberg. Keseberg was one of the few Donner party survivors who managed to reach a set of lake cabins along with a woman named Tamsen Donner. Nobody knows exactly what happened next, but Keseberg is suspected of murder. Rescuers found him at the cabin, boiling parts of Ms. Donner's body in a pot on the fire. He calmly admitted eating her and that he found her delicious, the best flesh he'd ever tasted.

Keseberg wasn't convicted for his suspected crime, but his life went badly anyway. (Surprise, surprise.) He briefly opened a

Sacramento restaurant. (What a career choice!) But the restaurant was soon burned to the ground. Keseberg lived out his life in shame and poverty—despised.

ALFRED PACKER, THE COLORADO CANNIBAL

Officials at the Los Piños Indian Agency on Cochetopa Creek, Colorado, in April of 1874 couldn't believe their eyes when they saw Alfred Packer stumbling sick and half-frozen into their offices. And the survival story he told them was pretty wild. Seems Packer and a party of six left on an ill-advised trip in the fall of 1873 and got trapped by winter storms. According to Packer, while he was away, scouting out a route home, a fellow traveler killed everybody. Poor Packer returned to find the killer roasting human meat, and was forced to kill the cannibal in self-defense. Trapped in the wilderness, Packer then had to live on the bodies of his murdered companions.

When officials went to the campsite and found the murdered, hacked-up, half-eaten bodies of Packer's former companions, they didn't believe his story. Packer was jailed briefly. He escaped, was recaptured and imprisoned for 17 years. After his parole, Packer lived the remainder of his life in Colorado in relative peace. He died—get this—a devout vegetarian.

* * *

PUTTIN' ON THE RITZ

So while we're talking people-*as*-food, let's talk food *named for* people. Escoffier, world-famous chef at the Ritz-Carlton in London, created several treats inspired by important ladies of the day: Peach Melba for opera diva Nellie Melba; strawberries Sarah Bernhardt for the famous actress; and Cherries Jubilee to celebrate Queen Victoria's 50th year on the throne. But then, he had a little help from an absolutely *killer* kitchen staff.

On the night Germany invaded Belgium in 1914, Escoffier's had a young Vietnamese assistant on staff named Ho Chi Minh. Escoffier saw something exceptional in his hardworking kitchen helper and later promoted him to pastry chef. However, Ho Chi Minh was more interested in politics than pastry. In the end, he had a whole city named after him. Escoffier has only a sauce—a delicious sauce, but just a sauce—as his namesake.

Between the two rebellions he led against Canada, Louis Riel was a schoolteacher in Montana.

DOUBLE-CROSSED BY A DEAD MAN

*The British soldier who was crucial to the
Allies' capture of Sicily didn't know a thing
about it—he had already been dead for days.*

WHERE TO NEXT?
After the Allies' successful campaign in North Africa during World War II, British Intelligence planned and executed an elaborate deception to fool the Germans about where their next objective would be. Winston Churchill put it bluntly: "Everyone but a bloody fool would know it's Sicily." The island was the perfect base for an invasion of Italy, but its rough terrain favored a defender. The Allies needed a plan that would prevent Hitler from reinforcing Sicily's defenses.

EWEN AND ARCHIBALD'S BOGUS ADVENTURE
To direct attention away from Sicily, the Germans had to be fooled into believing the Allies were about to invade elsewhere. First a bogus plan was prepared that involved an attack in the Balkans and the invasion of Sardinia. A method had to be found to allow German Intelligence to discover the plan, and that problem was solved by two junior British officers named—how British can you get?—Lt. Commander Ewen Montagu and Squadron Leader Sir Archibald Cholmondley. Both were members of the XX (Double Cross) Committee, the counterespionage arm of British Intelligence.

THEY DON'T CALL IT INTELLIGENCE FOR NOTHING
The idea was to disguise a dead body as a staff officer, to plant high-level documents with falsified invasion plans, and then allow it to fall into German hands. They considered dropping the body from a plane over German occupied territory with a partially opened parachute, but abandoned that idea since an autopsy would show that he had died long before. The Double-Cross team decided to make the corpse a victim of a plane crash at sea because he would be expected to have been floating in the sea for

several days. Montagu and Cholmondley selected a man who had died of pneumonia because he would have fluid in his lungs, and if an autopsy were performed, it would appear that he had died of drowning. They eventually found a body of a man in his early thirties who had been physically fit until his death, and received permission from his family to use the body with the understanding that his identity would never be revealed.

MEET MAJOR MARTIN
They created an identity for him: Captain (and acting Major) William Martin of the Royal Marines, born in Cardiff, Wales, in 1907, and assigned to Headquarters, Combined Operations. The corpse was outfitted in an officer's uniform with service ribbons and appropriate military identification. To make his identity more credible, Major Martin was given a photo of his fiancée along with a couple of love letters and even a receipt for an engagement ring. He was also supplied with theater ticket stubs, pound notes, loose change, keys, a statement from his club for lodging, some bills, and letters from his father. They chained a locked briefcase to him with official papers that subtly revealed the fake invasion plans and showed that Major Martin was flying from England to Allied headquarters in North Africa.

BURIAL AT SEA
On April 30, 1943, the submarine H.M.S. Seraph surfaced about a mile off the Spanish coast. Spain was selected for the drop because of the German military intelligence network in place there, and Allied intelligence's confidence in the Spanish government's willingness to cooperate with the Germans. Major Martin, secretly encased in dry ice, was brought up on deck. The captain ordered everyone below deck except for his officers. They outfitted Major Martin with a life jacket, read a prayer, then dumped his body overboard. A few hours later the dearly departed was spotted and recovered by a Spanish fisherman.

BURIAL ON LAND
After some delay and diplomatic shuffling, the Spanish government eventually returned Martin's briefcase, apparently unopened. Once the documents returned to London, however, microscopic examination of the paper revealed the briefcase had indeed been

---

In the 1980s, Prime Minister David Lange made New Zealand a nuclear-free zone.

opened, and the papers presumably photocopied. Major Martin was buried a few days later in Huelva, Spain with full military honors, surrounded by floral tributes from his heartbroken fiancée and family. Back in London, the June 4 edition of *The Times* noted Martin's death in the casualty lists.

JOHN DOE REDEEMS HIMSELF

The German intelligence operatives were completely fooled. "The authenticity of the captured documents is beyond doubt," they reported. The Allied invasion of Sicily began on July 9, 1943. Montgomery's British Eighth Army and Patton's U.S. Seventh Army attacked the southern tip of Sicily and met limited resistance. Most of the Germans' defenses were concentrated along the north coast. By the time the German High Command realized they had been deceived, the battle for Sicily was nearly over.

After the war the deception was revealed and there has been a great deal of speculation as to Major Martin's identity. It was never disclosed, but according to Montagu: "He was a bit of a ne'er-do-well, and...the only worthwhile thing that he ever did he did after his death."

*　　*　　*

TEN FACTS TO KNOW ABOUT WWII

1. WWII started with the German invasion of Poland on September 1, 1939.
2. Adolf Hitler's aborted plan to invade Great Britain was called Operation Sealion.
3. The Battle of the Coral Sea was the first naval battle fought only between aircraft carriers.
4. Okinawa was the last battle of WWII.
5. Outnumbered Canadian troops surrendered Hong Kong to the Japanese on Christmas Day 1941.
6. The heaviest tank of WWII was the German Tiger II.
7. Russian forces fought and won the Battle for Berlin, bringing an end to the war in Europe.
8. On D-Day, the Canadians came ashore on Juno Beach.
9. The Japanese built the two biggest battleships of WWII: *Yamato* and *Musashi*.
10. The last *Führer* was Admiral Karl Donitz.

Technically, the first American president was John Hanson of Maryland.

DIRTY SECRETS IN THE HISTORY OF HYGIENE (Part II): RUB-A-DUB-DUB

"Give us this day our daily bath" could be a motto of modern life.
But bathing habits have changed drastically
over the course of human history.

The ancient Roman baths are legendary for good reason. They were huge marble and tile structures that weren't just for bathing: The more luxurious ones had gardens, libraries, and even lecture halls. The grandest baths were named for the emperors who built them: the baths of Caracalla, for instance, covered nearly 28 acres.

A SOCIAL OCCASION
The Roman baths were gathering places for exchanging news, playing board games, or exercising with dumbbells and medicine balls. People would spend whole days there, like at Disneyland. Entry fees were low and children were admitted free (so they weren't *that* much like Disneyland).

RUNNING HOT AND COLD
Bathers had the choice of several different types of baths. The frigidarium (brrrrr!) was the cold water bath. The tepidarium contained—as you might guess—warm water. The caldarium was hot, hot, hot. A bather might start with the tepidarium, get very warm in the caldarium before finishing his bath off with an invigorating plunge (ah!) into the frigidarium. Because the aqueducts supplied a constant stream of water to Rome, it was no big deal to empty and refill the pools with fresh water every day.

ON GOOD BEHAVIOR
During the time of Julius Caesar (100–44 B.C.) mixed bathing was prohibited. Later the rules were relaxed and the sexes bathed together. To keep order, there were rules. Rule number one was "Don't stare." The second rule was to behave as though fully dressed. And some people may have actually managed to do that.

Winston Churchill was once a war correspondent in Cuba, India, and Sudan.

But as Rome declined, the baths became places for licentiousness and orgies. Maybe this was why the early Christians thought of bathing as sinful. In fact, after the decline and fall of the Roman Empire in the fifth century, bathing became rare.

THE FAMOUS TURKISH BATHS

Meanwhile, in the East, they had a different attitude. Islam embraced bathing as a purifying ritual. The bath (*hamam*) was often adjacent to the mosque where Mohammedans worshipped. Mohammed himself recommended a hot bath both for the joys of personal cleanliness but also as a fertility aid. But not because of shared bathing; that was forbidden in Turkey, both then and now.

The Ottomans built gorgeous baths with domed ceilings and marble fountains. Private homes didn't have baths, so everyone, rich and poor, just like in Rome, came to the public baths. And just like Rome, the Turkish baths had a cold room, a hot room, steam baths, and resting rooms with refreshments. Wealthy matrons were known to spend the whole day there, gossiping and checking out prospective brides for their marriageable sons.

SOME STINKY EUROPEANS

So while the rest of the world—the Arabs, Chinese, and Japanese—were taking regular baths as both a cultural and spiritual habit, medieval Europeans were opting for pungency. St. Francis of Assisi proclaimed an unwashed body to be a pious body. St. Agnes, a follower of St. Francis died at age 13 without ever having washed. Queen Isabella of Castile (of Isabella and Ferdinand fame and as devout a Christian as they come) boasted that she had taken just two baths in her life—at her birth and before her wedding.

Queen Isabella may have covered her stench with perfumes, but other Europeans preferred not to be so piously filthy. Medieval paintings show wealthy families and their friends bathing together in large tubs while musicians played for them.

A HOT TIME IN THE OLDE TOWNE

For a lot of 12th and 13th century Europeans, bathhouses were the place to be. These bathhouses had large hot water pools and in most cities money for bathing was included as part of a worker's salary. The baths were run by a guild, just like every other occupation. Visits to the bathhouse became a regular family practice.

Of Canada's 36 Fathers of Confederation, two of them were named John Hamilton Gray.

Boys would run through the streets announcing when the water was hot.

TOO HOT TO HANDLE

The sexes bathed together. Add a lot of drinking and feasting (at the same time) and you've got about as much fun as a Middle Ager could have. Bathing was the most popular amusement of the time. But eventually, things got a little too hot, so mixed bathing was all of a sudden prohibited.

By the 14th century, "bathhouse" was pretty much synonymous with "brothel." Bathhouse keepers checked customers for signs of syphilis and refused entry to anyone who was obviously suffering from the disease. So the bathhouses stayed, but they weren't as much fun as they used to be.

EARLY AMERICAN BATHING BEAUTIES

Four hundred years and a lot of scientific progress later, doctors started encouraging people to bathe. John Wesley, founder of the Methodist church, sermonized that "cleanliness is next to godliness." But old habits died hard, especially in the New World.

In early America, a lot of people thought bathing was a health hazard. In 1837, Boston forbade bathing except on specific medical advice. In part, bathing was rare because preparing the bath was so difficult. Early Americans had to haul a tub into the kitchen, draw water from the well or spring and heat it over a wood fire. The whole family might take turns using the same water until it became questionable whether the last to bathe was getting cleaner or dirtier.

WASHING IN WASHINGTON

During the presidency of John Quincy Adams, the presidential bathtub was the Potomac River. President Adams took his bath in the river just before sunrise. On one morning, someone absconded with the presidential clothes and Mr. Adams had to shout until he attracted the attention of a young boy who ran to the White House for more.

THE DUSTY TRAIL

Bathtubs were rare in the Wild West. In 1871, Tucson, Arizona boasted 3,000 people, a newspaper, a brewery, two doctors, several saloons—but just one bathtub. Pee-ew!

One of Canada's "founding fathers" was an American: William P. Howland of Paulings, NY.

WASTE OF A GOOD BASKETBALL TEAM

*How the king of Prussia overcame short-man syndrome
with the help of his royal guards.*

Frederick William I must have been quite a sight. An all-round psychopath known as the "drill master of Europe," the king of Prussia was very short and weighed about 280 pounds, with a 102-inch waist—the original butterball. In case his bulging eyes, purplish complexion, and homicidal temper didn't make enough of an impression, he smeared his face with bacon grease (he thought it would make him look more intimidating—maybe—but we bet it made him look more like a butterball). To add to his image he carried a rattan stick around and was in the habit of beating anyone who crossed him with it—or anyone within reach, whichever came first. An all-around delightful guy.

A TALL STORY, BUT TRUE

Frederick, who ruled from 1713–1740, made up for his lowly stature through his hobby, the giant Potsdam guards. Every man in this special honor guard—headquartered near the royal residence at Potsdam, just outside Berlin—had to be at least 6 feet tall and most were over 7; some reached almost 9 feet.

Given Frederick's personality, there weren't a lot of volunteers for the guards. So Prussia sent agents all over the world to kidnap big guys. They brought back doctors, lawyers, diplomats, monks, and soldiers from other nations' armies. A tall priest was kidnapped in Italy while he was serving mass. One of Frederick's most expensive prizes was an Irish giant, spirited away from England at a cost of £1,000 (worth more than $100,000 today).

LIFE AND DEATH AS A POTSDAM GUARD

Frederick's oversized acquisitions tended to be uncooperative. Life in the guard was squalid, and about 250 guards escaped every year. Those who were caught had their noses and ears sliced off. Several times the guards tried to burn down Potsdam, but it wasn't until the king died that the troop was mercifully disbanded.

In 1926, Joseph Goebbels demanded that Hitler be expelled from the Nazi Party.

THE MONSTER THAT PHILO MADE

His invention changed the world—but was it for the better?
Philo T. Farnsworth certainly didn't think so.

The invention that probably did the most to change modern society is something most people have never heard of, invented by someone most people have never heard of either. The invention is the dissection tube—the thing that makes your television work—and its inventor was Philo T. Farnsworth.

A BOY AND HIS LIGHT SWITCH

Philo was the son of a Mormon farmer. When his family moved from Utah to Idaho in 1919, 11-year-old Philo was surprised and delighted to find that his new home was wired for electricity (he was pretty thrilled about the flush toilet, too). From the moment he flicked his first light switch, Philo became obsessed with all things electrical.

MISTER FIX-IT

By age 13, he was a self-taught electrical engineer. And the handiest guy on the farm. When a generator blew, Philo came to the rescue. He built motors effortlessly from spare parts. And all the while he devoured newspaper and magazine articles about new ideas in electronics—and worked on how he could improve those ideas himself.

PUTTING THINGS IN FOCUS

It was an article about Scottish inventor John Logie Baird and his work with cathode rays that made Philo zero in on what would turn out to be his life's work. Baird had been trying to reproduce real images on a screen but so far had produced nothing but blurs of light. From the moment young Philo read about Baird's work, he was obsessed with the transmission of images onto a screen. He thought of nothing else.

That's why, while plowing a field one day, it was only natural that the thought came to him that electrons could scan an image

---

Hitler and Mussolini installed a fascist government in Spain that survived them both.

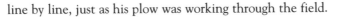

line by line, just as his plow was working through the field.

HOW YOU GONNA KEEP HIM DOWN ON THE FARM?

It took Philo another seven years to translate his idea into a working televison system. On September 7, 1927, he successfully sent a single line from his camera—which he called an image dissector—to friends who were looking at a glass receiver tube. They had just witnessed the first-ever transmission of an electronic television picture.

BATTLING THE BIG BOYS

Philo's euphoria over his invention was short-lived. Within a few years, he was embroiled in a legal battle with the Radio Corporation of America (RCA). The company didn't want to pay Farnsworth royalties to produce television sets, so they instigated a legal battle over who was the rightful inventor of television: a Russian immigrant they'd hired—one Vladmir Zworykin—or our own Philo T. Farnsworth. After much analysis and testimony the U.S. Patent Office awarded primacy of invention to Farnsworth.

A TELEVISION APPEARANCE

In 1957 Philo appeared on televison himself, as a mystery guest on the quiz show, *What's My Line?* The mystery guest was someone with a unique claim to fame. It was up to a panel of four people to figure out exactly what that was. When asked if he was the inventor of something that could be painful when used, Philo said, "Yes. Sometimes it's most painful."

Philo thought he'd created a monster—a way for people to waste a large portion of their lives. He wouldn't allow his own children to watch television because he thought it would ruin their "intellectual diet."

* * *

SPEAKING OF HEALTHY HABITS

Did you know Henry Ford was a vegetarian? Meat was expensive at the time; his decision to eat vegetables characterized his moderate lifestyle. Well not too moderate: as his automobile empire grew, he and his wife Clara moved to a 1,300-acre property. Of course, they had it landscaped to include a huge vegetable garden.

WHEREWORDS: A QUIZ (Knight Life)

The knightly news. Where did all these words that we associate with those guys in shining armor come from? Choose the best answer, then check it against our answers on the next page.

1. CHIVALRY
a. Corruption of "shebalry," the protocol of the court of the Queen of Sheba.
b. Hebrew "shiva" for "seven," the number of knights per order.
c. From the Latin "caballus" via French "cheval," meaning "horse."

2. DRAGON
a. In honor of Ottoman leader Torghud Draghon, who fought a legendary fire-breather.
b. The serpent, Drakon, described in Homer's *Iliad*.
c. The dragon's mythical breeding grounds in Dragholn, Denmark.

3. TOAST
a. Old English "tost," the salute a knight would give before battle.
b. It was named for a piece of burnt bread that the Romans dropped into their wine glasses.
c. 12th century Spanish philosopher Mauro Tosti, known for his long speeches.

4. CAMELOT
a. For pagan King Camaalis, whose castle was by the River Cam.
b. From "complot," meaning the "conspiracy" against Lancelot.
c. King Arthur named it himself, for the "camellias" growing there.

5. NEMESIS
a. From Greek mythology, she was the "goddess of retribution."
b. Latin contraction of "ne" + "amecus," meaning literally "not friends."
c. After "Nemausus," the river that fed the great aqueducts of Rome.

6. GRAIL
a. The medieval word, "grayle," meaning "treasure."
b. "Graal," a "cup," supposedly the cup that Jesus drank from at the Last Supper.
c. The Greek word for the Golden Fleece that Jason quested after.

7. GARGANTUAN
a. The gargantey, a small duck that eats the equivalent of its own weight every day.
b. The 8th century Mongol ruler "Garga," who, at 7' tall, weighed in at 700 pounds.
c. From Gargantua, a giant-hero in a work by Rabelais.

8. JOUST
a. After Sir Joustier, who founded the Knights Templar in 1118.
b. The Latin word "juxta" meaning "nearby."
c. It was the name of Galahad's magic lance.

Voltaire dismissed France's Canadian colonies as "a few acres of snow."

1-c. "Chivalry" has links to the words "cavalry" and "cavalier," not to mention the Spanish "caballero," or horseman. The word originally referred to a group of horsemen at arms and eventually came to mean the system of knighthood.

2-b. Agamemnon carried a shield with a picture of a dragon as he led the Greeks in the Trojan War.

3-b. The Greeks were the first to toast each other as a pledge of friendship, but the Romans named it from their custom of dropping a piece of burnt bread into a glass to counteract the wine's acidity.

4-a. Camelot's exact location (if you believe there really was a Camelot) is thought to be a place called Camalat, in Somerset, England, named for the pagan King Camaalis.

5-a. Nemesis was the Greek goddess of justice or revenge., so a "nemesis" was someone who avenged or punished. Shakespeare used it in Henry VI. "Your kingdom's terror and black Nemesis? O, were mine eyeballs into bullets turned..." (Talk about revenge, wishing your eyes were bullets.)

6-b. In medieval legend, the Holy Grail was a cup or chalice, believed by the Christians to be the chalice of the Last Supper. Its magical powers provided food and healing, but it could only be found by the purest knight. In Arthurian legend, that's Galahad.

7-c. French writer François Rabelais used the folk tale of Gargantua to write his 16th century satirical masterpiece, Gargantua. The word "gargantuan" first appears there, describing the giant who as an infant drank the milk of 17,913 cows, combed his hair with a 900-foot-long comb, and once ate six pilgrims in a salad.

8-b. Early medieval tournaments consisted of melees, or mock battles, fought by knights on horseback. This evolved into the joust, in which two horsemen charged until they were "nearby" each other and, with their lances leveled, tried to unseat their opponent.

*　　*　　*

The knight's bones are dust, and his good sword rust;
His soul is with the saints, I trust.
Coleridge (1772–1834)

THE REAL JEKYLL & HYDE

*The 19th century's most remarkable literary creation was based
on 18th century Scotland's most unlikely criminal…*

In 1886 Scotland's most famous man of words, Robert Louis
Stevenson, introduced to a fascinated world his short story *The
Strange Case of Dr Jekyll and Mr Hyde*. This tale of a respected
physician who transforms into a deranged and dangerous criminal
was the first fictional appearance of the now well-worn split
personality crime theme. Stevenson got the inspiration for his
investigation into man's darker side from a similarly respected
fellow Scotsman.

THE TWO SIDES OF DEACON BRODIE
William Brodie was born into an upright 18th century Edinburgh
family and grew up as the model of respectability. He followed his
father into the cabinetmaking trade, and by his mid twenties had
established himself as a fixture among the upper crust of Scottish
society. He was also the deacon of the local chapter of the Mason's
Guild as well as an Edinburgh city councilor.

Brodie loved to gamble. And he had ongoing relationships
with two prostitutes. Inevitably the gambling debts started to pile
up and, when his two mistresses began to produce little Brodies,
the good deacon found himself in desperate financial straits.

CASING THE JOINT
In the course of his legitimate daytime activities, Brodie visited
his rich clients in their homes. He started making wax impressions
of the house keys he came across, and checking out the houses for
items of interest. He'd return in the evening to gather up the
goods. His life of crime served two purposes: it was a solution to
his money worries, and he liked the thrill of it all (as most
gamblers do).

Brodie teamed up with a locksmith by the name of George
Smith and together they stole everything in Edinburgh that wasn't
nailed down. In contrast to his elegant and cultured cohort, Smith
was a small time crook with few redeeming qualities. When two
more local criminals with similar dispositions were recruited into
the gang, the undoing of William Brodie began.

Norman Schwarzkopf's dad was a leading investigator in the Lindbergh baby kidnapping.

THE HEIST

Brodie detested incompetence, but his most daring job—an attack on the headquarters of the Scottish Customs and Excise—was plagued with inefficiency. Brodie, dressed in black and acting as if he were playing a role in a pageant, stood guard outside with Ainslee as the other two made their way inside. Ainslee got cold feet and the usually cool Brodie canceled the job.

A large reward was offered for the capture of those who had dared to even try to steal from the Scottish taxpayer. John Brown decided to turn king's evidence. He told the disbelieving authorities that the man behind the raid was none other than the highly respected Deacon William Brodie. The police were dispatched to Brodie's apartment—but only so they could officially discount the preposterous suggestion that he could be involved.

THE EVIDENCE

But what they found there substantiated Brown's accusation. Skeleton keys, a burglar's black suit, and several pistols were catalogued and taken to headquarters for further examination. Brodie himself was nowhere to be found. He'd fled to Holland, intending to set sail for America. But as he boarded the ship (in top hat and tails), he was approached by two Dutch police officers. They escorted him back to dry land and extradited him back to Edinburgh to face his accusers.

Dressed in a three-piece suit and top hat, Brodie gazed fixedly at his accusers. He answered questions with a haughty carelessness. He seemed completely untroubled by the fate that awaited him—death by hanging.

THE EXECUTION

As he stood on the gallows that he himself—in his role as city councilor—had designed, Brodie offered up his own prayer (which is too hypocritical for us to repeat). Then he bravely beckoned for the hangman to perform his task.

A trickster to the end, Brodie had one last card to play. The night before he'd rigged his clothes with wire from neck to ankle to take the jerk of the rope; the silver tube he'd stuck down his throat was supposed to prevent his neck from breaking. However the trick failed and Deacon Brodie breathed his last that October 1, 1788.

When Britain adopted the Gregorian calendar, Oct. 4, 1582 was followed by Oct. 15.

MORE BOUNCE TO THE OUNCE

*It's hard to think of a substance more useful than rubber.
It's on the bottom of your shoes, in the tires of your car, and
in the balloons at your birthday party.*

There's a story that Christopher Columbus was the first
European to discover rubber. When he was in Haiti, he
noticed some boys playing with a rubber ball. The local
people took Columbus into the forest and showed him how, when
they cut the bark of certain trees, a milky white liquid (latex, to
you) bled from the cut. When the latex dried, it was solid and
spongy. Besides the balls the kids were playing with, the Indians
also made waterproof shoes and bottles from the strange substance.
But if he brought some of it back with him to Spain, he never
mentioned it.

RUBBER BOUNCES ALONG... BUT SLOWLY
It was mentioned here and there by some Portuguese and Spanish
writers in the 16th century. In the 1730s two scientists, Charles de
la Condamine and François Fresneau, made an official report to
the French Academy of Sciences on rubber's characteristics and
properties. Now the Europeans were curious enough to mount
expeditions to the Amazon to try to find some more.

INNOVATIONS
In 1770 an English chemist named Joseph Priestly discovered that
the substance rubbed out marks from a pencil—what the English
came to call a "rubber," and what Americans call an "eraser."

Then, in 1832, Scottish chemist Charles MacKintosh started
manufacturing his soon-to-be-famous "mackintosh" raincoats. But
rubber remained nothing more than a curiosity because of the way
it reacted to the elements: cold made it extremely brittle, and heat
made it sticky.

A GOOD YEAR FOR GOODYEAR
All this changed in 1839 when American inventor Charles
Goodyear accidentally spilled a mixture of rubber and sulfur onto

The Roanoke settlers who vanished may have been massacred by Pocahontas's father.

a hot stove. Now the rubber stayed firm, whether it was hot or cold. This process of mixing and heating rubber was called vulcanization, after Vulcan, the Roman god of fire.

THEY'VE GOT AN AWFUL LOT OF RUBBER IN BRAZIL
The miracle of vulcanization made rubber a hot commodity. At first, almost all the latex was harvested in the Amazon Basin. Brazilian merchants were making a fortune, while the rest of the entrepreneurial world watched them hungrily.

IT WASN'T REALLY STEALING
That is until, in 1876, an English botanist, Sir Henry Wickham, brought some back to England. He told Brazilian customs officials that the 70,000 rubber tree seeds he was bringing to England were botanical specimens for the royal plant collection. And they were dumb enough to believe him.

TRICKY, TRICKY
But once the rubber tree seedlings were old enough, the English government sent them to Ceylon and Malaya, where they were plunked into the ground. By the turn of the 19th century, large rubber plantations in the Pacific Rim supplied most of the world's natural rubber.

NOT THE KIND YOU WEAR ON YOUR FEET
Rubber changed the way people lived, not the least of which was in the area of contraception. In the 1860s, a medical entrepreneur named Edward Bliss Foote marketed a one-size-fits-all "womb veil." At about the same time, the first rubber "caps" for men were manufactured. These innovations were soon followed by full-size condoms, known as "rubbers."

IS IT REALLY RUBBER?
During World War I, when the Allied blockade prevented Germany from getting the rubber it needed for tires, German scientists set to work on an artificial substitute. By the time World War II broke out, rubber was even more strategically important, but good synthetics were still prohibitively expensive. When Japan seized control of most of the rubber-producing islands of the Pacific Rim, effectively cutting off the U.S. supply, the search for synthetics was fast and furious. Within a few years, good synthetics made from petroleum were in wide use. Today, it's hard to find the real thing: Almost all "rubber" in manufacturing is synthetic.

IMMANUEL KANT TRIES COMEDY

A great philosopher tries to make you laugh.

When philosopher Immanuel Kant claimed that human beings could never grasp the ultimate nature of reality, he changed the face of philosophy forever. That's what they say, anyway.

THE YUCKS

When he wasn't pondering the nature of reality, he spent a lot of time on the subject of laughter. In his *Critique of Judgment*, he said, "Laughter is an affection arising from strained expectation being suddenly reduced to nothing."

But then, he tried to prove it by telling some jokes:

- An Indian at an Englishman's table in Surat saw a bottle of ale opened, and all the beer turned into froth and flowed out. The repeated exclamations of the Indian showed his great astonishment. "Well, what is so wonderful in that?" asked the Englishman. "Oh, I'm not surprised myself," said the Indian, "at its getting out, but at how you ever managed to get it all in." ("At this we laugh," added Kant, "and it gives us hearty pleasure.")

- Did you hear the one about the sailing merchant who had to throw all his goods overboard in a storm? He "grieved to such an extent that in the selfsame night his *wig* turned gray."

- A wealthy man died, and his heir had difficulties conducting his funeral. Complained the heir, "The more money I give my mourners to look sad, the more pleased they look."

Hang on to that day job, Immanuel.

During World War II, German U-boats sank 23 vessels in Canada's St. Lawrence River.

IT'S ALL GREEK TO ME

Ten Greek Philosophers Worth Knowing

So, there you are at the Philosophy Department mixer at your local university, trying to make small talk. Don't panic: you can impress that bookishly cute graduate student with the knowledge of ancient Greek philosophers you'll learn about right this very second. It's quick, it's easy, and no one needs to know just where you got the info. Ready? Here we go.

Thales: Regarded by most philosophy types as the "First Philosopher," this guy (c.625–547 B.C.) did it all. He was a statesman, an astronomer, and a mathematician—he predicted an eclipse and he suggested that sailors use the constellation Ursa Minor to sail by (a good idea, since the North Star is in it). But his big idea was that everything was ultimately made out of water. The details are wrong, but the idea that there's something that everything has in common is an important one—the first step toward a universal "theory of everything" that motivates scientists even today.

Anaximander: Thales thought that water was the universal element; Anaximander (610–c.545 B.C.) said it was a substance called "apeiron," a sort of weird nothingness out of which certain qualities (hot or cold, wet or dry) could be extracted. This is a freaky, abstract kind of thought, and that's precisely why it's interesting—it's an attempt to describe nature using theory, rather than something that can be explicitly touched and seen. Anaximander also suggested humans evolved from fishlike creatures, beating that smug twerp Darwin by a couple of millennia.

Pythagoras: Yes, that Pythagoras, the one whose theory about triangles gave you such a headache in geometry class. So it should come as no surprise that Pythagoras (580–500 B.C.) declared that everything in the universe was fundamentally mathematical, right down to our souls, which he believed were exceptionally purified numbers. Imagine going to heaven and finding out you're a "3." No, it doesn't make sense to us either, but that doesn't mean it wasn't influential; if you've got a "lucky number," you're playing with a faint echo of Pythagoras' teachings.

The United States paid Russia just two cents an acre for Alaska.

Heraclitus: Heraclitus (540–480 B.C.) gets credit for being the first Western philosopher to have the idea that opposites define each other—what is "hot" without "cold"? "Happiness" without "sadness"? Yes, you figured this one out in high school, while you were (ahem) "listening" to Pink Floyd's "Dark Side of the Moon." But Heraclitus did it first, and he believed that interaction of opposites helped give the universe structure and balance. He wasn't too far off—just ask Newton, who noted that "For every action, there is an equal and opposite reaction." That's not just an observation, it's a law of motion. *Duuuude.*

Empedocles: This guy claimed he was a god, and legend has it he jumped into a volcano to prove it, at which point, of course, he died a painful, flaming, screaming death. The legend isn't true, but the guy's dead now in any event, so there goes that whole god thing. Anyway, Empedocles (490–430 B.C.) is the fellow who gave us the four "classical elements"—earth, air, fire, and water—from which everything was supposed to be made, in varying amounts. This was incorrect, but people kept believing it, more or less, for the next couple thousand years. Empedocles is also considered the father of rhetoric and of medicine.

Democritus: Democritus (460–c.370 B.C.) was, along with his mentor Leucippus, an "atomist"—a proponent of the idea that everything we can see is made of countless little bits of matter we can't see, and that these little bits were ultimately indivisible. As it turns out, Democritus was pretty much exactly right on all counts (it's not a coincidence we call the smallest bits of organized matter "atoms"), although it would take another two millennia until chemist-philosopher John Dalton made any headway into explaining the details. Blame it on the Dark Ages.

Protagoras: If you've ever met someone who likes to argue for the sake of arguing, you've met a spiritual descendant of Protagoras (c.490–421 B.C.), who's gone down in history as the first "Sophist"—a breed of philosopher that argued there was no objective truth, and that everything had to be viewed through its relationship with man ("Man is the measure of all things," is his famous quote). This sort of flagrant moral relativism (that's what it was called) didn't make Protagoras very popular; he was booted

---

The Union Ironclad *Monitor* was the first ship to have a flush toilet.

out of Athens for his beliefs (or lack thereof). However, that's not the worst thing Athenians ever did to a philosopher.

Socrates: Here's the worst thing Athenians ever did to a philosopher—made him suck down a cup of poison. They did it to Socrates (469–399 B.C.), arguing he was corrupter of the youth of Athens because, you know, he asked them questions. And then they started thinking. Can't have that. Actually, Socrates' big innovation was that fact he asked questions—using them in a process known as "dialectic," by which truth was to arise by critically examining the statements of those around him. It's a process still used today. All we know of Socrates comes from the writings of his contemporaries, notably...

Plato: The big cheese of Greek philosophy, Plato's big idea was the concept of "forms." These were perfect, totally realized versions of everything (horses, trees, sitcoms, bathroom reading material, etc.) against which the versions we actually see in our lives are but poor copies. Plato (c. 427–347 B.C.) communicated this idea in his famous "Parable of the Cave," in which men chained to face one direction see shadows on a cave wall and think the shadows to be true representations of the world, when in fact they're just twisted, flickering shadows (the idea being we're all chained cavemen, the real world is flickering shadows, and the "forms" are the real objects). Theoretically you can be trained to perceive the forms, but it might take more time than you've got.

Aristotle: The good news is that Aristotle (384–322 B.C.) was a dazzling thinker, writing exhaustively on subjects ranging from astronomy to logic to politics to theology, and he had a ton of really interesting ideas which continue to inform science and philosophy right to this day. The bad news is that he wasn't right about everything, but was considered such an authority that Europe (or more accurately, the Catholic Church, which borrowed heavily from Aristotle for its brand of philosophy known as Scholasticism) more or less took him at his word on things scientific for right up to the Renaissance. Eventually they got over it, mostly, but we probably lost a few centuries spinning our wheels. And this is why you don't have your own personal rocket car to the moon right now.

WHAT A WAY TO GO! IMMORTAL, BUT DEAD

Strange and unusual events surrounding the deaths of famous people.

Aeschylus: 456 B.C.
The founder of Greek tragedy died when an eagle mistook his shiny bald head for a rock and dropped a tortoise on it to crack the shell. According to legend the shell remained intact.

Attila the Hun: A.D. 453
The King of the Huns died of a bloody nose. He ate and drank heavily at his wedding feast the night before. Sometime during the night he choked to death on the blood, some say probably from overexerting himself with his new young bride.

King John: 1216
This king of England was such a glutton that he eventually died of dysentery, caused by too much fruit and cider.

Ivan the Terrible: 1584
The notorious Russian czar saw a comet and believed it to be a sign that he would die. His body became swollen, but his doctors couldn't find the cause. He died a short while later of his mysterious illness.

Tycho Brahe: 1601
The Danish astronomer was such a stickler for good table manners that it cost him his life. After a couple of hours of heavy drinking, he needed to relieve himself, but instead he sat down at the table for dinner with guests. He felt increasingly uncomfortable, but the etiquette of the day forbade leaving the table during dinner. His bladder burst, and he died 11 days later.

Jean-Baptiste Lully: 1687
The French composer was conducting his orchestra so vigorously that he stabbed himself in the toe with his baton. The injury became infected, but he would not allow his doctor to amputate the toe. After a few weeks the doctors told him they would have to amputate his entire leg in order for him to survive, but he refused that as well. He died soon after.

U.S. Major General John Sedgwick: 1864

During the American Civil War, General Sedgewick was on the front lines, trying to calm his troops. "I tell you they cannot hit an elephant at this distance," he said. Just then he was hit in the head and killed by a sharpshooter's bullet.

Chang and Eng Bunker: 1874

The famous "Siamese twins" were really Chinese. When they joined up with P.T. Barnum, they became American citizens and took the last name, "Bunker." When Chang died of bronchial trouble, Eng died of fright because he thought he would die, too.

P.T. Barnum: 1891

America's greatest showman, known for his classic line, "There's a sucker born every minute," wanted to read his obituary before he died. The *New York Evening Sun* was happy to oblige and printed it under the title "Great and Only Barnum. He wanted to read his Obituary; Here it is." The 80-year-old Barnum obliged by dying two weeks later.

John Jacob Astor: 1912

The multimillionaire had the misfortune to book passage on the maiden voyage of the *Titanic*. Chivalrous to the end, Astor gave up his place next to his wife in one of the few lifeboats and said, "Goodbye dearie, I'll see you later."

Harry Houdini: 1926

The legendary escape artist was known for his ability to take a strong punch to the stomach, but Houdini was surprised by a blow from a student who had come to see one of his lectures. His died of a burst appendix.

Isadora Duncan: 1927

Always the flamboyant dresser, the early practitioner of modern dance broke her neck when she went for a ride in a sports car and her long scarf got caught in one of the rear wheels.

Elvis Presley: 1977

The King of Rock and Roll was found dead by his girlfriend in a fetal position on the floor of his bathroom. His extensive drug use had caused a heart attack that struck while he was sitting on the toilet.

Robert E. Lee and Ulysses S. Grant served on the same side of one war... the Mexican War.

MONUMENTAL WASTE OF EFFORT: THE MAGINOT LINE

The best offense is a good defense, but a bad defense is just offensive.

To fully understand the Maginot line and its complete and utter uselessness, we need to step into the Way Back Machine and set the dial for February 21, 1916. On that day, German forces began their attack on Verdun, France along the Meuse River; the rationale for doing it (other than the general fact there was a war going on, and they had to attack something) came from German General Erich von Falkenhayn, who believed that the Verdun attack would force France to exhaust their resources defending their position. Soon they would be out of brie, and Paris would fall!

THE MONUMENTAL RUNNER-UP

This would be a correct assessment, as far as it went. Unfortunately the Germans did not consider the possibility that they might also hemorrhage men and supplies, which they did, in vast amounts. All told, about 800,000 men lost their lives in Verdun, in more or less equal measure on both sides, and at the end of it, Verdun was back in French hands. So I suppose you could call it a draw. But isn't that just like World War I: Lots of people getting killed, but a lot of nothing actually getting done.

WHAT AN I-MAGINOT-ION!

Be that as it may, that battle and others like it scarred the French psyche after World War I. Perhaps ascertaining, and correctly, that the Treaty of Versailles was going to go the way of Marie Antoinette's head, and that the Germans would once again come calling, the French tried to figure out the best way to avoid that scenario. The answer came from André Maginot, minister of war in the late 1920s and early 1930s: Let's build a wall, and keep those nasty Germans out!

In the War of 1812, the U.S. burned down Toronto and the British burned down Washington.

IT'S INVISIBLE

Well, not exactly a wall, but a line—the Maginot line, a series of interconnected fortifications that spanned the entire French border with Germany, from Sedan to Wissembourg: about 150 miles. There were 50 discrete forts on the line, all within cannon shot of each other, with blockhouses interspersed between them. Each of these forts was a marvel of defensive design, with the thickest concrete and best defensive weapons the world had to offer.

TAKE THE TOUR

Each fort held up to 1,000 personnel, and thanks to an immense labyrinth of connecting underground tunnels, men and supplies could be shuttled back and forth without exposing them to enemy fire or prying eyes.

Within the underground spaces were barracks, storehouses, and recreation areas; it was even air-conditioned. It was said that the Maginot line was more comfortable to live in than any French city you could name. At the very least, no one was peeing up against a wall when they couldn't find a bathroom.

BETTER THAN EURODISNEY?

By any critical standard, military or architectural, the Maginot line was a wonder. It was, in fact, the largest single construction event in European history. Think of it as the French version of the Panama Canal (especially since the real French version of the Panama Canal, attempted in the 1880s but laid low by poor financing and malaria, was such a bust).

CHUCK ADDS HIS TWO FRANCS

As far as anyone could see, there were two itsy-bitsy minor problems with the Maginot line. The first was purely philosophical: By committing so many men and resources to the defensive nature of the line, the French ran the risk of being lulled into a false (and smug) sense of security. They should also be preparing offensively as well. Charles de Gaulle suggested to his superiors that France should have an army that was both mechanized and mobile instead of sitting in a bunker waiting for the enemy to tromp into its sights. He was suggesting this course of action through the very beginning of 1940; he was not very popular for doing it.

THE ENDS OF THE LINE
The second itsy-bity little problem was that the Maginot line only covered the border of Germany; it stopped in the east at Switzerland and in the west at Belgium. No one would be especially worried about something happening at the Swiss end: Switzerland was and is famously neutral (its motto: "We'll take money from anyone.") and in any event, it's not real easy schlepping tanks over the Alps.

WHAT! MOI, WORRY?
But what about Belgium? Well, you see, the French had thought about that whole Belgium thing, but they weren't worried. They had already talked to the British, and everyone agreed that if the Germans, for some nutty reason, just happened to come through Belgium, the Allies would mount a ground offensive and everything would take place there (it had worked so well in World War I, after all!). And anyway, getting into France through Belgium meant going through the hilly forests of Ardennes, which were thought to be impassable for tanks and heavy weaponry and equipment. So there you have it. Nothing to worry about.

WHAT'S "SLAM DUNK" IN GERMAN?
The French were so fixated on the superiority of the Maginot line that it was literally impossible to consider that it could be defeated, and the Germans (who may have been genocidal curs, but were not stupid) used this to their advantage in May of 1940. First, the Germans kept their Army Group C facing the Maginot line as a diversion, to keep the line's 41 divisions of French troops where they were. Then the Germans launched their blitzkrieg into the Low Countries on May 10, wiping out any resistance, Allied or otherwise, in the space of days, and giving the Germans the corridor they needed to swing around the Maginot line and enter France through Ardennes. What about the impassable forests? Not so impassable after all; the tanks and heavy artillery took to the roads while the German troops trekked through the trees. Over the river and through the woods, past Maginot's line we go.

ALL OVER THE MAP
The Germans made it to French soil on May 12 and encountered little resistance; the Franco-Belgian border was the least defended frontier the French had, and what troops were there had little in

the way of artillery defenses or antiaircraft guns. By the 13th, German troops were across the Meuse; a few days later they were swarming all through France. The French finally pulled some troops out of the Maginot line, but it was too little, too late. By the time of the German offensive at Somme on June 5, the 49 French divisions that weren't walled in on the line faced 130 German infantry divisions as well as ten divisions of tanks.

THE FRENCH: TOAST

On June 9, the Germans began driving towards the Swiss frontier, utterly isolating what troops remained on the Maginot line. And the troops in the line couldn't do anything to stop it. Inasmuch as the French considered the Maginot line impregnable, all the big guns faced towards Germany. They couldn't be turned around. The Germans entered Paris on June 14, and after that, it's all just Nazi collaborators, Vichy France, and Charles De Gaulle going, "I told you so."

SURRENDER? NEVER!

The few Maginot line apologists (and there are some) note that the Maginot line worked as advertised—indeed, it worked so well that the Germans had to find another way into France! However, one must consider that the point of the Maginot line was not to keep the Germans merely from attacking through their mutual border with France, it was to keep them out, period. On this ultimate and ultimately solely relevant criterion, the Maginot line is an immense and colossal failure, a testament to what happens when you combine a lack of imagination with a complacent worldview. The Maginot line is, in fact, hubris defined, poured into concrete, and set in the ground.

THE PROMISE FULFILLED

The Maginot line is still there (it's hard to dispose of 150 miles of concrete fortresses). The blockhouses and fortresses are now used for varying purposes, from homes to wine cellars to discos. One imagines that André Maginot might find it a bit humiliating to see a portion of his grand idea serving as an all-night warehouse for young, beer-swilling Euro-trash, but then, if you can't beat 'em...

PROVEN WRONG BY HISTORY: PART II

More ill-conceived comments by the supposed intelligentsia.

THE TELEPHONE

"This 'telephone' has too many shortcomings to be seriously considered as a means of communication. The device is inherently of no value to us."

—**Western Union internal memo, 1876**

THE AIRPLANE

"Heavier-than-air flying machines are impossible."

—**Physicist Lord Kelvin, president, Royal Society,1895**

"Aeroplanes are interesting toys but of no military value."

—**Marshal Ferdinand Foch, Professor of Strategy, École Superieure de Guerre**

"Man won't fly for a thousand years."

—**Wilbur Wright, to his brother Orville after a disappointing flying experiment, 1901**

ROCKETRY

"Professor Goddard does not know the relation between action and reaction and the need to have something better than a vacuum against which to react. He seems to lack the basic knowledge ladled out daily in high schools."

—**1921 New York Times editorial about Robert Goddard's revolutionary rocket work**

THE RADIO

"The wireless music box has no imaginable commercial value. Who would pay for a message sent to nobody in particular?"

—**David Sarnoff's associates in response to his urgings for investment in the radio in the 1920s**

THE BOMB

"The bomb will never explode. I am saying this as an expert on the subject."

—**Admiral Daniel Leathy advising President Harry Truman during the American atom bomb project, 1945**

During the War of 1812, the British took Detroit without firing a shot.

HOW MOSQUITOES CHANGED HISTORY

They may be small, but they're powerful. Mosquitoes have been manipulating the course of human history since its very beginnings.

1,600,000 B.C. Africa—Our ancestors take their first upright steps. Thanks to mosquitoes, they are already infected with malaria.

500 B.C. India—Brahmin priest Susruta deduces that mosquitoes are responsible for the spread of malaria. No one pays any attention for the next 2,400 years.

323 B.C. Babylon—Alexander the Great is felled by a mosquito, dying from malaria at the age of 33. His dream of a united Greek empire collapses within a few years, and widespread malarial infection contributes to the decline of Greek civilization.

A.D. 410 Rome—Marauding Visigoths finish off the Roman Empire, already undermined by a fifth column of malaria-spreading mosquitoes in the low-lying areas surrounding the capital. Shortly afterward, Alaric, leader of the vanquishers, is vanquished in his turn by a treacherous mosquito.

1593 Africa—Mosquitoes send yellow fever and malaria to their relatives in the New World via the slave trade, setting the stage for epidemics that would decimate both colonial and aboriginal populations.

1658 England—Bitten by a Royalist mosquito, Oliver Cromwell dies of malaria, paving the way for the return of the British monarchy.

1690 Barbados—Mosquitoes spread yellow fever to halt a British expedition en route to attack the French in Canada.

1802 New Orleans—Napoleon sends troops to reinforce France's claim to Louisiana and put down a slave rebellion in Haiti. Of the 33,000 soldiers, 29,000 are killed by mosquito-borne yellow fever. Louisiana becomes part of the U.S.; Haiti becomes independent.

In the 1620s, the Dutch had a colony on the lower tip of Manhattan.

1902 Stockholm—British army surgeon Dr. Ronald Ross receives the Nobel Prize for establishing the link between mosquito bites and malaria.

1905 Panama—Mosquitoes almost succeed in halting construction of the Panama Canal, as panicked workers flee a yellow fever epidemic.

1939 Colorado—DDT is tested and found to control mosquitoes and other insects. Mosquitoes eventually develop resistance to the chemical; humans don't.

1942 Dutch East Indies—Japanese troops seize the islands that provide most of the world's quinine, then the only reliable malaria therapy known, hoping mosquitoes will become their best allies in fending off Allied forces. Nearly half a million U.S. troops in the East are hospitalized with malaria between 1942 and 1945.

1965–1975 Vietnam—Mosquitoes infect as many as 53 U.S. soldiers per thousand with malaria every day.

1995 Geneva—The World Health Organization (WHO) declares mosquito-born dengue fever a "world epidemic," while deaths from malaria rise of 2.5–3 million a year.

*   *   *

Besides malaria and dengue and yellow fevers, mosquitoes have been in the news for a carrying a whole host of new and deadly blood-borne diseases.

Until 1999, West Nile virus, originating from the Nile River valley, had not previously been documented in the Western Hemisphere. The virus causes encephalitis, an inflammation of the brain, and can be transmitted by mosquitoes. West Nile was found in "overwintering" mosquitoes in the New York City area in early 2000, a sign that the virus is permanently established in the U.S. In the year 2000, 21 cases of the illness were reported, including two deaths in the New York City area.

The world's oldest parliament, Iceland's Althing, was founded in A.D. 930 by Vikings.

IT'S NOT EASY BEING MARCO POLO

We would never have heard of Marco Polo if it weren't for the book he wrote about his adventures. It made him world-famous, but not in the way he'd hoped.

THE ADVENTURE BEGINS

Marco Polo was born around 1254 in Venice, Italy. He picked up the traveling bug from his father and uncle who had already explored Asia when Marco was just a bambino. That was where they met the great Kublai Khan, who was to figure so importantly in Marco's life.

Marco was about 17 when he and his father and uncle set off on their most famous expedition. They traveled first by ship, then overland through Armenia, Persia, Afghanistan, into China, and across the Gobi Desert. Four years after they'd begun, they reached Shang-tu, the summer residence of Kublai Khan, emperor of the Mongols and conqueror of all China.

MR. POPULARITY

The great and powerful Khan took an immediate shine to Marco. He liked him so much that he insisted that the entire family stay: he didn't say for how long. It was an offer they couldn't refuse, so the Polos stayed on, and from Marco's account, didn't seem to mind. They put their hopes of returning home on the back burner.

The emperor set them up as major players in his court and made sure they had all the comforts of home. Marco's father and uncle worked enthusiastically for Khan, probably as military advisers. Marco mastered three or four languages and was sent on fact-finding missions from one end of China to the other. Part of his job was to visit recently conquered regions and report back to Khan about them. But the Polos never let Khan forget that they didn't want to stay forever.

HOME SWEET HOME

It wasn't until 17 years later that Kublai Khan consented to let them go home. On their way, they were to deliver a Mongol

The U.S. invaded Canada twice, once during the Revolution and once during the War of 1812.

princess who was betrothed to a Persian prince. It took them so long to get to Persia—two whole years—that when they arrived, they were told that the groom was dead. But it turned out that his son was available, so the princess married him instead.

The Polos arrived in Venice in 1295, richer than they'd left, though they would have been fabulously wealthy if they hadn't been robbed in Turkey on the way. They'd been gone for 24 years and had almost forgotten their native tongue. Which made it difficult to convince their relatives—who had long ago given them up for dead—of who they were.

ONE MORE ADVENTURE

But Marco's adventures weren't over. Italy was divided into rival city-states in those days, and Venice was at war with Genoa. Marco joined up, and in 1298, was captured as a prisoner-of-war and thrown into a Genoese jail. That's where he met a writer of romances named Rusticiano of Pisa. The two hit it off, and Marco soon began dictating the story of his travels.

He took the manuscript with him when he left prison a year later and published it under the title, *Description of the World*. Marco intended it to be the ultimate geography book. Most of it was based on his own firsthand experience of life in the Mongol empire, but some of the remarkable places he wrote about, like Japan and Ethiopia, were descriptions based on hearsay, told to him by relatives or acquaintances he'd met on his travels.

And even though printing hadn't been invented yet and each copy had to be written by hand, the book was an instant success and was eventually translated into all European languages.

Great, right? Wrong.

THE PROBLEM WAS...

No one believed a word of it. How could such things be true? According to the book, everything in China was bigger, faster, richer, more splendid, more civilized. How could the Kublai Khan host a banquet with 40,000 guests? And who would believe that there were people living south of the equator when the whole world knew it was uninhabited? Obviously, the book was a fantastic, romantic fable. So fantastic and imaginative that the buzz went out. Everyone wanted to read it. Kublai Khan joined the ranks of mythical hero-kings. And, against his will, Marco joined the ranks of great storytellers. Nothing he could say would convince anyone otherwise.

Because the book mentioned such vast distances and such immense riches, it was nicknamed "The Millions." And Marco, to his humiliation, was nicknamed "Marco Millions." After that, in carnivals throughout Europe there was always a clown called "Marco Millions" who told the most extravagant lies.

THE ADVENTURE ENDS
Marco had experienced enough adventures to last a lifetime. He lived the next 20-odd years quietly in Venice with his wife, Donata, and his three daughters. He spent his time managing his fortune, which on his death—ironically—proved to be smaller than he'd boasted.

The curse of Marco Millions followed him for the rest of his life. When Marco lay on his deathbed at age 70, his friends begged him to admit that he'd made it all up. He answered with irritation, "I have not told half of what I saw."

HUNDREDS OF YEARS LATER
Historians eventually proved Marco Polo's claims to be largely true. In fact, Christopher Columbus owned a copy of the book and was so inspired by it that he used it to convince Queen Isabella and King Ferdinand of Spain to fund his voyage to "Asia." The object of his exploration was to find evidence of the Great Khan and the treasures that Marco Polo described.

If Marco Polo hadn't been imprisoned in Genoa—the birthplace of Christopher Columbus, by the way—he might never have written of his travels. And the New World might have been discovered by someone else. We Americans owe a lot to Marco Polo. So how do we show our appreciation…?

MORE HUNDREDS OF YEARS LATER
In 1928, a Eugene O'Neill play called *Marco Millions* opened to raves at New York's Guild Theater. According to the review in *Women's Wear Daily*, the character of Marco Millions was "a smug idol of overstuffed self-sufficiency…."

Sometimes a guy just can't win.

COWBOYS?
WE CALL 'EM SISSIES!

Those weather-beaten, tall-in-the-saddle cowboys are the epitome of manliness. What if we told you that sometimes, after the sun went down, they loved to boogie?

After weeks and months of riding the range, eating beans and biscuits cooked over a fire made from cow chips, sleeping in the bunkhouse or on the ground, a cowboy was ready to have some fun. And there wasn't much that a cowboy liked better than goin' to a dance. Yup. A dance. ('Course, in some places it was called a hoedown or a shindig or a stomp, but it was still a dance.)

I HEARD IT THROUGH THE GRAPEVINE
The hospitality of the West was as big as the sky. And when somebody decided to give a dance, they didn't send messengers or invitations. The word went around, that's all, and if a cowboy heard about it, he could consider himself invited. He'd ride 60 miles to get there if he had to. But first he had to get slicked up.

AT THE BUNKHOUSE
Most every cowboy had something resembling "Sunday-go-to-meetin' clothes." These were dug out and laundered. Boots were greased till they were shiny. The cowboys shaved themselves and cut each other's hair—only to get covered with trail dust on the way there. But they didn't notice as they joined upward of 100 people who were also making their way to the dance.

BEEF ON THE BARBIE
Part of the lure was the "chuck"—what a cowboy called his food. This particular barbecue supper would have been days in the making. And all the womenfolk would bring fresh-baked pies and cakes and doughnuts. Enough to feed a cowboy army. Washed down by coffee from a pot that sat on the stove all night. But the food wasn't the reason why the cowboys had come from miles around.

Benjamin Franklin preferred the turkey to the eagle as the American national bird.

SWING YOUR PARTNER

After supper, the tables and chairs were moved aside and the fiddler warmed his fiddle. That signaled the start of the dance. Dancers took their places and the "caller" called the steps. The couples on the dance floor would somehow manage to follow calls like:

> Choose your partner, form a ring,
> Figure eight, and double L swing,
>
> Swing 'em once and let 'em go,
> All hands left and do-see-do.
>
> You swing me and I'll swing you,
> And we'll all go to heaven in the same old shoe.
>
> Swing your partner before you trade,
> Grab 'em back and promenade.

Everybody was a little bashful at first, but after a while even the shyest cowpoke was out there rompin' and stompin'.

NO WALLFLOWERS

Just like anywhere in the old West, there were never enough women to go around. Every last woman, no matter what her age or allure, got to dance till her feet were sore, but there was still a shortage. Those cowboys loved to dance so much they found it impossible to sit out an opportunity to "stomp." And the dances were "square dances" and required a certain number of couples to complete the set. What to do?

ARE THERE ANY VOLUNTEERS, HONEY?

It's a simple solution. When there weren't enough womenfolk to go around (which was pretty much all the time), some of the rootin'-tootin' manly-man cowboys would tie bandannas around one arm. This meant that they were willing to play the part of a female dancer—to dance what they called "lady fashion." And so they did, long into the night.

For 20 years, Rudolf Hess was the only occupant of Berlin's Spandau Prison.

THE QUEST
FOR LONGITUDE

A quest for a geographical unit of measurement doesn't have the same romance factor as a quest to slay a dragon. But finding an accurate gauge of longitude opened up the world, whereas slaying dragons never did anybody any good (least of all the dragons).

Now, you do remember longitude, don't you? Yeah, we know. Fourth grade was a long time ago for us, too. Look, find a globe. Now, on the globe, you'll notice the planet is sliced up by a bunch of lines going two separate ways. The horizontal lines are called "latitude." They tell you how many degrees you are north or south of the Equator, remember? Duh!

The vertical lines, by process of elimination, are longitude. They tell you how far east or west you are, using the longitude line that runs through Greenwich, England (for no really good reason) as the prime meridian. By using longitudinal and latitudinal coordinates, you can find any spot on the globe.

LATITUDE-FATITUDE
The catch is getting an accurate reading of your coordinates. Latitude has never been too much of a problem; humans figured out early on that the Sun's path reaches higher or lower in the sky depending on how far north or south on the planet you are on any particular day. If you know what day it is, simply take a reading of the Sun's position at high noon, do the math, and presto—you know where you are, in a northerly or southerly sort of way.

WHERE AM I?
This was a perfectly serviceable arrangement for a time, but as humans and their ships navigated farther and farther from the shore, however, it became apparent that there was a need. Traditional methods of measuring longitude were laughably inaccurate. Take, by way of example, the method in which distance was measured by counting how many rope knots, spaced about 50 feet apart, slipped out of a sailor's fingers in 28 seconds (thus the nautical term for speed, "knots").

Two small Alaskan islands were the only part of North America occupied by the Axis.

This would be fine as long as you traveled in a direct straight line and were constantly gauging your speed. But no one on a ship ever did either; the former because of waves, cross-currents, and winds, the latter because, oh, I don't know, the sailors were busy singing sea shanties and dancing the hornpipe. This way of measuring distance was known as "dead reckoning," most likely because if you reckoned by it, you might end up dead.

WANTED: A CLOCK

While latitude only required the knowledge of the date and the ability to determine the angle of the Sun, longitude required another determining dimension: the knowledge of the exact time at a place that was not where you were (let's call this place "Greenwich, England"). Due to the rotation of the Earth, noon comes at different times at different places east and west on the planet. If you spotted the Sun at high noon wherever you were, and then noted the time difference between you and Greenwich, you could determine your longitudinal distance from that point. What you needed was a clock, set to Greenwich mean time, that kept excellent time.

This was no problem if one was on land. By the 17th century, thanks to the principle of the pendulum, there were some reasonably accurate clocks in Europe. However, pendulum clocks aren't practical on sailing ships, particularly the rickety deathtraps people used to cross the seas back then. A ship that's rocking and rolling on the waves is really not the ideal place for a timepiece that uses pendulum motion.

A COOL 20,000 LBS.

After a navigational mishap in 1707 that killed thousands of sailors (English navy ships thought they were farther west than they were and tore open the bottoms of their ships on coastal rocks), the British Parliament offered a reward of £20,000 to the person or persons who could provide an accurate system of longitudinal reckoning. Twenty thousand pounds was an astounding sum of money at the time (compare 10 million dollars, which itself was a huge sum until all those Internet IPOs), and the contest coordinators, among them Sir Isaac Newton, found themselves wading through some really stupid ideas.

Only a tenth of one percent of all people on wagon trains were killed by Indians.

THE STUPIDEST IDEA

For example, one suggested stationing warships in permanent positions across the Atlantic; at midnight Greenwich time, they'd send up fireworks that could be seen for 100 miles around. Ships at sea could take their reading from there. Of course, this solution assumes there was a practical method for the "firework ships" to know when it's Greenwich time; obviously, were that the case, there would be no need for the ships at all. The entries became so cockamamie that the "quest of longitude" became a shorthand phrase for insanity.

THE HERO OF THE PIECE

The ultimate hero of the "quest of longitude" was a very unlikely fellow indeed: a certain John Harrison, a self-taught clockmaker and a carpenter by trade. Harrison did three things. First, he replaced the pendulum with balance springs. Second, he made the springs with a combination of metals to compensate for shrinkage and expansion. Finally, for the wood casings and other wood parts of the timepiece, Harrison used a tropical wood that was self-lubricating to reduce friction. At the end of it, Harrison had created the first timepiece that could keep accurate time at sea.

He took the first version, the H1, on its maiden voyage to Lisbon in 1734 (and got so violently seasick he never sailed again). Harrison went through three variations of the timepiece before developing the ultimate winner, the H4. In 1761 the H4 went from England to Jamaica and back—six and a half weeks—and only lost five seconds. The contest board was so skeptical of the achievement they made the clock do it again. Even then, they only gave Harrison half the prize. It took the direct intervention of King George III (you might remember him as the supposedly "mean, crazy king" from whom American colonials sought independence) to make the board cough up the remaining dough.

IT'S ABOUT TIME

Harrison not only created the means to establish positions at sea, he also gave the world the most accurate time measurement it had ever seen to that point. He understood that it's not just where you are, it's *when* you are. In this sense, the quest of longitude was also another quest entirely: the quest for time. Timing is everything when you're looking for your place in this world.

Harald Fairhair united Norway as part of a campaign to impress a girl.

MEN IN SKIRTS

*It may sound like heresy, but the Scottish kilt is not an
ancient tradition. And it was the ingenious creation—
not of a Scot, but an Englishman!*

How many men, not just in Scotland, but all over the
world, are proud to wear the tartans of the Scottish clans
of their ancestors? How many of these men occasionally
put on a kilt to show their pride in this ancient heritage? They're
all the victims of one innovative industrialist and two ingenious
con men.

WHEN IS A KILT NOT A KILT?

The modern garment called the kilt was invented around 1727 by
an Englishman named Thomas Rawlinson. Before that date, the
Highland Scots' traditional dress was a plaid knee-length thing
belted at the waist, kind of a cross between a blanket and a shirt.
(In fact, the Gaelic word "plaid" means "blanket.") Rawlinson
owned an ironworks and thought his employees' cumbersome
blankets interfered with their efficiency. So he invented the kilt.
To encourage his workers, he started wearing one himself. It
caught on so well that Parliament banned it in 1745 as a threat to
the British way of life. Suddenly, every Scot wanted to wear one.

Meanwhile, the English fell in love with Highland mythology
and costume. Sir Walter Scott's novels of Highland adventure
were bestsellers, and the Highland Society of London became very
influential. The real Highland Scots had become a despised under-
class, but British Army generals and great lords and landowners
could now be seen wearing kilts and listening to the bagpipes.
Even the English royal family started dressing up in kilts—a tradition that survives to this day.

WHEN IS A PRINCE NOT A PRINCE?

Enter our two con men, tall, charming, aristocratic young men
who called themselves John and Charles Edward Stuart. They
arrived in London in the early 1800s, and started telling people
that they were the secret—but legitimate—grandsons of Bonnie
Prince Charlie. His wife, the Princess Louise, fleeing his drinking,
had run away to a convent. They claimed that while she was there

---

The Tombstone gunfight was actually in front of a photography studio, not the O.K. Corral.

she gave birth to their father in secret. Dear old dad had told them the whole story, and here they were to claim their birthright.

Their ambition was to convince London society of this outrageous story, but when that didn't work, they moved to Scotland, where they found a much better welcome. Soon, some of the leading aristocrats of Scotland were treating them like royalty. They now called themselves Sobieski Stuart, "Sobieski" being the name of the Polish royal family, a connection they claimed through their alleged grandmother, the same Princess Louise.

They set themselves up as authorities on Scottish tradition and started publishing various books about it, based on ideas they invented themselves. There were books of history and traditional tales, but their real stroke of genius was to announce that their father had a Latin manuscript from the 16th century describing the costumes of the Highland clans. They produced what they said was a copy of this remarkable document, and soon they had all of Scotland rushing to put on what they said was the authentic version of Scottish costume. Eventually, in 1842, they published an expensive illustrated book of this material, and ever since, the fantasy world they created has been accepted as the true tradition of the Highlands.

WHEN IS A TARTAN NOT A TARTAN?

At the time, there were perhaps two or three tartan patterns that were traditionally associated with a particular family or clan. Which is probably where the Sobieski Stuarts got the brilliant idea of including a catalog of "family" tartans in their book. Of the 76 tartans they illustrated, over 50 were invented by them, the others being various patterns they had found in Scotland. Their invented patterns are now accepted by hundreds of thousands of people around the world as proud family history, and the number of tartans in use has expanded to over 2,000. In fact, there's nothing to stop anyone from inventing new ones.

In 1838, a grateful Scottish aristocrat, Lord Lovat, had told them they could have the home of their choice on his estates, and they chose the romantic island of Eilan Aigas, where they designed and built a suitably grand hunting lodge, complete with antlers, weapons, and armor on the walls, and (of course) busts of the Stuart kings, their ancestors. By the time their book came out, their triumph was complete. They sat on thrones, kings in all but name, while the flower of the Scots nobility, dressed in the costumes they had invented for them, knelt before them on the flagstones.

WHEN IS A KING NOT A KING?

They weren't satisfied, though. They foolishly decided to convince Queen Victoria to accept their claim to the throne, and she was not amused. When she rejected them publicly, they were frozen out of English society. Denounced as liars and charlatans, their fabricated world fell apart, and they disappeared as suddenly as they had arrived. They were last heard of heading for Prague, where they disappeared from history, too.

Final Irony: If Scotland ever gets its independence, the national imagery it chooses is sure to be the Sobieski Stuart version.

* * *

GREAT SCOT!

Though Alexander Graham Bell would have preferred to be remembered for his work with the deaf, we honor him as the inventor of the telephone. Alexander was born in Edinburgh, Scotland, in 1847. His grandfather was a speech therapist who helped stammerers. Bell's dad created "visual speech," a picture-based system for teaching the deaf how to make sounds. He wrote textbooks on how to speak correctly. Alexander's mother was a musician, although she had lost her hearing at age 12.

Alexander, who had the gift of playing music by ear from an early age, had planned on becoming a musician. He even taught music and speech at a boys' school. The business of talking and hearing was somewhat of a family preoccupation.

It was his knowledge of music and his experience working with the hearing impaired that helped Bell invent the telephone when he was only 29. The first phone call was made on March 10, 1876. Bell called his assistant, Mr. Watson, in the next room to tell him "Mr. Watson, come here. I want you."

Annie Oakley lived long enough to teach soldiers marksmanship during World War I.

TAKING NOTE: MUSICAL NOTATION

If you're not a musician, the musical notation on sheet music looks as confusing as an algebraic formula. But for musicians it's a clear and concise road map that shows the way: with it, any competent musician can play a piece he or she's never heard before, and deliver it more or less as the composer intended.

A lot of the details of our current musical notation evolved over the centuries, but the fundamentals can be traced back to one person: Guido of Arezzo, an Italian monk who lived between 990 and 1050.

BEFORE THERE WAS GUIDO

Guido didn't wake up one day with the idea of musical notation whole and perfect in his head. There'd been some rudimentary forms of musical notation known to the Western world for centuries. In Guido's own time, a system of notation known as "neumes" were used as guides for Gregorian chants. Neumes were squiggly (but vague) little notations that told the singers to "sing high here" or "sing low there." They were okay for people who already knew the piece of music, but pretty useless if the singer or musician didn't. Musicians still had to learn musical pieces by ear, from other musicians. Building up a repertoire of tunes could take years.

A BETTER MOUSETRAP, MUSIC-WISE

Guido's innovation was to refine the "staff"—the parallel lines that are used to denote a particular pitch. The rudimentary version that was already being used had only two lines for the C and F notes. Guido added two more lines, one below the C and one between the C and F. Presto—a staff that clearly showed the relationship that each neume (and each musical note) had with the others around it. Guido liked to say that his innovation could help train an ecclesiastical singer in just one year, as opposed to the ten years that had previously been required (all that memorization, remember).

Among the cities founded by Vikings were Dublin, Ireland, and York, Great Britain.

KICKED OUT OF A BAND OF MONKS

Guido's new-fangled musical ideas got pretty much the same reception that other musical rebels from Mozart to Eminem received in their time: the older generation didn't much cotton to it. He was kicked out of two monasteries because the other monks didn't like his style (today we would say he left the group because of "creative differences").

TALENT WILL OUT

But Guido was getting pretty famous. Pope John XIX heard about Guido's new ideas and invited him to Rome. Guido taught the pope how to read music, which so impressed the pope that he urged Guido to stay in Rome. But the climate wasn't good for Guido's health. So he went back to one of his old monasteries where he was welcomed back (as you might imagine, given the pope's being Guido's biggest fan and all) with open arms.

DO, RE, MI, FA, AND SO ON...

Guido also created another musical innovation: the system of naming scale degrees—"re," "mi," "fa," "sol," and "la." Guido did it by composing a hymn to St. John the Baptist, and having the first syllable of each line fall on a different tone. He called them: ut, re, mi, fa, sol, and la. "Ut" was eventually changed to "do," which Rogers & Hammerstein no doubt appreciated; the final tone "te" (also known as "ti") was added later.

LIFE AFTER GUIDO

With the basics of Western musical notation in place, other innovations followed. The five line staff became standard in the 16th century; the current shape of musical notes followed in the 17th. Many of the words and signs that describe tempo and dynamics were standard by the 18th century.

And there are still new notations being added, as composers attempt to describe recent musical innovations such as microtones (musical intervals in between the conventional half-step intervals) and computer-generated music.

GRAZIE, GUIDO!

But still and all, the way most music is expressed today owes a direct debt to that Italian monk of a thousand years ago.

FOOD A MILLENNIUM AGO

*A truly grueling tale of what your average
late-medieval peasant could expect to find on his table
after a hard day's work in the fields.*

WHAT'S FOR LUNCH? I'M STARVING!
Finding enough food to eat in the year A.D. 1001 was a
problem. There were long periods, particularly in
winter, when no fresh food was available. Not to mention the
total of 20 famines in Europe during the 10th century, some lasting three or four years. As a result, people gorged themselves
whenever they had the chance because they never knew when
another opportunity to eat might arise.

HELLO, GRUEL WORLD

The staple of Joe Peasant's diet was gruel—what we'd call oatmeal
today—which nutritionists now tell us is much healthier than
eating a diet of mostly red meat. When vegetables were in season,
people ate cabbage, carrots, peas, and various garden greens. They
picked apples, pears, and nuts right off the trees.

THE STAFF OF LIFE

Bread was made from wheat, rye, or barley, and the flour was
baked without removing the bran. Sounds healthy enough, eh?
Unfortunately, the bread consumed a thousand years ago was full
of impurities. So not only was it coarse, it was often infested with
weevils and mold. Consequently, everyone's teeth were bad to
rotten, and most people suffered from foul breath.

CRAZY ABOUT BREAD

Worse than all that were outbreaks of ergotism, a fatal illness
caused by eating rye infected with a fungus parasite. The fungus
contained "ergotamine," which when baked was transformed into
a deadly hallucinogen. The infected parties suffered symptoms
resembling madness and had no idea what was wrong with them,
after which they died.

The Battle of Bunker Hill was actually fought one hill over, on Breed's Hill.

THAT'S ONE SPICY HORSE MEATBALL!

A millennium ago, horses were just beginning to replace oxen as the quintessential farm animal. But they were still desirable as a source of protein and were eaten with gusto—and probably a generous helping of mustard. Salt, pepper, cloves, and other spices were all the rage during the Dark Ages; they not only preserved food, but also killed the rotten taste after the food had spoiled.

FOUR AND TWENTY BLACKBIRDS

In addition to horses and the odd rabbit or pig, birds were eaten with regularity. People ate cranes, storks, swans, crows, herons, loons, and blackbirds. Sometimes birds were served in a pastry like the "four and twenty blackbirds baked in a pie," from the well-known English nursery rhyme "Sing a Song of Sixpence." It was said that cooks could tell if a pie was done by its sounds of crackling and "singing," much like that of a blackbird.

MINIMALISM MEDIEVAL-STYLE

Setting the medieval table was easy because there were no plates. Even the great nobles, who generally spread out tablecloths for their meals, went without plates. Instead—is Martha Stewart listening?—meals were served on round, flat slabs of bread. Bread plates had the advantage of soaking up drippings, and of being edible. When plates eventually came into vogue, it was customary to share your plate with the person sitting next to you.

Guests were invited to bring their own knives. Spoons and forks were introduced in Europe much later. Folks in the eastern Mediterranean had been using a two-pronged fork for centuries, but it wasn't till 1071 that a Greek princess who married the doge of Venice brought the custom—and the fork in question—with her. Rich Venetians took it up as the fashion, but the custom stayed in Venice for centuries before the rest of Europe noticed.

GROG: BREAKFAST OF CHAMPIONS

To wash down their rather simple meals, peasants of the day drank. And drank. In fact, a thousand years ago, alcoholic beverages were a diversion and comfort to households among all classes. Wine was the favorite drink of the nobility and wealthier middle class. But everyone drank beer, even for breakfast, and the alcoholic content was three to four times higher than today's suds.

Nazi Germany did invade the United Kingdom, but only as far as the Channel Islands.

Mead, a kind of beer made from fermented honey, was popular in northern Europe and packed a wallop stronger than a kick from an irate mule. It could have an alcohol content of up to 18 percent.

IT'S A BEER-ACLE!
Beer was such a prized commodity in those days that one Swedish king chose, among several prospective brides, the one who could brew the best beer. A Swedish queen, St. Brigitte, was rumored to have repeated the miracle performed by Christ, but with a slight variation: Brigitte changed water not into wine, but into beer.

KEEP YOUR HANDS ON YOUR CHICKEN BONE, BUDDY!
As far as table manners were concerned, a manual of etiquette intended for gentlefolk (royalty, nobles, and the wealthier classes in general) reminded them not to break wind while at the table, neither to hawk and spit on the floor, nor to pick their noses or scratch their heads looking for lice. And, particularly in the case of males, not to fondle the breasts of the women next to them.

THANK YOU FOR THE FOOD WE EAT
None of this concerned the lowly peasants, who scratched and picked their way through the same monotonous meal of gruel day after day and considered themselves lucky if they could fill their bowls to the brim. (Excuse me, dear wyfe, might ye biggie-size that gruel combo for me?)

*   *   *

LET MY CHICKENS GO!

Leonardo da Vinci felt so strongly against people eating animals that he often purchased live poultry and then set the birds free.

He wrote, "I have, from an early age, abjured the use of meat, and the time will come when men such as I will look on the murder of animals as they now look on the murder of men."

General George Patton placed fifth in the pentathlon at the 1912 Olympics.

THE OLYMPICS EXPOSED

If you wish we could return to the ancient Olympics when athletes played for love of the game instead of medals, when sportsmanship was king... Oh, dear. Uncle John is going to disllusion you again.

The first Olympic Games were held in 776 B.C., but their real beginnings are shrouded in myth. Legend tells us that Herakles (who later made a Roman name for himself as Hercules) won a race on the sacred Greek plain called Olympia. He decreed that the Olympian race should be re-enacted every four years.

NAKED GAMES
A big difference between the ancient Olympics and the modern games is that back then there were no commercial logos on the athlete's clothing because nobody wore clothing: the ancient games were played in the nude.

The first competitors wore shorts, until 720 B.C. Then, according to the ancient writer, Pausanias, one guy tossed his trunks so he could run faster. After the shortless guy won, clothing was abolished.

ROUGH, TOUGH, AND IN THE BUFF
Some historians think it may have been the militaristic Spartans who pushed for nudity. They trained in the nude (both men and women, the latter—naked women in public!—being very contro-versial). But the Spartans were top athletes, so the other city-states may have wanted to imitate them.

MORE NAKED GAMES
The first Olympic games were just races, but more sports were added as the years went by: the pentathlon, horse races, chariot races, and the pankration, which was a combination of boxing and wrestling. At one time or another, there were 23 Olympic sports events. While nudity may have helped the runners, it didn't help the Olympian jockeys much. They were bare and rode bareback— no saddles, no stirrups. Controlling the horse was a challenge!

Only four Western Hemisphere nations sent troops to World War II.

PEACEFUL ENEMIES

There was one more very important reason for the "undress" code: without their clothes athletes couldn't hide any weapons. At the time, the Greek city-states were often at war. But during the Olympic festival, they called a truce so that everyone could travel to Olympia safely.

Hostilities, weapons, and armies were forbidden. Even the death penalty was suspended. All the same, nobody really trusted anybody else. The games had their roots in warfare and the athletes were prepared for battle as well as for sporting competitions. For the most part the Olympic truce held.

WHEN MEN WERE MEN AND WOMEN WEREN'T ALLOWED

Women weren't allowed to watch the men's games, much less compete. This supposedly had more to do with the religious aspects of serving Zeus than it did with nudity. Women had their own races anyway, at Olympia in honor of the goddess Hera (a.k.a. Mrs. Zeus), where they could be just as naked and win their own darn laurel wreaths. By the way, any woman caught watching at the male Olympics was thrown headfirst off the cliffs of Mount Typaeum.

ANCIENT MAULERS

War and women were forbidden in the ancient Olympics, but violence was allowed. Some of the early Olympic games probably made professional wrestlers look like sissies. Entrants could trip, punch, and kick their opponents, even in their, um, private parts. Pankration entrants could also break fingers for a quick win, and one pankratiast became so good at this that he was called "Finger Tips."

THOSE RICH ATHLETES

Today's millionaire pros are cousins to the ancient Olympians. We may like to think of Greek athletes as idealistic amateurs, but the word "athlete" is derived from Greek words meaning "one who competes for a prize." Aristotle, Plato, and Socrates whined about the declining morality that money brought to the Games. Galen, a Greek physician asked, "Are athletes to be worshipped like kings because they have large incomes?" Hmmm.

MORE THAN THE KEY TO THE CITY

Olympic competitors had to pay their way into the Games—and it wasn't cheap. They also expected payment for the glory they brought to their cities. In 6 B.C., Athens offered bonuses equal to around $600,000 today. Athenian champions got front row seats at the theater and free meals in the city hall for life. They even made money by doing "appearances" at other festivals.

A SHOW OF STRENGTH

Athletes trained hard. By the sixth century they were hiring coaches. There were fads involving diet and exercise just like today. Athletes from Croton in Italy believed in a meat diet, and beans were a no-no. The greatest wrestler of the ancient Olympics, Milo of Croton, supposedly ate 40 pounds of meat and bread at one meal, washing it down with eight quarts of wine. It worked: Milo won himself 32 titles in his career.

SLEAZY POLITICS

Then as now you couldn't keep politics out of the games. Politicians gave speeches between the races (but it's not known if people hung around to listen). Campaigning politicians sponsored chariots to gain popularity with the crowds. There were even violent political disputes over which city should control the Sanctuary of Zeus in Olympia where the games were staged.

THE MORE THINGS CHANGE

Despite all its problems, the Olympics did promote cherished ideals of peaceful competition and individual achievement. In A.D. 395, Emperor Theodosius I banned them during a purge of pagan festivals. But he couldn't kill the spirit of the Olympics and, in 1896 in Athens, the modern Olympics began. This time everyone wore clothes, but they still have problems that are an awful lot like the ones the ancient athletes used to face.

*   *   *

TELL THEM TO COME BACK LATER

The ancient Greeks gave the Olympics top priority. Even when the Persians were invading in 480 BC and the survival of the Greek city-states was endangered, thousands of spectators watched the finals of boxing bouts at the Olympian stadium.

The future Pope John XXIII was an Italian sergeant during World War I.

HEY, WHAT ABOUT THOSE FREEMASONS?

Ah, yes, the Freemasons, that mysterious secret society that does whatever it does when those Masons go inside those temples of theirs. Probably nothing good, involving scary initiation rites and sacrifices to pagan gods and strip poker and such.

Who are these guys, and what are they doing in there? And are they really running the world? Well, they might be. Or—and this is a wacky, zany theory here, but just go with it for a second—they could be what they claim to be, which is an innocuous fraternal and social organization that currently has millions of members all around the world. Let's take a look and see which is more likely.

LAND OF THE FREEMASONS

The most probable origin of the Freemasons has the organization incorporating in 1475 in Edinburgh and consisting of masons (stone workers) and wrights (woodworkers). Members from other crafts were allowed to join, starting with coopers (barrel makers) in 1489. "Modern" Freemasonry is generally agreed to have begun with the creation of the Great Lodge of London in 1717. Over the centuries the organization drifted away from its original trade association and became more of a club for men of various professions and callings, although the Freemasons' symbols and official gear (including a stonemason's apron) recall the early days.

THE MEMBERSHIP LIST

The question regarding Freemasons in history is not who has been one but who has not. Freemasons in American history range from Benjamin Franklin and George Washington to Colonel Harland Sanders (yes, the chicken guy) and Michael Richards, a.k.a. "Kramer" from Seinfeld. Several United States presidents were Freemasons, the most recent being Gerald Ford, as have been numerous senators (including Strom Thurmond), representatives (including Davy Crockett), and Supreme Court justices (including William Howard Taft, who was also a president). So while

Freemasons as a group may or may not rule the world, there's little doubt that individual Freemasons have had their hand at the wheel quite a bit.

However, the thing that makes people suspicious about Freemasons is not membership rolls, but the rituals that have sprung up within the group over the years, the "initiation rites" and ceremonies and various "levels" that Masons can achieve by going through them. These rites are supposedly secret and paganistic, with one of the big sticking points being the Mason's conception of a "Great Architect of the Universe" ("God" to most of us). Freemason detractors suggest that this "Great Architect" is not a generalized representation of a higher being, as the Freemasons claim, but a manifestation of Baal, god of the Canaanites, i.e., not the same God that gets play on Sundays. Freemasons, it should be noted, roll their eyes at this allegation.

Be that as it may, the Freemasons have fueled a great deal of resentment over the years, and at one point even spawned a political party, named, appropriately enough, the Anti-Masonic Party. It was formed after the mysterious disappearance of bricklayer William Morgan in 1826, who was allegedly preparing a tell-all book about the Freemasons' secrets and rituals. He was never found, and the rumor was the Freemasons did him in.

A FREEMASON UNDER EVERY BED
The Anti-Masonic party had some success on the state and local level, and even managed to help former United States President John Quincy Adams get elected to the House of Representatives in 1830. However, as a national political party, it was something of a bust. Its 1832 presidential candidate, William Wirt, carried only Vermont and was fourth in a field of four candidates. (The winner, Andrew Jackson, was a two-term Grand Master of Masons for Tennessee; his primary opponent, Henry Clay, was a Grand Master of Kentucky.) Ironically, it turns out that Wirt, the standard bearer for the Anti-Masonic party, had been a Mason himself! Man, those guys were everywhere.

MASONS VS. KNIGHTS
Even today, Freemasonry arouses the suspicions of many branches of Christianity, most notably the Roman Catholic Church, which until very recently would excommunicate members who joined

Masonic clubs. It's no longer an automatic out, although membership in the Freemasons and the Roman Catholic Church is seen as mutually incompatible. (Catholics with a burning desire to join a social fraternity have the Knights of Columbus, which is an association explicitly connected to the church.) Freemasons, of course, strenuously object to the idea that their group is a paganistic cabal dedicated to taking over the world, but isn't that exactly what a paganistic cabal dedicated to taking over the world would say?

Who wants to get in the middle of a fight between a paganistic cabal dedicated to taking over the world and the One True Church? You'd get squashed like a tick. Rather than choosing sides on this matter, we'll just give you a couple of Web links and let you figure this one out on your own.

Here's the entry on "Freemasonry" from the Catholic Encyclopedia: *http://www.newadvent.org/cathen/09771a.htm*.

And the Freemason point of view, from Mason Edward L. King's informational site: *http://www.masonicinfo.com/*.

* * *

THE HERETIC QUOTA

The Inquisition began in the 12th century, a time when the pious worried that some non-Christian religious sect might spread across Europe. Pious nobles in France, England, and Italy set about rooting out potential dangers to the true Church, kicking convicted heretics out of office, turning them out of their homes and businesses—and oh yeah, burning them alive. The Inquisitors and their methods varied through four centuries, but one thing never changed: convicted heretics had their property confiscated.

Capital punishment wasn't the norm until the 13th century. Maybe that was when the Church realized that a business could be made out of punishing heretics. Suddenly the death rate increased enormously, and so did the profits on the Vatican balance sheet. Catholic Popes, beginning with Lucius III in 1184, handed out local Inquisition rights in European provinces like so many fast-food franchises. The Vatican handed down quotas for local Inquisitions insisting that they burn a certain number of heretics and seize a given dollar amount of property each season.

U.K. Prime Minister Alec Douglas-Home played world-class cricket.

MATA HARI,
THE SPY WHO WASN'T

Mata Hari went down in history as the exotic dancer who loosened many a lip in the service of the Germans during WWI. Far from it—the social climber never passed a single French secret to the Germans, though she was shot by a firing squad in 1917 for her supposed crimes.

Mata Hari's name has passed into the language along with famous femme fatales like Jezebel and Delilah—women who used their beauty to enslave and betray powerful men. But the story of the real Mata Hari played out differently than what's remembered about her.

A LITTLE DUTCH GIRL

Mata Hari was born Margaretha Geertruida Zelle in Leeuwarden, Holland, in 1876, and it sounds like she was a wild one from the beginning. She met husband-to-be Rudolph MacLeod through a personals ad in the newspaper and soon after joined him at his post in faraway Java. A couple of years of his company proved to be enough. She fled to Paris to begin her exotic dancing career.

LIFE UPON THE WICKED STAGE

She was an immediate success. Parisian audiences flocked to her naughty, titillating performances to glimpse the exotic "Oriental" dancer who shed her veils in a naughty titillating way. Mata was intent on bigger things and tried to launch a serious professional dancing-acting career. She was even booked into a few Italian opera houses, but people just wanted to see her unveil herself. She was the "entertainment" at several notorious private parties, too.

39 AND HOLDING

By 1915 Hari's career was fading fast (like the rest of her). She was doing less and less dancing on the stage and more and more of the horizontal boogie with a steady stream of men who passed through her bedroom. Recently unearthed French files give away the names of dozens of Mata Hari's lovers while she hovered at 40, including composer Giacomo Puccini, Baron Henri de Rothschild,

---

Two British prime ministers are named in the Beatles' song "Taxman."

French Minister of War Adolphe-Pierre Messimy, affluent German landowner Alfred Kiepert, and last but not least, German military attaché Major Arnold Kalle.

TARTS CAN'T WIN

That last affair is probably the one that killed her. In 1917, Mata Hari was arrested by the French and accused of spying for the Germans. They produced decoded messages outlining a German plan to hire Mata Hari as a spy. But not only were the French unable to produce any evidence of secrets she'd handed over, several high-ranking French officers testified that Mata Hari had tried several times to give information on German activities to French counter-intelligence agents.

AN ERROR IN ACCOUNTING

Mata Hari claimed that the German messages were an attempt by the aforementioned Major Kalle to pay her on the military's tab—the guy was padding his expense account! No matter. She was convicted of spying for the Germans and executed by firing squad in 1917. Rumor has it that she threw open her blouse to distract the squad from firing. In truth she went bravely, still a slut, but with her blouse buttoned up.

POSTMORTEM

Prosecutor Andre Mornet admitted 40 years later "There wasn't enough [evidence] to whip a cat." (Those French say the darndest things, don't they?) Mata Hari was forbidden to call any civilian witnesses during her trial, and the evidence she was convicted on was spotty and contradictory at best. Historians pin the blame on anti-German hysteria (of which there was lots at the time) and also the vindictiveness of Mata Hari's prosecutors, who were probably punishing her for doing it with Germans. The French have some funny ideas about sex (and everything else).

*   *   *

TOUGH COOKIE

Nancy Hart was a spy for the Confederate army. At 20 years old, she was captured and imprisoned by the Yankees. She stayed on her best behavior till one of the guards came to trust her, relaxing his vigilance around her. She stole his gun, shot him and escaped.

THE POPE WAS A LADY

The ninth century Pope John VIII was brilliant, kind, musically
talented... and female. At least that's what some historians say.
Others dismiss the tale as pure myth.

Although the story of the female pope has several versions, here's how it usually goes. An English woman named Joan (or Jeanne) resented the fact that she wasn't allowed to get an education. At the time, book-learning was thought to be unnecessary and even harmful for a woman. So Joan disguised herself as a man, probably as a monk, and called herself John English (in other stories, John of Mainz).

A VERY SPECIAL LITTLE LADY

She went to Athens to study, where she impressed everyone with her scholarship. Then she moved on to Rome, where she taught science, became a secretary in the Curia (the central administration arm of the Roman Catholic Church), and eventually was made a cardinal. As before, her abilities attracted the attention of scholars. Her conduct was also considered flawless.

Joan—still in disguise, of course—was elected pope. Over the next two years, five months, and four days, she handled that position very well. But one day she gave herself away. During a solemn procession through the streets of Rome, the pope got down from her horse and—to the horror of onlookers—gave birth to a child, then and there.

Here's where the story diverges: some versions say she died in childbirth or soon afterward. Others say a furious mob tied her to the tail of a horse, dragged her through the city, and finally stoned her to death. Yet another version has her immediately deposed as pope, but living out a long life—and doing penance, lots of penance. That particular story ends with a touch of irony: her son grew up to be a bishop.

SEZ WHO?

A female pope was first mentioned during the ninth century by a historian called Anastasius the Librarian. And in fact, Joan's name turns up in some early lists of the popes. To further back up the story, several versions were written down by Dominican record

---

The throne of Ethiopia's Menelik II was actually an electric chair imported from the U.S.

keepers during the 13th century. One of them was a report written by Martin of Troppau, a Dominican friar from Poland in 1265. In it, Martin named names, gave details, and placed Joan's papacy in the 9th century. Since he'd served in the Curia as chaplain to a pope, his story was widely believed. Dominican friars like Martin were prominent in European universities, and Dominican nuns were the scholarly type as well, so maybe the idea of a studious woman wasn't as foreign to the Dominicans as it was to most everyone else of that time. But time passed, and by the 17th century, Catholic historians were repudiating the story and questioning Joan's existence. (But those darn Protestant historians went on telling the tale.)

Those who stand by the story of Pope Joan offer details as bizarre as this one. Supposedly, right after Joan's reign, a new inspection was made mandatory for papal candidates. A prospective pope had to sit on a chair shaped much like a toilet, where his sex could be checked from below, either manually or visually. Another story says that since the day Pope Joan gave birth, papal processions have avoided using the street she was on at the time. The *Catholic Encyclopedia* explains that the street is just too narrow for a procession of papal proportions.

STAR OF STAGE, SCREEN, AND FICTION?

Real or imagined, our controversial heroine was played by Liv Ullmann in the 1972 film *Pope Joan*. She (Joan, not Liv) has also turned up on tarot decks and in playing cards. In fact, a card game called Pope Joan was popular in Scotland during Victorian times.

It's said that the story was originally a Catholic morality tale that was used to justify keeping women out of the priesthood—and out of the papacy—especially if they were going to have babies in the street like that. It was only later that anti-Catholics turned the tables and started to use the story as propaganda.

According to Vatican records—and there's lots of them—all the popes are accounted for and there's no Joan among them. The John VIII they list has a very complete biography: he was born in Rome, served as pope from 872 to 882, involved himself heavily in politics, bribed the Saracens to keep them from invading Rome, and was assassinated by his own relatives. As juicy a pope story as they come…except for Joan's.

PARDON ME, FRITZ, IS THAT MY LEG DOING THE POLKA?

One day in the year 1278, you're a normal German peasant, getting your typical day's worth of abuse from landowners, clerics, wealthy merchants, crazed neighbors, the wife, and kiddies. The next thing you know—Pow!—you're easin' on down the road, just a-twitchin' and a-dancin' like an extra in some 13th century road company of The Wiz. Bad booze? Or something more sinister?

The day started out quietly enough. You woke up at five, milked the cows, rethatched the roof with another coat of dung, then got chased a mile by that crazy Müeller kid with the mismatched eyes.

EASE ON DOWN THE ROAD
Now it was time to shop and maybe relax for a few hours in town. You pulled the goose quills out of your neck (courtesy of young Müeller, a superb marksman despite his insanity), brushed yourself off, and headed into town for a quick brewski with the boys and to pick up victuals for the evening meal.

LET'S DANCE!
On your way into town, you run into nearly 200 townspeople near the Maas River Bridge. For some bizarre reason, they're all doing some crazy jig, looking like they escaped from the local laughing academy. You feel suddenly compelled to join in! In minutes, you're all thrashing your bodies around randomly, arms hitting heads, legs kicking all willy-nilly, bodies dragging on the ground. Wait until the hausfrau hears about this, you think.

A VISIT TO ST. VITUS
Suddenly, the bridge gives out with the weight of all you dancers, and nearly the entire cadre is wiped out in the river. But you and about 10 others survive! "Mother of Mercy!" you scream, and rightly so. The town priest has you and the others in tow and is bringing you posthaste to the chapel for some blessing or other.

The visit to the chapel, dedicated to St. Vitus, is miraculous.

In 1892, Annie Moore from Ireland became the first immigrant processed at Ellis Island.

As soon as you enter the still, dark sanctum, all dancing subsides as quickly as it had begun. *Cured!* screams the priest. *Cured!* rejoins the small saved band of ex-dancers.

IT'S JUST A PLAGUE
Your experience that morning will be forever recorded as the mystery of St. Vitus' Dance—and the saint whose chapel you were brought to will be forever known as the patron saint of those afflicted with what was once called the "Dancing Plague."

HISTORICAL AND HYSTERICAL
But this sort of thing didn't just happen in this one accursed spot in Germany. During the Middle Ages, there were incidents all over Europe where large groups of people displayed what can only be called hysterical behavior, that is, physical symptoms caused by mental anxiety of some kind. Dancing mania was frequently a symptom of this hysteria. It's been documented in psychiatric journals and books, jam-packed with tales of tormented people nearly dancing themselves to death.

THINK "CHOREOGRAPHY":
The term "dancing" in describing this disorder comes from the Latin word "chorea" and is characterized by involuntary jerking movements of the extremities. There is a medical condition called chorea, but most experts agree that the medieval involuntary dancing was undoubtedly a psychological phenomenon.

LETTING OFF STEAM
But the infectiousness of it (like what happened to you when you saw everyone dancing near the bridge) is a sure symptom of mass hysteria, brought on—most experts agree—by the oppressiveness of life in the Middle Ages. It was a way for the downtrodden peasant to escape the social pressure cooker for a while.

TONY 'N' TINA'S WEDDING
The lively Italian dance called the tarantella had its roots in dancing mania, too. The name "tarantella" comes from one of two sources: Historians can't decide if it was named for the town of "Taranto" (where an early outbreak occurred), or if the victims thought it was caused by the bite of a "tarantula." Either way— leave it to the Italians—the onlookers got out their mandolins and tambourines and set it to music. Now the tarantella is a staple at Italian weddings on both sides of the Atlantic.

The Uruguayan navy once defended Montevideo by firing Edam cheese cannonballs.

BREAKING THE MOLD: DISCOVERY OF PENICILLIN

The closest competitor is the discovery of vulcanized rubber, which led to our ability to sit around during the hottest part of the day in five-mile traffic jams. But as much fun as that is, not dying a terrifying, stench-filled death at the microbial hands of some bacteria is even better.

Make no mistake, a stench-filled bacterial death was a serious possibility for just about everyone well into the 20th century. Serious strides were made in the general sanitation of the planet in the 19th century (thanks to Joseph Lister, who, among other things, convinced doctors that wearing a perpetually bloody smock as a badge of competence was actually carrying germs from one patient to the next), but sanitation only goes so far.

THE POOP ON BACTERIA

Bacteria are teeny little things, and they can get into places they're not supposed to be with surprising rapidity, where they are happy to procreate until they kill you. This isn't very smart on the part of the bacteria (killing one's host tends to cause the food supply to tap out), but it's not like bacteria have brains, and anyway, they live for about 20 minutes. What do they care?

DOUGHBOYS ATTACKED ON ALL SIDES

Come with us now to the battlefields of the First World War. Nasty little war, that one, with lots of soldiers wallowing in mud and getting shot, bayoneted, or gassed every now and again. If they were lucky, they'd die right there in the mud; if not, they ran a very good chance of dying in the hospital—not from their wounds directly, but from the infections those wounds inevitably bred. Doctors knew bacteria were the culprits in many soldiers' deaths, so researchers were assigned to discover antibiotics. Scotsman Alexander Fleming was one of them.

THE POOP ON THE PETRI DISH

Fleming wasn't much help on the antibacterial front during World

---

Genghis Khan conquered more land than Alexander the Great, Napoleon, & Hitler combined.

War I (neither was anyone else), but in 1928 he noticed an odd thing in one of his petri dishes, which had been swabbed with *Staphylococcus*, the nasty little bug that can cause everything from boils to toxic shock syndrome. The dish had been contaminated—some sort of airborne something had managed to get into the dish before Fleming sealed it off—and whatever it was that was in there with the staph was killing it off something fierce.

If Fleming had been a bug-eyed drone, he would have tossed the sample, because contaminated samples were supposed to be ditched. But Fleming was a scientist, thank God, and he knew he'd found something.

A FUNGUS AMONG US

Penicillium notatum was what he found. The penicilli were releasing some sort of chemical (which Fleming, in a burst of stunning originality, decided to call penicillin) that killed bugs dead, and not just a few bugs—we're talking all sorts of bacteria. Deader than Marley's ghost. How? By screwing with the bacteria's assembly process. In order for bacteria to survive, they have to build a cell wall as they reproduce; penicillin keeps the bacteria from building these walls. The bacteria die, exposed to the elements. It'd be sort of sad if they weren't in fact trying to kill you.

THE POOP ON ANTIBIOTICS

Incidentally, this is how antibiotics work—by messing with the assembly process. The best way to keep bacteria from using your body as real estate is never to let them lay down their subdivisions in the first place.

SUCCESS STORY

The catch—there's always a catch with these things—is that naturally occurring penicillin (a.k.a. as Benzylpenicillin or penicillin-G) isn't very stable and, thus, isn't very useful. Fleming found the wonder drug, but he couldn't do anything with it. Frustrated, he shelved his penicillin research in 1931. Penicillin has to wait until Oxford researchers Howard Florey and Ernst Boris Chain manage to synthesize a stable form of penicillin. It performs as promised and in 1940, penicillin debuts and starts kicking microbe ass. Fleming, Florey, and Chain get the Nobel in Medicine in 1945. They were all also knighted. Fungus was very good to them.

TSK, TSK, TSK

Fungus has been very good to all of us—not too many of us die from sore throats anymore. However, don't get cocky. Human beings, convinced as we are that anything worth doing is worth overdoing, have spent the better part of the last 60 years wantonly misusing antibiotics in lots of dumb ways. We use antibiotics for viral infections, which is pointless. We feed antibiotics to animals to who aren't sick to make 'em bigger and fatter. We take antibiotics only until we feel better instead of following the directed medication course. (If you feel better, you are better, right?)

TB OR NOT TB

The result is that we've bred some amazingly drug-resistant strains of bacteria. We've got some TB bacteria running around these days that is, in fact, resistant to every single antibiotic we can throw at it, even the incredibly toxic antibiotics that hurt you as much as they hurt the bug.

NO SOAP

And it's not just TB, of course: *Streptococcus*, *Staphylococcus*, and *Pneumococcus*, heck, all of the really popular coccuses have virulently drug-resistant strains out there. *Enterococcus faecalis* and *Pseudomonas aeruginosa* are just waiting to poison your blood. And here's a thought for you: streptomycin-resistant *e.coli* has been found in the diapers of today's infants.

Thing is, streptomycin hasn't been used to treat much of anything for three decades. It's evolution, baby. Anyone who doesn't believe in the process is going to be mighty surprised when an ear infection sends them to the morgue. But what can I do about it, you ask? Well, for one, stop using that stupid antibacterial soap. You're just making things worse, you know.

PERHAPS THE GREATEST IRONY

All the benefits that we've gotten from antibiotics could be wiped away because of our own deliberate misuse of them. It'd be like Prometheus giving man fire, and then, after watching man burn down a forest or two, just to see the pretty lights, deciding that maybe he should take it back. It's an accident we got antibiotics, but when we lose them, it'll be our own damned fault.

Printing pioneer Johannes Gutenberg was actually a goldsmith.

THE REAL BRAVEHEART

*Movie fans will never forget William Wallace, the Scots rebel
leader that Mel Gibson portrayed so convincingly in
Braveheart. But was Wallace nearly forgotten
in Scotland until Hollywood rescued his legend?*

Randall Wallace, the producer of the 1995 film *Braveheart*,
was researching the production in Scotland when he
visited the Wallace Memorial at Elderslie, Renfrewshire.
The producer talked to local teens sitting near the statue and
asked them what they thought about their hometown's great hero.
The kids had no idea the statue represented William Wallace; in
fact they'd never heard of him.

WILLIAM WHO?
They know who Wallace is now. And in Wallace's rising historical
fortunes, it's easy to forget the darker, bloody side of his battle to
free Scotland. Wallace was the great leader of Scotch resistance
against the English - who also wiped out villages, burned down
churches, and flayed his enemies to make battle ornaments.

DEATH, LIES AND THE MOVIES
Artistic license was taken with Wallace's family history in *Braveheart*. One brother was written out completely, and another, along
with Wallace's father, was conveniently axed early so as not to get
in the way of the action. The historic accounts of Wallace's life
were also slanted to make storytelling easier. Accounts written in
Scotland made Wallace a noble conquering giant; those written in
England called him a murderer and outlaw.

WALLACE'S STORY GETS VERSE
Braveheart is based on a view of Wallace presented in the *Scoticho-
rum* of Walter Bower. Bower wrote it in the 1440s, 135 years after
Wallace's death, and his main source was anti-English propaganda
where Wallace got excellent, but not always accurate press.
Bower's account was the source for a romantic epic poem, *The
Wallace*, by "Blind Harry." The poem became Scotland's national
myth for several hundred years. In some Scottish homes it held an
honored place near the Bible.

The last battle of World War I was fought in what is now Zambia.

WILL THE REAL WILL PLEASE STAND UP?

But what's the scoop on the real, non-mythologized Wallace? Well, for one thing, remember his statue? It might be in the wrong hometown. Most of the facts about 13th century Scotland are hazy, but modern research indicates that the great man was actually born in Ellerslie, Ayrshire. The name "Wallace" means "Welsh," and he was probably a descendant of Welsh-speaking immigrants who came to live in West Scotland. William was the son of a knight and minor landowner. He was not a noble, but he was an educated member of the prosperous Scottish upper classes. In *Braveheart*, Mel Gibson could have portrayed a well-dressed, well-heeled, brilliant, 13th-century warrior (though fans would have missed all that wild hair and face paint).

A STIRLING VICTORY

Wallace was a brilliant commander. A high point of his military career was the Battle of Stirling Bridge of 1297 where the Scots were badly outnumbered. Stirling Bridge was very narrow, allowing few soldiers to cross at once. The outnumbered Wallace managed to split the English forces in two; the English who had crossed to the north side of the bridge had no room to maneuver, and they were cut off from retreat. Wallace's men slaughtered some 5,000 English that day; and the despised English treasurer's flayed skin made a belt for Wallace's sword.

WALLACE WAS NO ANGEL

Wallace led his army into the English border region of Northumberland. Here the darker side of Wallace's story emerged. The English commanders had tried to subdue Scotland by burning and pillaging it. Now, Wallace and his men sacked the English cities for food to take back to starving Scotland. They burned towns and killed the inhabitants so that the English soldiers would find no help if they returned. (And Wallace knew they would try to return). The great Wallace and his men were as merciless in Northumberland as the English had been in Scotland.

WALLACE WAS NO FOOL

In the summer of 1298, when King Edward I led a large army through the area into Scotland he rode through a barren landscape. Thanks to Wallace, who'd laid waste to Northumberland, the approaching English army was almost starved out.

A NOBLE KNIGHT BUT NOT A NOBLE

Sometime in early 1298, Wallace was knighted, most probably by Robert Bruce, Earl of Carrick, and he became sole Guardian of Scotland. In the Middle Ages it was an amazing achievement for a mere knight to become more powerful than nobles were, but Wallace was a man of amazing achievements. Still, his rapid rise as one of the most powerful men in Scotland made him enemies. Independence was restored in Scotland (thanks to Wallace), and Robert Bruce was enthroned as king.

But in 1305, Scottish noblemen who were less entrenched against the English than they were against Wallace handed him over to England and Edward I.

MARTYRDOM IN ENGLAND

The English took Wallace to London for a show trial. Maybe the worst mistake King Edward I ever made was to have his old enemy tortured, mutilated, disemboweled and hacked to pieces in public. Edward I made Wallace a martyr in Scotland, and a symbol of Scotland's quest for independence. Wallace's life (darker side and all) came to stand for bravery in the pursuit of freedom. As the 18th century Scottish poet Robert Burns said: "The story of Wallace poured a Scottish prejudice into my veins which will boil along till the floodgates of time shut in eternal rest." Wow. And Burns hadn't even seen Mel Gibson.

*   *   *

Robert the Bruce, once deemed a turncoat by the Scots, ended up a greater hero than Wallace. He repeatedly made and broke peace with the English. But in 1304, Bruce made a treaty with the church to help him gain the Scottish throne, and the support of the people. In 1305 he went to Scone to claim the throne and was crowned King Robert I of Scotland. A number of battles ensued with mixed results. After one bloody defeat, he hid in a dark cave to escape the English army. As the famous legend has it, while he sat there depressed at his failures, he saw a tiny spider trying to climb its silken thread to its web, and repeatedly tumbling back down. Yet, the spider continued its struggle. Bruce was so inspired by the spider's tenacity that he grabbed up his sword and shouted "If at first you don't succeed—try, try again!"

Before climbing Mount Everest, Edmund Hillary was a New Zealand beekeeper.

THE TOOTH ABOUT DENTURES

Chew on the strange history of false teeth.

Whether you want to chew someone out or just chew your dinner, you gotta have teeth—even if they're false. Dentures, as single teeth, whole plates and partial bridges, date back more than 2,000 years to the Etruscans. As early as 700 B.C. hippopotamus and whale ivory provided the materials for skilfully crafted chompers. Sadly, the Etruscan age was the high point of mouth gear until the 1800's.

ANCIENT DENTISTS PUT THE BITE ON YOU

Ancient Greeks and Romans were inordinately proud of their dentures, consisting of an imitation tooth bound to a real tooth with gold wire. They were proud, and poorer, since the work cost a fortune. (Some things never change.) The truly rich ancients got dentures made from gold, silver, agate, and mother of pearl.

DENTURES TO DIE FOR

Queen Elizabeth I resorted to stuffing the gaps in her royal grin with cloth. In later years, there would be the distasteful (yes, pun intended) practice of using teeth of the dead. During the Battle of Waterloo, bags of teeth were retrieved from fallen soldiers.

FANGS A LOT

In 1774, French dental wizards Duchateau and Dubois de Chemant crafted the first set of porcelain dentures. People looked forward to a great improvement on their old dentures, which were often hinged with springs, and had the embarrassing habit of popping out of a person's mouth.

A WOODEN SMILE

Unfortunately, the new "technology" was of little use to George Washington, who was known to have suffered greatly with his teeth. And "wooden" you know it; those famous presidential choppers were never made of wood. Various materials, yes, but not wood. This was proven in 1999 when a touring exhibit of Washington artifacts included his "artificials."

Catherine of Aragon was both a widow and a virgin when she married Henry VIII.

DENTAL DRUGGISTS

In 1808, Giuseppangelo Fonzi forged on with a single porcelain tooth held in place by a steel pin. Claudius Ash improved on the original porcelain in 1837, and the use of dentures took hold in the U.S. Meanwhile the business of dentistry was getting a "shot in the mouth" with the invention of anaesthetics. Ether was used successfully by dentist William Morton in 1846, although nitrous oxide, first identified and experimented with in the 1790's, would prove to be the pain-blocker of choice.

PUTTING THE BITE ON CRIME

Due to improved dental health services, fewer people wear dentures. But improvements in denture components over the years has been a bonus for crime investigators. As early as 1849, the body of a Dr. George Parkman was identified from his dentures. False teeth are generally not soluble in acid, which helped convict John Haigh in 1949, for the acid bath murder of a Mrs. Durand Deacon. She'd been wearing her dentures when she was killed.

A GLOWING SMILE

People suddenly discovered that their patented pearlies glowed so nicely because they contained uranium. Uranium's use for false teeth was patented in 1942. Why, you ask? Because natural teeth fluoresce under "black light," and so does uranium. The amount of uranium in false teeth in the U.S. was only .05 percent by weight. Still, it bombarded the inside of the mouth with eight times the normal level of background radiation. Its prolonged use was likely a result of the mistaken idea that it improved one's appearance. This theory went out the window when it was discovered that some dentures did not fluoresce white under the lights, but red, yellow, and green. The government (acting with reassuring speed) revoked the federal exemption for uranium's use in the mid-1980s.

CHIPPED TEETH

Japanese dentist Hisashi Kishigami, who cleans a large number of dental prostheses, started microchipping them. Not only does it ensure they return to their rightful owner, but it has been a valuable resource in identifying lost senile or Alzheimer's victims, (if they remember to put their dentures in) and in identifying the deceased. (Don't forget to die with your dentures on.)

BAD HISTORY! BAD!

*Or, 11 Reasons Why You Shouldn't Get Your
History from Hollywood.*

A night at the movies is a fine way to amuse yourself and support America's $6 billion a year film industry, but it's a bad way to learn anything useful about history. Even when you throw out the obviously historically inaccurate comedies or special effects-laden fantasies, the supposedly more "accurate" genre of historical drama is still chock-full of bad history or history "reedited" to make the story less confusing, more exciting, or to accommodate the availability of Mel Gibson. Even Oscar-winning films are replete with inaccuracies that would make your history teacher throw up. As proof, here are ten mostly recent historical dramas that have played fast and loose with the past.

Pearl Harbor (2001): Before the attack on Pearl Harbor in the film, Japanese Zeros are shown flying low over wholesome American kids playing baseball; they would have to have gotten up pretty early to play ball, since the attack occurred just before 8 A.M. Commander-in-Chief of the Pacific Fleet Admiral Husband Kimmel is likewise shown golfing, as if to emphasize his utter unpreparedness for the attack. In fact he was nowhere near the greens when the attack occurred. (Kimmel, the Navy's fall guy, was relieved of command after the attack; he's since been exonerated.)

Movie heroes Ben Affleck and Josh Hartnett are shown taking flight and doing battle with attacking Japanese Zeros; in the real world, it was Army pilots Kenneth Taylor and George Welch who managed to get into the air. Later, Affleck and Hartnett fly in Doolittle's raid over Tokyo; no actual pilots flew in both battles. Affleck is also shown serving in Britain's Eagle Squadron. While the squadron did include Americans, they were all civilians.

Final small inaccuracy: In one scene a sailor displays a dollar bill with the word "HAWAII" on it; those bills, introduced in Hawaii so they could be declared illegal if the Japanese invaded, came out in July 1942—long after the Pearl Harbor attack.

During WWI, Germany offered Arizona, New Mexico, and Texas to Mexico to change sides.

Thirteen Days (2000): The film in which Kevin Costner averts nuclear war during the Bay of Pigs, with a little help from John Fitzgerald Kennedy (JFK). Most historians and participants of the event suggest that Costner's character, JFK adviser Kenny O'Donnell, was not nearly as pivotal a character in the crisis as he's shown to be. Indeed, several critical scenes in the film show O'Donnell doing things he never did in real life—taking Bobby Kennedy to meet the Soviet ambassador, giving pep talks to pilots before they overfly Cuba, and having a moment with JFK himself before a Kennedy television address.

The film also had an embarrassing flap over its newspaper ads, which featured F-15 Eagle fighter jets and a Spruance class destroyer. But neither of these saw military service until the 1970s. The error was on the part of the ad agency, not the film producers. Stupid ad agencies.

Gladiator (2000): This Oscar-winning toga flick is a historical mess right down to the Latin somebody chipped into the Coliseum. First off, there is no historical general to match Russell Crowe's Maximus. There was of course a real Marcus Aurelius, whose son was named Commodus. However, Commodus didn't smother Marcus Aurelius to death when he learned he wouldn't be chosen as emperor, if for no other reason than he already was emperor (or more accurately co-emperor) when his father died in A.D. 180. Moreover, while Commodus did in fact enjoy prancing about as a gladiator, much to the scandal of the higher classes, he was not killed by a revenge-crazed former general during gladiatorial battle. His real death in 192 is even weirder: He was strangled by a champion wrestler hired as an assassin by his advisers.

Oh, and the Roman Empire didn't become a republic again after Commodus's death, as intimated in the movie. Commodus was succeeded as emperor by one Publius Helvius Pertinax, who lasted all of three months before his assassination. Tough gig.

The Patriot (2000): Neither Mel Gibson's character Benjamin Martin nor the chief baddie William Tavington are actual historical characters, but both are based loosely on real people: Francis "Swamp Fox" Marion and British Lieutenant Colonel Banastre Tarleton, respectively. The operative phrase here is "loosely," since Francis Marion owned slaves and loved a good fight (a far cry

In the 1570s, the Spanish were defeated by a Dutch army on ice skates.

from Gibson's Martin, who was reluctant to go to war and paid free black citizens to work on his plantation).

Tarleton, while earning the nickname "Bloody Ban," didn't set fire to churches while the parishioners were still in them. He also didn't die in the film's climactic Battle of Cowpens; he lived until 1833.

The Battle of Cowpens, it should be noted, hadn't nearly the amount of heavy firepower as is portrayed in the film. There were only two light cannons, brought by the British. Other than that, it was muskets and swords—still bloody enough. Incidentally, British commander Lord Cornwallis, portrayed in the movie as a somewhat stuffy older man, was actually only 42 at the time of the battle, in which he did not take part. The British forces were led by Tarleton, who led badly—he lost 600 out of 1,500 men, while the colonists lost a mere 72. Oops.

U-571 (2000): You know that part in the movie, when the crack team of U.S. soldiers launches a surprise attack on a German submarine and steal the sub's Enigma code generator? Never happened. The U.S. had no part in capturing the naval Enigma machine; that honor belongs to the British, who clambered aboard the German sub U-110 on May 9, 1941, to recover a working Enigma machine, its cipher keys, key books, and other cryptological records.

The Germans subsequently made their naval Enigma machines more complicated (they were sneaky that way), requiring the Brits to perform the same maneuver again on October 30, 1942, when British sailors boarded the U-559. Two soldiers drowned in the attempt to bring up the sub's Enigma machine, but the signal key books were retrieved, which allowed the Allies to crack the naval Enigma code. Americans did board the German sub U-505 in 1944, retrieving sensitive papers, maps, and whatnot (earning the leader of the boarding crew, Lt. Albert David, the Congressional Medal of Honor), but it just wasn't the same.

There was a German submarine with the designation U-571 that patrolled the waters off the U.S. Eastern shore, sinking several merchant ships between 1942 and 1943. It sunk in the North Atlantic on January 28, 1944, after getting into a fight with an Allied aircraft and losing. All hands were lost.

Elizabeth (1998): Lots of people in this film are in the wrong place at the wrong time, or simply shouldn't be there at all. Bishop Stephen Gardiner, shown leading the Catholic Church opposition to Queen Elizabeth, died three years before she was crowned. Sir William Cecil was not an old man when Elizabeth came to the throne, as he is in the film, but a spry 38; he remained one of the queen's closest advisers until his death in 1598. Sneaky Francis Walsingham, portrayed as two or more decades older than the queen, was in fact only one year older. Robert Dudley, Elizabeth's fallen lover in the film, never really fell, but rather remained one of the queen's closest friends until his death in 1588. Other time-slip issues include Elizabeth's excommunication by the pope, which happened far later, in 1570.

Amistad (1997): While the majority of the characters in this retelling of the famous slave ship rebellion are based on real-life people, Theodore Joadson, played by Morgan Freeman, is not. The *Amistad* is shown making port in the winter; in the real world, it made port in August 1839. (Interestingly, in 1839, slavery was still legal in Connecticut, where the *Amistad* made port; a general emancipation in the state was not enacted until 1848. The film rather conveniently doesn't bring up the fact of a northern state still allowing slavery.) The film also shows the leader of the Africans, Cinque, peppering his lawyers (who included former president John Quincy Adams) with legal questions and helping create the defense. But there's no real evidence that he did this.

Braveheart (1995): Oh, lots to complain about here, but for the sake of keeping things brief, let's focus on the film's portrayal of the relationship between William Wallace (hunky Mel Gibson) and Princess Isabella (sultry Sophie Marceau). In the movie, she's seen negotiating with Wallace for English king Edward I before she eventually jumps his bones and ultimately (one assumes) places his child on the English throne as Edward III.

Wallace was captured by the English and very messily dispatched (the movie got that right) in 1305. Isabella was born in 1292, making her 13 at the time of Wallace's death. She didn't wed Edward II until 1308—by which time, incidentally, he was already king. (Isabella would, however, play a primary role in deposing her husband in 1327.)

The movie fiddles with the death of Edward I, who died in 1307, not immediately after Wallace's death, and certainly not due to apoplexy from the idea of a Scotsman one day gaining his throne. Also, it should be noted that Edward I wasn't in the habit of throwing his son's gay lovers out of windows.

Hoffa (1992): Jimmy Hoffa's bosom buddy in this flick, Bobby Ciaro (played by director Danny DeVito), goes through every bump and turn of the union boss's tumultuous career with him. That's loyalty, or would be if Bobby Ciaro actually existed, which he did not—he's an alleged composite of several different real-life people. This film also shows Hoffa (and Ciaro) getting snuffed in Hoffa's car and then being tossed into the back of a moving truck, never to be seen again. Since no one actually knows what happened to Hoffa (except possibly those few what did it to him, and Hoffa himself, all too briefly), this is also total fiction.

JFK (1991): So many historical inaccuracies that it's hard to know where to begin. For example, the film features David Ferrie (Joe Pesci) confessing knowledge of the Kennedy assassination; in real life Ferrie consistently denied knowing anything. In presenting Dealey Plaza evidence, the film contends 51 people heard shots from the "Grassy Knoll," while the U.S. House Select Committee notes only 20. The film presents witness Lee Bowers telling the Warren Commission about seeing a "flash of light" and "smoke"; Bowers actually told this to author Mark Lane well after his Warren Commission testimony. The film has the Dallas mayor changing the motorcade route; the route was planned for days and was even published in newspapers. And so on and so on. People will be fighting about this one for years to come.

Fat Man and Little Boy (1989): This re-creation of the birth of the nuclear bomb features a scene in which scientist Michael Merriman, working with others prior to the bomb's creation, stops an inadvertent nuclear reaction from detonating. As a result he receives massive radiation exposure and expires. This would be sad if "Michael Merriman" were a real person, but he's not; he's yet another "composite" character designed to push the plot along. An event like this did happen, bringing about the death of a real Manhattan Project scientist—Canadian physicist Louis Slotkin, but it happened in 1946, nine months after the nuclear bombs from which this movie gets its name were dropped on Japan.

DIRTY SECRETS IN THE HISTORY OF HYGIENE, PART III: SMILE

Taming Mr. Tooth Decay

Before toothbrushes, there was the twig. You'd take your twig and chew the end to form a sort of bristle. When the bristle end wore out, you'd cut it off and repeat the process. As late as the 19th century, people brushed with a twig and table salt.

THE BRUSH

The earliest toothbrushes were invented in China (where else?) around 1500, and came to Europe during the 1600s, where they soon became all the rage. Before then, Europeans had mopped their teeth with rags or sponges dipped in sulfur oil or a salt solution. Sometimes the rag or sponge was fastened to a stick (now there's progress). The Chinese version consisted of hog's bristles tied to a piece of bamboo or bone. In 1938, nylon filament developed by DuPont became state-of-the-art for the bristle.

TOOTHPASTE THEN

The tastiest toothpastes used by the ancients were powdered fruit, honey, or dried flowers. But imagine brushing your teeth with pastes made from these revolting recipes: mice, the head of a hare, or lizard livers. Spanish and Dutch writings from the 14th and 15th centuries suggest that urine was saved and used to clean the teeth. Chalk was a popular ingredient in the 1850s. Soap was added to toothpastes in the early 1800s. The foaming action in toothpastes is created by adding a trace of detergent.

FLUORIDE THEN AND NOW

In 1931, Dr. Frederick McKay, a Colorado dentist, confirmed the link between fluoride and reduced tooth decay. In 1956, Proctor & Gamble was the first company to add fluoride to toothpaste in its Crest brand. After years of controversy, fluoride is embraced by virtually all purveryors of toothpaste. How far we've come.

When Anne Boleyn was beheaded, so was her wolfhound.

THE REAL
BODY SNATCHERS

Don't go to weep upon my grave,
And think that there I'll be;
They haven't left an atom there,
Of my anatomie.

I f medical science was going to advance at all—this is during
the Age of Enlightenment—it depended on doctors improving
their knowledge of human anatomy. The medical establishment needed bodies to practice on and to study. Most countries
allowed medical colleges to acquire unclaimed bodies of criminals
for anatomy practice. But this supply was insufficient. What to do?

DIGGING FOR ANSWERS
Once again the human mind, powered by greed, triumphs! The
solution was the ghastly practice of body snatching, that is,
digging up the recently dead and selling them to surgeons for use
in anatomy class. Sometimes medical students and surgeons did
their own digging, but they were generally too busy—just like
now—to spend their time traipsing around cemeteries. So the
profession of body snatching was born. They answered to the
elegant name "resurrectionists" or the decidedly less elegant "sack
'em up men." By the late 1700s, London and Edinburgh had
become the body-snatching capitals of Great Britain.

JOB DESCRIPTION
It was a relatively safe career. The only real risks were the danger
of contracting contagious diseases from corpses, or of being discovered and attacked by outraged crowds. Hardly any body snatchers
went to prison: Under British law, a corpse was not considered
property, so taking one wasn't theft.

The resurrectionists could be prosecuted only if they took
goods from the grave, like the shroud, or if they entered a cemetery that was private property. Even so, most of them were in
cahoots with wealthy and prominent doctors or universities, so
they often had access to good lawyers.

Charles Bonaparte, grandnephew of Napoleon, founded the FBI.

MODUS OPERANDI
They typically worked in groups. They—excuse the expression—haunted funerals, pretending to be mourners, so they could return later knowing exactly where the dearly beloved was buried. Using a narrow-bladed wooden shovel to minimize the sound of scraping metal, they only shoveled out the area over one end of the coffin, hopefully the end with the corpse's head. When they struck the casket, they pried off the end of the lid, tied ropes to the cadaver, and jerked it out. Then they filled the hole back in.

A BUSINESS LIKE ANY BUSINESS
Entrepreneurs like Ben "Corpse King" Crouch of London trained rookie body snatchers in the ways of the dark profession. His teams patrolled London's burial grounds in search of the newly dead, and their nightly take was even recorded in a ledger like some ghastly corporation. Like any capitalist enterprise, competition could be fierce, and gangs often battled with each other over fresh graves. Some enterprising body snatchers signed exclusive contracts with particular schools or surgeons.

A NEW WRINKLE
The famous team of Burke and Hare modernized the business in even more monstrous ways. They cut out the back-breaking part of the operation—digging up bodies—by just killing people outright. In 1828–29, these two enterprising fiends murdered 16 men, women, and children in Edinburgh and sold the fresh bodies to a delighted Dr. Robert Knox, one of the finest surgeons in the city as well as, apparently, one of the most gullible.

THE FALL GUY
Gullible or not, when Burke and Hare were finally nabbed, a wide-eyed Dr. Knox feigned ignorance of their murderous system, but his denials didn't satisfy the mob and he fled Edinburgh.

Hare testified against his partner and walked away scot-free. Burke was convicted of murder and executed. Afterward, in the ultimate irony, he was publicly anatomized at the medical college. His skeleton is on display at the University of Edinburgh, and a wallet made from his skin still graces the museum at the Royal College of Surgeons.

ENOUGH CADAVERS TO GO AROUND

Burke and Hare's horrific crime spree inflamed public sentiment and compelled the British Parliament to pass the Anatomy Act of 1832. This law improved medical schools' access to legal cadavers and pretty much put the British resurrectionists out of business.

THE AMERICAN WAY

The practice continued in the United States, where most states refused to pass such laws. American body snatchers, like their British brethren, were particularly fond of preying on the poor and indigent because there were so many of them. They were less likely to have family claim their bodies, and they were often dumped in shallow graves in potter's fields—a body snatcher's buffet.

ALL CORPSES AREN'T CREATED EQUAL

But democracy meant that upscale dead people weren't safe from the attentions of the resurrectionist either. In one celebrated case, in 1878, the missing corpse of Congressman J. S. Harrison turned up at the Ohio Medical College. Harrison was none other than the son of President William Henry Harrison and the father of President Benjamin Harrison. This notorious event prompted some states to enact anatomy laws. But only some. A lot of other states maintained that the state had no business involving itself in legislating that sort of stuff. So grave robbers had free reign to continue their nasty ways in many parts of the United States. Certain American medical schools regularly acquired their cadavers, no questions asked, from shadowy body snatchers as late as the 1920s. And, who knows, perhaps even more recently than that.

* * *

Down the close and up the stair,
But and ben wi' Burke and Hare;
Burke's the butcher, Hare's the thief,
Knox the man who buys the beef.

* * *

The grave's a fine and private place,
But none, I think, do there embrace.

In 1940, German spy Josef Jacobs became the last person executed at the Tower of London.

HISTORY'S GREATEST TRAVEL BARGAIN

*An ocean voyage to sunny beaches and unspoiled pine forests
with all expenses paid by the British government.
Who could ask for anything more?*

In the 1780s, English citizens demanded that Parliament solve the problem of overcrowding in the "hulks"—rotting ships along the Thames River that were used as prisons. The government would have liked to hang more prisoners, but was afraid that it might create unrest. The old practice of shipping felons off to "the colonies" had ended with that pesky American Revolution.

BON VOYAGE
Australia was an English colony, but it had no settlers. And therefore commercial potential. So why not offer some lucky prisoners a change of scene? Eleven ships left England on May 13, 1787, for a voyage that would continue halfway around the globe. This first fleet carried 730 convicts, including over 100 women. In January of the following year, the prisoners landed in New South Wales and founded the settlement that would become Sydney, Australia.

THE NOT-SO-LUCKY WINNERS
It was like a bad scene from *Survivor*. The prisoners were separated from their families and everything familiar by thousands of miles of ocean. They were dumped into a vast wilderness without the proper clothing, supplies, or tools. Who were these imprisoned pioneers? Although the intent was to export violent criminals, many were merely desperately poor folk who had been found guilty of stealing food or clothing.

TROUBLED IN PARADISE
Over the next 50-plus years, thousands of convicts were sent to Australia. Assigned to work for the government, private settlers, traders, they built the early immigrant settlements and provided the labor for the new agricultural economy. Life was grim for prisoners in New South Wales, too. Reports received in England

claimed that the system had turned prisoners into slaves. By the 1830s, the practice of transporting prisoners down under began to die out. By that time, the convict population, now paroled and released, accounted for the majority of settlers.

TASMANIAN DEVILS
But it was Van Diemen's Land, now called Tasmania, that gave the Australian settlement plan its truly evil reputation. This was where the "troublemakers" went, arriving at the picturesque city of Port Arthur, the penal colony once known as "hell on earth." Once there, convicts were sentenced to hard labor, sometimes in chain gangs hauling lumber and working in quarries. Punishment for minor infractions was severe, and lashings with the infamous cat-o'-nine-tails were common. Life was so brutal that some men made suicide pacts. One man would agree to kill another, then would escape himself by going to the gallows.

GREAT ESCAPES
Naturally, escape became a favorite pastime. In 1822, a convict named Alexander Pearce escaped with some other prisoners. When he arrived in civilization, he was asked where the rest of the guys were. He confessed that he'd survived by eating them!

Some convicts stole weapons and took off into the wilderness to become outlaws (and cultural heroes) called "bushrangers." They didn't have to do much to win the support of the general population, since most of *them* had once been prisoners, too.

STRANGER THAN FICTION
In Charles Dickens' famous novel, *Great Expectations*, the hero Pip gets money from a convict who made his fortune in Australia. Dickens' fiction was based on fact. Many former felons became Australian success stories. They created everything from farms and ranches to newspapers and great architecture.

THE INCREDIBLE HULKS
For years, the Aussies kept quiet about their ancestors' origins in the "hulks" of England. But times change. Now, descendants of the first fleet dress up in historic costumes to celebrate the day when a weary group of prisoners landed in what the Aussies affectionately call "Oz." *Dahling*, it has become *trés chic* to flaunt your ancestors who once traveled courtesy of the king!

In the 1800s, New Zealand had both a gold rush and a jade rush.

STOMPED TO DEATH BY "LITTLE BOOTS"

Caligula was the emperor of Rome from A.D. 37 to 41
He's remembered as a vicious and cruel despot, a sadist, and a
megalomaniac—and those were his good points!

Gaius Caesar grew up in a military camp where his father's soldiers nicknamed him "Caligula" ("Little Boots") for the child-size military boots he wore. His father, Germanicus, was a great Roman general and adopted son of Emperor Tiberius.

LITTLE ORPHAN CALIGULA

In a scenario so Roman you can almost hear the lions munching on Christians: Germanicus's military victories made him so popular with the Roman public that Tiberius got jealous and had him killed. Later on, Tiberius killed Caligula's mother, Agrippina, and the rest of Caligula's brothers.

SNEAKY LITTLE SON OF A GENERAL

For reasons unknown to historians, Caligula was spared and went to live with Tiberius on the island of Capri. Eventually Caligula gained the confidence of Tiberius so that when the emperor died, he named Caligula and his grandson Gemellus joint heirs to the throne. Caligula had no interest in sharing power, so he managed to get the Roman senate to declare Tiberius's will invalid and to choose him as emperor.

HAIL, CALIGULA!

For the first six months he was a good ruler, but that all changed when he became ill with what was called at the time "brain fever." This may have been an attack of encephalitis, which can cause a marked character change resulting in behavior similar to schizophrenia. Anyway, after the illness, Caligula's character changed all right: He became a vicious tyrant. Historians believe that he probably became insane. Witness the following.

THE POSTER BOY FOR BRAIN FEVER

From then on, he racked up a series of exploits that only a total wacko could think up.

The Zulu army that beat the British at Isandhlwana included a regiment in their 60s.

- He banished or murdered most of his relatives and had people tortured and killed while he watched. He would sometimes eat dinner at the same time.
- He declared himself a god and had temples erected and sacrifices offered to himself.
- He had his horse, Incitatus, made a senator.
- He was hated and despised by the Roman senate because he conducted treason trials in which many senators, both guilty and innocent, were condemned to death. One unlucky official was flogged with chains for several days while Caligula watched, and was finally put out of his misery only because Caligula was offended by the smell of the gangrene that developed because of his injuries.
- He quickly emptied the Roman treasury to support his lavish lifestyle, building projects, and the games he staged for the citizens. To refill it, he introduced new taxes. He also began to acquire the property of the wealthy citizens of Rome by forcing them to bequeath him all of their property and then having them killed.
- He was married four times and cheated openly on all of his wives—with both men and women. He even committed incest with his own three sisters. Whenever Caligula kissed the neck of his wife or mistress, he'd say: "This lovely neck will be chopped as soon as I say so."
- He proclaimed his mastery of the sea by building a three-mile-long bridge on top of hundreds of boats lined up across the Bay of Naples. He then crossed the bridge by chariot, and claimed that he had ridden across the waters like the god Neptune.
- He planned to invade Britain and so marched his troops to the northern shoreline of Gaul. But instead of crossing the channel, he ordered his men to collect seashells, which he called the spoils of the sea. Then he returned triumphantly to Rome expecting to be welcomed as a hero.

FAREWELL, CALIGULA!

The Roman people finally had enough and were ready to give "Little Boots" the boot. Caligula and his fourth wife were killed by the officers of his guard, who—just to prove that brutality wasn't only the province of emperors in ancient Rome—also smashed his infant daughter's head against a wall. He was succeeded as emperor by his uncle Claudius, a kinder, gentler emperor. But compared to Caligula, who wouldn't be?

The Boer War was the first time motorcycles and trucks were used in war.

HISTORICAL HINDSIGHTS

Some very smart people can be downright cynical about history.
Keep the following quotes in mind as you leaf through
the olden days as Uncle John remembers them.

"History is a pack of lies about events that never happened told by people who weren't there."
—**George Santayana**

"History is more or less bunk."
—**Henry Ford**

"History is nothing but a parade of crimes and adversities."
—**Voltaire**

"I often think it odd that [history] should be so dull, for a great deal of it must be invention."
—**Jane Austen,**
Northanger Abbey

"History (n.): An account mostly false, of events mostly unimportant, which are brought about by rulers mostly knaves, and soldiers mostly fools."
—**Ambrose Bierce,**
The Devil's Dictionary

"The past actually happened but history is only what someone wrote down."
—**A. Whitney Brown**

"God cannot alter the past, but historians can."
—**Samuel Butler**

"Historian: an unsuccessful novelist."
—**H.L. Mencken**

"History is indeed little more than the register of the crimes, follies, and misfortunes of mankind."
—**Edward Gibbon**

"History is mostly guessing; the rest is prejudice."
—**Will and Ariel Durant**

"Happy the people whose annals are blank in history books!"
—**Thomas Carlyle**

"History, Stephen said, is a nightmare from which I am trying to awake."—**James Joyce**

Despite his name, Bernardo O'Higgins was the first president of Chile.

THE GREAT LEAP BACKWARD

*China goes into the steel business
and calls it the "Great Leap Forward."*

In the mid-1950s China's Chairman Mao Tse-Tung realized that he was the leader of a backward country. He looked at Britain, France, America, and the Soviet Union, and saw that there was one crucial area where China was a long, long way behind— steel production. If China was to become a modern country, it needed to start producing as much steel as its competitors.

MAN OF STEEL
Like most Chinese people of his time, Mao didn't know much about science or technology. He consulted his advisers, and one of them came up with a brilliant idea. They would build small blast furnaces in every village. The peasants could convert their iron plows and sickles into high-quality steel that could be used to build warships, bridges, and factories, and China would enter the 20th century. Within 15 years, Mao foresaw, Chinese steel production would equal that of the United States.

MAJOR MELTDOWN
The peasants didn't know much about science and technology either, but they did what they were told. Soon enough every village square had a tall, conical "blast furnace." Tons of precious fuel were used up to melt good tools into useless black lumps of slag. But excitement was running high.

THE CHAIRMAN DROPS IN
Chairman Mao spent most of his time at his luxury villa, reading in bed or lounging by his swimming pool. But every now and then he would go by special train to inspect the progress of the steel production at some provincial village. No one wanted to tell him that his great plan wasn't working, so they sent another train on ahead, loaded with imported steel girders. They'd stack the girders up in the village square before the chairman arrived and tell all the villagers to pose proudly beside the pile. Mao was delighted at

---

Darius I of Persia connected the Nile to the Red Sea with a canal.

the progress his country was making. He'd take a quick look around, congratulate everyone on how well it was going, and get back on his train.

THE RESULTS
When harvest time came around, all the tools had been melted down, and the best the Chinese could do in the time they had left over from steel production duty was to try pulling the plants up with their hands. Most of the crops rotted in the fields, thus beginning a famine that lasted until 1960 and killed an estimated 30 million people.

NOT AS DUMB AS HE LOOKS
Mao eventually realized that there was no steel. Now there was no food and no agricultural tools either. Communist China, which had been making fair progress since the revolution in 1949, went into a sudden decline. The Great Leap Forward brought China's economic development to a standstill for another 15 years.

*   *   *

Chinese Technology
However, among other things the Chinese invented:
Gunpowder and guns
Magnetic compass
Printing
Earthquake detector
Fan
Fireworks
Football
Harnessing animals
Kites
World's first robot
Wheelbarrow
Cast-iron ploughs
Spaghetti
Rudder

A ziggurat tower called Etemenanki may have inspired the Tower of Babel story.

THE REAL LEGACY OF CHRISTOPHER COLUMBUS

*Don't read this if you want to go on thinking of
Columbus as some big hero.*

Christopher Columbus's real legacy isn't Columbus Day. It isn't even the wonderful city of Columbus, Ohio. No. In discovering a New World, Christopher Columbus sounded the death knell for an old one. Here's what they left out of those elementary school history lessons.

OLD WORLD MEETS NEW

The Arawak people of the Bahama Islands were minding their own business on October 12, 1492, when a big strange-looking boat approached one of their idyllic beaches. The men who got off the boat were impressive: They looked like gods with their shiny metal clothing and white skins. And even though the leader spoke harshly and pulled out a dangerous-looking long metal thing, the Arawak went out of their way to treat their visitors with kindness.

They presented the strangers with parrots, balls of cotton, spears, and lots of other expressions of good will. Their captain, Christopher Columbus, was quick to take note of this extraordinary kindness. After recording in his log how generous the natives were, he went on to say, "With 50 men we could subjugate them all and make them do whatever we want."

MAN WITH A MISSION

Columbus was looking for gold. So when he noticed that most of the natives wore tiny gold ornaments in their ears, he took some of them by force (the natives, not the ornaments) and brought them to his ship. He demanded to be led to the gold. The Arawak led him to Hispaniola, where he left 39 crew members who were supposed find the gold. Then he took more Indian prisoners and returned to Spain to report to Ferdinand and Isabella that he had reached Asia (what a dummy) where he'd found "great mines of gold and other metals."

To free their emperor, the Incas filled a 23 x 16 room with nine feet of gold.

WRONG, WRONG, WRONG

He was wrong, of course, on all counts. But his report was encouraging enough to get a second expedition underway–this time with 17 ships and more than 1,200 men. The avowed intention of this voyage was to get as many slaves and as much gold as humanly possible.

SERVES THEM RIGHT

On reaching Hispaniola, Columbus learned that his 39 crewmen had been killed by the natives after taking women and children as slaves for sex and labor. Columbus was further incensed when he found that there was very little gold here. Knowing that he had to show some dividend for the expensive expedition, he sent his men out on successive waves of slave raids. Five hundred natives were carried back to Spain; 200 died en route.

OOH, HE'S A TOUGHIE

But Columbus was still intent on finding that gold. He had to repay his investors. He returned to South America and, on the island of Haiti, ordered all persons 14 years of age or older to collect a minimum quantity of gold every three months. Those who failed had their hands cut off and bled to death. This, despite the fact that the only gold around was in the form of dust on the edges of streams.

I'LL TAKE CASSAVA

The natives who tried to escape were hunted down with dogs and killed. Mass suicides took place across the islands; hundreds of natives took cassava poison rather than fall into Spanish hands (or in Columbus's case, Italian). The Arawak, who Columbus had first encountered, killed their infants to spare them from the inhumanity of the Spaniards.

GOODBYE, OLD WORLD

In unwittingly discovering a New World, Columbus thus also sealed the fate of an old one. For thousands of years the natives of the Americas had lived in relative peace and harmony. The real legacy of Christopher Columbus is that he sounded the death knell for that way of life.

TIE ONE ON

Codpieces and drawstring pants come and go, but over the centuries, the necktie and its antecedents persist, hanging about a man's neck like a noose done in a four-in-hand.

The necktie has never been anything but a pointless strip of cloth, born to dangle and sway and wait for a use. Yank on one, you half expect a ticket to issue forth from the mouth of the wearer.

VANITY, THY NAME IS LOUIS

In fact, ties can be traced back, like so many pointless things, to the idle vanity of a king. And in this case, the king who knew more about idle vanity than any before or since: Louis XIV, the Sun King. Seems in 1660, Louis was reviewing a regiment of bad-ass Croat soldiers, who wore brightly colored silk handkerchiefs around their necks. Why? Who knows? Maybe the Croats were worried they'd get separated at court and needed some conspicuous item of clothing to find each other later, like wayward second-graders on a field trip. Whatever the reason, Louis saw the regiment and their handkerchiefs, and just had to have one: a regiment of bad-asses, that is, not a handkerchief. He already had some of those.

THE KING'S REGIMENT

So he got one, because who was going to tell Louis no, and he called them the "Royal Cravattes" ("cravatte" derived from "Croat" in French) and gave them fancy handkerchiefs for their necks. That was that. The king had spoken. Everyone started wearing ties. If it happened today, the bad-ass Croats could probably sue for copyright infringement. But this was the 17th century. What were you gonna do!

CARRIED TO EXTREMES

Men got stupid with the cravats. By the early 1800s, cravats were stuffed around the neck as if the head were being surrounded by tissue for transport in a box. Some guys couldn't move their necks at all; like whiplash victims or HR Pufnstuf, they had to rotate their whole bodies to look around. And some of these boys wore

---

The St. Nicholas on whom Santa Claus is based was from modern-day Turkey.

two cravats at the same time; one imagines they needed servants and a system of mirrors so they could navigate the street. There were a hundred different ways to tie a cravat, some of which could take hours. Perhaps for this reason, fiddling with someone's cravat was a dueling offense.

EVEN TIES CAN BE FASHION VICTIMS
The best you can say about today's iteration of the necktie is that at least it's not aggressively stupid. One does not wear it wrapped around one's jaw, or more than one at a time. Even the horrifyingly wide ties in the '70s had a rational basis for their lateral expansion—they were merely keeping pace with the expanding lapels of the time. Mocking a '70s tie is purely a case of blaming the victim. They didn't want to go wide. They had no choice.

YES, BUT WHAT DOES IT DO?
Be that as it may, it still doesn't take away from the fact that the tie does not now serve, nor has it ever served, any useful purpose. At least bell-bottoms and Nehru jackets kept your extremities warm. Tie manufacturers would dispute this assessment of their products' usefulness, of course. No industry can be trusted to be an objective observer of its product's place in the universe—particularly one that has a literal chokehold on men's fashion.

LIFE AND DEATH SITUATIONS
Men simply do not realize that the tie is there at all their major life events. It's there when you graduate from high school and college. It's there at your wedding. It's there at your children's baptisms and bar mitzvahs. And when you die, they stick one on you and, like a pharaoh taking a prized but aggravating cat into the next world, you are both stuffed into the ground together. The only reason men aren't born with ties is the grudging acknowledgment by the tie industry that looping the umbilicus into a Windsor knot around the neck of a fetus might cause brain damage. Which would limit tie purchases later in life.

THE LOYAL OPPOSITION SPEAKS
Tie enthusiasts, the Quislings of men's attire, point out that ties allow for some individuality in an otherwise regimented world of men's business attire. But really, now. It's not individuality ties provide, it's the illusion thereof, and a poor one at that.

The 1898 book *Futility* eerily presaged the 1912 sinking of the Titanic.

AND IS SHUT UP

Wear your Jerry Garcia tie all you want, you still have to file the same reports as Ted, three cubicles down, wearing his $6 polyester blend from Sears. A tie with Edvard Munch's *The Scream* silk-screened upon its narrow width will not stop you from your dark suspicions that The New Guy makes twice what you do, with half the experience.

And anyway, you wouldn't wear a single one of those ties to a performance review, so what does that say. Tie enthusiasts also point out that ties accentuate a man's verticality. Well, if you want to accentuate your verticality, go on a freakin' diet, already.

A RAY OF HOPE

Men wear ties, because so far as they know, men have always worn ties; it's what men do. If they knew that the tie got started as the passing fancy of the foppiest of the Great Kings of Europe, it probably wouldn't change a thing; the dress code is always dictated from above. Will they ever stop wearing them? Probably not. The best we can hope for is that ties don't start hampering neck movement again, and that if they do, we can somehow take out those tie wearers before they infect the rest of us. Their peripheral vision would be shot, you know. They would never see it coming.

*   *   *

Codpieces

The codpiece could be equated with the padded bra, what you see is not what you get. It started innocently enough…The codpiece began as a flat piece of material to cover the slit in men's trousers and, therefore, the genitals. As jackets got shorter, the focus on the area between a man's legs grew. Now additional protection was required to protect the "unmentionables." The codpiece grew to do double-duty as a place for men to store "other" valuables. Once breeches became wider, the need for codpieces decreased. The extra "room" in trousers developed into pockets. Although codpieces were no longer a fashion statement, men still needed a place for their valuables. Pockets met this need.

Confucius was appointed Minister of Crime and wiped out crime in the Lu Province.

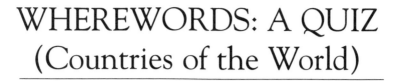

WHEREWORDS: A QUIZ
(Countries of the World)

Everybody comes from somewhere, but how did these somewheres get their names? Choose the explanation you like best, then check it with the correct answer on the next page.

1. THE PHILIPPINES:
a. Tagalog word "filip'pi," for "erupting volcanoes."
b. Magellan named in honor of King Philip II of Spain in 1542.
c. The New Testament book of the Bible, Philippians.

2. BOLIVIA:
a. South American revolutionary leader, Simon Bolivar.
b. Bolvana, mythical Inca paradise.
c. Spanish "bolina" for "shining" and "via" meaning "way."

3. INDIA:
a. The word "indian," for the country's highest caste or class.
b. Feminine form of "Indio," one of the twin gods of fertility.
c. The Indus River, from the Sanskrit "sindhuh," for "river."

4. ARGENTINA:
a. "The Argenis," a poem by Brazilian poet Gabriel Marquez.
b. The Latin word "argentum," meaning "silver."
c. Spanish explorer Juan Argento, who died a hero there

5. PORTUGAL:
a. Latin "portus cale"; it was a Roman "port."
b. Considered the front "porch" to the "house" of Spain.
c. Legendary Spanish chieftain P'Ortuga whose troops rid Lisbon of the Huns.

6. CHINA:
a. Genghis Khan named it for his wife "Ka'china."
b. The Chin (Qin) dynasty that unified China.
c. From Persian word "chini," for the "porcelain" made there.

7. FRANCE
a. The early German invaders, the Franks.
b. Its earliest ruler, Emperor Francis I.
c. Named for Pope Franciscus.

8. AMERICA:
a. From Latin "americ" for "abundant."
b. "Mer ika," the Algonquian name for "tall boat."
c. Named after early Italian navigator Amerigo Vespucci.

There was a New Australia in Paraguay in the 1890s.

1-b. Magellan named the Philippines for the king of Spain. The 7,100 islands comprising the Malay Archipelago were Spanish colonies from 1521 to 1898.

2-a. The popular Venezuelan-born soldier and statesman known as "the Liberator" led Peruvian nationals in their fight for independence in the 18th century.

3-c. Some of the earliest humans on planet Earth lived along the banks of the Indus River in northwest India.

4-b. The Spanish claimed the region in the 1500s and named it, in Latin, for the tons of silver that washed out of underground deposits and were carried downstream by the Silver River ("Rio Plata" in Spanish).

5-a. Romans conquered the native Celts here around 200 B.C. The name stuck.

6-b. The Chin (Qin) dynasty ruled China from about 221 to 205 B.C. The name stuck.

7-a. Gaul was part of the Roman Empire (they called it "Gallia,") when the Germanic tribe, the Franks, conquered the area in 486.

8-c. A German cartographer, Martin Waldseemuller, who literally put America on the map, named the area for Vespucci, who argued that—despite what everyone else thought at the time—the American continent was not part of the Indies. Way to go, Amerigo!

*   *   *

"The history of every country begins
in the heart of a man or a woman."

O Pioneers! by Willa Cather

"National injustice is the surest road to national downfall."
William Gladstone

The Carib Indians, for whom the Caribbean is named, now survive mostly in Dominica.

MOST LOPSIDED WAR: THE SPANISH-AMERICAN WAR

Hey, they started it.

Actually, they did. A little-known fact about the Spanish-American War (as if any fact involving this war is perennially on the lips of Americans) is that Spain declared war on the United States first, on April 24, 1898. The United States, furious at being caught napping on this issue, declared war the very next day—and then backdated the declaration to April 21. Take that, you lousy Spaniards!

ADIOS, ARMADA!

This Battle of the Declarations was, alas for our sadly incompetent Iberian antagonists, the very last thing that the Spaniards won. A week later, George Dewey and a fleet of American battleships steamed into Manila's harbor and sank the entire Spanish Pacific fleet like they were shooting fish in a barrel. Which, considering the Spanish fleet was anchored and silent, was exactly what they were doing.

BULLY FOR YOU, T.R.!

A couple of months after that, Americans landed in Cuba. Teddy Roosevelt had resigned as Secretary of the Navy to lead his "Rough Riders" into battle—proof that downward mobility isn't always a bad thing for one's career. The Rough Riders forced the Spanish fleet into a retreat that found it beached and burning up and down the Cuban shore line. The whole war took less than four months, and at the end of it, America got Guam and Puerto Rico for free, and bought the Philippines at a cut-rate price. Oh, and in all the hubbub, we somehow managed to annex Hawaii. Apparently, some folks there are still sore about that.

YOU BIG BULLIES!

Spain never had a chance. Oh, sure, Spain could kick around Cuba, whose bid for independence, and Spain's brutal repression

---

The Parthenon was nearly destroyed in 1687, when it was used to store gunpowder.

thereof, had started this whole sorry shebang. But like the third-grade bully who terrorizes the kindergartners but cowers under the pummeling fists of the sixth-grade bully, Spain got spanked by superior firepower—and a country that was itchin' to use it. Yet another little-known fact about this war was that for years, the United States had a contingency plan to kick Spanish butt up and down the entire Western Hemisphere. It was called the "Kimball Plan"—the national equivalent of the sixth-grader waiting for that third-grader to rough up a younger kid, so he'd have a legitimate excuse to beat him up and take his lunch money.

WHY IT WAS THE BEST

The Spanish-American War was America's debut out of the ranks of the second-raters. All our other wars up to that point (those couple of wars with Britain, that nasty intramural squabble between the states) had been fairly even slug-fests. Even that war with Mexico wasn't entirely a blowout, although giving up two-thirds of their territory had to hurt 'em.

The Spanish-American War, by contrast, was a slam dunk. We lost more people fighting the Filipinos, who apparently didn't much cotton to the Americans buying their country for a lousy $20 million, than we did fighting the Spanish. (What? You don't remember the Phillipine-American War, which lasted three years and cost 4,200 American lives? Funny about that.)

Since 1898, we've participated in other lopsided wars, of course, most recently that one in the Persian Gulf, where the casualty ratio between Them and Us was something on the order of 100 to 1. But in those wars, we had help, and we didn't come away with any real estate to speak of—real estate being, of course, the gold standard in war gains.

*   *   *

"To fight and conquer in all our battles is not supreme excellence;
supreme excellence consists in breaking
the enemy's resistance without fighting."
The Art of War by Sun-Tzu

Now an art gallery, the Louvre used to be a royal palace.

THE CRUSADER FOLLIES

*After capturing Jerusalem at the end of the First Crusade
(1096–1099), the question became how long the new
Christian Kingdom of Jerusalem would last.*

While the leaders of the First Crusade were back in
Europe triumphantly showing off their captured religious relics, the Muslims in the Holy Land were
winning battles and slowly taking their lands back from the
crusaders who'd been left behind. The crusaders still held
Jerusalem, but the loss of other lands was beginning to cause serious concern.

ST. BERNARD TO THE RESCUE
In response, a Second Crusade was organized in 1147, inspired by
the preaching of the silver-tongued St. Bernard of Clairvaux, the
leading figure in the western Church (but not the St. Bernard the
dog is named for).

So with high hopes for a great, glorious victory over the
Muslims (also called Saracens), King Louis VII of France (with a
force of 15,000 men) and King Conrad III of Germany (20,000
men) set out for the Holy Land. Both were crackerjack administrators, but unfortunately, they had very little idea what they were
doing when it came to running military campaigns in foreign
lands. (Uh-oh.)

EASY PICKIN'S FOR THE GERMANS
The French took a leisurely pace, so the Germans were the first to
arrive in the Constantinople metropolitan area where they took
what they wanted from the locals, their fellow (though Greek
Orthodox) Christians, without paying. Whole villages packed up
their possessions and moved out of the way of Conrad's army
rather than risk losing everything.

CONRAD THE CLUELESS
By the time Louis and his slowpokes reached Constantinople, the
Germans had already crossed the Bosphorus strait into Asia
Minor. The Byzantine Emperor Manuel had advised Conrad to
hug the coast, so the Byzantine fleet could provide them with

---

The Three Magi are said to be interred in a cathedral in Cologne, Germany.

supplies as they marched. But the emperor's advice was ignored. Instead, Conrad decided to take his army right through the heart of Asia Minor—home turf for the Turks. He couldn't possibly have made a worse choice.

EASY PICKIN'S FOR THE TURKS

Constantly harassed by Turks, hungry, exhausted, and very thirsty, Conrad's men finally found a small stream that must have looked like an oasis. Actually, it was more like a trap. Without any semblance of discipline, the Germans broke ranks and ran toward the stream. Waiting for them there was a large Turkish force who knew a good opportunity when Allah presented it to them. They swarmed all over the hapless Germans who, in their disorganized state, never really stood a chance. Conrad's army was cut to pieces, nine out of every ten men lost. Conrad himself barely managed to escape with his life.

CRUSADING ISN'T EASY

King Louis, along with the pathetic remnants of the German force, took Emperor Manuel's advice and wisely stuck to the coast of Asia Minor as he marched south toward Palestine. Still, his army had to endure the hardships of a rugged mountain crossing and repeated attacks by the Turks. By the time the crusaders reached Antioch—which, like Jerusalem, was still in Christian hands—their numbers had been cut in half.

I'LL TAKE DAMASCUS

They set off for Damascus in July of 1148. The leaders of the Crusade—which now included Louis, Conrad, and the ruler of the Christian-held sections of Palestine, King Baldwin III—decided to attack the city from the west. The orchards to the west of the city, where the crusaders made their camp, would supply them with plenty of timber, food, and water and would be a good position from which to launch an assault.

MILITARY INTELLIGENCE

They were doing just great—the fall of Damascus was imminent—until they made a huge strategic blunder (yes, another one). They'd received reports that the eastern wall of the city was less fortified and they knew that a large Muslim relief force was on the way, so they decided to shift camp to the eastern side of Damascus.

Hey, Indiana Jones! Many believe that the real Ark of the Covenant is in Ethiopia.

They now found themselves sitting on an exposed site with no water and little food. And it turned out that the intelligence they'd received was untrue.

So the Muslims quickly took advantage of the crusaders' tactical blunder by occupying the western side of the city. This, of course, made it impossible for the crusaders to return to their original location. They'd managed to place themselves in a position from which they could only withdraw, which is exactly what they did.

LOSERS

The crusaders' siege of Damascus, which had lasted all of four days, had come to a very abrupt end. In the face of this huge failure, their only real choice was to call it quits and return home, shame-faced and empty-handed. Of the 35,000 men who'd begun the Second Crusade, only a fraction made it back home. In contrast to the First Crusade, which had never lost its focus on the ultimate goal of taking Jerusalem from the Muslims, the Second Crusade had repeatedly taken its eye off the ball. The resources put into the Second Crusade were huge. The return on the investment was zero.

* * *

THE END IS NEAR!

Late in the year A.D. 999, as the hours ticked down toward the new year of 1000, people throughout Europe held their collective breath. What would the new year and millennium bring? Many believed it would herald the Last Judgment and the End of the World, and pilgrims converged on Jerusalem where they thought the final battle between good and evil would take place.

Some of those pilgrims were thrown to their knees in mid-journey by a thunderstorm. They recorded the event for posterity, believing the thunder to be the voice of God announcing the Day of Judgment.

Meanwhile, in September 999, a meteor appeared in the skies above England, shining with a light so brilliant it turned night into day. This caused a lot of doubters to quit the nonbelievers' team and start playing for the other side.

At least nobody had to worry about their computer crashing!

Of the 22 people at the opening of King Tut's sarcophagus, 21 were alive 10 years later.

COFFEE KLATCH

It's 6:00 a.m. and as you crawl out of bed, bleary-eyed, the most press-
ing question in your mind is: where did my morning java come from?
Okay maybe not. But we're going to tell you anyway.

A long time ago—way before Starbucks—people told each other these legends about the origins of coffee.

Story #1: According to an ancient Ethiopian legend, a goat herder named Kaldi discovered coffee while in the pasture with his animals. When he saw that his goats were acting frisky after eating berries from a certain tree, he decided to experiment on himself. Kaldi enjoyed the effect so much that he told the local monastery about it. The abbot who ran the place thought the "magic berries" were a work of the devil and threw them into the fire. The burning beans caused such a lovely aroma that the monks rescued them from the flames. The monks began to use the beans in religious ceremonies and for medicinal purposes.

Story #2: The Arabian legend is very much like the Ethiopian, except, of course, in this story Kaldi is an Arab instead of an African. It features the same frisky berry-eating goats, and Kaldi trying some, too. But in this story, a tired and hungry learned man named Aucuba just happened to be passing by and saw Kaldi and his goats jumping around. Since he was hungry, he ate the berries and—miraculously—wasn't tired any more. Aucuba was so impressed that he took some of the berries, sold them, and became a rich man. No one knows what happened to poor Kaldi who, we guess, didn't have any of that entrepreneurial spirit.

JOE IS BORN
The earliest written record of coffee was in around A.D. 900 by an Arab physician-philosopher named Rhazes. Rhazes thought that coffee (which he called "bunchum") contained a substance that could cure disease. But you didn't drink it—the berries were dried, crushed, and mixed with fat to form a ball that was eaten.

FOR MEDICINAL PURPOSES ONLY
So coffee was originally used by the "general public" as medicine. Only religious Muslims used the bean in a beverage. But by the

13th century, Arabian coffee houses (called "qahveh khanehs") served it as a drink to anyone who had the money to pay for it. A lot of Muslims were so upset at the public use of this "holy beverage" that they threatened death to anyone who frequented these dens of sin. But you know what it's like when you gotta have that cuppa java. It didn't keep the café crowd away. And those coffee fans must have (excuse the pun) spilled the beans, because the word about coffee started to spread.

THE TRAIL OF COFFEE

Europe: European travelers brought back the news of an unusual black beverage called "qahveh." (Get it? Coffee.) By 1615 Italy was importing it. Its debut caused a commotion among the Italian clergy who thought it was the "bitter invention of Satan." (What is with these religious guys?) Pope Clement VIII eventually gave his papal approval. Over the next 80 years, coffee drinking and coffeehouses spread from Italy to other parts of Europe. In 1690 the Dutch managed to smuggle a few plants to the Netherlands where the first European coffee cultivation began. Thus ended the Arabian monopoly on the coffee trade.

The New World: In 1723 a sneaky son-of-a-gun named Gabriel Mathieu de Clieu stole a coffee plant from the Jardin des Plantes, a botanical garden in Paris, with the intention of bringing coffee to America. Historic records say that on the voyage he encountered violent storms, pirate attacks, and a severe water shortage on board. It is almost a miracle that he and his treasured plant survived the voyage. It was from this one plant that the growth of coffee spread through the New World.

Brazil: Coffee finally made its way to Brazil in 1727. Francisco de Melo Palheta, a Brazilian army lieutenant, was sent by his country to arbitrate a boundary dispute between French and Dutch Guiana. Both countries were cultivating coffee (progenies of de Clieu's stolen coffee plant), but they weren't allowing the export of seeds or seedlings. Palheta wanted his country to be part of the lucrative coffee trade, so he endeared himself to the wife of the governor of French Guiana. She was so impressed with how he handled the arbitration that on his departure she presented him with a bouquet. Hidden in the bouquet were coffee seeds and cuttings. Palheta brought them to Brazil, where they flourished, beginning the now well-known Brazilian coffee industry.

To prevent warfare with rivals, Ottoman sultans had the right to kill their brothers.

THE AMBLING ROOM

The search for World War II's greatest treasure is still going strong.

It's been called the largest piece of jewelry ever created. Some experts estimate its worth at over $100 million; others say it's priceless. Fortune hunters have looked for it at the bottom of the Baltic Sea, in a Lithuanian lagoon, buried in a silver mine, and in the treacherous world of art thieves. Forget about diamonds and gold! The hunt for World War II's most compelling treasure centers on tree sap! Even though scholars insist it was destroyed, pieces of the amber room have recently come into the hands of the cops. Funny. You'd think it wouldn't be so hard to find a room.

ARE YOU LISTENING, MARTHA STEWART?

The treasure was created at the beginning of the 18th century when the king of Prussia, Frederick I, and his architect came up with a novel form of interior decoration. They decided to have Frederick's study in Berlin's Royal Palace paneled in amber.

Amber, the petrified resin of ancient trees, has always been popular. Ancient Egyptians wore it; decadent Romans gambled with amber dice; and wealthy Europeans in Frederick's day wore amber jewelry and ate off amber bowls and plates. But an entire room of amber—that was an historic first.

WE MEAN FOREVER

The project took years to complete. The finest craftsmen in Europe engraved the amber and pieced together intricate mosaics to make four panels that lined Frederick's study. By 1713 Frederick owned the most magnificent amber creation the world had ever seen. Unfortunately, he didn't have a lot of time to enjoy it; he died the same year. The next king, Fredrick Wilhelm I, was nick-named the "Soldier King." And you know those military men: they don't have much use for art treasures. So when Russian Czar Peter the Great came to Berlin in 1716 and admired the Amber Room, the new king had it dismantled and gave it to him.

PETER THE PROCRASTINATOR

Peter had about as much use for it as Frederick Wilhelm I: he put the room in storage, and there it stayed until Peter's daughter,

---

Hemorrhoids may have cost Napoleon victory at Waterloo. He couldn't ride his horse.

Elizabeth, ascended to the throne in 1741. The czarina was a woman of art and fashion; she saw the Amber Room as a fixer-upper with literally tons of potential. She installed it in the Catherine Palace in the town of Pushkin, and set her favorite architect, Bartolomeo Francesco Rastrelli, to work.

GOING FOR BAROQUE

The new Amber Room was a dazzler: gilt everywhere, wall mirrors, chandeliers, the whole bit. The room in the Catherine Palace was a larger space than Frederick's original study, so additional jewel-encrusted panels were added. These included four Florentine mosaic scenes fashioned from gems like jasper, marble, jade, onyx, and quartz. Remember these mosaics; they'll be turning up later under very suspicious circumstances. Also among the furnishings were display cases containing precious amber objects like chess sets, candlesticks, and jewel boxes, but it was the chamber itself that knocked the guests' silk leggings off. A British ambassador called it the eighth wonder of the world.

BARBARIANS AT THE GATE

By the beginning of World War II, the Amber Room had been the pride of the Catherine Palace for almost 200 years. It had been restored periodically because of damage from sudden temperature changes. Anyway, for some reason—either the fragility of the amber or the speed at which the Germans were advancing—in 1941, the Soviet government evacuated the Amber Room's contents to a hiding place in Siberia, but left the panels. Workers camouflaged the walls with layers of paper, cotton, and gauze.

The Germans knew what they were looking for. Paper, cotton, and gauze didn't fool them; Hitler wanted the Amber Room "returned to its homeland." Soon after the Wehrmacht tanks rolled into Pushkin, German art experts arrived at the palace. They took the panels with them. The panels next showed up at a castle in Königsberg, East Prussia. Within four years the Soviets advanced on Königsberg, and it was the Germans' turn to play "hide the Amber Room." If they did stash it, no one ever found it: the Amber Room was never seen again.

In 1659, England fined people five shillings if they were caught celebrating Christmas.

THE MULTIMILLION DOLLAR QUESTION

The fate of the Amber Room remains a question. Is it at the bottom of the Baltic Sea? Or in a lagoon? Was it buried in a silver mine? Has it fallen into the hands of art thieves? Or did it simply go up in smoke? The conflicting scenarios all have supporting evidence and eyewitness testimonials. Some Amber Room hunters think that when enemy troops surrounded Königsberg, the Germans evacuated the treasure by sea. Support for this scenario comes from witnesses who, in early 1945, saw suspicious crates being loaded onto the steamer, the *Wilhelm Gustloff*. The ship was sunk by a Russian submarine, so the *Gustloff* (and perhaps the Amber Room) lies on the bottom of the Baltic Sea. Other water-oriented hunters say the treasure isn't far from Königsberg. Locals near the Lithuanian town of Neringa witnessed some SS soldiers hiding a number of crates on the Baltic shore. The water level rose and the crates (perhaps filled with amber) now lie at the bottom of a murky lagoon.

SHIPMENT TO NOWHERE

Other hunters found clues that led underground. Erich Koch, the Nazi official in charge of East Prussia, had a great interest in the Amber Room and may have sent it to his hometown of Weimar, Germany. Evidence shows that the art-loving Nazi sent over half of Königsberg's many looted artworks home to Weimar. Some believe that, in Weimar, the art treasures were loaded into phony Red Cross trucks, then hidden in mines or bunkers. After the Allies imprisoned Koch, witnesses quoted him as saying, "where lies my treasures also lies the Amber Room." He died in 1986, so he isn't saying anything else—about anything.

DRILLING FOR AMBER

Another clue is a Nazi document ordering the Amber Room sent to Saxony, Germany. In December 2000, German and Czech search teams were separately tunneling into opposite ends of the old, caved-in Nicolai Stollen silver mine that lies under Saxony and crosses the border under the Czech Republic. Each competing team followed different advice given by SS informants as well as local witnesses who recalled seeing the SS at the mine in 1945. The two teams are still at it.

When Dickens visited the U.S. Senate, he was appalled to see the senators spitting tobacco.

DUMMKOPFS!

Some art historians think the raiders of the Amber Room are wasting their time. They say no one will find the treasure because it's destroyed, kaput! Amber burns at 300° F, so when the Allied bombs devastated Königsberg, they set fire to the amber panels.

A KNICK HERE, A KNACK THERE

Remember those four Florentine mosaics that were made for the Catherine Palace and then hidden in Siberia in 1941? German police confiscated one of them in Bremen, Germany, in the mid-1990s. A pensioner was selling it for over $2 million; he'd inherited the panel from his father who'd served in Hitler's Wehrmacht. Experts believe the mosaic was stolen before 1944, but the fuss led a housewife to wonder if an amber chest she bought in East Germany also belonged to the Amber Room. Old photos revealed that it did. Around the same time, Christie's auction house sold off a soldier's head made of amber and believed to be from the Amber Room. So Fred and Elizabeth's stuff is back on the market.

LET'S CALL IT "CATHY'S PALACE"

Meanwhile, back at the Catherine Palace, craftsmen are re-creating the Amber Room. Nearly 300 years after Frederick Wilhelm I's gesture of goodwill and good riddance, Germany and Russia are together again, this time to create another masterpiece. The new Amber Room is set to open in 2003, and if they handle the publicity right, the joint may soon be jumpin' with Bermuda-shorted tourists from all over the world.

* * *

"The bee enclosed and through the amber shown,
Seems buried in the juice which was his own."
Martial

"I saw a flie within a beade
Of amber cleanly buried."
Robert Herrick

"Pretty! in amber to observe the forms
Of hairs, or straws, or dirt, or grubs, or worms."
Alexander Pope

Before it realized he was a Marxist, Wall Street gave Fidel Castro a ticker tape parade.

8½ NOT-SO-VICTORIAN THINGS ABOUT QUEEN VICTORIA

Since she's become the symbol of stuffy propriety,
people have forgotten that Queen Vicky was kicky.

1. SHE HAD A THING FOR AN OLDER MAN

Victoria's father died soon after she was born, leaving her in search of father figures. In 1837, when she became Queen, Victoria developed a crush on the prime minister, handsome, 58-year-old Lord Melbourne. She decided that to get up to speed as queen, she'd need him to advise her at least 6 hours a day. One contemporary observed that Victoria's attraction was "sexual, though she does not know it." The young Queen was devastated when Melbourne's government fell, forcing her to deal with a new (and presumably less debonair) prime minister.

2. SHE FOUND "FUN IN BED"

So much fun that portions of Vicky's diary concerning beddy-byes with her hubby, Prince Albert, had to be destroyed after her death. She described her wedding night as "most gratifying and bewildering" (to Lord Melbourne, of all people). When her doctor mentioned birth control after her ninth child was born, she responded, "Oh, Sir James, am I to have no more fun in bed?"

3. SHE WAS A LOUSY PARENT

The one thing Victoria disliked about sex was that it led to babies, whom she once called "nasty objects." The busy Queen and her husband farmed the kids out to wet-nurses and nursemaids. The children continued to be bothersome even when they were grown up; they had to be married off and supported with money begged from Parliament. Albert thought that a few should be dumped on the unsuspecting colonies.

4. HER SUBJECTS WANTED TO KILL HER

Well, quite a few of them, anyway. A few months after her marriage, Victoria became target practice while out in her carriage

---

To ensure an heir, Henry VIII had six wives. But he still ended up with no grandkids.

with Albert. Fortunately the assailant missed, but he wasn't the last to try. Among Vicky's more colorful assassins was a crazed midget who took a shot with a gun that was loaded with tobacco. A would-be assassin shot at Vicky in the train at Windsor station and was pummeled by schoolboys from Eton. And a former soldier varied the routine by hitting Victoria over the head with a brass-knobbed cane.

5. SHE WAS A STALKING VICTIM
Victoria had a royally obsessed stalker, "The Boy Jones," as he was known in the tabloids. Young Edward Jones first broke into Buckingham Palace when he was 15, spending three days skulking about, pilfering from the Royal Kitchen and reading Victoria's letters. A skillful lawyer got him off with a promise never to do it again. But after two years of good behavior, he was caught lurking under Victoria's couch. Altogether, Jones broke into the royal quarters five times. Increasingly harsh sentences didn't stop him until they finally sent him off to sea. Except for one brief desertion, Jones wasn't heard of again.

6. VICKY WAS KICKY
True, she got a bit stuffy after her beloved Albert died in 1861. But in her earlier years, Queen Victoria gambled, drank and once got so excited at a horse race that she broke a window in the Royal Box. As a single Queen, she stayed up later and later until dinner was being served at one in the morning.

7. HER STIFF UPPER LIP QUIVERED
When poor, devoted Albert pushed off at only 42, Victoria went a bit odd. A certain amount of hysterical grief was natural, but the Queen wore black for the rest of her life, made a cult of his memory, and kept his rooms exactly as they had been when he died. She even had the bed linen changed regularly and his nightshirt put out every evening. What bothered her subjects most was her avoidance of public appearances. Even when her oldest son, Bertie, was married she arrived late, watched from behind a screen in a private stall and cleared, out once the ceremony was over.

Until 1399, the first language of English kings was French.

8. SHE CARRIED ON WITH HER SERVANT AND ALMOST LOST THE THRONE

While Victoria hid out, her more cynical subjects assumed she was doing the fling with her Scottish servant, John Brown. The Queen loved her Scottish retreat of Balmoral where she and the kilted Brown tramped through the heather. (But was she a tramp?) Brown did sleep in the chamber next to Victoria, and she ran her household as Brown saw fit. He told her family and advisers to buzz off. Some began referring to the Queen as "Mrs. Brown." Anti-monarchy feelings grew, and the public soon saw Brown as Rasputin with a brogue. When the Queen traveled to Switzerland in 1868, rumors spread that she had secretly given birth to Brown's child—a pretty amazing feat, since she was 50. The public turned sympathetic again when the Queen and Bertie each became ill, and Brown became a hero when he foiled assassination attempts on his queen. After Brown died, suspicious historians noticed that she had his diary destroyed.

8 1/2. HER NAME IS A BYWORD FOR EROTICISM

By the time she died in 1901, she'd been around so long that everyone thought Victoria was wonderful, and wonderfully proper. So why is it that the most common name in the history of Playboy Playmates is Victoria—more popular than Cindy, Jenny, or Kim?

* * *

VICTORIAN WEDDING SUPERSTITIONS

A Victorian rhyme said that a bride must wear, "something old, something new, something borrowed, something blue, and a silver sixpence in your shoe." "Something blue" went back to Biblical times, when Israeli brides wore blue ribbons to show their fidelity. The purpose of "something old" and "something borrowed" was to get good luck from articles belonging to a happily married woman. "Something new" referred to the belief that a new gown was lucky. A "silver sixpence" in her shoe brought the bride a wealth of love and happiness. The Victorian bride had one choice for her dress: "Marry in white, choose right." Once dressed, she had to avoid looking in a mirror as she went out the front door (never the back!) starting with her right foot. On her way to the ceremony, the bride tried to meet a chimney sweep (which meant happiness) and not a funeral procession (which meant doom).

In the 1920s, Canada's Director of Military Operations had a plan to invade the U.S.

CAROUSING CHARISMA

The Intoxicating Life and Times of Sir John Eh?

While other countries have heroic founders such as George Washington, King Arthur, or Simon Bolivar, Canadians have the brilliant but all-too-human Sir John A. Macdonald who enjoyed much of life through an alcoholic haze—then wound up supporting the temperance movement.

THE TEEN-AGED LAWYER
Born in Glasgow, Scotland, in 1820, John Macdonald arrived in Kingston, Ontario (then known as Upper Canada) with his family when he was five. The future Sir John practiced law at only 17, supporting his mother and sisters when his father died. The young lawyer had wit, a good grasp of psychology, and an encyclopedic memory.

FROM COLONIES TO CANADA
John went into politics, and soon had the goal of uniting the British North American colonies into a new country. The fact that the inhabitants of Upper Canada were soured on Lower Canada, and Lower Canada returned the favor, didn't faze him. On Canada's official start date, July 1, 1867, Macdonald became Canada's first prime minister and, with a few interruptions, stayed in charge until his death in 1891.

THE FLAWED FOUNDER
Sir John was no saint. His regime was often marked by scandal and he spent a good part of his career in the pocket of big railway interests. Despite his flaws, Sir John Eh? (pronounced long a), as he's affectionately known, is still beloved.

SLOSHED IN THE SENATE
The best known stories about Macdonald concern his heavy drinking. Even in the days when both the House of Commons and the Senate had a bar directly beneath, and fully half the Members of Parliament (or MPs) were drunk by the late evening, Sir John stood out (though not necessarily up).

It took Britain just 38 minutes to defeat Zanzibar in an 1896 war.

A NAUSEATING SPEECH
On the way to an election event, Sir John imbibed a great deal. As a consequence, Sir John actually vomited on stage while his opponent was speaking. When his turn came to address the audience, Macdonald apologized: "I don't know how it is, but every time I hear my opponent speak it turns my stomach." The crowd loved it.

DO AS I SAY, NOT AS I DO
When party members complained about the heavy drinking of another MP, Macdonald chewed him out: "Look here, McGee, this Government can't afford two drunkards, and you've got to stop."

IT'S THE ECONOMY STUPOR
Sir John gave a speech late at night after a liquid dinner. The speech made little sense, so the reporter covering it visited Macdonald the next day asking for help in reconstructing his words. As the reporter read his notes, Sir John jumped up and gave the entire speech, correctly. The reporter thanked him and as he left, Sir John handed out a kind warning: "Never report on a public speaker when you are drunk."

WE WANT BOOZE NOT BIGOTS
Sir John knew his failings made him more popular with some voters. Referring to a bigoted political rival, Macdonald told a group of cheering workmen, "I know...that you would rather have John Eh? drunk than George Brown sober."

A SCANDALOUS MEMORY
When a government commission looking into a complex real estate scandal called Macdonald to testify, he was on one of his binges. Macdonald had shaking hands and bleary eyes, and commission members sighed, giving up hope of anything useful. Sir John then proceeded, without any hesitation or reference to notes, to give all the details of the transaction, going back 20 years, including exact dates.

A SOBERING EXPERIENCE
In later life, during his happy second marriage, Macdonald curtailed his drinking and even gave support to the temperance movement.

THEM'S FIGHTIN' WORDS: AT SEA

The days of sailing warships and the defeat of the Spanish Armada resulted in some important contributions to the English language.

One hundred and thirty Spanish ships sailed from Lisbon, Portugal, but only 76 of them returned after the English navy overpowered them in the Battle of the Armada. It had been the first gun duel between ships propelled only by sails, and it became the model for all future naval actions up to and including the Battle of Trafalgar more than 200 years later.

armada
The term **armada**, Spanish for a "fleet equipped with arms," came into English from that famous encounter of 1588 and eventually came to stand for a fleet of virtually any vehicles (ships, planes, trucks) that move with a common purpose.

taken down a peg
In the aftermath of this great victory, England's pride in its navy rose considerably, and flags and pennants to indicate the rank and status of a ship's commander came into greater use. Flags were hoisted and secured to a series of pegs on the mast; the higher the flag, the more important the ship's commander. When a command was handed over to a subordinate, the flag was **taken down a peg or two** so as to fly lower on the mast. Today this expression still means deflating or humbling someone.

the cut of the jib
Another indication of a ship's status that dates from the same period was the **cut of the jib**, the "jib" being a triangular sail that flew from the foremast. Its particular shape indicated the type of vessel and sometimes its nationality. From this we get the phrase "the cut of his/her jib," meaning a person's outward appearance or demeanor; "I don't like the cut of his jib" thus judges someone on that basis.

first-rate
In the seventeenth century Royal Navy warships began to be rated

on a scale from one to six, based on their size and the weight of ordnance (weapons, etc.) they carried. Horatio Nelson's flagship *Victory*, which weighed 2,163 tons and mounted 100 heavy guns, was ranked as a **first-rate** ship. Later this term simply came to mean "excellent," and it is still used in this way.

turn a blind eye
Lord Nelson himself contributed another very familiar idiom to our language. During the siege of Copenhagen in 1801, Nelson was second-in-command of the English fleet and was ordered to withdraw. Eager to continue his attack, he pretended not to see the flagship's signals to retreat by putting his glass to the eye that had been blinded in the Battle of Calvi. His attack forced the French to surrender, a naval victory second only to Trafalgar. Ever since, the term to **turn a blind eye** has meant to deliberately ignore or overlook something.

clearing the decks
When a battle was anticipated, the crew prepared by **clearing the decks,** that is, removing or fastening down all loose objects on deck that might get in the way of the guns or injure a sailor. Today, of course, we use this term loosely, simply meaning to get things out of the way so as to prepare for some other activity.

battening down the hatches
One of the preparations for either military action or bad weather was **battening down the hatches**. It consisted of fastening down canvas over hatches with strips of wood called battens. Later the phrase came to mean preparing for chaos or violent confrontation.

at close quarters
If the enemy boarded a ship, the combat that ensued was called **in or at close quarters,** that is, the crew were in close contact with the enemy. Later the term came to be used for any crowded or confined space.

cut and run
Sometimes, of course, a ship faced overwhelming odds and had to retreat quickly. Occasionally this need could be anticipated. In square-rigged ships, sails were secured with light ropes that could be easily cut to let them fall quickly, enabling the ship to sail at once. From this practice we have the term **cut and run,** for making a hasty exit.

Four of Mary Todd's brothers fought for the Confederacy. Her husband was Abraham Lincoln.

by the board
Retreat could also be hastened by jettisoning some of the supplies or cargo. These materials were said to have gone **by the board**— that is, fallen overboard and carried away. Today we still speak of something that has fallen out of use or been discarded as having gone by the board.

scuttlebutt
One thing not readily discarded was drinking water, which was kept in a lidded cask called a **scuttlebutt**. The name combined scuttle, for a hole in a vessel, with butt, for a large cask. The hole in the cask allowed access to the contents. Probably because crew members gathered around the scuttlebutt to drink and chat (like the office water cooler of today), the name eventually came to mean gossip, as in "What's the scuttlebutt about setting up a new department?"

deliver a broadside
Heavily armed sailing ships had considerable firepower. They could deliver a broadside, that is, simultaneously discharge all the artillery on one side of the ship, and cause enough damage to blow an enemy out of the water. On land, however, **delivering a broadside** came to mean delivering a volley of verbal abuse, whereas to "blow out of the water" means to effect a resounding defeat in sports, business, or other competition.

son of a gun
The gun deck of square-rigged ships became the source of another common expression. Wives of Royal Navy crewmen occasionally were permitted to go on long voyages with their husbands, and not surprisingly some of them would become pregnant. The only safe place to give birth was behind a canvas shelter rigged up between cannons on the gun deck, so a baby boy born in this way was dubbed a **son of a gun,** an term that also hinted at a question of who the father was. In any case, the term was adopted in civilian life and it survived long after the British Admiralty outlawed the practice of wives living on board, around 1840.

Spain found so much silver in the New World that the inflation ruined its economy.

DEATH OF A REVOLUTIONARY

The story of Che Guevara, or…
who was that guy on all those posters?

Say "revolutionary" and the image is automatic: the uniform, the beret, and the determined, soulful look of Ernesto "Che" Guevara. Che was the Elvis of revolutionary struggle for disaffected youth of the 60s and 70s. Even before his death, Che was the ultimate radical. Mao, Lenin, and Castro had sold out the cause to run morally questionable governments. Not Che.

THE DOCTOR'S CURE

The Argentinean doctor (Che studied medicine at Buenos Aires University) was Fidel Castro's second-in-command in the Cuban Revolution. After fighting with Castro from 1956 to 1958 in a seemingly impossible struggle against the dictator Fulgencio Batista, the impossible happened. They won. Che was rewarded with top jobs, including minister of industry, president of the National Bank, and permanent representative to the United Nations in New York. Rather than enjoying life at the top, he gave it up to lead guerrilla wars to help the oppressed.

WE ALL WANNA CHANGE THE WORLD

Truth was Guevara was too radical for Castro. Che saw the Cuban takeover as a stop on the road to world revolution, but Castro had a nation to run. When Che attacked the U.S.S.R. for deserting revolutionaries and the U.S. for imperialism, Castro saw Che as trouble. When Guevara wanted to pick up his rifle again and start peasant wars against the imperialists, Castro decided to let him.

Che's first target was the Belgian Congo. In 1965 he got Castro to let him lead a small Cuban force in the huge African country. He thought the locals would rise up and join him in a revolution against their Belgian colonial oppressors. The untrained locals melted away when faced with the Belgian mercenaries. The country fell to Mobutu Sese Seko, one of Africa's most corrupt leaders.

Portugal was the last country to hold on to its African colonies, losing them in the 1970s.

GUEVARA REMAINS UNCHANGED

Guevara returned to Cuba; but the Congo hadn't discouraged him. He disappeared from Cuba and entered Bolivia with a false passport in the fall of 1966. Once again, Che figured that peasants would rise up against the capitalist oppressors. This time, he was dead wrong. Che's guerrilla force in Bolivia included Peruvians, Cubans, and Argentineans as well as Bolivians. The government announced that a gang of foreign bandits was roaming the countryside. The peasants' reaction was simple fear. When Guevara's men arrived, the locals fled. The revolutionaries became hungry and desperate. Guevara fought on. He'd trained in guerrilla war in Mexico in 1954 with Captain Bayo, a veteran of the Spanish Civil War, and he was a star pupil. In the summer of 1967, his men carried out guerrilla raids against the Bolivian Army and proved they could strike almost at will, even without popular support.

ENTER THE GREEN BERETS

Then the Chief of the Bolivian Armed Forces got help—from the 8th Special Forces division of U.S. Army Forces. A 16-man team of Green Berets arrived to train and equip a unit of Quechua Indians, the 2nd Rangers Battalion. The Battalion was dedicated to wiping out Guevara's force—and Guevara. So was an American CIA task force. A Cuban-American CIA officer, Felix Rodriguez, posed as a Bolivian Army officer to witness the kill.

On October 8, Guevara and his men were surrounded, and after a brief firefight it was all over. Guevara, wounded in the leg, was captured. Bolivian soldiers carried Che on a stretcher to the nearest town. The Bolivian Army announced on the radio that Che had been killed in the battle. Rodriguez went to tell Che he was going to be executed. The noncommissioned officers drew straws, and a Bolivian sergeant shot Guevara dead. Che stood up to die. He defiantly said that he preferred death under the guns of the oppressor. Death guaranteed his fame. If he hadn't been killed, the Bolivian insurrection might have failed. By shooting him, the Bolivians and CIA turned him into a martyr and a hero. Soon his image was an inspiration to young people worldwide. Still, it was a sad end for the soldier who had dedicated his life to bringing power to the powerless. He lost the chance to fulfill his dream of revolution. All he got was his picture on a lousy T-shirt.

Nkosikazi Nomzamo Madikizela is better known under her married name, Winnie Mandela.

THE STICKY HISTORIAN

*Psst! How would you like to watch acts of sex and violence from over
25 million years ago? All you need is a special specimen of fossilized tree
sap—better known as amber. The catch is that the ancients who were
caught in the act are…well…bugs.*

Millions of years ago, while eating, hunting, killing their
prey, and even while having sex, insects were trapped in
the sticky resin of trees. Over centuries this resin hardened into honey-colored, translucent stones called amber. And
when amber contains what the scientists call "inclusions" of
anything from flies and mosquitoes to flowers and frogs, it
becomes a picture of prehistoric life, frozen in time.

TINY BUBBLES
Amber traps air bubbles, too, and scientists think they might hold
a clue to the mystery of what killed off the dinosaurs. The bubbles
tell us that 67 million years ago, Earth's air contained 35 percent
oxygen to today's 21 percent. Was that 35 percent oxygen level
crucial to dinosaur life? Evidence in amber shows that the oxygen
in the atmosphere began to fall significantly at the end of the
Cretaceous period—the era when the dinosaurs disappeared from
the earth.

AMBER GOES HOLLYWOOD
In the movie *Jurassic Park*, scientists extracted dinosaur blood
from the stomach of a mosquito that had been encased in amber.
The DNA from that blood was used to clone packs of dinosaurs
that roamed the park and terrified everybody, on-screen and in the
audience. It should come as no surprise that the science in the
movie wasn't completely accurate. The *Jurassic Park* amber was
discovered at a fictional amber mine in the Dominican Republic.
But amber from the Dominican Republic was formed 30 to 50
million years ago, when dinosaurs had already been extinct for
more than 15 million years.

WHAT'S OLD IN NEW JERSEY
But amber that was formed in the age of the dinosaurs does exist.
Scientists at New York City's American Museum of Natural

History have collected 93-million-year-old amber fossils at a secret site in New Jersey.

PREHISTORIC CLONES?

Scientists don't know if reality will ever catch up to the movies. A couple of examples: In 1995, researchers at California Polytechnic State University revived *Bacillus* bacteria spores from the stomach of a bee encased in amber. The bee's estimated age was somewhere between 25 to 30 million years. If prehistoric bacteria can live again after millions of years, what other ancient creatures might someday revisit Earth? On the other hand, the British Museum of Natural History reports that the DNA stored in amber fossils is too corrupted to use for cloning. Still more scientists disagree and continue to investigate the extraction of DNA from amber fossils and the possible re-creation of prehistoric life.

CAVEAT AMBER

The success of *Jurassic Park* inspired a new worldwide industry in fake amber fossils. Con artists have created fossils out of plastic; they look just like like amber and supposedly contain prehistoric insects, feathers, or the hair of ancient mammals. So, how can you tell if amber is real or not? One good way is to stick a heated needle into your so-called "amber fossil." If you smell burning plastic, you just bought a fake.

*   *   *

UNZIPPED

We thought this was a cool story, but couldn't fit it in anywhere. It has nothing to do with amber, but with something else that's sticky. Swiss mountaineer George de Mestral was out hiking with his Irish pointer on a fine summer day in 1948, when he noticed little burrs sticking to his pants and clinging to his dog's fur. The tenacious burrs inspired de Mestral to race home, neglect his burr-infested dog, and examine the burrs under a microscope. He noticed hundreds of little hooks clinging to the fabric and thought he might be on to something that would replace the zipper. The idea "stuck" in his head—he "clung" to his idea for years and finally had it patented in 1955. It took several years for the public to get "hooked," but eventually Velcro (a combination of the words "velvet" and "crochet") "caught on" and became a multi-million dollar industry.

VAN GOGH: AN EAR FOR TROUBLE

Pained expressionist? Embarrassing failure? Insane artist?
All of the above? The real story on that ear incident.

Vincent van Gogh was born in Holland, when it was still called Holland, in 1853. From his early youth he was thought to be strange, even freakish. He was a failure at everything he tried, except painting.

HE'S GOT "PROBLEMS"

Twice in his life he tried to cultivate romances with women who rejected him outright. The woman he finally took to his bed was a prostitute, a fact that scandalized his family. He chose to throw in his lot with the poor and downtrodden; he completely rejected all aspects of middle-class propriety. He was prone to volatile mood swings and mental breakdowns. A weirdo, plain and simple.

WASN'T HE THE "EAR" GUY?

Ask people what they know about van Gogh and you will, more than likely, get some vague reference to an ear-chopping incident. Not surprising, considering he chose to immortalize this chapter in his life with a self-portrait that shows off his heavily bandaged ear. But why did he do it in the first place?

AU REVOIR, PARIS!

By 1888, the 35-year-old van Gogh was sadly disillusioned with life in Paris. Besides being a misfit, he was a failure: he couldn't sell any of his paintings. So he moved to Arles, in the south of France, where he planned to establish an artist's colony. He invited fellow painter Paul Gauguin to live with him. From the outset, the relationship between the two was volatile to say the least. Van Gogh was a foreigner to all of the normal social graces of decent living—a thing that annoyed the heck out of Gauguin. On Christmas Eve, 1888, the two men got into an argument; the argument became a brawl. Vincent attacked Gauguin with a razor, but Gauguin managed to ward off the blow. Van Gogh fled to his room.

It nearly bankrupted England to ransom Richard the Lion-Hearted after he was kidnapped.

EAR TODAY, GONE TOMORROW

Vincent proceeded to get hopelessly drunk. He soon came to regret his fiery display towards Gauguin. In his drunken stupor he concocted a way that he could make amends—he would cut off his ear (yeah, that's the ticket!) as a show of remorse. Holding a razor in his right hand, he stood before a mirror and sliced through his left ear from the top of the lobe working down at an angle.

FOR ME? YOU SHOULDN'T HAVE!

Van Gogh gift-wrapped the severed portion of his ear in a hand-kerchief and took it down to his local bordello where he, covered in blood, sought out Rachel—a prostitute he had a crush on—and handed her the package. The poor girl fainted, the brothel was thrown into turmoil, and Vincent fled. The police found Vincent asleep in his bed the following morning.

THE NOT-SO-FUNNY FARM

He spent the next 12 months in an asylum, but they weren't big on rehab back then. Two years later he ended his life with a self-inflicted gunshot wound to the chest. His work, of course, and the romantic story of this tortured artist antihero have gone on to become legend.

*   *   *

EAR ANATOMY

Pop quiz, hot shot. You listenin'? It's Audiology 101 and you've got the cheat sheet. Here's everything you need to know.

External ear: Focus, dude, focus! The external auditory canal and auricle concentrate the sound, kinda like that big horn on old hand-crank record players you see in old-timey movies.
Middle ear and eardrum: Check out these cool bones! Malleus, incus, and stapes—that's hammer, anvil, and stirrup, respectively. They form the amplifier in your own internal stereo system.
Inner ear: This is where the action is. The cochlea is a snail-shaped bone which—presto-change-o!—transforms sounds into nerve impulses. All the other stuff in here helps you balance.
Mastoid air cells: These weird air pockets also help amplify the sound, sort of like an echo change. So you really do have a hole in your head after all.

From 1958 to 1961, Egypt and Syria were one country called the United Arab Republic.

TO HILL AND GONE

*The San Francisco cable car doesn't just carry people. It also carries
the distinction of being an official National Historic Landmark.
Here's the story of how it first came to be.*

On a fateful rainy day in 1869, Andrew S. Hallidie watched
as four horses struggled to pull a streetcar up one of San
Francisco's steepest hills. About halfway to the top, one of
the horses slipped on the wet cobblestones. The driver applied the
brakes, but the chain snapped, and the car slid backward to the
bottom, dragging the poor horses to their doom. At that moment,
Hallidie decided to do something about it.

NOTHING ORDINARY ABOUT HIM
Andrew Hallidie wasn't just an ordinary bystander. His father was
an inventor who held several patents for "wire rope," the forerunner of wire cable. Young Hallidie had inherited his father's inven-
tiveness. His sense of adventure had brought him from England to
California, where he prospected for gold for a few relatively unsuccessful years, tried blacksmithing, then turned to building bridges,
the suspension kind that used lots of his father's wire rope.

THE RIGHT MAN FOR THE JOB
Hallidie held a patent on the "Hallidie Ropeway," a steam-
powered cable line he'd invented in gold territory. The ropeway,
also called a tramway, transported cars full of ore across mountain-
ous areas on a wire rope that had a tensile strength of 160,000
pounds per square inch. At the time of the streetcar accident,
Hallidie lived in San Francisco and owned a company that manufactured—guess what?—wire rope.

MAN WITH A PLAN
Hallidie's idea for a cable-operated streetcar began with laying a
moving cable in a groove in the street. He attached a grip to the
cable: when it grasped the cable, the car would move forward;
when it released, the car would stop. He spent the next couple of
years trying to drum up financial backing, during which the
project became known as "Hallidie's folly." Folly or not, Hallidie
finally raised enough money to build an experimental line.

Idris I was the first and only modern king of Libya. Muammar al-Qaddafi deposed him.

TRIAL RUN

At 4 a.m. on the foggy morning of August 2, 1873, Hallidie and a small group of engineers gathered for the first trial run. Hallidie chose the very early hour to minimize his embarrassment if it didn't work. The driver, known as a gripman, climbed onto the car, but as he looked down, the fog parted for one dramatic moment and he saw the bottom of the hill far below. He stepped down from the car and said, "I have a wife and kids at home," as he backed away.

NOW WHAT?

No one else volunteered, so Hallidie climbed into the car himself and took hold of the levers that operated the grip. The car glided smoothly down the hill. When it reached the bottom, he turned the car around, and made it back up the hill—all without mishap. A Frenchman in a nightcap who had watched from a window threw a bouquet of flowers onto the roof of the cable car; he was the only member of the public to witness the maiden voyage of the San Francisco cable car.

BUILD IT AND THEY WILL COME

That afternoon, it seemed like the entire town turned out for the first public run. And before even watching to see if it worked, 90 intrepid San Franciscans climbed onto the car built for 26 passengers and took the first official ride, perched on the roof and hanging off the side of "Hallidie's folly." For the next century or so, San Franciscans rode the cable cars to and from work or shopping. Now, of course, they take buses or cabs, or even cars, when they want to go across town. It probably never occurred to Andrew Hallidie that his invention would become one of the most popular tourist attractions in the world.

* * *

OTHER COOL LOCAL INVENTIONS (IN NORWAY)

The paper clip was patented in 1899 by Norwegian Johan Vaaler. Norway didn't have a patenting system then, so Vaaler got his patent issued from the U.S. In the 1940s, during the Nazi occupation, Norwegian soldiers weren't allowed to wear buttons with the king's initials. As a show of nationalism, the Norwegians fastened their coats with paper clips. Wear with pride!

In the 1970s, Grenada fell to Marxists after its prime minister became fixated on UFOs.

THE REAL ROBINSON CRUSOE

Alexander Selkirk was the real-life castaway who inspired the famous Daniel Defoe novel with the mouth-filling title: The Life and Strange Surprising Adventures of Robinson Crusoe, of York, Mariner. *But Selkirk's story is entirely his own.*

IF IT'S TUESDAY, IT MUST BE MÁS A TIERRA

The sailors were just putting ashore at a small, supposedly deserted island off the coast of Chile when they were startled by a wild man dressed in goatskins running toward them along the beach. The man could barely make himself understood, but over the next days, as the ability of speech slowly came back to him, Alexander "Wild Man" Selkirk told them the story of how he had survived for more than four years—without human companionship—marooned on the island of Más a Tierra.

HOW HE GOT THERE IN THE FIRST PLACE

Selkirk was born in Scotland in 1676 and ran off to sea almost as soon as he learned how to run. By age 27 he'd landed a job as first mate on the ship, *Cinque Ports*, which means "five ports" in French, a fine name for a ship except that if you pronounce "cinque" it sounds just like "sank." Not a good word to use around any kind of seafaring vessel. The men who sailed the *Cinque Ports* were privateers, a fancy word for pirates paid by their government to prey on other countries' merchant ships. The captain, William Dampier, was a highly skilled mapmaker, but an incompetent and foolhardy sailing man.

THE ANGRY SEA

The *Cinque Ports* was positioned to sail around Cape Horn, the southern tip of South America, and had already tried three times. In the best of weather, rounding the Horn was dangerous, but this was the middle of storm season. The men were sick, tired, and talking of mutiny. But Captain Dampier couldn't wait to get to the Pacific Ocean where rich Spanish and Portuguese ships plied the waters, begging to be captured and looted. Selkirk argued with

---

On July 4, 1776, George III wrote in his diary, "Nothing of importance happened today."

the captain that the ship was battered and badly needed repair, but Dampier was adamant. He forced the men to try again. This time the *Cinque Ports* made it. The ship limped to the island of Más a Tierra to pick up food and water.

Selkirk thought now that they would rest a bit, then repair the ship. But Captain Dampier was anxious to get going again. Selkirk argued some more, to no avail. Then he made the most important decision of his life. Afraid that the ship would sink, he asked to be relieved of duty. He would stay on Más a Tierra, a known stopping place for fresh water, fruit, and crawfish. Selkirk was sure another ship would be along shortly. He was young, 27, healthy, and too optimistic. So in October 1704, our hero put ashore with his clothes, bedding, a firelock rifle, gunpowder, bullets, tobacco, tools, a kettle, a Bible, mathematical instruments, and some books. By the time the longboat pulled away, he began to doubt his decision. He called after the boat, but it was too late.

THE LONELY GUY

For the first few weeks our castaway constantly scanned the horizon for ships. The solitude terrified him, and he fell into a depression. He despaired of ever being rescued. His depression lasted eight months. He knew because he counted the days by carving notches in the trees.

He wasn't entirely alone. Herds of wild goats roamed everywhere. The island was overrun with cats and rats that had come ashore from other ships. He killed the goats for food, and, eventually, clothing. The rats gnawed him while he slept, but once he shared his meat with the cats, they protected him from the rats. He began to settle in.

The island was a tropical paradise with a perfect climate, plenty of fresh water and fruit, and virtually everything Selkirk needed. He used the island's pimento trees to build two huts; one he used as a living room and bedroom, the other as a kitchen. He kept a fire going on a nearby hill so he could signal a passing ship. Over the years ships did come by, although they rarely got close. Twice, Spanish ships put down anchor, and twice Selkirk decided not to risk being seen. Better to stay alone on the island than be killed or sold into slavery, a certainty for a captured English seaman.

The writings of Confucius were nearly lost when China's emperor tried to burn them all.

AS TIME GOES BY

Selkirk eventually moved from his huts to a cave. When he ran out of powder for his rifle, he had to chase the goats if he wanted meat. His diet also included crawfish, fruit, pimentos, goats' milk, and even some turnips that sailors had sown there. He kept himself busy and in good spirits reading, singing, and praying. He was in the best physical shape he'd ever been in his life. His shoes had worn out long ago, so he went barefoot. When his clothes wore out, he replaced them with a goatskin coat and hat. He must have looked like a wild man, indeed.

SAILS IN THE SUNSET

Finally, in early 1709, the wild man saw an English flag atop the ship at anchor in his harbor. He ran to meet the longboats. The ship that rescued Selkirk was the English privateer, *Duke*. Its captain, Woodes Rogers, described the rescue in his 1712 book, *A Voyage Around the World*.

By a strange coincidence, the pilot of the *Duke* was none other than William Dampier, the captain of the *Cinque Ports*, who had left Selkirk on Más a Tierra four years earlier. No hard feelings on either side. Dampier vouched for Selkirk's seamanship, so he was given a position of responsibility on the *Duke*. When Selkirk helped to capture a richly loaded Spanish merchant ship, Captain Rogers rewarded him by making him the ship's captain for the return home to England.

HIS SHIP COMES IN

When Selkirk got back to England in 1711, he told his story to essayist Richard Steele, who published it the following year. Daniel Defoe read the story and was inspired to create his own story of *Robinson Crusoe*.

Thanks to the Spanish ship, Selkirk returned to Scotland a wealthy man. But he was as unfamiliar with money as he was with civilization. He made a home for himself in a cave, where he tried to replace the tranquility and solitude of Más a Tierra. Finally, Selkirk returned to the sea as first mate on the man-of-war *Weymouth*. He died at sea, age 45, after drinking water infected with a tropical disease. Más a Tierra is now known as Robinson Crusoe Island. It's a tourist attraction, just three hours by plane from Santiago, Chile.

Winston Churchill was one-sixteenth Iroquois.

TOMBSTONE TERRITORY

Only Uncle John could bring together the likes of Alexander the Great and Al Capone. Here's what's engraved on the tombstones of some famous folks.

Alexander the Great
A tomb now suffices for him
For whom the world was not
 enough

**William H. Bonney
"Billy the Kid"**
Truth and History.
21 Men.
The Boy Bandit King—
He Died As He Lived.

Alphonse Capone
My Jesus Mercy

Nicolaus Copernicus
Stand, Sun, move not

Emily Dickinson
Called Back

Sir Arthur Conan Doyle
Steel True, Blade Straight

Wyatt Earp
…that nothing's so sacred as honor
and nothing's so loyal as love

Ralph Waldo Emerson
The passive master lent his hand,
To the vast Soul which o'er him
 planned.

Benjamin Franklin
The Body of B. Franklin, Printer
Like the Cover of an old Book
Its Contents torn out
And Stript of its Lettering &
 Gilding
Lies here. Food for Worms

For it will as he believ'd
appear once more
In a new and more elegant Edition
Corrected and improved
By the Author.

Robert Lee Frost
I had A Lover's Quarrel With The
 World

Gustavus III, King of Sweden
Happy at last

"Wild Bill" J. B. Hickok
Killed by the assassin Jack M'Call
in Deadwood, Black Hills Aug. 2d
 1876
Pard, we will meet again in the
Happy Hunting Ground
To part no more,
Goodbye

John Keats
This Grave
contains all that was Mortal
of a
Young English Poet
Who
on his Death Bed
in the Bitterness of his Heart
at the Malicious Power of his
Enemies
Desired
these words to be engraved on his
Tomb Stone
'Here lies One Whose Name was
writ in Water.'

The speeches of England's George VI were carefully written to minimize his stammer.

C. S. Lewis
Man must endure his going hence.

Anne and Charles Lindbergh
...If I take the wings of the I
morning
and dwell in the uttermost parts of
the sea....

Jack London
The Stone the Builders Rejected

Henry Wadsworth Longfellow
Gone are the living, but the dead
 remain,
And not neglected; for a hand
 unseen,
Scattering its bounty like a
summer rain,
Still keeps their graves and their
remembrance green.

Roger Maris
Against all Odds

Karl Marx
Workers of all lands unite.
The philosophers have only
interpreted the world in various
ways; the point is to change it.

Mary Ann "Polly" Nichols
Victim of
"Jack the Ripper"

Edgar Allan Poe
Quoth the Raven,"Nevermore."

Buford Pusser
He Walked Tall

Babe Ruth
May
That Divine Spirit
That Animated
BABE RUTH
to Win the Crucial
Game of Life
Inspire the Youth
of America

Robert III King of Scotland
Here lies the worst king and the
most miserable man in the
kingdom.

William Shakespeare
Good friend, for Jesus' sake forbear,
to dig the dust enclosed here!
Blessed be the man that spares
 these stones,
and cursed be he that moves my
 bones.

George Bernard Shaw
I knew if I stayed around long
enough, something like this would
happen.

Percy Bysshe Shelley
Nothing of him that doth fade
But doth suffer a sea-change
Into something rich and strange

William Butler Yeats
Cast a cold eye
On life, on death
Horseman, pass by

King James I was one of history's first anti-smoking zealots.

THE 100 YEARS' WAR

*The Hundred Years' War wasn't really one big war that lasted
100 years. It was a lot of small wars interrupted by long periods
of peace, with characters fascinating enough to spark the imagination of William Shakespeare.*

The Hundred Years' War was a bunch of wars between the
years of 1337–1453 that summed up the attempted English
invasion of France. It was a great try, but in the end the
English failed. Historians began lumping together all the sieges,
raids, and battles that took place during this period under one title
for the sake of historic simplicity, only since the late 19th century.
Before then each battle was known for its own name. Long years
of truce interlaced the hundred years of on-again, off-again fighting. Each battle typically lasted only about one day, with often less
than 3,000 soldiers on each side. All the major battles put
together only took up 2 weeks of the infamous hundred years.
Sieges (blockades) were far more frequent and comprised many
years of hand-to-hand combat.

THE FEISTY YOUNG KING

Edward III of England (son of Edward II and Isabel of France) was
only 14 years old when he became King of England in 1327. After
his father's death, the Queen and her longtime lover, Roger
Mortimer, the Earl of March, ruled England. But, their reign
didn't last long. In 1330, the young King Edward III had his
mother's lover, Mortimer, detained and executed for causing strife
in the family. Edward went on with his military pursuits, which
he found more interesting than royal administration and policy
decisions. Not surprising for a teenager. For the most part, he left
those issues up to his trusty barons.

BLOOD RELATIONS

Queen Isabel, Edward's philandering mother, was England's link to
France. Her brother Charles was the King of France. When
Charles died without an heir to the French throne, people naturally assumed that one of Isabel's sons in England would inherit
the throne. Surprisingly, on his deathbed Charles bequeathed the
throne to Philip VI—both his and Isabel's first cousin.

Sweden had a Charles VII, but no Charles I, II, III, IV, V or VI.

BUT DO THE ENGLISH SPEAK FRENCH?
During these times, nationality and language was not a barrier to
the royalties of both France and England. They spoke the same
language, Anglo-Norman French. A thriving language during this
period, Anglo-Norman French bridged the syntax of English and
French.

EDWARD'S QUEST FOR FRANCE
Since the 11th century, England claimed ownership to territories
in northern France across the English Channel, but the French
wanted the land back. In 1337, Philip VI of France took back the
Duchy of Guyenne, an English domain in France. Edward, of
course, wanted the land back and was willing to fight for it.

THE ENGLISH WREAK HAVOC
The first stage of the Hundred Years' War was marked by victorious land battles for the English, including the battle of Crécy
(1346), battle of Poitiers (1356), and the siege of Calais
(1346–1347). Calais, the major port of entry into northern
France, was a particularly tactical win and brought the English in
closer contact with their Flemish allies. The second stage took
account of declined military activity after 1380 and vast raids by
the English in French towns and cities. French people, unlike the
English, saw warfare in their communities as their towns were
pillaged and looted.

A REALITY-BASED MIDSUMMER'S NIGHT DREAM
The events that followed this bleak period inspired Shakespeare to
write his famous play, *Henry V*. As the war dragged on, the English
were forced back by the French so that they occupied a narrow
strip of coast in northern France. But, soon enough Henry V
succeeded Edward as King of England and went on the offensive
again. His big victory at Agincourt was followed by an era of
peace when he married the French princess, Catherine. Their son
was to rule both England and France, but with Henry's death in
1422, the war between the two countries continued.

ROYAL DISORDER
With Henry V's union with the French royalty, a royal strain of mental disorder was introduced to the English royal family. All those generations of marital match-ups between the two countries' royal houses finally caught up to them!

WHEN IT'S OVER
In this seemingly never-ending story of wars, it wasn't until the year 1565 that England lost its final toehold in northern France at Calais. This marked the end of England's hunger for territories in France. In the years after the war, the English continued to beef up their naval military that served them well against France.

WAR SKEPTICS
Thankfully, common laws of war prevented the mass murdering that took place in crusading wars. But even so, the devastation that did take place opened the proverbial floodgates to thought and criticism of war in intellectual circles.

FEASTING ON KNIGHTHOOD AND DEATH
The prestigious culture of knighthood flourished during the years after the Hundred Years' War, reaching its pinnacle in the court of the 15th century dukes of Burgundy. The end of the war also saw an upsurge of cultural interest in death, and the virtues of death represented in war such as nobility, glory, and grandeur. This can be seen by the revival of grand, individualized tombs as well as increasingly expensive and lavish funeral processions for the dead.

* * *

ANGLO-NORMANIZATION
The Battle of Hastings in 1066 sealed the Norman (i.e., north French) conquest of England. The Bayeux Tapestry commemorates William of Normandy's victory. Or does it? Commissioned by William's half-brother for display in the Bayeux Cathedral in France, the 231-foot-long tapestry was actually stitched by the famed English needleworkers of Canterbury. They sure made the battle look like hard work for the noticeably ugly Normans, and there surely was a wistful hint of nostalgia in the closing line: "The sun set on the field—and on Anglo-Saxon England."

In 1941, Mongolians staged history's last full-scale cavalry charge. German tanks flattened it.

ANAGRAMS

It's a form of wordplay that's probably been around as long as the first alphabet. The trick is to rearrange the letters of a word or phrase to form a new one. That's the easy part. What's more remarkable is when the new phrase describes the original in some way. Like these historical examples...

PRESIDENT CHARLES DE GAULLE
becomes...HE'S LARGE AND ILL-PERSECUTED

FRENCH REVOLUTION
becomes...VIOLENCE RUNS FORTH

ENGLAND'S QUEEN VICTORIA
becomes...GOVERNS A NICE QUIET LAND

THE LEANING TOWER OF PISA
becomes...WHAT A FOREIGN STONE PILE!

DISRAELI
becomes...I LEAD, SIR

THE VERSAILLES PEACE CONFERENCE
becomes...ALLIES CONVENE HERE; PERFECT CASE

NICHOLAS THE SECOND, CZAR OF RUSSIA
becomes...ZEALOUS ANARCHISTS DO SCORN CHIEF

TOWER OF LONDON
becomes...ONE OLD FORT NOW

JEANNE D'ARC, MAID OF ORLEANS
becomes...AS A MAN, REJOINED OLD FRANCE

SAINT GEORGE AND THE DRAGON
becomes...HA! A STRONG GIANT ENDED OGRE

FLORENCE NIGHTINGALE
becomes...FLIT ON, CHEERING ANGEL

PERSHING'S AMERICAN ARMY
becomes...RACE IN, SAMMY, GRASP RHINE!

VENETIAN GONDOLIERS
becomes...RIDE IN LAGOON EVENTS

ROOSEVELT'S ROUGH RIDERS
becomes...GOV. R'S TRUE HERO SOLDIERS

CATHERINE DE MEDICI
becomes...HER EDICT CAME IN: DIE!

DANTE GABRIEL ROSSETTI
becomes...GREATEST BORN IDEALIST

THE MONA LISA
becomes...NO HAT, A SMILE

The death of George V was timed so that it would make the better morning newspapers.

THE ANCIENT CITY OF KING SOLOMON?

The ancient ruins of once-rich Great Zimbabwe are the largest in Africa south of the Sahara. The Europeans who discovered it in the 19th century couldn't believe that "mere African savages" could have built it. So who did?

The ruins of Great Zimbabwe lie in an isolated position near the Limpopo River in present-day Zimbabwe, central Africa. They're so impressive that when Rhodesia (formerly Southern Rhodesia) became independent, the country took its new name from these amazing remains. Because by then, the answer to the secret—who had built this colossal edifice?—was known.

WHAT A RIDICULOUS IDEA!
But for over a century of fascination to Europeans—during which so many probed, dug and in fact demolished so much archeological evidence—only one thing seemed clear to them: no way could this remarkable achievement have been built by, in their words, "mere African savages!"

JUST GREAT
The enormous buildings are the largest ancient ruins south of the Sahara. The "Great Enclosure" is over 100 yards across and nearly 300 yards in circumference. The walls are about 36 feet high and up to 20 feet thick. Within the enclosure is a tower, 35 feet high and 20 feet wide at the base—and it's solid, with no spaces within! (There's still a mystery as to its use.) All around the Great Enclosure are other stone complexes. Over a million granite blocks were used in the building, all closely fitted together using no mortar.

FRANCE-SIZED
Eventually it was found that Great Zimbabwe was the center of an enormous ancient kingdom, with some 200 other areas of stone buildings and monuments that made up a once-thriving nation about the size of France. Estimates showed that the population of the complex could have been around 20,000.

DIGGING FOR TREASURE

Even though there are rivers nearby, the "city" wasn't built near them—a major inconvenience in the African climate. But it was apparently built right on top of very rich gold and copper mines—pretty good alternative reasons.

The area was fabulously wealthy in its time. Amazingly, artifacts from India and China have been found there, evidence of enormous trading power, via the east coast of Africa.

WHO DONE IT?

The various theories were weird and wonderful. Could this be the fabled site of King Solomon's mines? Did the Phoenicians, via where the Suez Canal now is, move down the east African coast? They certainly had the building and trading skills. What about the Arabs? They'd been building trading cities down the east coast for centuries—did they also spread inland? What about that preacher, Prester John, the fabled white ruler of Ethiopia?

IT'S A DATE

The dating of Great Zimbabwe suggests that the major building was carried out around A.D. 1100, which rules out King Solomon and the Phoenicians for a start. Prester John has since been proven never to have existed, and the walls have since been shown not to be Arab-built.

As one of Sherlock Holmes's favorite sayings goes, "Once you have got rid of the impossible, what is left, however improbable, must be the answer." Could it have been those "mere African savages," after all?

THE LOCALS

The major tribe in the area today is the Shona. A simple understanding of the Shona language (something the early explorers didn't seem to think of) shows that "zimbabwe" means "houses of stone"—which would have been a pretty logical indication. A look at the history of the Shona shows that the tribe came into the area around A.D. 500, and has been dominant there ever since.

RUINING THE RUINS

Of course, the early Europeans couldn't comprehend such a thing and, in their desperation to reach the expected original (i.e. non-

African) ruins—and, of course, to get at some of that gold and copper—they carved through and destroyed a lot of archaeological evidence that might have told them the full story much earlier.

TAPPED OUT

Great Zimbabwe and the surrounding lands were in fact developed and built by the Shona. They probably reached the height of their economic strength around A.D. 1500. After that, with its gold and copper resources tapping out, trade with the Arabs (who handled the Shona's import-export trade with Asia) declined and eventually fell away altogether.

INDEPENDENCE DAY

Until the 19th century, its story had been lost. But now it's at least partly known again. And when the "Rhodesians" gained their independence, they were more than proud to rename their country Zimbabwe, reflecting on their peoples' former glory.

*   *   *

CHIEF SEATTLE'S SPEECH

It is the most stirring and often quoted of native American speeches, supposedly delivered by Chief Seattle in 1854. In it he refers to the earth as his mother and the rivers as the blood of his ancestors. He also expressed his grief at having seen "a thousand rotting buffaloes on the prairie, left by the white men who shot them from a passing train."

Yet these words were never spoken by that famous chief. They were, in fact, the invention of a Hollywood screenwriter by the name of Ted Parry who gave them to a Seattle-like character in the 1972 movie *Home*. Since then millions of people have associated the speech with the real Seattle.

MY HEROES!

*In 1800, Spain controlled all of the present United States west of the
Mississippi, and everything south of it to the bottom of South
America—except for Brazil, which belonged to Portugal.
Less than 25 years later, all of Latin America was independent.
How did an entire continent-and-a-half change hands so quickly?*

The colonists of Latin America had a few chips on their
shoulders, and we don't mean nachos. For one thing, the
Creoles—the colonists who were white but had been born
in the New World—were feeling shut out of their own government. Most of the power was held by royalists (supporters of the
European kings and queens) who'd been born in Europe.

If you weren't white, you had it even worse. Native Americans toiled for a living on farmlands stolen from their ancestors.
Most blacks were slaves. The economy was in lousy shape. *Dinero*
was tight, and local industries were suffering under high taxes and
high shipping costs. All in all, the colonists were getting a little
caliente under the collar. There had been a few attempted rebellions here and there during the 18th century, but they fizzled out
pretty quickly. By the turn of the century, the successful revolutions in the United States and France gave colonists new hope.

OPPORTUNITY KNOCKS
In 1807, Napoleon sent French troops to occupy Spain and Portugal. While Spain was otherwise engaged, the colonists decided to
take advantage of the distraction. Over the next several years,
rebellions broke out from one end of Latin America to the other.

A SIGN FROM HEAVEN
Paraguay achieved a shaky independence in 1811. That same year
a revolution in Venezuela started out well. But in 1812, when a
violent earthquake hit hard in areas held by Venezuelan rebels,
but left the royalists' territory mostly untouched, a lot of revolutionaries took it as a sign of God's disapproval. From then on
things went from bad to awful. Morale hit an all-time low.

HERO NUMERO UNO
Enter José de San Martín, the lesser-known of two great leaders of

---

The people of India and the Mayans were the only ancient people who knew about zero.

Latin American independence, but a very important hombre in his own right. San Martín knew that for independence to last, it had to happen throughout Latin America, not just in one state. In 1817 he led an army of Argentines and Chileans across the Andes, and after a year of fighting took Chile from the royalists.

OLÉ FOR OUR SIDE!

Using his new position of power, he then tried to negotiate peacefully for a new government in nearby Peru. The lengthy negotiations failed, and San Martín's troops were on the move again. This time the royalists ran away, and San Martín and his men were cheered by the populace as they marched unopposed into Lima in 1821.

UP NORTH IN SOUTH AMERICA

Meanwhile, the tide was also turning in the northern end of the continent, thanks to the other hero of this story, the extremely famous Simón Bolívar. Bolívar had been a leader of the failed rebellion in Venezuela, and after its final defeat in 1815, he had fled to Jamaica. But the fearless Bolívar had just begun to fight. He gathered an army in Haiti and returned to Venezuela in 1816. In just three years he liberated not only Venezuela but also the lands that are now Ecuador, Colombia, and Panama. In 1819 these became a single nation called Great Colombia. It was later split into smaller countries, but Bolívar became its first president.

AT LEAST THEY DIDN'T CALL IT SIMONLAND

In 1823, the new government of Peru invited Bolívar to come over and take charge—of the whole country. Who could turn down an offer like that? Upper Peru later became an independent country in 1825, under a constitution that Bolívar himself drew up. The new nation was called Bolivia in his honor.

LET'S HEAR IT FOR OUR HEROES

The success of San Martín and Bolívar inspired more revolutions throughout Latin America. Mexico and Central America declared their independence from Spain in 1821, and Brazil severed ties with Portugal in 1822. Even though Bolívar's dream of a unified Latin American nation never came to be, he and San Martín helped bring an end to imperialism in the Americas. Except for Canada, of course, but that's another story.

In 1864, the top U.S. income tax rate was 3%.

WHY DO THEY CALL IT THE DARK AGES?

Do you know when the Dark Ages were?
Don't feel bad; not even the experts agree.

The Dark Ages started around the late 5th century, when Rome fell, and ended sometime between the 8th and 11th centuries, when the Middle Ages semi-officially started.

CASTING SOME LIGHT ON THE DARK AGES

There are two main reasons for calling this period the Dark Ages: 1. Less is known about this time than other eras, because fewer books and writings survived. Ergo, we're in the dark about the age. 2. That era always seemed barbaric and chaotic to historians. Most of the folks living then were illiterate and half-starved. The phrase "Dark Ages" describes the way people were living: in the dark.

To put things in perspective, remember that Rome had ruled most of Europe for around 800 years. When it collapsed, so did all the organizations that ruled Europe, the Middle East, and North Africa in its name. With no more administrators or armies to keep order, everything came apart. Food couldn't be distributed, and most money was worthless. Barbarian invaders smelled easy pickings and moved in. As if the barbarians weren't bad enough, a plague that started in Constantinople in 542 spread throughout Europe, and by 594 had killed half the population of Europe.

BACK TO BASICS

People moved away from the cities, abandoning the niceties like roads, baths, sewage systems, and other municipal services. They spent most of their hours scrambling for food, and had no time for learning, art, or any of the finer things in life.

Most scholars prefer "Early Middle Ages." Calling such a big chunk of centuries "dark" implies that nothing worthwhile was going on. That's not true. Christianity was spreading, monasteries and churches were being built, feudalism was forming, and—as we've already pointed out—there were plagues, invasions, and famines. Sounds like it was a great time to be alive doesn't it?

In 1978, Emilio Marco Palma became the first person born in Antarctica.

NEW WORLD ORDER

*King Tut never smoked a cigarette. Mark Antony never gave
Cleopatra a box of chocolates. Montezuma never ate pork chops.
Were they all health fanatics? Well, not exactly...*

During the lifetimes of ancient folk, tobacco did not exist in
Egypt, cocoa had never been seen in Rome, and pigs didn't
live in Mexico. In fact, many of the plants and animals
that cover the globe today weren't widespread until the voyages of
Columbus redrew the ecological map of the world.

THE PRE-COLUMBIAN MENU
Before 1492, no Englishman ever ate corn, and no Native American ever rode a horse. There were no wheat fields waving across
the Great Plains. You couldn't get your Italian grandmother's
recipe for tomato sauce because no one in Italy had ever seen a
tomato. You could look your entire life, but you wouldn't find a
banana in Guatemala, an orange in Florida, or a peach in Georgia.
If you ordered fish and chips in London, you just got fish because
there were no potatoes.

TRAFFIC JAMS ON THE ATLANTIC
Columbus's voyages of discovery changed the world by creating
rush hour on the Atlantic Ocean. Explorers, conquistadors,
missionaries, and settlers moved back and forth between the New
World and the Old. They carried plants and animals from their
homelands to the Americas, and they brought what they found in
the Americas back to Europe. Farms and kitchens on both sides of
the Atlantic would never be the same again.

WILD INDIANS START HORSING AROUND
When European settlers came to the Americas, they wanted to
feel at home, so they brought a lot of home with them. First and
foremost, they could not have conquered and settled the New
World without their single greatest import—the horse. Mastery of
the horse gave Europeans the advantage of speed and mobility. It's
not a coincidence that the last Native Americans to be conquered
were the Plains Indians of North America who adopted the trusty
horse after the Europeans arrived.

As a Member of Parliament, Isaac Newton only spoke once. He asked for an open window.

Cattle, pigs, goats, sheep, and donkeys—not a one of them existed in the Americas before they arrived from Europe. The new settlers also brought their own crops, and plenty of them. They imported wheat and other small grains like oats and barley to the fertile plains. They brought bananas, sugar cane, rice, and citrus fruits to the American tropics. Before European colonization, there was not a lot of coffee in Brazil. In fact, there was none.

AMERICA'S APPLES WERE A BUNCH OF CRABS

Fruits such as pears and peaches were unknown in the Americas, and the only apples were wild crab apples. Colonists introduced popular flowers like the All-American daisy and vegetables like cucumbers, cauliflower, cabbage, and onions. Even that old Southern staple, black-eyed peas, originally came from the Old World. Settlers also brought the dandelion, which keeps gardeners busy on weekends as they pull them out of their lawns.

THOSE A-MAIZE-ING NEW WORLD VEGGIES

Native Americans had their own collection of unique crops that Europeans had never seen before they got off the boat in the New World. The crops that made the greatest impact on world history were corn, the potato, the tomato, and tobacco.

But there were other New World crops, including the lima bean (Can you believe anyone liked lima beans enough to take them home?), sweet potato, pineapple, avocado, cranberry, and squash. Even though Halloween had been celebrated in the British Isles since ancient times, they never had a decent jack o'lantern until the Europeans got pumpkins from Native Americans. Plenty of flowers were also distinctively New World like zinnias, marigolds, dahlias, sunflowers, and the poinsettia.

MAKE CHOCOLATE, NOT WAR

From South America came cinchona bark, used to make quinine for treating malaria. Quinine saved lives, but most people would argue that the greatest gifts the Old World got from the New were the fragrant vanilla bean and the delectable cacao bean—source of chocolate. Aztecs, portrayed as savage warriors and practitioners of human sacrifice, were particularly fond of vanilla and chocolate. It was the Aztecs who first proved that old historical truth—no sooner do you settle down to relax with a nice cup of cocoa than a bunch of conquistadors arrive uninvited on their warhorses.

Florence Nightingale carried around a pet owl named Athena.

LIFE INSURANCE WITH YOUR LATTE?

Imagine the patrons at your local coffee place wearing big, curly Louis XIV wigs. Got it? Well, you're looking at the beginnings of the world-famous insurance company, Lloyd's of London.

You can't get a cup of coffee these days without being surrounded by mobile professionals sipping cappuccinos and busily avoiding going to the office by talking on cell phones and tapping laptops. Guess what? They did that in the 1600s too.

WHERE EVERYBODY KNOWS YOUR NAME

In the late 1600s, worldwide commerce was standard business for the merchants of Great Britain. Countless ships bearing treasures such as tea, sugar, spices, and timber rode the world's waves. The merchants who owned these vessels were always worried that a storm, pirates, or a captain's miscalculation off an uncharted shore would send their expensive ship and its expensive cargo to the bottom of the drink. Worried merchants often gathered to shmooze and pick up the latest information on all the ships at sea. Their favorite meeting place was Lloyd's, a London coffeehouse.

LATTE LLOYD

Edward Lloyd opened his cramped little cafe in 1687 on Tower Street near the Thames River. London coffee shops had specialty customers, like writers, bankers, or wool traders. Located near the docks, Lloyd's was a natural haven for those in the maritime trade. Later, when Lloyd moved his shop to more upscale digs on Lombard Street, he brought his shipping clientele with him.

THAT'S USING THE OLD BEAN

Lloyd served a fine cup of java to the coffee-crazed Londoners of the 17th century. But as he scanned his cafe full of hand-wringing ship owners (all wondering if their frigate of cinnamon or cloves had made it safely around the Horn), Lloyd saw an opportunity. He hadn't survived the dictatorship of Oliver Cromwell, the Plague, and the Great Fire by being a dunce. Lloyd thought of a way to make his customers pay for more than just a mug of java

---

Antonio de Egas Moniz won a Nobel Prize in medicine for developing the lobotomy.

and a dish of sherbet—and pay handsomely.

MOVE OVER STARBUCKS

In 1696, he started a publication called "Lloyd's List" that printed information on ship movements and conditions at sea. Lloyd's List contained dispatches from a network of reporters around the world. This info wasn't exactly timely—this was centuries before the telegraph or telephone, but any knowledge of weather conditions in distant seas or the geography of ports where no charts existed was invaluable. Lloyd's List grew larger over the years and became the established fount of information for London's shipping community. Lloyd's coffeehouse was known to be a better, faster, and more reliable source of maritime information than the Admiralty. Better yet, it was always open.

BUSINESS BLOSSOMS AMONG THE BEANS

In addition to becoming a source of information, the crowded tables of Lloyd's spawned a new breed of entrepreneurs. These smiling gents watched Lloyd's roomful of wealthy maritime merchants desperately trying to minimize their risks, and they saw a gold mine. They decided to sell peace of mind, and they offered to cover any potential loss of ship or cargo (because of storm, or pirate, or act of God) in return for an up-front payment called a premium. Lloyd's coffeehouse had given birth to the insurance salesman.

GOING TO THE OFFICE—FINALLY

Edward Lloyd died in 1713, but his business survived and continued to prosper. In 1771, a group of 79 coffeehouse underwriters joined together to form a company called The Society of Lloyd's. This was the official start of Lloyd's of London. Three years later, these insurance men finally moved out of the backroom of the coffeehouse into real office space.

AVOIDING THE OFFICE—AGAIN

No doubt, from that point forward, the insurance men used the coffeehouse not as their office, but as a place to go to avoid going to the office.

A SNOWBALL'S CHANCE

*Like many British eccentrics, Geoffrey Pyke at first
appears normal when viewed in Who's Who,
but on closer examination...*

Geoffrey Pyke was captured trying to sneak into Berlin during World War I and tossed into a German prison camp. By carefully noting that the sunlight momentarily blinded his guards every day at one certain location, Pyke managed to escape. That and a few other escapades made him something of a celebrity back home. Once the second World War loomed, the British decided to take advantage of his offbeat genius.

WACKY BUT WORKABLE

Assigned to the War Office as a scientific advisor, Pyke threw himself into devising clever and sometimes practical ways to help the war effort:

- Motorcycle sidecars that carried stretchers.
- Motorized sleds that carried torpedoes.
- Writing "Officer's Latrine" in German on a motorized cart British commandos were to use so the Nazis would leave it alone.
- Disguising British agents as avid golfers, then sending them throughout Germany to secretly gather signatures on a poll to convince Hitler that his people didn't want to go to war.

But the concept that propelled Pyke from fascinating oddball to military legend was the one he hit on while pondering one of the great problems of the war.

PYKE'S TOUR DE FORCE

Allied shipping was being cut to pieces by the merciless and precise German submarine fleet. Henry Kaiser's innovative line of Liberty Ships—cheap, mass-produced cargo ships—couldn't keep up with the appetite of the Wolf Pack subs. What was needed was some kind of strong military presence, a way of providing air cover so the merchant ships could get through safely. Something simple to assemble, that could carry long-range aircraft, and that wasn't so expensive that it drew valuable resources from the battlefront.

ICE IS NICE

Pyke's vision was marvelously absurd: an ice ship 600 feet wide, 4,000 feet long that would carry aircraft, munitions, and crew. According to War Department sketches, the ships were to look like aircraft carriers on steroids: flat-decked monsters that could carry, repair, and launch all kinds of aircraft. In one illustration, a planned ice-ship made the regular steel-hulled carrier—the largest ship in the war—look like a dinghy.

ON THE ROCKS

Pyke envisioned a special system mated to the refrigeration equipment so the bergs could spray out super-cold water to literally freeze enemy forces in their tracks. The project was code-named Habakkuk after a Biblical prophet who said, "I am doing a work in your days which you would not believe if told."

THE FLY IN THE OCEAN

The stumbling block to Pyke's incredible plans was that the frozen giants of the sea would—on a nice day—turn to mid-Atlantic slush. Pyke fixed that: he mixed a special combination of wood pulp and water, then froze it. The result was a rock-hard substance that melted very slowly, just what was needed to keep the ice ships afloat. It was named "Pykrete," after Pyke and concrete.

Pyke's boss, Lord Mountbatten showed it to his boss, Winston Churchill, and the deal was done. In 1943, a site was found—a secret boathouse on Patricia Lake in Canada—and testing began. The (comparatively) little ice ship was a complete success—in other words, it didn't melt all through a hot summer. But by this time the battle of the Atlantic had been virtually won. Pyke's project was abandoned.

After the war, Pyke worked to help staff England's fledgling National Health Service. But as he grew even more eccentric, he began to feel that his genius wasn't being recognized. In 1948, he took an overdose of sleeping pills and said goodbye to an unappreciative world.

The first New York to California flight, in 1911, took 49 days.

CLASS OF THE HEAD

How did sailors ah… go in old ships? They lacked flush toilets—even bathrooms—on Columbus's voyages or Drake's raids. The answers, however, are in plain view.

For the first few millennia of seafaring, the sea itself served as a portable potty. Sailors simply grabbed onto a sail and commenced "hanging out" over the edge. On a rough sea, this could be an occasionally dangerous occupation, not to mention embarrassing: ships were small and generally traveled within sight of land. Perhaps this explains why voyages usually paused each evening at a port.

THE END OF FREESTYLING

After the 17th century, ships added urinals called "pissdales." A metal basin built of lead or copper, the pissdale was fitted to the bulwarks (that's a wall lining the perimeter of the deck to you landlubbers). A lead-lined hole through the bulwarks allowed liquid to escape. Aw! But going over the rail was so much fun!

Enter the "beakhead," or more simply, the "head." The head, a structure at the very front of the boat, was ideal for the latrines. It was easy to get to, even for lubbers. It allowed a, ahem, "free drop" and was exposed to water during rough weather, which meant that it would be self-cleaning (bonus!). The location was so logical that "head" became synonymous with a ship's latrine, even today.

There were even special heads for officers. Certain seats more toward the side were enclosed in booths. Primarily intended for petty officers, theses "roundhouses" were also much preferred by the men during storms.

DOUBLE DUTY

For whalers, the extremely long time spent at sea meant that the crew had to get creative when it came to keeping clean. To this end, the crew urinated into a urine barrel. (Sailors with venereal diseases were excused from this duty.) The collected urine was then used to wash clothes. Urine contains ammonia, one of the few substances that sailors could use to remove oil or grease—a problem when rendering a whale. Talk about piss and vinegar!

In 1792, 1,200 free blacks sailed from Nova Scotia to found Sierra Leone in Africa.

CRUSADE OF THE STARS

The Second Crusade (1147–1148) failed to accomplish anything in particular, so the movement went into a 40-year funk. But the crusades staged a comeback—better than ever and with a star-studded cast.

The holy city of Jerusalem that the crusaders had fought so hard to capture fell to the Muslims in 1187. This set the stage for what turned out to be one of the most interesting of all the Christian campaigns (1189–1193).

THE FREDDIE, DICK, AND PHIL SHOW

Just like the good old days of Pope Urban II (who started the whole crusade thing), Europe reacted with wild enthusiasm in 1189 to the news that a new Crusade against the infidel Saracens was about to be launched. Three of medieval Europe's most illustrious monarchs would lead the charge to regain the Holy Land: Emperor Frederick Barbarossa of Germany, King Richard the Lionhearted of England, and King Philip Augustus of France.

FOOLHARDY FREDDIE

Emperor Frederick was nearly 70 years old. He'd governed Germany well for 36 years, but his strong and flamboyant personality sometimes led him into scrapes. He was an experienced crusader—he'd been on the Second Crusade 40 years earlier. By early May 1189 he had assembled one of the largest crusading armies—if not the largest—ever to take the field. His army began its march on May 11, 1189.

DASTARDLY DICK

By the time the Third Crusade got under way, Richard was nearly 33. His courage and resourcefulness showed up best on the battlefield and on campaign. He was the finest Crusade commander since Bohemond (of the First Crusade), and possibly the best of all. In fact, in single combat he was unrivaled in skill and bravery.

But he was also vain about his looks and loved pomp and display. He was also devious and self-centered. Richard sold everything he could to pay for the high cost of raising and transporting a huge army to the Holy Land. (This apparently included just about everything in England that wasn't nailed down.)

Scalping was originally a Dutch idea, not an Indian one.

FRIENDLY PHIL

Philip was the youngest, still in his mid-twenties at the start of the campaign. He wasn't attractive, clever, or well-educated, but he had a kind of practical intelligence and a strong disposition toward equity and fairness. He didn't have Frederick's strong religious fervor. He was in fact more interested in acquiring Champagne (the province, not the drink), as well as Aquitaine and Flanders—all territories controlled by the English. This made Richard his natural enemy. But when the Crusade finally set out from France in July 1190, the two kings rode side by side, smiling and pretending to be the best of friends. In reality, though, Richard completely overshadowed Philip. And Philip resented it.

PHIL'S ILL

Philip and Richard parted company at Lyons, in southeast France. Philip decided to take his army over the Alps to Genoa, on the northwest coast of Italy. Richard marched south through France to Marseilles, where he hired several ships to transport his army to Genoa to link up with Philip's forces. From Genoa, the two armies would sail together in a huge fleet to the Holy Land. Philip got there first, but he'd had a rough journey over the Alps and was ill and in low spirits. His spirits sank even lower after hearing news of the fate of the third monarch, Frederick.

FRED'S DEAD

Frederick had already made it to southern Asia Minor, when he stopped near a river and decided to take a swim. He was a vigorous old man with tremendous stamina, but he was also something of a show-off. In any case, he ran into some serious difficulties in midstream (he may have had a heart attack) and drowned. Dispirited and leaderless, his entire army turned around and trudged back to Germany. Only a few made it back though; most of them were slaughtered by the Turks or died of plague.

ACHEY AT ACRE

In June 1191 the crusaders landed at Acre, a key fortress city on the northern Palestinian coast that the soldiers of the First Crusade (1096–1099) had conquered and then lost several years later to the Muslims. Another crusader army garrisoned in Palestine had been besieging the fortress for two years without success when Richard and Philip arrived. They were just drawing up the

Josef Stalin's son died in a Nazi German prison camp.

final details for a major assault on the Saracen stronghold when Richard fell seriously ill (it was probably malaria). Though weak and listless, he had himself carried to the forward lines on an inspection tour and shot several arrows at the tower watchmen.

NEIGHBORS, GOOD AND BAD

Meanwhile, a shrewd, skilled warrior-prince named Saladin and his powerful Muslim army were camped on the hills above Acre. When Saladin heard that Richard was sick, he chivalrously sent him a gift of fruit and snow.

Even though they succeeded in breaching the walls, the crusaders' first assault came to nothing. Philip ordered a second attack a few days later, which also failed. There was much hard and vicious fighting, centered around the crusaders' siege engines, the huge towers that the crusaders wheeled over to the walls of besieged cities. Soldiers then used a covered bridge (to shield the men from mortal dangers like rocks and arrows) placed near the top of the tower to climb across and onto the city walls. In those days, kings and princes would occasionally give pet names to their siege engines. Richard brought his favorite siege engine, which he affectionately called "mategriffon," "the Greek-killer," and Philip brought his "Bad Neighbor." Bad Neighbor battled against a similar engine mounted on the walls by the Saracens. It was called, menacingly, "the Evil Kinsman."

THE SURRENDER OF ACRE

The fighting grew more and more desperate, but Saladin wouldn't send his main army against the crusaders. (He may have been waiting for fresh troops from Egypt.) In any case, this put the beleaguered defenders of Acre in a very bad position. So bad, in fact, that they were forced to beg the crusaders for a truce. The Saracens had just one request—that they be allowed to leave the city unharmed, with just the clothes on their backs. This gave the crusaders a chance to show Christian mercy in action.

RICHARD THE HARD-HEARTED

King Philip was prepared to accept the terms of surrender, but Richard rejected them outright. The portrait that some historians have painted of the gallant king who behaved with courtesy and a certain amount of respect for his enemies has no real foundation. Richard hadn't come all the way to the Holy Land to mount a

---

During World War II, the German-sounding sauerkraut was renamed "liberty cabbage."

difficult, costly siege, only to let his enemies walk away scot-free. About 6,000 Saracens from Acre surrendered and were taken prisoner. At Richard's order, more than 3,000 of the Muslims—men, women, and children—were executed on a hill near the city, in full view of Saladin and his men.

PUT UP YOUR DUKE!

Richard installed himself in a palace in Acre and flew his battle flag. When a minor player, Duke Leopold of Austria, set up his flag beside Richard's, soldiers under Richard's command tore down the flag and tossed it into a ditch. Leopold was offended by this outrageous insult—and Richard had a new mortal enemy.

A KING'S RANSOM

On July 31, 1191, King Philip left Acre by ship and returned to France, leaving most of his army behind in Richard's command. Richard pressed on and won back considerable portions of the Holy Land for Christianity. But in the end he decided not to attempt an attack on Jerusalem. He considered the city impregnable.

Worse yet, Richard fell into hostile hands on his return journey to Europe. Interestingly enough, these were not Muslim hands. Instead, they turned out to be the vengeful hands of a certain Duke Leopold of Austria. With a keen eye on the bottom line, Leopold released his royal captive only after England had forked over the staggering sum of 100,000 pounds—quite literally a king's ransom.

* * *

IN THE LOOP

Loopholes were originally those slit-type windows in the battlements of castles. They were wider on the inside, so archers could shoot from them while being protected by the very narrow opening on the outside. They became obsolete when gunpowder made castle and city walls unimportant as protective devices.

Even though no one could have escaped through them, the word came to mean an outlet or means of escape. Of course, today a loophole is a clever way out of a situation, especially one that has to do with the law.

English and Portuguese troops have never faced each other in combat.

DON'T LET YOUR DAUGHTERS GROW UP TO BE POETS

Lady Ada Lovelace brought a poetic perspective to mathematics. Maybe that's why she could work out complicated computer programming before a computer had even been built.

L ady Byron was terrified that her daughter Ada might turn out like her father. When Annabella Milbanke married the poet Lord Byron in 1815, he was already famous as the creator of the brooding, defiant romantic hero. He was as deeply melancholic and determined to follow his own passions as the characters he created.

"MAD, BAD, AND DANGEROUS TO KNOW"

That's Lady Caroline Lamb's oft-quoted appraisal of Byron, and, as one of his lovers, Lady Lamb ought to know. Byron's amorous dalliances also included his half-sister, Augusta Leigh, and a long string of other ill-advised love affairs.

A year after they were married, Lady Byron went home to her parents, taking baby daughter Ada with her. In spite of her husband's furious protests, she managed to get a legal separation. Stories about Byron's affairs and rumored bisexuality aroused so much public moral indignation that Byron left England, never to return. Taking no chances that her daughter might grow up to be a poet, Lady Byron hired a series of tutors to educate little Ada in mathematics and science, as well as reading and writing. By the time she was 13, Ada knew more about math than her tutors did.

HOW TO TRAP A MAN WITH MATH

It wasn't as odd as you think for girls to study math in the mid-1800s. Magazines like the *Ladies Diary* encouraged women to develop their wit as well as their beauty, and actually had special sections that posed math problems. (Imagine trying that on the *Elle* gang.) And women were regularly writing for scientific publications around the same time.

His pacifist parents raised Dwight David Eisenhower to hate war.

ANALYTICAL ENGINE

At a dinner party one night, Ada—by then married to the earl of Lovelace, and with three young children—heard inventor Charles Babbage talk about his calculating machine: the Analytical Engine. She was hooked. The engine wasn't finished, and wouldn't be built in their lifetimes. Though neither she nor Babbage would ever see it, they both understood how it could work.

She translated an Italian article about it, and added a footnote of her own that discussed the difference between a simple calculating machine and the Analytical Engine—a difference like that between pocket calculators and computers today. Babbage suggested she add more of her own ideas, which turned out to be three times as long as the original article and were published in 1843 in *Taylor's Scientific Memoirs*, a serious science journal. Apparently Ada Lovelace inherited something from her father after all. Her powerful imagination allowed her to make leaps beyond the available information. Aware that Babbage had based his designs on a weaving loom, she wrote in a letter, "The Analytical Engine weaves algebraic patterns just as the Jacquard loom weaves flowers and leaves."

CREATING A COMPUTER IN HER MIND

Lady Lovelace described how the engine could produce important sequences of numbers, how it could deal with symbolic sequences (such as algebra), how it could have a memory, and how subroutines could be built in for special tasks. She predicted it could be used to compose music and produce graphics. She even considered artificial intelligence, and she explained why A.I. wouldn't work. In fact, her ideas were so good that a lot of people consider her the first computer programmer. (In 1979, a U.S. Department of Defense software language was named after her.)

After her work on the Analytical Engine, Lady Ada's social life broadened to include a wide range of interesting contemporaries: Charles Dickens, Michael Faraday, Charles Wheatstone, Sir David Brewster, and her old pal Charles Babbage. But she suffered from recurring illnesses. Unfortunately, she turned out to be like her famous father in another way. Like Byron, Ada Lovelace died at the very young age of 36.

MAGNIFICENT FAILURE

This page, like billions of other printed pages read worldwide, owes its existence to a bankrupt, small-time German businessman.

Johann Gutenberg borrowed 150 gulden from his cousin in 1448 and set up the world's first book-printing operation in his hometown, Mainz, Germany. He had no idea of how rapidly his idea would spread. By 1500, more than a thousand print shops in Europe were using his technique, and several million books had been printed. Yet Gutenberg's business never printed more than 300 copies a day, and by 1458 he was bankrupt.

FASTER AND CHEAPER

Gutenberg never planned to produce large editions or flood the market with bestsellers. He just wanted to find a way to compete with expensive, handwritten copies of the Bible, and other sacred texts, for rich clients. This work was traditionally done on parchment made from sheepskin and was a slow, pricey process. Gutenberg's idea was to mechanically turn out a cheaper alternative.

EAST MEETS WEST

At the time of Gutenberg's big idea, printing was being done on a limited scale using the Chinese invention of woodblock. In Europe, woodblock printing had been used to print patterns on fabric, pictures, and then pages of books. The process involved engraving each page on a block of wood—in reverse!

JUST HIS TYPE

Woodblock printing was difficult, time-consuming, and the quality of printing was poor. It just wasn't a moneymaker. So Gutenberg invented a printing technology of his own—moveable metal type. By setting a standard size and format, Gutenberg could design a new method for producing letters. Rather than engrave each page individually on a block, he made hard metal punches for letters. The punches were used to form molds in soft copper. Molten lead was then poured into the molds to make lead type. The lead letters were stored in different drawers, then lined up in wooden forms to make up a page. The forms could be used over and over and disassembled after a job was done so the letters could be

---

Neither Germany nor Italy were united as modern countries until the 1800s.

reused. Gutenberg also used good-quality paper rather than expensive parchment. This paper had been available in Europe since the 12th century. Cheaper than parchment, it was made from rags and wood fiber. He made ink from soot, linseed oil, and egg whites to produce a solid black print on moistened paper. A wine press squeezed the paper and type together, and this system was used until the 1800s, when an iron press was developed.

BESTSELLER—180 COPIES SOLD

Aiming to compete with handwritten manuscripts, Gutenberg wanted each book to be an exclusive, luxury product. After printing, his books were hand-finished with painted initial letters and illustrations. Although he'd invented the tool for mass production of books whose pages could be exactly alike, the world wasn't ready for them. If Gutenberg had mass-produced cheap texts, he couldn't have sold them—most people in Europe couldn't read.

Gutenberg's bestselling book was the famous Gutenberg 42-line Bible. It was so clear and legible, some readers said sorcery was involved. Printing came to be known as "the black art" because of its magical results and because printers got covered in ink. Printers' assistants were called "printer's devils"; the term continued in use until hot-metal printing disappeared in the 1970s.

After his business failed in 1458, he opened a second print shop in 1459, but this closed by 1462. Gutenberg's 42-line Bibles are priceless now. He made about 180 of them, but few have survived. Still, Gutenberg's invention survived. As different Christian churches tried to establish their own versions of the Bible in the following centuries, printing came into its own. Churches and learning institutions ordered huge numbers of books. In Germany the spread of printed books (especially Martin Luther's translation of the Bible) helped establish a standard written language in Germany. Gutenberg's invention was changing the world. People were learning to read.

A BESTSELLER WITH NO ROYALTIES

Gutenberg died in 1468 without profiting from his amazing invention, but we reap the profits every time we read a book.

One of Theodore Roosevelt's sons was named Kermit.

WHAT WERE THE WARS OF THE ROSES?

When King Richard II of England got back from a trip to Ireland, there was somebody else sitting on his throne.

The Wars of the Roses were fought between two branches of the Plantagenet family, the Yorks and the Lancasters. The Yorks ruled Britain for almost 250 years, from 1154 to 1399—and were successful enough to add Scotland and Wales to the list of countries under British rule. But In 1399 Henry Bolingbroke, of the Lancaster branch, took the throne from his cousin King Richard II, a York.

OUR STORY BEGINS...

Henry threw Richard in prison, where he died, possibly by starving himself. The whole episode ticked off Richard's branch of the family to no end. They kept pretty quiet because Henry, now King Henry IV, and his son, Henry V, were popular kings (the younger added lots of territory to the British Kingdom including most of France). Tensions were kept to a minimum between the Lancastrians and Yorkists for a long time after Henry IV took the throne.

REMEMBER THE RICHARD!

It was during the reign of the next king, Henry VI, that England lost control of her holdings in France (thanks in part to Joan of Arc) and unrest began to brew. Add to that questions of Henry's sanity (cuckoo!) and you had real trouble. Around 1452 or so, it was remembered how Henry VI's grandfather had taken the throne from Richard II. That was all the Yorkists needed.

"WE'RE A-FEUDIN'!"

The two branches of the Plantagenet family started carrying on. They sniped at and feuded with each other whenever time and distance permitted. The Lancasters assumed they were the rightful rulers because, let's face it, possession is nine-tenths of the law. The York side aimed to even the score for Richard's sake, and for the next 20 years, Merrie Olde England wasn't all that merry. Each skirmish between the Lancastrians and the Yorkists was another War of the Roses.

St. Patrick wasn't Irish. He was a Brit kidnapped by Irish pirates.

THE TIDE TURNS

Finally in 1471, something came of all this feuding. Henry VI was finally deposed (and probably murdered by the Yorks). The Yorks took over and put their own Edward IV on the throne. Things were decidedly merry again until Edward died, leaving behind only an infant son. His name was also Edward, naturally, and he took over the throne as Edward V. But because he was a baby, Edward Jr., wasn't particularly intimidating. The boy's uncle, Richard, one of the folks not intimidated in the least by the boy king, seized the throne as Richard III and little Eddie was never seen or heard from again. Richard III ruled until 1485, during which there were more skirmishes between the Yorkists and Lancastrians, and bad feelings grew throughout the kingdom.

SO LONG, RICHARD

Richard III was generally disliked, and you know what happens when subjects aren't happy with their monarch. On August 22, 1485, Henry Tudor defeated King Richard III's forces at the Battle of Bosworth (which is famous because it signaled the end of the Wars of the Roses and because it only lasted two hours, which must be some kind of record). Crowned King Henry VII, he married Elizabeth, the daughter of Edward IV, to unite the two branches of the family. Their son was the famous Henry VIII.

SHAKESPEARE GETS INTO THE ACT

If you're still confused about all the Henrys, Richards, Planta-genets, Yorks, Lancasters, and Tudors—not to mention the Edwards—you're not alone. Shakespeare devoted seven plays to trying to set the record straight as to the history of the Wars of the Roses. The plays, titled after the Henrys and Richards involved in the wars, and are known as Shakespeare's history cycle.

BUT WHY THE WARS OF THE ROSES?

Those of you who've been paying attention may be asking your-selves, "Yes, but why were they called the Wars of the Roses?" Very simple. Because each family, or "house," had a symbol: the Lancaster's was the red rose, the York's was the white. When Henry VII took the throne, he designed what's called the "Tudor Rose," a rose with alternating red and white petals signifying the unification of the houses of York and Lancaster.

It was probably Francis Hopkinson, not Betsy Ross, who designed the U.S. flag.

PROVEN WRONG BY HISTORY: PART III

Gives new meaning to eating one's words. Want fries with that?

OIL DRILLING

"Drill for oil? You mean drill into the ground to try and find oil? You're crazy."

—Drillers whom Edwin L. Drake tried to enlist to his oil-drilling project in 1859.

BACTERIOLOGY

"Louis Pasteur's theory of germs is ridiculous fiction."

—Pierre Pachet, Professor of Physiology at France's Toulouse University, 1872.

SURGERY

"The abdomen, the chest, and the brain will forever be shut from the intrusion of the wise and humane surgeon."

—Sir John Eric Ericksen, British surgeon, appointed Surgeon-Extraordinary to Queen Victoria, 1873.

THE STOCK MARKET

"Stocks have reached what looks like a permanent high plateau."

—I. Fisher, Professor of Economics, Yale University, 1929.

FEDERAL EXPRESS

"The concept is interesting and well-formed, but in order to earn better than a 'C,' the idea must be feasible."

—A Yale University Management Professor in response to Fred Smith's paper proposing reliable, overnight, delivery service. (Smith went on to found Federal Express.)

EVERYTHING ELSE

"Everything that can be invented has been invented."

—Charles H. Duell, Commissioner, U.S. Office of Patents, 1899.

Until 1832, Old Sarum had two members in Britain's parliament, but nobody lived there.

WHEN CHILDHOOD WAS BORN

Forget Sesame Street. Forget cute. Forget "Let Mommy kiss your boo-boo." There were days when boys couldn't be boys, and a girl didn't enjoy being a girl.

SHORT PEOPLE GOT NO REASON

Once upon a time, there was no such thing as childhood. There was infancy and, oh, sure, there were a lot of short people who looked like what we know as children, but once they hit five years old or so, they were expected to behave like adults. As soon as a kid was able, he or she would be apprenticed to the family business, be it a farm, bakery, or blacksmith's shop. By seven years old—what the Roman Catholic church considers the "age of reason"—children had reached full adulthood.

AW, QUIT YER WHININ'!

Sociologists agree that a typical 10-year-old in almost any period before the 20th century was more mature and independent than today's 25-year-old. The concept of childhood, and the associated protections and innocence, didn't surface until the 15th and 16th centuries, and then only among the privileged classes. The idea took centuries to filter down to the rest of society.

YOU SAY YOU WANT A REVOLUTION

When the Industrial Revolution hit, kids who weren't working city streets selling papers and shining shoes found work in factories; farm kids found employment in mills and mines. All worked under the same miserable and dangerous conditions as adults.

SIDE TRIP TO ENGLAND

Charles Dickens didn't have to go very far for story ideas. Children in Great Britain whose parents couldn't support them (or who had no parents at all) were called "pauper children." The government was supposed to arrange for them to become apprentices, to learn a trade, and be cared for. But thousands were turned over to mill owners, with no one to intercede for them or keep track of their status. Some parents even sold their children to mill owners for a period of years. The lucky ones who stayed at home still worked long hours to supplement the family income.

THE WHEELS OF PROGRESS
In 1802, England passed the first child labor legislation, but it only applied to pauper apprentices and wasn't enforced in any way. Over the next 76 years, it was followed by a series of "Factory Acts" that gradually strengthened inspection of conditions, shortened work hours, and raised the minimum age for working tykes.

REPORT TO THE COMMISSIONER
When Parliament set up a commission in the 1830s to investigate problems, a young textile mill worker testified that since the age of eight he had worked from 6 a.m. to 8 p.m., with an hour off at noon. However, when things were especially busy, he worked 16 straight hours, from 5 a.m. to 9 p.m. Another boy, whose parents sold him to a mill owner, testified that child laborers were locked up in the mill night and day. A few dared to escape, but if found, they caught the Dickens, if you know what we mean.

BACK IN THE U.S.A.
Child labor problems first became an issue in the U.S. in the 1850s, mostly in large northern cities like New York. And the problems grew as industrialization increased. Add to that the increasing immigration at the turn of the century, and the South's late and slow industrial development, and you've got a system that screamed for reform.

It wasn't until the early 20th century that a serious child labor movement was born. Activists fought against a system that allowed six-year-olds to work 16 hours a day, even if the little darling was bringing home a whopping two cents a week.

NOW, THAT'S PROGRESS
Naturally, the factory and mill owners fought like crazy against these do-gooders. That is, until they realized that new machinery could do the job more efficiently than children—and do it for free. So, as more and more factories and mills were mechanized, the movement gathered steam. In the U.S., it wasn't until 1938 that a law was passed forbidding anyone under 16 to hold a job

---

Tiny Morocco was the first country to recognize the U.S. as an independent country.

(except for 14 and 15 year olds who are permitted to work in certain occupations after school). But as these little laborers were liberated from the workforce, a huge, new problem loomed. What to do with children who now had nothing to do all day? Crime was rampant in the cities, mostly committed by bored kids.

SCHOOL DAYS, SCHOOL DAYS

"I know!" said somebody, "Let's put them in school, that'll keep them off the streets." The idea caught on. And that, ladies and gentlemen, is how compulsory public education was born, and with it, the segregation of children from the rest of society. Our present-day concept of childhood had almost arrived. Just one more thing was needed to complete the picture.

HI, MOM!

The continuing trend toward mechanization was forcing women out of work, too, leaving the men to do all the heavy lifting. So moms stayed home and the kids became more and more dependent on them. Finally there was someone who could answer those burning questions: "What's for dinner?" "Did you see my other sock?" "Can I sleep over at Kimberly's?"

And this of course—after World War II when the "boys" returned home—gave rise to that perfect ideal of the nuclear family of the 1950s, made up of a dad, a mom, and 2.7 kids.

The rest, as Uncle John says, is history.

*   *   *

KEEP SMILING

The yellow smiley face is as round as the name of the man who created it. Harvey R. Ball, a World War II veteran and graphic artist. Ball gave birth to his grinning brainchild in December 1963 as a commission for the State Mutual insurance company, who wanted to boost company morale. He received $45 for his work of art. The smiley face spread like wildfire and the rest is history. Harvey passed away on April 14, 2001, at the age of 79, but his smiley face will live on. Maybe forever.

When slavery ended, some 40,000 African Americans became cowboys.

HENRY THE NAVIGATOR

*Our story begins sometime around the third century, when
Europe lost the continent of Africa...*

The ancient civilizations of Egypt, Greece, and Rome had known that south of Africa's Sahara Desert there was a large area populated by black people. As the Dark Ages descended and closed Europe off for a thousand years of ignorance and superstition, they forgot. By the seventh century, Muslim Arabs had overrun Egypt and all of North Africa. Europe was still picking up the pieces (and none too successfully) after the fall of Rome and didn't have time to look for black Africa, even if they'd known it was there. Besides, the Arabs made North Africa a stronghold no one dared cross, cutting the rest of Africa off, just as if it had slid into the ocean.

ENTER OUR HERO

Years after the curtain had descended across Africa, in 1394 a man was born whose delusions would change all this: Portuguese Prince Henry, known to history as "Henry the Navigator." Henry was famous for a few things, among them the fact that he never got on a ship. However, he was single-handedly responsible for a long series of Portuguese voyages of exploration which, nearly 100 years later, would result in Portuguese ships sailing around the African coast, with Bartholomew Diaz rounding the Cape of Good Hope in 1488, and finally discovering it was possible to reach East Africa and India by sea. All these Portuguese sailors were graduates of Henry's School of Navigation. And he kept the voyages going in the face of war, debt, and disaster. Why? Not because he wanted to explore Africa. He was in search of paradise.

RUMOR #1: In the 14th century, the Garden of Eden was thought to be a real place, and it was believed that God had appointed a Christian monarch by the name of Prester John (which means "Priest John") to guard it. He was supposed to rule over a land of fantastic riches somewhere in East Africa. In fact, there was a kingdom there called Abyssinia, which had been Christian for a thousand years, but it was cut off from the rest of the Christian world by those darn Arabs.

If people asked Al Capone what he did for a living, he would say he dealt furniture.

RUMOR #2: Based on another legend that said the Nile River had a western branch that emptied into the ocean on the West African coast, Henry sent a bunch of ships to explore the coast, go up the river, and find Prester John and the Garden of Eden.

RUMOR #3: The Arabs said that beyond the terrible Cape Bojador on the northwest coast lay the Green Sea of Darkness— the beginning of the end of the world. The land changed to desert, the sun burned everything black, and there were great sea monsters. No one had ever returned from there. Was Henry afraid? Heck no. He was going to stay home.

LUCKY 15TH

He sent out 15 expeditions between 1424 and 1434, until finally, one brave captain, Gil Eannes, managed to round the fearsome Cape Bojador. He and his crew were eaten by huge, ugly sea monsters and that's the end of the story. (Just kidding.) They actually put ashore on the coast of the Sahara. They didn't find people, but brought back a few hardy plants as proof of their accomplishment. The next voyages went farther down the coast. Since the Portuguese (and pretty much everyone else) thought that the earth was uninhabitable in the region below the Sahara, it caused a sensation when the 1441 expedition found real, live black people. No one in Europe had even known they existed. But it barely made an impression on Prince Henry. He still wanted to find Prester John.

THE RIVER, THE PROBLEMS

In 1445 one of his expeditions at last found the great river he'd been looking for—the Gambia. Two problems: Henry's money was running out, so it would be ten years before he could finance an expedition up it. The second problem was that the Gambia wasn't connected to the Nile and wasn't very navigable for very far (but this would be discovered later). Henry's contribution was huge. Literally. He died hopelessly in debt in 1460 at the age of 66. but, with all his dreaming, he'd found a whole new continent and a whole new race of people. He'd also opened a new chapter in world history. Portuguese explorers and seamen inspired by Henry, and trained at his school of navigation, went out and established the most extensive empire in the world, an empire that dominated European trade for the next 150 years.

Connecticut, Georgia, and Massachusetts waited until 1941 to ratify the Bill of Rights.

THE SWAN KING'S CASTLES

Was the so-called mad king Ludwig just a genius born in the wrong place at the wrong time? Or was he really nuts?

Ludwig II of Bavaria is remembered as "the mad king." He was pronounced unfit to rule by reason of insanity in 1886, and removed from the throne by court officials. While lots of sane kings leave behind a forgotten list of battles and ugly fields of tombstones, Mad Ludwig's legacy still enchants the world.

THE PALACE CLOSET
Madness aside, Ludwig's day-to-day problem was that he was living in the palace closet. He was a youthful monarch in Victorian Europe, and was expected to have a wife and children, but he was a homosexual. Ludwig tried to escape from the impossible pressures of his monarchy into a fantasy world of castles and horses and mountains. In the end his fantasies killed him.

THE LITTLE PRINCE
Ludwig became crown prince at age three. Granddad Ludwig I had to abdicate the throne after giving too much power to his mistress, dancer Lola Montez. Daddy Maximilian took the throne, and Ludwig's childhood became an endless, lonely preparation for becoming king. Little Ludwig had some happy times with his governess who read him fairy tales. Mainly he was isolated with his younger brother Otto in a cold, military environment. The future ruler's program involved daily lessons from 5:30 a.m. to 8 p.m. The stress was on military training, but for Ludwig it was just plain stress.

THE SWAN KING
When Maxmillian suddenly died in 1864, the shy, handsome teenager was presented to the public as their new monarch. They adored him, and Ludwig adored them back. "I carry my heart to the throne, a heart which beats for my people and which glows for their welfare," he wrote his old governess. In his mind, Ludwig was

---

The original Bill of Rights would have kept federal politicians from raising their own salaries.

now the Swan King, the hero of the fantasies and fairy tales his governess had taught him. Ludwig's idea of being a Swan King was reinforced by *Lohengrin*, a romantic opera by Richard Wagner about some "Knights of the Swan." One of King Ludwig's first official acts was to bring Wagner to Munich at his own expense. Ludwig's patronage helped the composer create his masterpiece, *The Ring of the Nibelungen*.

THE KING AND THE CLOSET

Aside from opera, Ludwig enjoyed dressing up in fine costumes, and driving through the countryside in carriages or winter sleighs, ideally with a handsome young man by his side. Unfortunately, it soon became clear that the handsome young king just wasn't interested in women. Rumors began to circulate about Ludwig's relationship with Wagner. The composer only cared about Ludwig's money and prestige, but in the public mind Wagner was just a male Lola Montez. Wagner was booted out of Munich.

BROTHERLY LOVE

The unhappy Ludwig hoped that he could burden his younger brother, Otto, with the glory of the Bavarian throne. He thought that Otto might give a more convincing performance as king—with a normal marriage and some children, for a start. Unfortunately, Otto was mad. As Ludwig wrote in 1871, "Otto did not take his boots off for eight weeks. [He was convinced he had boils on his feet.] He makes terrible faces and barks like a dog." The royal family had to accept that Otto had gone over the edge. He was taken away for a long life under guard until his death in 1916.

Ludwig tried to go through with an arranged marriage in 1867, but at the last minute he called it off—he'd met a handsome blond groom in his stables. Ludwig promoted the groom to master of the horse with responsibility for 500 horses, but that didn't stop his new infatuation from getting married. Ludwig was heartbroken. He developed a few more male relationships after that, but from now on there was only one important thing in his life. Ludwig spent his life building fairy tale castles suitable for the fantasies of a swan king.

UNIFICATION IN HIS SPARE TIME

Meanwhile, over in the militaristic German state of Prussia (the German states were still independent countries at that time)

The U.S. was the first independent country in the New World. Haiti was #2.

Chancellor of Prussia Otto von Bismarck decided to unify Germany. He said later that he couldn't have done it without Ludwig's consent, and so, without interrupting his Swan King fantasy, Ludwig helped create the German state, a momentous decision that eventually led to two World Wars.

While the rest of Europe was building factories and battle-ships, Ludwig was busy building medieval fairy tale castles: Neuschwanstein, Linderhof, and Herrenchiemsee. They were partly inspired by Wagner's operas, and partly by the medieval and rococo architecture that were everywhere in 19th-century Europe. Linderhof was Ludwig's favorite castle. Framed by lush gardens the castle grounds contained small buildings that incorporated the romance of Wagner's operas. Ludwig could stay in the Venusberg, inspired by the opera *Tannhauser*, or in the Gurnamantz's Hermitage from the opera *Parsifal*. But his fun didn't last; the powerful ministers at court who were ambitious for Bavaria resented money being thrown away on castles.

SHIPPED OFF TO SEE

In 1886, the ministers at court decided that enough was enough, and issued a proclamation saying that Ludwig was unfit to govern. He was driven from his palace in a closed carriage, and taken to a retreat by the Starnberg See lake near Munich. Three days later, he died under suspicious circumstances. He and the doctor attending him seemed to have drowned in shallow water while they were out walking. The mysterious death was never explained.

WAS THE SWAN KING A FEW FEATHERS SHORT?

Was Ludwig really loony? Some modern historians suggest that Ludwig was tortured by guilt about his sexuality and that led to deranged, obsessive behavior. But he may have always suffered from madness. As a boy, he tried to kill Otto by strangling him with a handkerchief. His diaries are full of paranoid, senseless ramblings. If Ludwig was mad, there was a magnificent method to his madness. He combined aspects of Wagner's operas, the aura of old German fairy tales, and the reality of mountains and forests— and made Bavarian magic. Ironically, the castles he built so obses-sively, and which his officials considered such a waste of money, today bring millions of dollars to Bavaria in tourist revenues. The impractical Ludwig actually created a viable business.

An army of cowboys called gauchos helped win freedom for Uruguay.

THIS SIDE UP

*Henry "Box" Brown got his nickname the old-fashioned way.
He earned it.*

In the 1850s, a man called Henry "Box" Brown toured England, speaking and sometimes singing to enthusiastic audiences. He showed them a panorama he'd created, called "Mirror of Slavery," a moving scroll with scenes from slave life—scenes that he knew firsthand. The pictures also showed the story of how Henry "Box" Brown got his nickname.

BORN A SLAVE

Born into slavery in America, he was separated from his family as a teenager and taken to Richmond, Virginia, to work in a tobacco factory. He worked hard and even earned a little money. He fell in love, got married, and had three children with his wife, Nancy.

A PROMISE MADE

Before he married, Henry asked his owner to promise never to sell Nancy or their children. The owner agreed, but a few years later changed his mind. Henry watched helplessly as his family was led away with ropes around their necks. They were being taken south, and he knew he'd never see them again. After that, if Henry Brown's life was going to be worth living, it would have to be in freedom. He worked out a bold plan, one that could easily kill him—even if it worked.

IN THE HANDS OF FATE

Henry Brown had a white friend, a carpenter, who built him a wooden crate, 3 feet long, 2½ feet deep and 2 feet wide. On the outside, the carpenter painted "THIS SIDE UP, WITH CARE." He addressed the box to a friend in Philadelphia, an abolitionist who was a member of the Underground Railroad. On March 23, 1849, Henry Brown folded up his 5-foot-8-inch, 200-pound self, and squeezed inside the box. He later wrote, "I laid me down in my darkened home of three feet by two, and… resigned myself to my fate."

The carpenter nailed the box shut and left it for the baggage handlers. He sent a telegraph to his contact in Philadelphia, saying that the box was on its way.

BOXED IN

Inside the box, Henry had a little leather bag of water and some crackers. Three tiny air holes let in some light and air. He carried a hand drill, but it turned out, he couldn't have used that drill even if he'd been suffocating.

HANDLE WITH CARE

Unfortunately, the baggage handlers didn't always pay attention to the words on the outside of the crate. The very first ones turned it upside down, so Henry Brown was resting on his head. He was tossed into a baggage car, but the box rolled over and he was right side up again.

DEFINITELY WRONG SIDE UP

The crate was put on a steamboat, upside-down again. Henry described his body's reactions to that: "I... found to my dismay, that my eyes were almost swollen out of their sockets, and the veins on my temple seemed ready to burst. I made no noise, however, determining to obtain 'victory or death,' but endured the terrible pain, as well as I could, sustained under the whole by the thoughts of sweet liberty. About half an hour afterwards, I attempted again to lift my hands to my face, but I found I was not able to move them. A cold sweat now covered me from head to foot."

RIGHT SIDE UP

At that point, Henry thought he might die inside that box. But finally somebody noticed the words on the outside and turned it over. The crate was next put on a wagon. Then it was thrown off, and landed upside down. "I seemed to be destined to escape on my head," Henry commented.

He listened in terror as workmen argued over whether they could fit such a big crate onto the next train. But finally they picked it up and shoved it into the baggage car—this time right side up.

ALL RIGHT INSIDE?

Twenty-seven hours after it was sent, Henry's box arrived in Philadelphia. It had traveled 350 miles. After three more hours, a group of Underground Railroad members picked it up at the station, put it on a wagon, and took it to a house.

The first European to set foot in Australia was a Dutch sailor who'd been blown off course.

The people who crowded around the box were afraid to open it at first. Finally, someone knocked on the box and asked, "Is all right within?" to which Henry replied, "All right." Henry's new friends were overjoyed, and hurried to pry the box open. Henry got up, shook himself, and immediately fainted.

FREE AT LAST
He was free, and from that day on he was called Henry "Box" Brown. He and a friend toured the free states with the box and the panorama, telling people what slavery was like. His book, *Narrative of Henry Box Brown*, was published later that year. But in 1850, the U.S. Congress passed the Fugitive Slave Act. Now, suspected slaves could be arrested in the Northern states and returned to their masters.

MR. SHOWBIZ
So Henry Brown took his panorama to England and gave antislavery lectures there. Later, around 1862, he switched to entertainments that included other singers and dancers, and even ventriloquists. He was last heard of about 1864, living in freedom in Wales.

*   *   *

SLAVERY FACTS

Slavery came about nearly 10,000 years ago because farmers needed help—free help, that is—on the fields.

Slavery came to America in the 1600s, but not all of the states allowed the practice. The ones that did were appropriately known as "slave states"; the ones that didn't, "free states."

By the middle of the nineteenth century, there were nearly four million slaves working for the upper classes.

From 1790 to 1800, the capital of the United States was Philadelphia.

RIDDLES:
A SERIOUS SUBJECT

*People in ancient cultures took their riddles
much more seriously than we do today.*

In about the ninth century B.C., the Greek poet Homer wrote about heroes who fought in battles, had amazing adventures, and struggled with gods that acted like manic-depressives. Homer's *Odyssey* is about a king's long journey home after the Trojan War: the monsters, magic, and seductive enchantresses he faced. But legend has it that Homer—the author of all these monumental epics—killed himself in frustration because he couldn't answer a simple riddle.

THE RIDDLE THAT STUMPED HOMER

The riddle in question was this, spoken by Greek fishermen: "What we caught we threw away; What we didn't catch, we kept." According to the story, Homer couldn't figure it out, and it drove him to suicide. If you don't get it either, don't even think about following Homer's example. We'll give you the answers at the end of this article.

The story might not be true (whether or not there even *was* a Homer is still in debate), but the ancient Greeks went wild for riddles. The word comes from a Greek root meaning "to give advice."

A RIDDLE FROM BABYLON

Apparently the Babylonians believed that riddles could teach. The oldest riddles we know of were preserved on an ancient Babylonian clay tablet that probably served as a schoolbook. Here's one: "Who becomes pregnant without conceiving, Who becomes fat without eating?" If you can't compete with Babylonian kids, just check the answers.

A RIDDLE FROM THE BIBLE

Judges 14:12–20 talks about a riddle competition that Samson started at his seven-day wedding feast/bachelor party (this was before Delilah started hanging around). He offered rewards to

---

those who could answer, but demanded the same rewards for himself if they failed. Here's Samson's riddle: "Out of the eater came something to eat; Out of the strong came something sweet." Samson wasn't really being fair. His riddle was based on a recent personal experience that only a few people knew about. He'd killed a lion earlier—just the sort of thing you'd expect him to do. Anyway, on the way to the feast, he'd seen a swarm of bees and honey in the lion's carcass. The riddle was unanswerable until Samson's wife coaxed the story out of him and passed it on to her relatives—the in-laws. Then the relatives replied with a riddle of their own, and the party went on from there. Check out the answer at the end of the story.

The Queen of Sheba supposedly asked King Solomon a lot of "hard questions" when they met. Some translators say that she was asking riddles—which the wise Solomon—of course!—was perfectly able to answer. (But everybody knows what they were really up to. Oh, you didn't know? Oh, yes, they were quite the item.)

A RIDDLE WITH NO ANSWERS

Riddles also appear in the Islamic Koran, the Indian Vedas, and the ancient oral traditions of most cultures. A related form called "koans"—such as, "What is the sound of one hand clapping?"— are central to Zen Buddhism. Don't look for the answer to that one at the end—there's no logical answer to a koan. It's just supposed to open up your mind.

RIDDLE CHALLENGES

Riddle contests were part of the Roman Saturnalia, a wildly festive weeklong pagan midwinter celebration. A master of riddles presided over the contest and awarded a laurel wreath to the winner. The losers had to drink their wine mixed with salt water. Yuck.

THE RIDDLE OF THE SPHINX

The most famous riddle of all (yes, even more famous than "Why did the chicken cross the road?") is the one that the Sphinx asked every human she met. She was a dangerous creature with a woman's head and breasts, a lion's claws, an animal body, a dragon's tail, and a bird's wings. She prowled the countryside looking for trouble. And if you couldn't answer her riddle, she ate you. That simple. Here goes: "What walks on four feet in the morning, two feet at noon, and three feet in the evening?" The only person who answered this correctly was Oedipus Rex, the king who married his mother (but he didn't know she was his mother) and poked his own eyes out when he found out. As for the Sphinx, once somebody came up with the answer, she killed herself. Making the streets safe for dummies like the rest of us.

RIDDLES, INTERNATIONAL

Riddles have been asked—and answered—all over the world and in a multitude of languages. Here are two from two radically different cultures.

From Iceland: "Who is the swift one that found me on the road? Neither the sun nor any other light shines on him. I have often seen him running alongside ships at sea. He needs no clothing or food, and is visible to all but tangible by none."

Got the answer? Well, here's an ancient Mayan riddle that has the same answer. "You see it but you can't grab it. It goes with you but you can't grab it."

THE ANSWERS

Even though we still tell riddles, nobody said that our minds or our senses of humor work in the same way the ancients' did. Keep that in mind as you read:

The Riddle That Stumped Homer: What did the fishermen keep? Lice, which they already had.

A Riddle From Babylon: The thing that "becomes fat without eating" is a rain cloud.

A Riddle From the Bible: The answer to Samson's set-up question is honey out of a lion.

The Riddle of the Sphinx: The answer is "a man"—who crawls at the beginning of life, walks upright in mid-life, and walks with a cane in old age.

Riddles, International: A shadow.

HIPPOCRATES, M.D.

*He's known as "the Father of Medicine" and all medical school gradu-
ates in the U.S. take the oath he wrote some 2,500 years ago.*

MY FRIEND, THE WITCH DOCTOR...
In the fifth century B.C., most people thought illness was
a result of evil spirits and preferred to take their medical
complaints to the local healer. So when Hippocrates hung out his
shingle on the Greek island of Cos, he had his work cut out for
him. But he persevered and soon began to build a practice. He
even established a medical school where he taught his newfangled
ideas to the future doctors of Greece. His biggest contribution was
that he treated patients based on scientific evidence. Well, mostly
scientific.

WHAT HIPPOCRATES WAS RIGHT ABOUT
Some of his beliefs and discoveries:
• the importance of moderation in all things—working, eating,
drinking, exercising, sleeping—to prevent disease
• the use of fasts and diets to cleanse the body
• warm baths and massage to maintain health
• the importance of fresh air and a good diet
• the danger of being too overweight
• that if a healthy woman stops menstruating and feels sick, she's
pregnant

Some of his innovations:
• putting his ear to his patients' chests to check their lungs
• aligning fractures
• popping dislocations back in
• draining pus (ick) from infections

Which sounds pretty obvious to us, but it was all incredibly
groundbreaking in 400 B.C. or thereabouts. In general,
Hippocrates took the holistic approach to healing way before it
got to be trendy.

WHAT HE WAS WRONG ABOUT
Given that society was just emerging from the muck of mysticism,

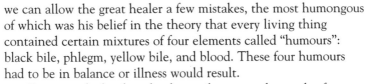

we can allow the great healer a few mistakes, the most humongous of which was his belief in the theory that every living thing contained certain mixtures of four elements called "humours": black bile, phlegm, yellow bile, and blood. These four humours had to be in balance or illness would result.

For example, he thought that epilepsy was the result of too much phlegm, which (hawk!) had to be removed gradually from the head. He also believed that young girls should sleep with a man as soon as possible to remove the impediment at the mouth of the uterus, and that pregnancy would bring a long-lasting cure by opening up the body so that excess fluids could move about freely.

Harumph, you're thinking. But this four-humour theory proved to be very popular and was still being used by physicians in the 17th century, while they largely ignored Hippocrates's very basic ideas on fresh air and good diet.

TAKE THE OATH, PLEASE

Highlights: the oath lists the responsibilities of the physician to the patient—to work for the good of the patient, to do him or her no harm, to prescribe no deadly drugs, and to keep confidential any medical information regarding the patient—and the rights of the patient under the physician's care. It warns doctors against overcharging (ahem!), overdressing, and wearing perfume. It encourages a pleasing bedside manner, but not too pleasing, because it forbids the doctor to have sex with patients.

CREDIT WHERE CREDIT IS DUE

Though Hippocrates gets all the credit, what's come down to us as his discoveries and beliefs is probably the collective results of the work of 60 or more students at his medical school. And even though he was wrong about a few things, he more than earned the title, "Father of Medicine," don't you think?

*   *   *

"Let medicine be thy food, and food be thy medicine."
Hippocrates

MY DINNER WITH ATTILA

*In A.D. 449 a Greek writer named Priscus of Panium visited
Attila the Hun's headquarters with a Roman embassy and
wrote a report about the banquet he attended there. It's been
translated by scholars, but never before by Uncle John.*

THE HUN? THAT'S NOT WHAT I CALL HIM.
The invitation said 3:00 p.m. sharp. And one does not
play around with the schedule of world conquerors. Especially when they've been nicknamed "the Scourge of God."
(That's what they call him in Hungary.)

The guests were a mixed bag: emissaries of the Roman Empire
(like me) rubbing elbows with local bigwigs and barbarians. I was
met at the banquet room door by a servant who handed me a
silver goblet filled to the brim with the local red. According to
custom, the guests were expected to say a prayer at that point, but
I couldn't help peeking around inside.

I was expecting something more primitive, but Attila surprised
me. The banquet hall, like the rest of the palace, was what we
ancient writers call "splendid." And instead of the familiar
(boring!) table-and-chairs setup, Attila had creatively opted for
wooden chairs that lined the walls. At first I thought, oh, no, not
another buffet, balancing plates on our laps! But I was wrong.
When we were ready to eat, the servants brought the tables in and
set them in front of us.

HIS SCOURGENESS

I'd seen Attila earlier that day, strutting around the palace
compound. At this moment, the great man sat in the middle of
the room on a couch. His oldest son sat on the couch, too, but
miles away from his parent. The young man just sat there, staring
at the floor. Which might have been out of respect, or maybe he
was as scared of Attila as some of the guests were.

I know you're dying to know what Attila looked like. He's
short and squat. He has a large head, deep-set eyes, a flat nose,
and a thin beard. At least one catty historian said he looked like
an ape. (It wasn't me!)

But what was he thinking when he got dressed that morning?

Watergate conspirator H. R. Haldeman ended up owning Sizzler restaurants in Florida.

The rest of us were dressed to kill—or at least to maim. Fancy swords, jewelry, the whole bit. Attila had opted instead for the natural look. Which is so B.C.! Instead of trying to compete with his guests—and god knows he's got spoils enough to do it—he wore the plainest clothes, no jewelry, no gold, no ornamentation of any kind.

ATTITUDE, AND PLENTY OF IT

The whole time, he had that fierce-warrior thing going. I wish he could have relaxed a little more—but when you're a scourge and all, you have an image to protect.

Then there's the drinking: to hang with Attila, you need a hollow leg. Between courses, he stood up and toasted every guest, one at a time. Everyone was expected to join in, of course, and then each of us had to toast him back, while the servants kept our goblets full. We were drowning in wine.

Considering our host was the barbarian of barbarians, the meal was downright sumptuous. Silver platters were heaped with the Hunnish version of the four food groups. While we chowed down, our host, still full of surprises, ate only meat. And only from a wooden platter.

WHAT, NO DANCING GIRLS?

At sundown, the servants lit the torches and the show began. Attila had lined up an unusual string of talent for our amusement.

First, two barbarians sang rousing songs they'd written about Attila and his amazing exploits, which moved some of the older warriors to tears. I felt a little stirred myself. Then a man who seemed to be deranged took the stage. He spoke gibberish—that was the extent of his talent. At first I didn't get it. But when the barbarians started whooping with laughter, I had to join them. Honestly, I laughed till my sides hurt. The next act was a Moorish dwarf (yes, that's right), whose talent was mixing up the languages of the Italians with those of the Huns and the Goths. The audience thought this act was even funnier than the last one.

A CHINK IN THE ARMOR

All the while, Attila never cracked a smile. That is, until his youngest son came in. He pinched the little guy's cheek and even dropped the fierce-warrior scowl for a second.

George W. Bush is the great-great-great-great nephew of 14th president Franklin Pierce.

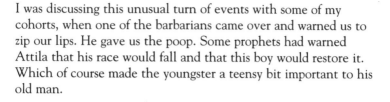

I was discussing this unusual turn of events with some of my cohorts, when one of the barbarians came over and warned us to zip our lips. He gave us the poop. Some prophets had warned Attila that his race would fall and that this boy would restore it. Which of course made the youngster a teensy bit important to his old man.

SHOW ME THE WAY TO GO HOME

I left in the wee small hours of the morning because I could not possibly swallow another sip of wine. Not so the barbarians. The party was still in full swing. And loud! Not that the neighbors would complain, of course.

*   *   *

HARES IN HISTORY

On June 4, 1951, the underdog home team, the Cleveland Indians, faced the favored New York Yankees. The Indians' prospects were so dismal that a local newspaper distributed lucky rabbits' feet to the Indian fans. The Indians won 8-2! What is it with those rabbit's feet, and why are they lucky?

Rabbits and their wild cousin, the hare, have been associated since pagan times with the fortunate aspects of spring, renewal, and fertility. In the Middle Ages, hares were associated with magical witches who were said to be able to change themselves into rabbits. Despite elements of witchery, the hare was still considered a lucky animal because of its many offspring and its burrowing habits. Fearing what lay buried under the earth, people admired the rabbit's ability to live underground and still survive.

Eventually the legends surrounding hares and rabbits, legends of fertility, the ability to survive evil, and magical powers, became associated with the "luck" in the left hind foot of a rabbit. Though not for the rabbit of course.

Pope Leo X had a pet elephant.

YE OLDE CRIME AND PUNISHMENT

From "No Parking" zones to "No Smoking" areas to the amount of water used in that porcelain receptacle you're sitting on, it sometimes seems as if our society operates under too many rules and regulations. Life didn't used to be like that, did it?

Come with us to Anytown, Germany, in the Middle Ages, where virtually everything was regulated, and where the regulations often varied according to social class. Take weddings, for instance, where the nobility could invite 48 people to their weddings, but servants or day laborers were only allowed 32 guests. And the wedding banquet, by law, had to start promptly at noon in summer or at 11 a.m. in winter.

THERE'S NOTHING FOR DESSERT!
Only two meals per day were allowed. The upper classes were permitted eight courses at each meal. The lower classes were restricted to five and were not allowed to serve a "confectionery," that is, something sweet, at the second meal of the day. The first meal could last no longer than three hours, which sounds like plenty of time for a meal, except that when the time limit was reached, everyone had to leave his seat immediately or be subject to a fine.

CRIMES AND MISDEMEANORS
Consider these "crimes" and the creative punishments imposed:

• Men or women who wore overly luxurious or elaborate clothing could have the forbidden garment stripped off them on the street.
• If a husband allowed his wife to rule the home or hit him, his fellow villagers would come to his house and remove its roof.
• The punishment for cursing, swearing, or blaspheming ran the gamut. In some places, the offender would have to run around the church's baptismal font holding a candle. For severe offenders, his tongue could be cut out.
• The poor soul who fell asleep in church was forced to wear a heavy wooden rosary and stand by the church door before the

---

Italy's notorious Medici family had a dollhouse inhabited by dwarves.

service for several of the following Sundays.

A fine was imposed for:

- Going to a fortune-teller
- Wearing a dress of more than two colors
- Wearing or making a dress with a neckline cut deeper than "the breadth of a finger below the little bone of the neck at the front of the collar"
- Arriving late for a wedding
- Serving wine or meals to guests after a baptism
- Being on the street at night without a lighted lantern

MAKING THE PUNISHMENT FIT THE CRIME

Public humiliation was a favorite way of teaching those darn miscreants a lesson. You may have heard about the practice of putting people in stocks or in the pillory in the town square for their offenses, but have you heard of these variations?

The Baker's Cage

Bakers who sold loaves of bread that were too light for the advertised size were placed in something called a "baker's cage" or "baker's chair," a seesaw device that dunked the baker in a pond. The number of dunkings was determined by the difference between the wrong weight and the right weight.

The Ass of Shame

Women who beat their husbands had to ride an ass through town facing backward. If the husband hadn't tried to defend himself, he had to lead the ass.

The Wheelbarrow

Lovers whose lascivious conduct had gone too far for the town authorities were sentenced in this way: the seducer had to push the object of his lust through the streets in a wheelbarrow while onlookers were encouraged to throw garbage at them.

The Barrel

Men who spent too much time and money on drink were paraded through town wearing a barrel painted with humiliating pictures.

The Neck Violin

A double iron collar, it was fastened around the necks of quarrel-

---

In 1794, Congress rejected a petition to make the U.S. bilingual—English and German.

ing women who then had to stand locked together in the public square until they agreed to stop bickering and keep the peace.

The Shame Flute
Pity the bungling musician who committed the terrible crime of playing music badly. He was tied to the pillory in the town square with his neck encased in the shame flute, an iron neck restraint with an instrument attached.

The Masks of Shame
These iron masks came in a variety of shapes, each designed to portray the person's offense. A gossip wore an iron mask with a long tongue. A person who stuck his nose into his neighbors' business wore a mask with a huge nose. If one behaved like a pig, he wore the pig's mask in public. The masks hid the wearer's face but in the small towns of the Middle Ages, where everyone knew everyone else, they did not provide anonymity. And to make sure that the townspeople came out for the public humiliation, the masks were fitted with large bells on top to announce the presence of a new victim.

AW, QUIT YER BELLY-ACHIN'
So the next time you have dessert at lunch, or arrive late for a wedding, or let your wife beat you up, just be happy you live in the 21st century, the century of "It's my own darn business."

*　　*　　*

"What does not destroy me, makes me stronger."
Nietzsche

Genghis Khan demanded 1,000 virgins a year as tribute from conquered territories.

THEY CALLED HER "LADY LINDY"

The first woman to make a name for herself in the air wasn't an "air hostess," which is what they called "stewardesses" before they called them "flight attendants." No, our girl was a pilot—and from all reports a darn... well... kind of average one.

In truth, Amelia Earhart was not considered a top-notch flyer. But she flew and she was famous, that's what's important. Especially since her first front-page exploit took place just 10 years after women had gained the right to vote. She became an inspiration to women everywhere. So what if she wasn't the best pilot on earth? She wanted something more than the traditional home and hearth, and she got it.

I'M AMELIA, FLY ME

Earhart was 31 when a friend of the powerful New York publisher George Palmer Putnam approached her with an idea. Putnam wanted to finance a flight that would make Earhart the first woman to cross the Atlantic in a plane. After which she'd write a book about it, and he'd publish it. That was the good news.

The bad news was that she'd only be a passenger. Putnam thought that, seeing as how it was only 1928, even that would be newsworthy. Earhart already had some experience as a pilot, but not enough. So the job of flying the plane, a trimotor Fokker called "Friendship," fell to Wilmer Stultz and Louis Gordon. Amelia was given the title "commander," but commander of pretty much nothing.

FIRST FLIGHT

On June 18, the Friendship took off from Nova Scotia, heading for Ireland. On the other side of the ocean, bad weather forced them to set down in South Wales. The fog had got the best of them, and there wasn't much fuel left, but, hey, they'd landed safely in Europe. And Amelia had made a name for herself.

LOVE AT FIRST FLIGHT

She had also made a friend in Putnam. More than a friend, really.

Ivan the Terrible blinded Russia's best architect so he couldn't build nicer buildings for others.

And since Putnam was married, tongues started wagging. In 1929, Putnam's wife went to Reno to get a divorce. Putnam and Earhart were married in 1931, and her book, *20 Hours, 40 Minutes*, was published soon after. Amelia's hubby worked hard to keep her name in front of the public, but she did most of the leg work. At his urging, she flew solo from the East to the West coast in 1928, where she attended the National Air Races in California, then returned to do a lecture tour to promote her book.

JUST US GIRLS

The next year, Amelia organized the first air race for women pilots, which the papers dubbed a "powder puff derby." That same year, Earhart and 98 other women pilots founded "the Ninety-Nines," an organization of women pilots.

LOOKIN' GOOD, AMELIA

Five years to the day after Lindbergh's flight, on May 20, 1932, Earhart flew solo across the Atlantic. When she landed in Londonderry in Northern Ireland she'd broken two records: not only was she the first woman to fly the Atlantic solo, she also was the only person to have crossed the Atlantic by plane twice. The 15-hour flight broke the previous record for speed that had been set by two British flyers 13 years earlier.

THERE'S NO STOPPING HER NOW

With the Atlantic under her belt, she turned her sights to the west. On her next solo flight, she crossed the Pacific, flying from Hawaii to California. After that, there was only one more record left for her to conquer. She wanted to be the first woman to fly around the world.

IF AT FIRST YOU DON'T SUCCEED...

On her first attempt in 1937, as she and her navigator, Frederick Noonan, were taking off, Amelia erred in judgment, and overcompensated for a dipping wing. The plane crashed, but Earhart and Noonan survived.

Undaunted, they tried again two months later. After 22,000 miles—with a mere 7,000 miles to go—they landed at Lae, New Guinea. When they took off again, it was the last time anyone ever saw them.

Nineteen hours and 30 minutes after leaving Lae, broadcasting

The Sumerians invented cuneiform writing in 3500 B.C.

on a strong signal, Amelia radioed, "We must be on you but cannot see you… gas is running low." One final voice transmission followed, one last position report. Then nothing.

YOU'RE INVITED TO A SEARCH PARTY

The Coast Guard began the search. President Franklin Roosevelt ordered nine Navy ships and 66 aircraft to join the effort, but no trace of the flyers or their plane was found. After the official hunt was called off, George Palmer Putnam instigated a further search, but to no avail.

YEAH, RIGHT

There are lots of theories—most of them wacky—about Earhart's ultimate fate. The most reasonable—but unlikely—is that she was on a spy mission for the U.S. Another just as unlikely scenario is that she purposely committed suicide. One popular rumor even claimed that Earhart was the voice of the infamous "Tokyo Rose," who broadcasted World War II propaganda exhorting American GIs to surrender.

Some physical evidence recovered on an uninhabited Pacific atoll points to a possible landing there, but even if true, it doesn't account for the remains of the pilot and her navigator.

AMELIA EARHART ABDUCTED BY ALIENS

The tabloids still periodically trumpet the uncovered "truth" of Earhart's fate. Until the real truth is comes to light, they'll go on claiming that she was on a secret mission or is still alive on a remote Pacific Island. And probably living with Elvis!

*   *   *

"Courage is the price that life exacts for granting peace with yourself."
Amelia Earhart

WHEREWORDS: A QUIZ
(Cities of the World)

We'll tell you where they are, you tell us where the names came from.
Then check your answer on the next page.

1. PARIS: The capital of and largest city in France.
a. The Trojan prince who abducted Helen of Troy.
b. It was the first "parish" in France.
c. The Parisii, the tribe of Celtic peoples, its first inhabitants.

2. TOKYO: The largest urban area and capital of Japan.
a. An anagram of the city it supplanted as capital: Kyoto.
b. Japanese for "eastern capital," which it has been since 1868.
c. After shogun Tokugawa Ieyasu, who captured it in 1601.

3. RIO DE JANEIRO: The former capital of Brazil.
a. For French explorer Admiral Jacques Janier.
b. From the Spanish word for "junior," or "little river."
c. It was named by Portuguese pioneers who landed there in "January" 1503.

4. ROME (in Italian, "Roma"): Italy's largest city and capital.
a. Julius Caesar named it for his first (and favorite) wife, Roma.
b. Named after Romulus, Rome's legendary founder and first king.
c. Latin word for "greatness."

5. CAIRO: The largest city in Africa and the capital of Egypt.
a. The Arabic word "al-qahira," which means "the victorious."
b. The Cairo root, staple of the north African diet.
c. A mythical oasis in *The Arabian Nights*.

6. CHICAGO: The third largest city in America.
a. Samuel Champlain named for his birthplace, Chicageau.
b. Lithuanian fur trapper Vlad Shkago, founded it in 1673.
c. Native American "checagou," refers to the smell of onions.

7. BOMBAY: The capital city of Maharashtra State in India.
a. WWI aircraft crew discovered it through the "bomb bay" doors.
b. Portuguese "Bom Bahia," for "beautiful bay."
c. The Latin word "bombyx," the raw silk the city is famous for.

8. SHANGHAI: The largest city in China.
a. Ancient Chinese characters that translate to "on the sea."
b. Admiral Chi'ang Kai, a hero in the war against Japan.
c. A centuries-old blessing and salutation, meaning "good luck."

A socialist wrote the U.S. Pledge of Allegiance.

1-c. Close to 10 million Parisians now populate the 41 square miles that have been variously controlled by the Germans, the British, Huns, and the Vikings. But they came after the original, indigenous clan, the Parisii.

2-b. Tokyo has been the capital of Japan since 1868, after the dynasty that ruled from the western city of Kyoto was overthrown. The emperor's court was transferred to Edo and the name of the city was changed to Tokyo. (Give yourself partial credit if you answered "a," even though it's just a coincidence that the names of the two cities are anagrams.)

3-c. In early 1503, gold-hungry Portuguese explorers sailed into Guanabara Bay to ring in the New Year and claim the area around the estuary for Portugal.

4-b. In Roman myth, Romulus was the son of Mars, the god of war. He and his brother Remus were left as infants to die in the Tiber River. They were rescued and raised by wolves. When they grew up, they argued over which of two hills to build the city on. A fight to the death ensued, and Romulus won.

5-a. When dissident Fatimid Muslims conquered Egypt in A.D. 696, they claimed the rich delta basin as their own and named it after their victory.

6-c. The Miami Indians called their village "Checaugou," named for a small river, which in turn was supposedly named for the odor of the wild onions that grew there.

7-b. Those Portuguese adventurers really got around. The city had been inhabited since prehistoric times, but wasn't called "Bombay" until it was captured by the Portuguese in the 16th century.

8-a. For more than 1,000 years this fishing port controlled China's access to the sea, hence the name.

During World War I, Charles De Gaulle was injured three times at the Battle of Verdun.

UNCOVERING UNDERWEAR

What our ancestors wore, and didn't.

H ave you ever wondered what people wore underneath their togas, hoopskirts, etc.? Let's take a peek:

WHEN IN ANCIENT ROME... OR GREECE OR EGYPT

- The Roman noblemen wore tunics and briefs under their togas. Women wore tunics, too, and breastbands that made them fashionably flat-chested.

- Female slaves in ancient Greece and Egypt often wore nothing but a necklace and a thong.

- King Tut's tomb contained 145 loincloths—diaperlike underpants.

BARE NAKED LADIES

- Women didn't wear panties until the mid-1830s. Before that, any form of pants was considered too masculine. Under those petticoats, everyone from Martha Washington to Marie Antoinette was naked.

- The hoopskirts of the 1850s and 1860s created a problem. The stiff frame that gave the skirt its shape flew up in a high wind. The solution? Pantaloons.

BOXERS OR BRIEFS?

- Men didn't wear boxers or briefs before the 20th century. Longjohns or union suits (so called because the undershirt and the drawers were united in one piece) were the way to go.

- In earlier days, the long tails of men's shirts did double duty as underpants.

In 1996, when Mikhail Gorbachev ran for the presidency of Russia, he got 0.5% of the vote.

BEST LIST OF BESTS

They've withstood the test of time, they've beaten out the competition, they're the all-time greats: Uncle John's choices for some of the best stuff ever.

Best **Writing Implement:** The computer. Because the idea of going back and retyping (or, hell, repenning) an entire book should fill any writer with suicidal horror.

Best Hat: The fedora. Any hat that can make a mug like Humphrey Bogart's look good has something going for it.

Best Method of Execution: The guillotine. You know, it was created to be a humane way of chopping off someone's head. Someone should have thought that point all the way through.

Best Means of Transportation: The locomotive. Probably the single most important tool in opening up North America, which is why the natives spent so much time wrecking the rails.

Best Use of the Wheel: In clocks, to provide accurate, standard measurements of time. Western Civilization as we know it would not be possible without it; you decide whether this is good or bad.

Best Phallic Symbol: The Washington Monument. Started in the early 1800s, paused during the Civil War (constructus interruptus), completed thereafter.

Best Useless Structure: The Eiffel Tower. It was built to represent progress. The French hated it. Insert your own punchline.

Best Cleaning Material: Soap. Just soap. Around for millennia, its use as a cleaning agent only really picked up in the last couple hundred years. In the 19th century, Justus von Liebig said that the amount of soap consumed by a nation was an accurate measure of its wealth and civilization. So, pick up a bar and lather up!

Best Use of Propaganda: Shakespeare's *Richard III*. As it happens, Richard III wasn't a hunchback or a mass murderer. (He wasn't a very nice guy, but who among royalty back then was?) Why such a nasty representation of Richard? Could be because the reigning monarch at the time was the granddaughter of the man who overthrew him. Just a guess.

Best Dance: The waltz. When it came out, it brought Vienna into chaos, as people neglected home and business to dance night and day and night again. (Because people loved dancing so close to each other! The horror!) Made the Macarena look like a blip. Which it was, but even so.

Best Drug: Nicotine. Percentage-wise, it's easier to quit heroin than nicotine. Although admittedly, heroin doesn't advertise in trendy magazines with young men with washboard stomachs sailboarding with hot chicks in bikinis.

Best Inappropriate Remark: "Let them eat cake." Purists note that Marie actually said "brioche," which is a sweet bread, and not exactly cake, but, you know, it's the thought that counts.

Best Board Game: Chess, which was introduced to Europe at the beginning of this millennium. Why is it the best? Because no one gives a damn that a computer can beat a human at Monopoly.

Best Use of an Unpleasant Climate by a Defending Army: Russia. Russian winters did in Napoleon and Hitler. Not bad. Oh, sure, the Russian soldiers helped. But look how successful they've been in warm-weather wars, and you'll know. It was the snow.

Best Proof the Human Race Is Not Merely a Festering Sore on the Face of This Over-Burdened Globe: Beethoven's ninth symphony, which is quite possibly the greatest artistic achievement the human race may accomplish. If all the universe gets out of us is that one piece of music, I figure we've paid our way. However, it means we've peaked. Let's try not to make the decline too steep, okay? Thanks.

* * *

Men occasionally stumble over the truth, but most of them pick themselves up and hurry off as if nothing ever happened.

Winston Churchill

The real John Birch was killed by the Chinese 10 days after World War II ended.

THE RICH HISTORY OF CHOCOLATE

Among the ancients, it was revered as the "elixir of the gods."

Today, it is the one sweet temptation that most of us find impossible to resist. Yet, for most of its 3,500-year history, it was not eaten but rather consumed as a beverage—and a cold one at that. Although its form and flavor have taken many twists and turns through the millennia, its appeal, once discovered, has been universal. So, why not treat yourself to a tour of the rich history of chocolate.

THE OLD GRIND

1500 B.C.: The Olmec civilizations of Guatemala, the Chiapas and the Yucatan regions of Central America cultivate the cacao tree and make use of its product by grinding the beans and then mixing with water.

MONEY GROWS ON TREES

A.D. 200: The Olmecs have been overthrown by the Mayan civilization. The vast cacao plantations are used as a source of currency, with the little black beans being traded for goods or services. The bean is only consumed by the ruling classes. By now the process of making the drink has become more sophisticated—the beans are roasted and then ground with water before spices such as chili are added. The resulting mixture is shaken until it develops a frothy top, at which point it is ready to be enjoyed.

A HEAVENLY DRINK

A.D. 1200: The Mayans have been supplanted by the Aztecs who heartily embrace the product of the cacao tree, even incorporating it into their mythology. Their god Quetzalcoatl is said to have pilfered a cacao tree from the heavenly realms and deposited it on the Central American plains ready to be converted into a health elixir and powerful aphrodisiac. Famed Emperor Montezuma enjoys the drink so much that he reputedly downs 50 goblets full every day (the amount of time he spends on the royal lavatory as a result of such liquid overload is not recorded).

Jimmy Hoffa was last seen alive at the Machus Red Fox restaurant.

WRONG CURRENCY

1502: Christopher Columbus, on his fourth voyage to the New World, takes possession of a Mayan trading vessel containing what he takes to be almonds and which function as a means of monetary exchange for the Native Americans. He thereby becomes the first European to encounter the cacao bean, though he scarcely gives it any attention and certainly never tastes it.

JUST A SPOONFUL OF SUGAR

1519–1544: Spanish explorer Hernando Cortes leads an expedition into the heart of Mexico in search of gold and silver. He is welcomed by the Aztecs and served their greatest delicacy—a cold, bitter drink that they call "cacahuatl." Cortes introduces this strange new brew to the Spanish court. It becomes an instant hit, even more so when sweetened with sugar. The Spanish would keep the secret of chocolate to themselves for the next 75 years.

ENGLISH COOKING

1579: The English let the chocolate opportunity slip through their fingers when they seize a Spanish cargo ship on the high seas. The British Buccaneers are surprised to find that the ship holds a cargo of what they take to be sheep droppings and set it on fire. Eight years later they get a second chance when another Spanish ship carrying cacao beans is seized. Again, however, they destroy the cargo, declaring it to be useless.

GOES A COURTING

1609–1643: The secret is out. Chocolate makes its way across Europe, causing a sensation among the royal courts who are first introduced to it. France's Sun King, Louis XIV is so taken with the delicacy that he appoints a representative to manufacture and sell it. The first book entirely devoted to chocolate is printed in Mexico. Throughout the French nobility, the aphrodisiac properties of the drink are highly regarded. Both Casanova and the Marquis de Sade are said to be prolific consumers.

FAST FOOD

1662: The Church of Rome declares that the consumption of chocolate, although highly nutritious and filling, is not considered to be food and can therefore safely be taken in its liquid form during periods of religious fasting.

Columnist and writer Ambrose Bierce vanished while following Pancho Villa.

JUST WHAT THE DOCTOR ORDERED
1765: Chocolate, by now highly regarded as a liquid delicacy and a medicinal remedy in Europe, makes its way to the United States where Dr. James Baker of Massachusetts begins a chocolate manufacturing plant. Cacao beans are ground into chocolate liquid and pressed into cakes that can be dissolved in water or milk to make drinking chocolate. At the same time, James Watt invents the steam engine in Europe, which will soon be applied to the mechanized manufacture of chocolate.

WARRANT FOR HIS ASCENT
1824: John Cadbury opens a grocery in Birmingham, England, selling roasted cacao beans on the side. Very soon he is concentrating solely on the cacao beans and, in 1854, receives a Royal Warrant to be the sole provider of chocolate to Queen Victoria. A century later Cadbury is the largest food company in the world.

BAR KING
1847: The modern chocolate bar is born when British manufacturer Joseph Fry mixes melted cacao butter into a paste that is then pressed into a mold and sold as a solid bar. Soon the public has become educated to eat, rather than drink their chocolate.

1893: Milton Snavely Hershey enters the chocolate business. The world is introduced to the milk chocolate Hershey bar, followed by Hershey's Kisses. His operations grow at such a rate he takes over the entire town of Derry Church, Pennsylvania, renames it Hershey, and turns it into the chocolate capital of the world.

1900 to present: The creation of chocolate delicacies becomes an art form. In 1908, the Swiss Toblerone bar is offered, in 1922 the European Chocolate Kiss, chocolate-covered cherries in 1929, and that old favorite—the chunky bar filled with nuts and raisins in the mid-1930's. During World War II, chocolate bars become standard issue item for the U.S. military. When man conquers Mt. Everest in 1953 and heads into space in the 1960s, the chocolate bar goes along. By the end of the 20th century, science acknowledges what the Aztecs knew all along—that chocolate is a powerful fighter against fatigue, giving the eater added strength and energy. But, the scientists found, that energy comes at a price —a one-and-a-half-ounce chocolate bar contains 220 calories!

GYPSIES: TRAMPS AND THIEVES?

There's the romantic vision of Gypsies: colorful folks in quaint caravans who play the fiddles, offer palm readings, and dress in scarves and bright peasant dresses, always cheerfully on the move.

And there's the less festive image of the Gypsies, which has them living outside the law in makeshift encampments and preying on good, upstanding folks, who nevertheless snuck in to gawk. The real story of the Gypsies, however, is something else again.

WHO ARE YOU CALLING A GYPSY?
First things first. To begin, they're not really Gypsies. They call themselves "Rom," or "Romany." "Gypsy" is just a title that was put on them by the *gadje* (in the Romany language that means "barbarian," and if you're not Romany, this means you) around the 16th century. The term "Gypsy" is inaccurate in any event—it's a shortened version of "Egyptian," based on the belief that Gypsies originated in the Nile delta. They didn't. They're originally from northern India. But you know those medieval Europeans; they weren't so good with the maps.

WORLD TRAVELERS
The Romany may have been from northern India, but they didn't stay there. By the 11th century they were in Persia (modern-day Iran) and by the 1400s could be found all over Europe. Today an estimated two to five million Romany live all over the world, including North America and Australia, although the majority still reside in Europe, with large numbers in the Czech and Slovak Republics, Hungary, Yugoslavia, Bulgaria, and Romania (which takes its name from Rome, the empire, not Rom, the people).

However, just because the Romany had migrated to Europe by the 15th century didn't mean that Europeans, notably twitchy concerning foreigners no matter what the era, were very pleased to have them there. It didn't help that the Romany, traditionally nomadic and organized in family-oriented bands, lived and worked

---

Pliny the Elder died of curiosity when he sailed too close to Mt. Vesuvius to get a look.

on the fringes of settled society. These social traits often made the Romany scapegoats for trouble (after all, they were just passing though). Romany were frequently labeled grifters, thieves, and witches, and were persecuted accordingly.

BY THE BOATLOAD

How? Well, for starters, they were given the boot a whole lot: Denmark, Norway, Sweden, France, and England are just some of the countries that had laws expelling the Romany from their borders between the 16th and 19th centuries. Much of the time, if the Romany didn't take the hint and came back, they could be killed, or shipped off in forced migrations to colonies in North and South America, Brazil, or Australia. The rationale of sending people you don't like or want to your own colonies is a little screwy, but the Europeans apparently figured it was better than having them on the outskirts of town.

A NICE HOUSE IN THE SUBURBS

Occasionally, a country would get it into its collective head to rescue the Romany from their lifestyle and make them "respectable" folks (without consulting the Romany on the matter, of course). In 18th-century Hungary, for example, Romany were made to settle and farm, and Rom children were taken from families to learn new trades. The Romany language was outlawed, as was their music (except on holidays). It didn't take, however, and forced assimilations in Spain were similarly unsuccessful.

HEY, JOIN THE CLUB!

If you thought things might get better for the Romany in the 20th century, you've clearly forgotten what a mess Europe was in that era. The Nazis, who didn't much like anyone who wasn't them, had it in for the Romany from the start. Not that the Romany were having a grand time of it before the Nazis came to power— The Romany were subject to discriminatory laws in Germany during the Weimar Republic as well. They were required to register with officials, prohibited from traveling freely, and frequently sent to forced-labor camps. The Nazis kept these laws in place and added to them, making the Romany subject to forced sterilizations and other horrifyingly racist laws.

THE "ARYAN" RACE

In one nasty bit of irony, the Romany were traditionally classified as "Aryan," though clearly not of the blond, angular variety which the Nazis had such a thing for. "Aryan" comes from the Sanskrit *arya*, which historically refers to the people of Northern India. The technical Aryan classification of the Romany pained Hitler and his toadies a bit, but not enough to give them pause. Indeed, other than the Jews, the Romany were the only racial group specifically targeted for extermination by the Nazis. By 1938, Romany were being placed into concentration camps, where they were often identified by black triangles (the mark of the "asocial"). During the course of World War II, somewhere between 200,000 and 500,000 Romany perished in the camps; an estimated 1½ million died between 1935 and 1945.

GIVE ME YOUR TIRED, YOUR POOR… BUT NO GYPSIES

Don't get too smug because you're an American, by the way. Anti-Gypsy laws were on the books at one time or another in Mississippi, New Jersey, Pennsylvania, Texas, Indiana, Georgia, and Maryland. In the late 19th century, Romany were even specifically barred from immigrating to the U.S.

BE P.C.

The Romany aren't as persecuted today as they have been in the past (at least, not in the U.S.), but stereotyping of the Romany still exists. You can even find some remnants in everyday speech. Anytime you say that someone has "gypped" you—that is, cheated or deceived you—you're using a racial slur: "gyp" comes from "gypsy." You probably didn't know that. Well, now you do.

* * *

NEW AGE GYPSY?

Admiring their nomadic, property-eschewing style as a type of independence, New Agers have latched onto gypsies, publishing books on so-called "gypsy" lore, legend, even medicine. Here at BRI, we have to agree with a contemporary Rom who writes, "There are four hundred books on the gypsies, but in all, not more than ten of which tell us anything new or true about them." Some people are just skeptical…

Frederick Douglass named himself for a character in a Sir Walter Scott poem.

MR. SAM, THE WHISKEY MAN

Samuel Bronfman knew how to make great whiskey, but more importantly, he knew how to sell it during prohibition.

Most of us know the big American tycoons of the 19th Century—Rockefeller, Vanderbilt, and J. P. Morgan. One 20th Century Canadian tycoon positioned his family up there with the most successful: Mr. Sam, the Whiskey Man.

STARTING WITH HIS SHIRT

Mr. Sam was Samuel Bronfman, third son of a poor Jewish immigrant to Canada from southern Russia in the late 19th Century. Like many fellow immigrants from Eastern Europe, the Bronfmans came with little more than the shirts on their backs. The family traveled to Canada's prairies to rebuild their lives and, if they got some "mazel" (that's Yiddish for "luck"), maybe they'd prosper.

WELCOME TO THE HOTEL MANITOBA

In 1903 the family used savings to purchase a small-town hotel in rural Manitoba, then a second in Saskatchewan. But by 1912, when Sam was 23 years old, the family used profits from the first two hotels, and bought a Winnipeg hotel to operate. The hotels really made their money from liquor sales, and temperance crusades were widespread in every Canadian province except Quebec. Mr. Sam saw legal problems coming. He started moving a step ahead of the regulators—and he stayed there.

YOU'VE GOT MAIL

In 1916 when Prohibition was enacted across Canada, except in Quebec, Mr. Sam (a step ahead) was set up in (guess where?) Montreal, Quebec. Local prohibition in Canada was strictly enforced in the provinces, but liquor trade between the Canadian provinces was federal and legal. Mr. Sam legally sold liquor to thirsty souls in prohibition-fettered provinces. He sold it from Montreal by mail-order. His business boomed, aided by the government.

The first language of African-American heroine Sojourner Truth was Dutch.

DOCTOR FEELGOOD

When the mail-order loophole closed, Mr. Sam was still a step ahead. By then he had a wholesale drug company, which was already doing business in various "liquor-based elixirs." Booze for "medicinal purposes" was legal across Canada. One doctor in British Columbia reportedly averaged 4,100 prescriptions monthly.

HERE'S TO YOU, MR. VOLSTEAD

When Prohibition came to the United States in 1919, Mr. Sam was ready. He'd established a string of "export houses" and warehouses along the Canadian side of the Great Lakes and across the prairies. American wholesale buyers would come to Canada, pay their money, and take delivery on the Canadian side. The Bronfmans paid the appropriate money in taxes to Canadian governments, which fully endorsed export sale of liquor. Where the liquor ended up wasn't Bronfmans or Canada's responsibility.

OFFSHORE BANKING

Naturally, there was opposition, since Bronfman was going against the Prohibition law. Based in Montreal, the whiskey man foresaw closure of the prairie and Great Lakes "export houses." American pressure and enforcement efforts were making business difficult. So Mr. Sam exported his liquor with a tiny French protectorate, the island of St. Pierre off Newfoundland. From there the (laundered) liquor went south. In 1923, more than 500,000 cases of liquor, mostly whiskey, went through St. Pierre. One thing you can say for Sam, he had plenty of chutzpah.

THE LOUISVILLE SLUG

By the 1920s the Bronfmans were major players in the international liquor trade. In Yiddish, "bronf-man" means "whiskey man," and Sam's name was proving prophetic. By 1923 he was blending house brand whiskey, and buying a Louisville distillery that was shipped, piece by piece, to Montreal.

BECOMING KOSHER

In 1928, the Bronfmans bought a financially troubled Canadian distillery, Joseph E. Seagram & Sons. Mr. Sam was now poised for the end of Prohibition, figuring that he needed years of lead time to properly age his whiskey, and be ready when legal markets opened. In 1935, barely two years after the end of Prohibition,

When the NAACP was founded in 1909, its only black officer was its newspaper editor.

Seagram's brands sold more than a million cases in the United States alone. They continue to be a world sales leader.

THE WHISKEY MAVEN
Mr. Sam studied to become a whiskey-making maven to ensure the Bronfman name was associated with quality. Sam directed the process of making his whiskey as well as directing the Bronfman business empire all his life.

THE SHIRT OFF HIS BACK
In 1939 Sam was elected chairman of the Canadian Jewish Congress, which he ran in as hands-on a manner as he did his liquor business. The Jewish Congress became a powerful political lobby, and still is today. (The Jewish Congress was recently a major player in forcing Swiss banks to return stolen accounts to Holocaust victims.) Sam's newfound talent—fundraising—generated tens of millions of dollars for Jewish causes. Mr. Sam once handed back a check for $250,000 with the scornful comment, "Get serious!" Then raised $25 million.

A FAMILY AFFAIR
When Mr. Sam died in 1971 at the age of 82, his two sons were already involved in the business. Mies van der Rohe designed the famous Seagram Building in New York City. Before the end of the century, the Bronfman Empire had expanded to include multi-million-dollar real-estate holdings, a substantial share of Dupont, and major interest in Universal Studios. Mr. Sam's family, thanks to his chutzpah, didn't have to worry about the shirts on their backs.

* * *

THANK YOU SIR, MAY I HAVE ANOTHER?

The delegates at the American Constitutional Convention had more than the country's well-being in mind when they were preparing the Constitution. A party bill from two days before the official signing shows the boys—only 55 of them, mind you—made quick work of 156 bottles of liquor, including eight bottles of whiskey.

THEM'S FIGHTIN' WORDS: KOREA

*A groundbreaking conflict (remember, we can't call it a "war")
that brought us a lot of now-familiar phrases.*

The Korean War was the first conflict for which an international organization recommended the use of force; the first war that couldn't be called a war because Congress never declared it to be one; and the first war in which jet fighters and helicopters were widely used.

bamboo curtain
Coined by *Time* magazine in 1949, it refers to the barrier of mistrust between China and its allies on the one hand and the non-Communist nations of Asia and the West on the other. The **bamboo curtain** was a counterpart to the "Iron Curtain" between the Soviets and the West.

police action
When communist North Korea attacked Haesong, South Korea, in June 1950, the United Nations demanded the attackers withdraw completely. When that demand was ignored, the Security Council decided to send in the troops. The U.N. didn't have a police force as such, but recommended that member nations take action, and 30 of them agreed to do so. President Harry Truman called out U.S. air and sea forces. He was acting without a vote of Congress because he was responding to a security measure recommended by the U.N. At a press conference, a reporter asked the president if the war could be called a **police action** under the United Nations's supervision, and Truman agreed that it could.

"Old soldiers never die; they just fade away."
The U.N. instructed its forces only to expel the aggressors and to do nothing more. Supplies were flowing to the Communists from Manchuria, behind the Chinese border, but the U.N. troops were not permitted to bomb enemy bases, airstrips, or supply centers because it might provoke an all-out war with the Soviet Union. Commander in chief General Douglas MacArthur voiced his

frustration loudly and publicly. In response, President Truman replaced him with General Matthew B. Ridgway—in effect ending MacArthur's military career. In a farewell speech to Congress, the general quoted a barracks song about old soldiers like himself.

to bug out
The term originated during World War II, but in Korea it acquired enormous currency. **To bug out** didn't just mean a retreat or withdrawal, but a fast pulling out, to avoid being killed or captured. Since the war it's been used more loosely for any rapid departure.

airstrike
The widespread use of jet fighters was new in this war, giving rise to the term **airstrike**, for attacks on enemy positions.

chopper
Helicopters saw a lot of action, too, and were nicknamed **choppers**, probably from the "chop-chop" noise made by helicopter rotors.

buy the farm
An air war called for training flights, generally carried out in American rural areas. When an air force training flight crashed on a farm, the farmer could sue the government for damages sufficient to pay off his mortgage and thus **buy the farm** outright. Since the pilot in such a crash usually died, he "bought the farm" with his life.

eyeball to eyeball
But Korea was primarily a ground war. When MacArthur's headquarters sent a dispatch to the Twenty-fourth Regiment to ask if they had contact with the enemy, they responded, "We is **eyeball to eyeball**." The message was widely quoted, and a decade later it was used with reference to the Cuban Missile Crisis, when the Cold War threatened to become a hot one.

M.A.S.H.
While attempts at peace negotiations went on for more than a year, some four hundred thousand casualties were inflicted on U.N. troops. Treating casualties was the job of the mobile army surgical hospital, or **M.A.S.H.**, which inspired a motion picture and long-running television series of the same name.

hooch
As in all wars, there was fraternization with the local populace.
From it came the use of **hooch** for a peasant shack or hut, or any
place where a serviceman might set up housekeeping with a
Korean woman. The word comes from the Japanese *uchi*, for
"house," and was also extended to mean a bunker or other front-
line living quarter. Later, it was widely used during the Vietnam
War.

brainwashing
The sick and wounded who were taken prisoner by the Chinese
were subjected to **brainwashing** to indoctrinate them with
Communist beliefs. The technique involved both physical and
mental torture to break down a soldier's loyalties and family ties.
The word itself is a translation from a Chinese term for "thought
reform," and the effectiveness of the technique was shockingly
demonstrated during prisoner-of-war exchanges when a number of
American soldiers said they did not wish to be repatriated. Since
then, the term is used to mean changing someone's outlook or
opinions, usually by underhanded means.

> Christine Ammer's book, *Fighting Words,* explores the
> linguistic legacy of armed conflicts over the centuries,
> from biblical times to the present.

*　*　*

CASUALTIES

The Korean War took the lives of nearly 4 million Korean people
(the majority, North Koreans). That's 10% of the population at
the time.

Chinese people were the next biggest losers, with about 1 million
casualties.

Nearly 55,000 Americans died in the conflict.

Tennessee Williams died after he choked on a nose-spray bottle cap.

BEST CRACKPOT RELIGIOUS LEADER: RASPUTIN

Grigory Rasputin was his own walking warning label.

Rasputin was the wrong guy at the right place at the wrong time. At the beginning of the 20th century, Imperial Russia was like a Jenga tower with one supporting strut too few. Rasputin didn't cause the czar to fall, but he sure helped to push.

THEY DON'T CALL HIM THAT FOR NOTHING

The name "Rasputin," wasn't his name, it was his condition: in Russian, it means "debauched one," and it was given to him after he built up a reputation, at a young age, for having a way with the ladies. You would think that being known as "Rasputin" would be a detrimental sort of thing—I mean, just imagine trying to meet people here if your name was "Greg Pervert."

HE CHANGES HIS WAYS (AS IF)

Rasputin experienced a religious conversion at the age of 18, which one could normally assume would have gotten him and his skirt-chasing ways sorted out. Au contraire. First, he joined a sect known as "Khlysty," which translates, roughly, as "the Flagellants." Not a good first step. Later he chose to pursue the closeness to God that only comes through what Rasputin described as "holy passionness," which could only be reached through sheer sexual exhaustion. This provided Rasputin the theological rationale he needed to do whatever he wanted to do with women.

MISTER ST. PETE

Fast forward to 1903. Rasputin is the toast of the St. Petersburg movers and shakers, who, with the spiritual dilettantism that inflicts the bored upper classes everywhere, regarded him the way celebrities in the 1960s regarded their swami. Sure, Rasputin was illiterate and he only bathed once a month, but there sure was something about him.

The day JFK was killed in Dallas, Richard Nixon was across town at a Pepsi convention.

THE TOP OF THE SOCIAL LADDER

Within a couple of years, Rasputin had found his way to the Czar
Nikolas II and Czarina Alexandra, and he endeared himself to
them by easing the pain of their hemophiliac son (historians think
by a form of hypnosis). He also told them that his destiny was now
tied to theirs; without him, they were doomed. The czar, never the
world's most courageous person, kept him around.

This is when things got bad. By day, Rasputin was the czar's
spiritual adviser; by night Rasputin wallowed in the orgy pit.
People complained. The czar had them transferred to Siberia.

HE'S OUT, HE'S IN

Finally the Prime Minister presented the czar with a formal report
on Rasputin's extracurricular activities. The czar booted Rasputin
for a couple of months, but the czarina would have none of that.
Rasputin was back, and the best the czar could do was shrug and
regard Rasputin as his wife's pet.

THE CZAR GOES TO WAR

World War I broke out, and the czar, perhaps wanting to feel like
he actually was in charge of something, went to command the
army in the field. The czarina was left to tend to internal affairs,
and stop that snickering. Rasputin was in the background, advising the empress. His advice on political matters was just about as
helpful as you might expect any advice coming from an ill-
educated, over-sexed, religious wacko might be.

IT'S A DIRTY JOB...

The Russian nobles, perhaps suspecting that the Proletariat Revolution was on its way and that Rasputin's "advice" wasn't going to
do much to help the nobles keep their lands or their heads,
decided to get Rasputin out of the way.

THE SUCKER WON'T DIE!

And thus it was in late December 1916 that Rasputin found
himself at the home of Prince Feliks Yusupov, lured there by the
promise that he'd meet someone's very attractive wife (no, really).
They fed him poison in tea and in cakes. He gobbled it down and
didn't blink. Then they shot him and cut off his instrument of
theological enlightenment. (No, not his brain. Yeesh.) He

managed to launch himself out the door. They shot him again, wrapped him in a carpet, and heaved his body into a river. At which point, of course, he died. Let's see you wiggle out of a wet carpet.

JUST LIKE HE SAID

But he was true to his word; the Romanovs and the rest of the nobility were all dead within a couple of years. The moral of this particular story is, if you're ever the emperor of the largest country on earth, and a strange-looking monk comes by and offers to heal your hemophiliac son, run. Just run. No good will come of it. It's a valuable lesson for us all.

*   *   *

FABULOUS FACTOIDS

Thanks to modern technology and a little thing called "DNA," scientists proved that Anna Anderson was definitively not the Grand Duchess Anastasia.

Only the first and the last Russian Czars were named Michael.

Russia's Catherine the Great? Not really Russian. She was actually born a minor German princess, a.k.a. Princess Sophie.

*   *   *

"Let them eat cake."   **—Marie Antoinette**
When a procession of Parisian paupers marched on Versailles in October, 1789, Queen Marie Antoinette reportedly scoffed, "Qu'ils mangent de la brioche," which was translated as "Let them eat cake." The quote was widely reported to showcase the Queen's callousness and to highlight just how out of touch with the sufferings of the people she was. But the quote is extremely suspect. In fact, it appeared in a publication by Jean-Jacques Rousseau more than 20 years before it was ascribed to the Queen. Additionally, brioche can refer to a type of bread that was served in the Royal household. So, the quote that was intended to make the Queen look bad was in fact, if she said it at all, meant in charity, not callousness.

Some believe that the Scottish rite of Freemasonry was founded by the Knights Templar.

TALKING 'BOUT THE TITANIC

*In 1890, a young immigrant traveled from Russia to New York in
steerage—the cheapest ship space there was. Years later,
a more elegant ship would bring young David Sarnoff
to the attention of the world.*

When his family moved to America, David Sarnoff—
future chief executive of RCA and NBC—spoke not a
word of English. When he was 15, his father died and it
was up to David to support the family, which he did by selling
newspapers and doing odd jobs. He even set up his own news-
stand. See? He was already a media guy.

SERENDIPITY STRIKES

One day, while looking for a newspaper office, young David
wandered into a telegraph company. They were looking for a
messenger boy. Why not, said Sarnoff. He got the job and taught
himself how to use the telegraph machine.

In 1906 he became an office boy for another company, the
Marconi Wireless Telegraph Company of America. By 1908 he
was a junior wireless operator for Marconi. A few years later, he
was promoted to run Marconi's New York City wireless station.

RADIO SILENCE

Sarnoff was at his station on the top of the Wanamaker Building
early in the morning of April 15, 1912. Meanwhile in the North
Atlantic, a chilling Morse code signal flashed out: "CQD, CQD,"
the general distress call for ships at sea, "Come Quick Danger."
(This was before the days when everybody used "SOS.") The chief
radio operator on the ship *Titanic* sent a more specific message
next: "Come at once. We have struck a berg."

THE GOOD NEWS, THE BAD NEWS

The message was picked up by another ship, the *Carpathia*, which
sped to the rescue. They took on board all the survivors they
could find. Then someone—and no one ever found out who—
broadcasted a message that all the passengers had been rescued

---

When Stalin became general secretary of the Communist Party, it was just a menial position.

and that the *Titanic* was being towed to port. The world breathed a sigh of relief. Hey, no rush to get there, everybody's okay.

THE OPERATOR PULLS THE PLUG

On the *Carpathia*, the wireless operator tapped out the names of survivors. Then his transmission went dead. He'd shut down his station and wouldn't communicate with anyone—not even the Navy cruisers that President Taft sent to the scene. You're wondering why, right?

SHOW ME THE MONEY

In those days, ship wireless operators weren't employees of the shipping line, but of the Marconi telegraph company. An investigation later discovered that Guglielmo Marconi himself, the "father of wireless" and owner of the telegraph company, had ordered radio silence on the *Carpathia*. It seems that Marconi had guaranteed *The New York Times* an exclusive story, and wanted to make sure they didn't get the news from anyone else. Meanwhile, The White Star Line, owners of the *Titanic*, insisted that everybody had been rescued. In fact, only about 700 of the more than 2,200 people who had been on the *Titanic* had made it.

GETTING THE TRUTH OUT

Faint ship-to-ship radio signals were still sending each other the *Carpathia*'s list of names. The young man on top of the Wanamaker Building picked up the signal and heard the news that some survivors had been rescued, but that no more were expected. He passed the list of names on, and they were picked up by other wireless operators from coast to coast. Sarnoff stayed at his station for 72 hours, passing on information to the world. For many people, it was the only valid source of news about the disaster. The media loved the Sarnoff story, and made a hero of the young immigrant.

SARNOFF'S BRAINCHILD

David Sarnoff stayed on when Marconi became Radio Corporation of America (RCA). Eventually, he got them to pay attention to his radical notion that radio waves could be used to bring music directly into homes. RCA started manufacturing and sending music to the "Radio Music Box," the worlds' first home radio. It marked the beginning of a long and successful career in radio and television broadcasting.

In his youth, Pol Pot learned to be a radio operator in Paris.

THE KING WHO STOLE THE CONGO

*How nearly a million square miles of valuable African
real estate came into the hands of the king of tiny Belgium.
Somebody should have slapped his wrists.*

Leopold II (1835–1909) was king of the Belgians. Confined in
the borders of his little kingdom, he dreamed of vast colonial empires. During the late 1800s, expansionist European
powers were claiming African territory as fast as they could. No
country could be great, Leopold, decided, without overseas
colonies. As a young man, he was fascinated by the history of the
Netherlands, a small country whose far-flung possessions in the
Far East made them rich and respected. Leopold wanted the same
future for Belgium. Too bad the Belgian people weren't interested.

A KING-SIZED DILEMMA
Belgium wasn't wealthy, and the Belgians had higher priorities
than dumping scarce resources down some tropical hole just so
their king could feel like a big man. Fretting at his subjects' lack of
vision, Leopold contemplated ways to create his own empire.

A KING-SIZED ATTENTION GETTER
News reached Europe that explorer Henry Morton Stanley had
just appeared at the mouth of the Congo River, after an unprecedented multiyear safari across Africa. Stanley originally achieved
international fame by finding Dr. David Livingstone in the vast-
ness of central Africa (and he always denied saying the famous
line "Dr. Livingstone, I presume."). Livingstone had not been lost
at all (he knew exactly where he was), but Stanley's African
exploits thrilled the Western world. And Stanley's trek down the
Congo attracted the rapt attention of the king of the Belgians.

A SCAM FIT FOR A KING
Leopold decided that the Congo was just the place for his empire.
Why, the mighty Congo River had the potential to be an African
Danube or Rhine! This big waterway slicing through the interior
of the continent was perfect for extracting raw materials out of the

jungle and shipping finished goods to thousands, perhaps millions, of new African customers. Leopold quickly formed the International Association for the Congo to cover his personal ambitions behind a corporate curtain. Then he hired Stanley to return to the Congo and negotiate treaties with local chiefs along the river.

A KING-SIZED THEFT

Time was of the essence. During the late 1800s, expansionist European powers were claiming African territory as fast as they could, and Leopold's European rivals also had their greedy eyes fixed on the Congo. The French were moving in from the north, and the Portuguese were restless in the south. Meanwhile Stanley traveled the river, meeting and signing treaties with the local chiefs. These Congolese chiefs were just being polite to Stanley. They had no idea that their mark on Stanley's papers would make a distant king believe he had the right to control their territory.

KING CON

Once Leopold had conned the Congolese, he had to con his European friends and enemies. He offered himself as the perfect compromise candidate to prevent a nasty superpower conflict over central Africa. He declared that the Congo would be a free trade zone open to the merchants of all nations. The British were satisfied; they certainly preferred Leopold to the French. The Germans were happy with anyone who wasn't British or Portuguese. The gullible Americans believed that the king wanted the Congo to be a state ruled by Africans.

As for the influential missionary lobby in all nations, Leopold swore to them that he intended to Christianize the Congo. He promised he would suppress the Arab-dominated slave trade that still existed there. The proper forces aligned behind him, and at the Berlin West African Conference of 1885, the Western powers gave the Congo to King Leopold.

KING CON GETS THE CONGO

In July 1885, Leopold declared himself sovereign of the Congo Free State. He had done what no other imperialist had managed to do, create his own personal colony. Over the next 23 years, Leopold sat in his comfortable palace in Brussels and exploited nearly 900,000 square miles of central Africa. Great for Leopold. Not so great for the Congolese.

Czechoslovakia, a Communist country, was the only one ever attacked by the Warsaw Pact.

THE MONARCH OF MISERY

Leopold created a freebooting army of European officers and African soldiers to enforce order and suppress rebellions. The king quickly forgot his promise of free trade; he declared the Congo his personal land, and the natural resources his private goods. The most valuable commodity to come out of the Congo was rubber, so Free State agents organized forced-labor collection by Africans. Failure to meet rubber quotas resulted in beatings with the *chicotte*, a nasty whip made of hippo hide. Worse, a lax rubber collector might have his hands cut off as an example to others that might refuse to make enough profit for the king's colonial government.

A HEART OF DARKNESS

In the late 1890s, reports of government brutality began to slip out of the jungles. British and American groups, particularly missionaries, investigated Leopold's Congo and discovered it was thoroughly rotten. The Congo Free State had become a savage organization that existed only to loot the Congo's natural resources by threat and violence. The brutal regime inspired Joseph Conrad's chilling classic *Heart of Darkness*, a story of the dehumanizing effects of power.

A KING-SIZED EMBARRASSMENT

The horrors in the Congo embarrassed the Belgian government in Brussels. Though there's reason to believe Leopold didn't condone the savagery of his agents, his rule allowed that savagery to flourish. In 1908, the Belgian government annexed the Congo Free State, removing the colony from the hands of the king. In 1909, Leopold II died, perhaps from shame.

AN UNHAPPY IRONY

In 1960, the Congo won independence from Belgium. Five years later, an army colonel named Mobutu took power and ruled the nation for 22 years, one year less than Leopold. Mobutu created a personal kingdom called Zaire. His government exploited the country's wealth and funneled it into his pocket. In May 1997, he was finally overthrown. Four months later, Mobutu died. Sound familiar?

Mao Zedong and Deng Xiaoping both died of complications from Parkinson's disease.

MR. JENNER AND THE MILKMAID

No, it's not the story of a romp in the hayloft,
it's about an old disease and an old wives' tale...

The first recorded mention of smallpox was by the Chinese in the twelfth century B.C. By the eighteenth century A.D. it was still one of the world's most dreaded diseases; it left scars and could blind and/or kill its victims.

THE MILKMAID IN QUESTION
In 1770s England, the only people who'd nurse smallpox patients were those who'd survived the disease and, therefore, couldn't catch it again. A teenage surgeon's apprentice, Edward Jenner, found out that the woman who was nursing one of his patients was also the man's milkmaid.

THE OLD WIVES' TALE MEETS...
She told him that even though she'd never had smallpox, she was immune to it because she'd had cowpox. (Cowpox affected cows and sheep; it also made people ill, but it was a mild disease compared to smallpox.) Jenner reported this to the surgeon, who told him not to listen to worthless old wives' tales.

... THE SCIENTIFIC APPROACH
But Jenner started to keep track of what happened to people who'd recovered from cowpox and were later exposed to smallpox. The milkmaid was right. Jenner eventually published a pamphlet stating that inoculations with cowpox would save people from dying of smallpox. Years of ridicule later, his ideas were accepted, and Jenner is now known as the inventor of vaccinations. Smallpox has been nearly wiped out, and countless lives have been saved with vaccinations—a word that's derived from the Latin word "vacca," meaning "cow."

Charles Lindbergh was actually the 61st person to fly across the Atlantic.

THE REAL LADY GODIVA

What is it about Lady Godiva that keeps our interest through the centuries?
That she was against taxing the poor people of her town?
That she had the courage of her convictions?
Of course not. It's because she went out in public with no clothes on.

THE IMPORTANCE OF REALLY LONG HAIR

Most of us are familiar with the story: Lady Godiva was concerned that her husband was taxing the people of Coventry too much and she told him so, over and over again. Finally, he said something like, "Sure honey. I'll lower taxes when you ride naked through the marketplace on your horse."

It was a bit of luck for Lady Godiva that extremely long hair was in style, because she decided to take her husband up on his dare. With her private parts covered only by her long tresses, Godiva climbed on her horse and rode through town. The punchline is that Lord Godiva was so impressed by her daring that he abolished all taxes.

WHAT'S WRONG WITH THIS PICTURE?

Historians object to the story for a variety of reasons. First, Godiva's story wasn't written until 200 years after the fact by someone who, for obvious reasons, wasn't there at the time. And second, the "marketplace" didn't exist yet; the town was more of a settlement, and the main street was just a dirt road in the 11th century, when the famous ride was supposed to have taken place.

What historians do know isn't much. Lady Godiva did exist and lived near Coventry. Her given name was Godgyfu, which means "God's gift." Not to be outdone in the Olde English name department, her husband was named Leofric. He was the earl of Mercia and a very powerful political figure. Godiva was a real Lady Bountiful, too. She and her husband built and endowed the monastery around which the town of Coventry grew up.

WHO STARTED IT

The first written mention of the story comes from Roger of Wendover, a historian and 13th century monk—but not one of the Lord and Lady's well-endowed monks. He describes the

Before founding the Boy Scouts, Robert Baden-Powell had been a spy in South Africa.

ride-that-never-was in detail:

> Whereupon the countess [sic]… let down her tresses, which
> covered the whole of her body like a veil, and then mounting
> her horse and attended by two knights, she rode through the
> market-place, without being seen, except her fair legs.

Without being seen? That's not the way we heard it.

WHAT ABOUT TOM?

The other version of the legend says that, out of modesty, Lady
Godiva asked the citizens of Coventry not to watch her while she
took her ride. But one man—Peeping Tom—couldn't resist. The
punishment for his impudence was severe. He was struck blind on
the spot. Which probably taught him a lesson. Or would have if
he'd existed in the first place.

The story of how Tom came to be is pretty silly. Some 16th
century mischief-maker salvaged a wooden statue of St. George
from the monastery when it closed down in 1539. He stuck the
statue in a window that overlooked the now-famous marketplace.
When anyone asked who that was at the window, the jokester
replied, "That's Tom. He's peeping at Godiva." How surprising is it
that a legend about a naked woman would expand to include a
guy peeking at her?

THERE SHE IS, MISS LADY GODIVA

The city of Coventry has been holding Godiva pageants for more
than 300 years. The main event is a reenactment of Lady Godiva's
famous ride. The first pageant, held in 1678, starred a maiden in a
pink bodysuit and a very long wig. She was accompanied by
costumed ladies-in-waiting, city officials, trade guild floats, and
those universal parade stalwarts, the fire brigade.

The pageant continued annually until 1854, when an event
that some people had been dreading—and others had been
hoping for—happened: a truly naked woman on a horse crashed
the pageant. Pandemonium ensued, and the pageant was
suspended for eight years.

The modern incarnation is called "Godiva Weekend," and
sounds suspiciously like what Americans know as a Renaissance
Faire. If you miss it, you can still see Godiva—naked, on horseback, and cast in bronze. Her statue gazes down on the modern
Coventry marketplace: a shopping center.

Because he supported violence, Amnesty International never adopted Nelson Mandela.

THE PHANTOM ARMY

We'll bet your history teacher never told you that one of the Allies' greatest weapons in World War II was a colossal hoax that Germany swallowed—hook, line, and sinker!

Behind D-Day's astonishing success was one of the most sophisticated deception schemes ever perpetrated on an enemy force. It went this way: Hitler knew the Allies were planning an invasion. And he was sure they'd cross the English Channel at the Pas de Calais (what the British call the Strait of Dover) to get to France, because it's the shortest distance between Great Britain and the continent. But a landing at Calais would put the troops smack dab in front of the strongest section of Hitler's "Atlantic Wall," a virtual suicide mission. So the Allies chose Normandy for the landings instead.

NOTHING UP MY SLEEVE...

This called for some fancy footwork. To mislead the Germans, General Dwight D. Eisenhower and his staff created a mythical 1st Army Group and based it in Britain near Dover, just across the channel from Calais. Eisenhower assigned George S. Patton, the American general the Germans most respected, to command this army that didn't exist.

THE PLOT THICKENS

To convince the Germans that the Phantom Army was preparing for invasion, Eisenhower's staff positioned inflatable tanks, balsa wood bombers, and canvas landing craft where the Luftwaffe could photograph them during aerial reconnaissance. Radio operators were assigned to generate routine radio traffic, and bogus intelligence reports and documents were "lost" and fell into the hands of the Germans. Local newspapers in the towns where the Phantom Army was stationed even carried false marriage and death notices.

STOP THE PRESSES!

One elaborate ruse included *National Geographic* magazine. The U.S. Army prepared a color spread depicting a variety of 1st Army Group insignias: shoulder patches and the like. When the magazine was published, they allowed some issues to be distrib-

---

Founded by Union army officers, the NRA was originally out to improve marksmanship.

uted, but then halted the printing, removed the bogus insignias, and released a revised version of the magazine.

THE BIG FAKE-OUT

The Allies continuously drew attention to the Channel coast near Calais. During the weeks before the invasion, Allied airmen dropped more bombs on the Pas de Calais than anywhere else in France. Naval units conducted protracted maneuvers up and down the coast.

On the night of the Normandy invasion, Allied planes dropped silver foil on the Pas de Calais which German radar picked up as an invasion fleet crossing the channel narrows. At the same time, a radar blackout disguised the real movement toward Normandy. All of these ploys were designed to convince Berlin that it needed to prepare for an amphibious assault on Calais.

"YOO-HOO! OVER HERE!"

By the time the invasion finally began, Hitler and his generals had been so thoroughly deceived that they believed the Normandy operation was a diversion. Instead of moving their reserve units to stop the Allies from reaching the beachheads, they continued to wait for what they thought would be the main attack at Calais. By the time that the Germans realized they'd been deceived, it was too late. Allied troops had breached the Atlantic Wall and were headed towards Paris. The "Phantom Army" had succeeded beyond anyone's wildest dreams. And without ever firing a shot.

*   *   *

"The Battle of Waterloo was won on the playing fields of Eton."

—The Duke of Wellington

When the duke was a boy at Eton College there were no playing fields, nor any organized sports. The supposed reference to the discipline, determination, and comradeship gained through such adolescent activity, therefore, falls flat. The quote was first ascribed to the duke by the French writer Charles de Montalembert in his treatise entitled "England's Political Future," which was published three years after Wellington's death. The Frenchman, however, never met the duke so it is highly likely that he invented the quote himself.

Tennessee teacher John Scopes was actually on the losing end of the famous "Monkey Trial."

THE HUNCHBACK OF NORTHERN FAME: THE STORY OF RICHARD III

Was Shakespeare's villain just a victim of artistic license?
Why did so many regular folk, especially in northern England,
want to clear the name of Richard III?

Shakespeare's Richard III is a villain you love to hate. An ugly hunchback, Richard succeeds in his ambition by arranging the deaths of his wife Anne, his brother George Duke of Clarence, his two nephews Edward V and Richard Duke of York, Henry VI, Henry's son Edward Prince of Wales, and anyone else who stands between him and the throne.

POOR RICHARD

Some folks—especially in the north of England where Richard had been in charge for many years—thought he was a terrific guy. After Richard's death, even with his enemies in power, city fathers at York referred to Richard as the "prince of blessed memory." A century later, Sir Francis Bacon reported that ordinary people of the north still grumbled that their Dick had gotten the short end of the stick. Was he a royal psychopath or a just and kindly ruler?

A FAMILY SQUABBLE

Richard was the last of a long line of Plantagenet kings who'd been ruling England since the middle of the 12th century. For several generations, two branches of the Plantagenets—the Lancasters and the Yorks—had been fighting over the crown. In 1462, the Yorks got it, in the person of Richard's older brother, King Edward IV.

THE GOOD BROTHER

Throughout his reign Edward IV struggled with rebels, always aided by the loyal Richard. Richard was given land and power in the north of England and seemed to be an ideal ruler. Then Edward died. His son, now Edward V, was only 12 years old. So good old Uncle Richard was named regent.

THE ROTTEN REGENT
When Edward IV died, Richard didn't mess around. He charged
down from the north, executed his potential rivals without a trial,
and soon had everything running like clockwork. There was one
small problem, a guy named Henry Tudor over in France was just
itching to cross the English Channel and grab the throne.

THE BAD UNCLE
But Richard grabbed the throne first. Claiming he'd stumbled
across evidence that Edward IV and Elizabeth's marriage wasn't
entirely kosher, he declared his brother's children illegitimate. He
imprisoned young Edward V and the younger Richard Duke of
York in the tower of London, and took the throne—though not
for long. Henry Tudor crossed the channel after all, and Richard
died defending his crown at the fatal Battle of Bosworth in 1485.

TRUTH VS. LEGEND
Those are the facts about Richard. What about the Shakespearean
plot?

A hunchback? Nope: Although he may have had one shoulder
slightly higher than the other, caused by years of swordplay,
Richard seems to have acquired most of his physical deformities
after death. In fact, his contemporaries said he was rather handsome, though not a hunk like his brother, Edward IV.

Murdered Henry VI? Maybe: Perhaps Richard killed Henry VI on
Edward's orders. Perhaps not. There's no evidence either way.
Richard was blamed for the murder of King Henry VI's son
Edward, the heir to the crown, but contemporary accounts say the
boy was killed on the battlefield.

Murdered his brother George? Unlikely: George had tried to overthrow his brother King Edward IV (talk about your dysfunctional
families!), and Richard gave his usual support to the king during
George's trial. But in private, Richard was reported to be
genuinely upset at the execution of his feckless brother, who may
have been suffering from some form of insanity.

Usurping the throne? Yep: The legitimacy of Edward's kids was
not as big a deal as Richard made it out to be. He'd seized the
throne, which seemed to be a sort of family tradition for the

squabbling Plantagenets. Perhaps he'd also had real concerns about the threat to England (and the Yorks) under a child king.

Did he murder his nephews? Jury's out: The biggest stain on Richard's reputation was the accusation that he killed the princes in the tower. Certainly he locked Edward V and his brother, Richard Duke of York, in the Tower of London, and after the summer of 1483, they were never seen again. But killing children wouldn't endear him to the public, whose support he needed. The boys' mother, the former Queen Elizabeth Woodville, who'd asked for the protection of the Church when Richard took the throne, decided to come out again—just at the time that the boys were supposedly murdered.

The other suspects and theories: If the princes were still alive after Henry VII became king, he might have done them in for the same reasons attributed to Richard. They weakened his claim to the throne. And the Duke of Buckingham is a major suspect in the royal tot killing. He had access to the children and (since he was also after the throne) a motive to get rid of them. Some believe that the princes were never murdered on purpose, but died in a botched escape.

A mystery through history: Mysteries still cloud the death of the princes. A child-murder would have made great propaganda, but nobody openly accused anybody else of murder. Buckingham could have justified his rebellion by accusing Richard of doing away with the tykes; he didn't. Richard could have added child murder to the other charges against Buckingham; he didn't. Or Richard could have produced the living princes to disprove the rumors that they'd been killed. (You guessed it, he didn't.) As for Henry VII, he never exploited the juicy gossip that the two kids had been offed by their Uncle Dick.

A hit man: Later writers claimed that Richard's actual hit man, Sir James Tyrrell, had confessed, in writing, to the crime, but the Tudors never made the supposed document public.

Make no bones about it: Perhaps the inability to produce bodies is what kept all three suspects from accusing each other. The bones of two children were found buried in the foundation of a staircase in the tower. But that discovery wasn't made until 1674. What-

---

ever happened to the two boys, Richard wins no prizes as an uncle or a regent. By imprisoning them instead of protecting them, he'd abandoned the princes to their enemies, even if he didn't kill them.

NOT GIVEN A FAIR SHAKE-SPEARE

But Richard didn't win prizes as the ultimate incarnation of evil, either. Up until 1483, he was an excellent and generous ruler, and a loyal brother, and nobody ever doubted his skill and courage as a warrior. One likely explanation was that, rather than being a murderous schemer, Richard was a decisive soldier, a man of action who wasn't good at mulling over long-term consequences. Once Edward died, Richard started making plans up as he went along. He may have ended up betraying his own principles—and in so doing, handed Shakespeare the makings of the villain we love to hate.

* * *

NOTABLE QUOTABLES FROM *RICHARD III*

"So wise so young, they say, do never live long."
Act ii, Scene 4

"The sons of Edward sleep in Abraham's bosom."
Act iv, Scene 3

"A horse! A horse! My kingdom for a horse!"
Act v, Scene 4

"My conscience hath a thousand several tongues,
And every tongue brings in a several tale,
And every tale condemns me for a villain."
Act v, Scene 3

WHO CONQUERED THE NORTH POLE?

*Most people believe Robert Peary tamed the great Arctic frontier in
1909. But a doctor named Frederick Cooke claimed to have beaten
him by over 12 months. Recent analysis suggests that
maybe neither of them made it.*

"**S**tars and Stripes nailed to North Pole—Peary." When
Robert Peary sent this telegram to the outside world on
September 6, 1909, he thought he was making history.
Imagine his surprise when he found out that rival explorer Frederick Cooke had announced five days previously that he had
reached the North Pole in April 1908—a full year before Peary.
This set the scene for a battle of egos that would rage for decades.
So, who really reached the North Pole first—Peary or Cooke?

IN THIS CORNER
To Robert Peary, the quest for the North Pole was an obsession.
The U.S. Navy civil engineer saw in the accomplishment the road
to fame, fortune, and immortality. After telling his mother of his
chosen course, he added, "I must have fame and cannot reconcile
myself to years of commonplace drudgery." It might sound a tad
grandiose to those of us who face commonplace drudgery every
day, but it actually comes off as humble compared to Cooke's take
on it.

AND IN THAT CORNER
Frederick Cooke, a physician from New York, wrote, "I saw myself
attempting to win in the most spectacular and difficult marathon
for the testing of human strength, courage, and perseverance, of
body and brain, which God has offered to man, until I stood
alone, a victor, upon the world's pinnacle."

TOP OF THE WORLD, MA!
Okay, so maybe a guy can't talk about conquering a pole without
sounding like he has delusions of grandeur. And it was obvious
that both had made genuine attempts to reach the North Pole.
The question was whether either had managed to go all the way.

FDR had a 25,000-piece stamp collection worth millions of dollars.

WALRUS GREASE, ETC.

Recent analysis of the diaries, journals, and field notes of Peary and Cooke may indicate that they both failed. The following discrepancies support this view:

- Peary's records never showed his claim to reach the North Pole.
- Peary's diary entries are remarkably tidy and display none of the walrus grease stains or poor penmanship to be expected from a man writing under extreme arctic conditions.
- Peary's diary pages for the days during which he claimed to be at the North Pole are inexplicably blank.
- During his testimony before Congress in 1911, Peary often contradicted himself and, when pressed for details of his expedition, he complained of memory lapses.
- Both men claimed to have traveled at incredible rates of speed—more than 15 miles per day over the roughest terrain on earth.
- Cooke's field notes betray an ignorance of mathematical concepts used to calculate latitude.
- A photocopy of a Cooke notebook shows that he doctored his accounts: writing over dates, renumbering pages, and erasing some of the entries.
- The sled that Cooke designed and used, though innovative (it could fold into a kayak), could probably not have stood up to the harsh conditions of the trip.
- Cooke had earlier faked a claim of climbing 20,000-foot Mt. McKinley.
- When interviewed, two of Cooke's Eskimo guides who remained at base camp claimed that Cooke was never out of their sight.

WHY WAIT?

Interesting, too, is the fact that Cooke didn't announce his "victory" until five days before Peary's announcement, even though he claimed to have reached the North Pole more than a year earlier. (Okay, it took him five months to get home, but still, it's kind of out of character for a man who claimed that he "stood alone, a victor, upon the world's pinnacle.")

SORRY...

Oh. Did you think we were going to tell you the answer? Well, heck, we don't know. The jury's still out. We'll just have to chalk it up as one of history's mysteries.

The presidential election of 1876 was even more heavily disputed than the election of 2001.

FIESTA!

In Peru and its neighboring countries, there is a special fiesta food: guinea pigs. Sixty-five million of the friendly little rodents get eaten every year (mostly fried).

Birthdays, weddings, no party would be complete without a tasty dish of fried guinea pigs, often decorated with the severed heads looking up at you cheekily from the plate. The Peruvians breed them at home, dozens at a time, keeping them running around on the floor; they are a part of everyday life. More than half the families in Lima have some. But apart from their value as food, the animals are also supposed to have magical qualities. Traditional healers use them in ceremonies to cure disease, and others use them in spells to drive away bad luck.

These modern traditions are all that's left of the guinea pig cult of the Incas. Archaeological evidence shows that guinea pigs have been domesticated in the Andes at least since 2,500 B.C., but they had a special place in the Inca civilization that the Spanish Conquistadors found when they arrived in the 15th century. According to a native chronicler, the Incas sacrificed a thousand white guinea pigs every July (along with a hundred llamas), in an offering to the gods that was supposed to protect the fields. These sacred beasts were about twice the size of today's pet shop variety.

The Spanish destroyed the Inca way of life, and the Catholic church was keen to stamp out the Inca religion too. So when they found that the whole country was overrun by sacred animals, regularly killed and eaten during traditional religious festivals, they suggested that the best thing would be to exterminate them. But the first bishop of Lima refused this request from the church authorities. He was afraid the natives would rebel. After all, the guinea pigs were an important source of food. So the Peruvians kept their guinea pigs. In Cuzco, the old Inca capital, there is a large painting of the Last Supper, which was part of the Catholic effort to convert the natives. They made an effort to include some local elements to get the message across. At such an important fiesta, there is only one possible dish that could have been served. Sitting in front of Jesus is a plate of fried guinea pig.

HER MAJESTY'S A PRETTY NICE GIRL

When you're the monarch of all you survey, people tend to talk about you behind your back, especially in sexual matters. We at BRI were curious about a few long-standing royal rumors.

CATHERINE, EMPRESS OF RUSSIA (1727–1796)
Background: Catherine the Great was born in Germany, married Peter III of Russia, and promptly threw him in jail, where he died under mysterious circumstances. She was famous for fostering European influences in her court. She even even claimed the French writer Voltaire as a pen pal. But she wasn't all that enlightened when it came to the Russian peasants, or serfs, as you'll see.

The Rumor: That Catherine's association with her horse went far beyond the usual owner-steed relationship.

The Truth: No. What the great lady liked best were horsemen, that is, the officers of her very own Imperial Horse Guard. Especially the young handsome ones.

How It Worked: Catherine would espy a cutie who then had to pass two tests. One was a physical exam, given by the court physician. The other test was of a sexual nature; one of Catherine's women friends would try the potentially lucky fellow out. If he passed both tests he'd be installed in the palace within easy reach of the empress. She rewarded her favorites with gifts of cash, pensions, and serfs. One of the luckier ones was given 4,000 serfs; equivalent to the population of a small town.

As she got older, her lovers got younger. Her last lover, when she was in her sixties, was 21.

Despite the fact that she gave people away as gifts—a practice we frown upon here at BRI—we still hold Catherine in the highest esteem. When she died of a stroke in her late sixties, she was on her way to our favorite room in the house: the toilet.

The CIA considered killing Fidel Castro by dosing his scuba gear with LSD.

ELIZABETH I, QUEEN OF ENGLAND (1533–1603)

Background: Power makes almost anybody sexy. Even a woman with a receding hairline, frizzy red hair, and gobs of white powder all over her face. No, not Mrs. Bozo the Clown… we're talking about Queen Elizabeth I. At least as she's been portrayed in her older years. But forget what she looked like. The people of England adored Elizabeth. She reigned for 44 years, during which she built her country into a major world power. She was a generous patron of progress and exploration. Under her sponsorship, Sir Francis Drake claimed the California coast for England. And Sir Walter Raleigh, one of her more serious suitors, named colonial Virginia after her.

But her name wasn't Virginia, you say? True. Raleigh was referring to one of Elizabeth's nicknames: "the Virgin Queen." Which fostered all sorts of rumors, especially the following.

The Rumor: That the Virgin Queen wasn't really a virgin.

The Truth: She probably was.

But Wait! Elizabeth is still pretty interesting since most historians think she may have been the champion sex tease of all time. She was quite fetching as a young girl and once she ascended to the throne—if you believe in power as an aphrodisiac—she also ascended to the title of most eligible bachelorette of her time.

She had some serious flirtations in her life, some of which ended in high drama. While just a teenage princess, for instance, she took up with the dashing-but-dumb Thomas Seymour. When his plans to stage a palace coup became known, Elizabeth's brother—King Edward VI—had him executed.

Most of the rumors that circulated about Elizabeth's virginity concerned her friendship with Lord Robert Dudley. He was her favorite male companion, and the two batted their eyelashes at each other for 30 years. (And occasionally bickered like a long-married couple.) But the experts believe that because the subject of her virginity was a constant source of speculation and because she lived a life where privacy was unheard of, any whisper of "the dirty deed" would have made it around the castle within minutes.

All her life, noblemen and princes from across Europe wooed and pursued Elizabeth, but she kept them dangling. As she got older, and England became more powerful, she was courted just as vigorously. She had the uncanny ability to convince any suitor that he just might be the one she'd share her throne with.

But Elizabeth knew only too well what could happen to a queen at the hands of a husband. When she was a child her father, Henry VIII, had her mother, Anne Boleyn, and her stepmother, Catherine Howard, beheaded.

ANNE BOLEYN, QUEEN OF ENGLAND (1507-1536)

Background: By all accounts, Anne wasn't the prettiest girl in the English court. But she had a cute, sexy way about her, which she put to good use to capture the heart of the lusty King Henry VIII of England. The problem was that Henry was already married. Anne refused to join the ranks of Henry's mistresses (which included her own sister, Mary). She wanted marriage and she kept up the heat until Henry wanted it, too.

When he couldn't persuade his wife, Catherine of Aragon, to divorce him, and couldn't persuade the pope to grant a divorce, Henry decided to start his own religion   yeah, that's the ticket. He called it the "Church of England" a.k.a. the "Anglican Church."

So Henry and Anne married and lived relatively unhappily for three years during which she gave birth to a girl who grew up to be Queen Elizabeth I (see above). But Henry wanted a son, and when he was sure Anne wasn't going to conceive one, he falsely accused her of adultery with five men, including her brother. The only fitting punishment for such crimes was execution.

The Rumor: That Anne Boleyn had three breasts. (How do these rumors get started?)

The Truth: Unproven, though one expert describes a large goiter on her neck that some myopic reporter might have mistaken for a breast.

So What?: Anne Boleyn's breasts were the least interesting thing about her. Remember those cute, sexy ways? They turned world history in a brand new direction.

The Europe that Anne Boleyn lived in was all about alliances, and the pope was a major player. The Protestant Reformation, which Martin Luther started, was already undermining the papal power. But it was strictly a grassroots movement until Henry stepped in. Up to that time, no monarch had risked incurring the wrath of the Vatican in such a big way. But Henry liked to take things to extremes. Take Anne for instance. Instead of just divorcing her (we wonder, would she have asked for alimony?), he overdid it and had her beheaded. He was just beginning to flex his royal muscles. As the years went by, he became as bloated with power as he was in his body.

Henry's break with the church signaled the beginning of its downfall as a major world power. It also legitimized the rise of the Protestant religion. And all because of one irresistible woman.

Anne was bewitching to the end. When she refused a blindfold at her execution, the executioner was so entranced by her eyes that he had to sneak up behind her to cut off her head.

JULIUS CAESAR, RULER OF THE ROMAN EMPIRE (100 –44 B.C.)

Background: What's a man… and by all accounts a ladies' man doing in an article like this? Read on.

Julius Caesar is the only ruler among these ladies who seized rather than ascended to or married into power. (Isn't that just like a man?) Born to the patrician class, the upper crust of ancient Rome, he was a poet, writer, brilliant general, and not in the least bit humble about it.

He conquered most of what is now central Europe, which made him terrifically popular with the populace, and that made the Roman powers-that-be very nervous. While they were deciding how to get rid of him, Caesar led his legions against Rome. Four years later, after he'd seized power, he declared himself, not emperor, but "dictator for life," a title that didn't embarrass him at all. Soon after that, a bunch of senators ganged up on him and stabbed him to death. That was on March 15, the famous Ides of March.

That's what can happen to people who live life that large.

The Rumor: That Caesar was an insatiable skirt chaser.

The Truth: Except for that time with King Nicomedes of Bithynia. Which is how he got the nickname "the Queen of Bithynia." Which is why he's included here, among the ladies.

The Lowdown: Caesar had a reputation as an inexhaustible heterosexual. It was well-known that he slept with the wives of other politicians and any queens of the female persuasion—Cleopatra included—he could lay hands on. A popular song of the time warned the Romans to lock their wives away because Caesar was in town. He even wanted to pass a law permitting him to marry any woman of his choice for the "procreation of children." And for the good of Rome, of course.

But in his youth, Caesar visited Bithynia, a Roman province in Asia Minor, and supposedly had a fling with the king. Most of the writers of the time mention it; one of them called Caesar "the Queen of Bithynia... who once wanted to sleep with a monarch, but now wants to be one." At any rate, other people were calling him "queen," too, and the name stuck.

Contrary to popular belief, homosexuality was not completely acceptable behavior in ancient Rome. A lot was made of the incident because Caesar, while exhibiting the leanings of a macho-macho man, was apparently a little—what shall we say?—effeminate.

But is it fair that one youthful indiscretion can spoil the reputation of an incorrigible man on the make? That's what can happen to people who live life that large.

EMPRESS DOWAGER TZU HSI OF CHINA (1835-1908)

Background: The last empress of China started out as a concubine, which, for a girl from the countryside, was not a bad place to start. Especially since, at the time, women in China were held in lower esteem than most farm animals. She was extraordinarily pretty, of course, or she wouldn't have been chosen to join the imperial harem, which due to hard times, was reduced to one empress, two consorts (minor wives) and 11 concubines.

Her real name is unknown. She received the name Tzu Hsi (which most westerners pronounced "Susie") when she joined the court. She gave birth to a boy, the emperor's only male heir, and with this stroke of biological luck she shot up through the ranks like a rocket. Now she was number two in prestige, just below the empress herself. Her son ascended to the throne when the emperor died, making Tzu Hsi the empress dowager, sort of a Queen Mum.

Just before she died in 1908, she chose her three-year-old

nephew, Pu Yi, "the Last Emperor," to succeed her.

The Rumor: That she was a homicidal nymphomaniac who held wild orgies in the Imperial Palace.

The Truth: It was a smear job, dreamed up by a British con man.

The Dragon Lady: Tzu Hsi may have been the most-maligned figure in history. The story of her sexploits, along with accusations of cold-blooded murder, was part of a fiendish plot concocted by Edmund Backhouse, the bad seed of an otherwise fine upper-class family. A swindler with good connections in China, he couldn't pass up the opportunity presented by the empress's death in 1908.

In two books published after Tzu Hsi died, Backhouse used forgeries and nonexistent documents to convince the world that the empress dowager was the true Dragon Lady, a sex-starved, ruthless monster who seduced and murdered her way to the Chinese throne. Backhouse even had the audacity to put himself at the center of some of his imaginary orgies with the Dowager Empress.

The public was more than willing to believe Backhouse's lies. For one thing, it gave them the opportunity to read pornography under the guise of historical fact. And the empress's barbaric ways went a long way to justify the British presence in China. Who better than the civilized Brits to save China from itself? Backhouse's lies were so completely accepted that even the respected writer Pearl Buck was taken in by him: She used his fabrications as fact in two of her own books.

Why did Backhouse do it? For one thing, there was money to be made. Stories of sex-starved Asian women sold a lot of copies. For another, there was fame to be had. The publication of the second book set him up as a Chinese scholar of international scope. On the other hand, at least one expert thinks he did it for the fun of it.

As for the country girl who became an empress, historians now say that she spent most of her time at the office. Do we dare suggest that she might have wished for a little more excitement in her life?

DARWIN'S COUSIN
AND THE APES

*Sir Francis Galton was a Victorian guy who lived with monkeys
for a while and liked numbers more than people. His numbers had
huge consequences for the course of the 20th century. But despite
his so-called mastery of statistics to chart the future of humanity,
he never had a clue about the future of his own work.*

Before he found his true calling, Sir Francis Galton
(1822–1911) spent an aimless youth as a mediocre student
and avid explorer of the exotic East. He set up house in
Egypt and Syria where he lived with slave girls, monkeys, and a
mongoose. However, he eventually tired of the decadent life of a
pasha and returned to damp England.

COUNT GALTON
Galton married a stern Victorian woman and settled down to a
long, unhappy life of trying to understand humanity by counting
things. He strove to use statistics to demonstrate important ideas
about life. Some of his work shocked his Victorian audience.

BEAUTY AND THE BUST
As a young man, he used statistics to study the fairer sex. While
living in southern Africa, for example, he studied the bust sizes of
indigenous women, who generally went topless. They wouldn't
allow Galton to measure by hand, so he observed them from a
distance, gauging their breasts with a sextant. When he returned
home, he continued the theme by creating a "beauty chart" of
England based on his own observations of the distribution of
attractive women in towns across the country.

GOD AS A STATISTIC
Galton also shocked society when he tried to prove that belief in
God's influence in human affairs was statistically unsupportable.
He collected numbers to demonstrate the fact that people who
prayed a lot, or who were prayed for (like the royal family), didn't
live any longer than anyone else. He also showed that ships carrying missionaries sank just as often as other ships. Galton did use

numbers for less peculiar purposes. For instance, he liked to collect meteorological data and was responsible for the first weather charts of Great Britain.

DABBLING LIKE DARWIN

Galton wasn't a professional scientist. He was a rich man who liked science and math and had the time to dabble. He decided to dabble in heredity. Heredity was a very hot topic in the mid-19th century, particularly after Galton's cousin, Charles Darwin, published *The Origin of Species*, his famous book on evolution. Galton was a firm supporter of his cousin's controversial theory, and he had a controversial theory of his own.

In those days, the concept of heredity was as plain as the nose on your face, that is, the nose you got from your mother's side of the family. However, no one knew with biological certainty how inherited traits passed from one generation to the next. The existence of genes was still unknown. Galton tried to demonstrate that parents transmitted not only physical characteristics such as hair color and height to their offspring, but also nonphysical traits like talent, intelligence, and even moral character. Successful people had successful kids because of biology.

SNOB SCIENCE

Galton decided that Britain, as the most powerful nation on Earth, must encourage their best and brightest to intermarry and have children. The government must make sure that successful people married each other to guarantee a constant birthrate of successful future leaders. Marriage between talented and less talented people would dilute the cream of the nation and doom Britain to a future in which they wouldn't rule the world!

Galton really meant that the government should keep upper-class bloodlines pure. It was obvious to him that the upper classes were the superior breed. After all, if the lower classes were smart, wouldn't they be upper class? (And spend their brilliant youth living with slave girls and monkeys?)

Eventually Galton had to face facts. The government wasn't going to regulate marriages. But his statistical work in heredity created a branch of science he called "eugenics." Eugenics continued after Galton's death and in the 20th century, flowered into a horror that he wouldn't have recognized.

SNOB SCIENCE SINKS TO NEW DEPTHS

Galton's idea that superior couples produced superior children was turned on its head in an attempt to purify populations by eliminating "undesirable" elements. Social activists sponsored eugenics progams in the United States. They tried, for example, to sterilize the handicapped and prevent them from reproducing. The Nazis based the Holocaust partly on eugenics theories of racial purity; they simply murdered any person or race that they believed to be inferior. These twists on the original concept of eugenics would have horrified even the elitist Galton.

JUST HANG UP

Oddly enough, though Sir Francis Galton blithely treated human populations as collections of numbers instead of people and laid the foundations for totalitarian eugenics in the 20th century, he also led the way in research on fingerprints. Fingerprints, being absolutely unique, are often seen as the ultimate expression of human individuality. But don't forgive Sir Francis too quickly, he also pioneered the use of questionnaires to collect statistical information for analysis. We have that darned Galton to thank every time an opinion pollster calls during dinner.

* * *

HITLER, A HYPOCRITE?

Despite his own merciless actions, Hitler chose to be a vegetarian. As hypocritical as this sounds, he believed that killing and eating animals was inhumane and cruel. He believed that by respecting the animals' rights and abstaining from eating meat, he was saving innocent lives. Too bad he didn't feel that way about humans.

The words "czar" and "kaiser" are both descended from the word "caesar."

HANDICAP?
WHAT HANDICAP?

A listing of famous people in history who didn't let their handicaps stand in the way of accomplishment.

L udwig von Beethoven, 1770–1827
Went completely deaf during his thirties, yet continued to write some of the world's greatest music.

Elizabeth Barrett Browning, 1806–1861
Incapacitated as a result of a childhood spinal injury and lung ailment. Became a renowned poet, political thinker, and feminist.

Thomas Edison, 1847–1931
Developed hearing problems early in life that became progressively worse as he grew older. Edison was one of the greatest and most productive inventors of his time.

Albert Einstein, 1879–1955
Unable to speak until the age of three, Einstein was thought to be "simple-minded" until it was realized that he learned by visualization rather than by the use of language.

Joan of Arc, 1412–1431
Though she suffered from narcolepsy—an uncontrollable urge to sleep—this visionary French peasant led the French armies to victory over the English at Orleans in 1429.

General Philip Kearney, 1814–1862
A famous American general who lost an arm during the war with Mexico and went on to distinguish himself in the Civil War.

Helen Keller, 1880–1968
Born blind, deaf, and mute, but graduated cum laude from Radcliffe in 1904. She mastered five languages and wrote six books.

Dorothea Lange, 1895–1965
Walked with a limp due to a bout with polio at the age of seven.

Lange spent her life traveling the world photographing the disenfranchised. She is most famous for her documentary images of American rural life during the Great Depression.

Lord Horatio Nelson, 1758–1805
Lost an eye and one arm, but went on to become an admiral and the hero of the battle of Trafalgar, where he destroyed the combined French and Spanish fleets.

John Milton, 1608–1674
Became blind at age 43, but went on to create his most famous epic, *Paradise Lost.* Considered by many to be the greatest English poet after Shakespeare.

Alexander Pope, 1688–1744
A hunchback who was the first English poet to enjoy contemporary fame throughout the European continent and to see translations of his poems into modern as well as ancient languages.

Wiley Post, 1899–1935
Despite the loss of one eye, he became one of the most colorful figures of the early years of U.S. aviation and made the first solo flight around the world in 1933.

John Wesley Powell 1834–1902
After he lost his right arm in the American Civil War, he became a science professor and explorer who developed an interest in preserving native American cultures. In 1879, he founded the Smithsonian Institution's Bureau of Ethnology to study and record the traditions of Native Americans.

Franklin Delano Roosevelt, 1882–1945
Lost the use of his legs after contracting polio at age 39, but went on to become the 32nd president of the United States (1933–1945). Roosevelt served longer than any other American president.

Charles Steinmetz, 1865–1923
A hunchback, this German-born American electrical engineer developed a practical method of making calculations of alternating current, thus revolutionizing electrical engineering.

Before Columbus, no Indian had type B blood.

Harriett Tubman, 1820–1913
As a child born into slavery, she was struck on the head by an overseer. The blow fractured her skull and caused episodes of narcolepsy for the rest of her life. She eventually escaped bondage and guided runaway slaves to freedom in the north for more than a decade before the American Civil War.

Josiah Wedgwood, 1730–1795
Suffered an attack of smallpox that eventually required the amputation of his right leg. This English pottery designer and manufacturer developed a scientific approach to pottery making, and his works are considered to be among the finest examples of ceramic art.

Woodrow Wilson, 1856–1924
Dyslexic from early childhood, Wilson served as president of the United States from 1913 to 1921. He also suffered a stroke during his term that left him partially paralyzed on his left side.

FAMOUS PEOPLE WITH EPILEPSY

Agatha Christie
Alexander the Great
Alfred Lord Tennyson
Alfred Nobel
Algernon Charles Swinburne
Aristotle
Blaise Pascal
Charles Dickens
Fyodor Dostoevsky
Edgar Allen Poe
Edward Lear
Gustave Flaubert
Hannibal
Hector Berlioz
Isaac Newton

James Madison
James Joyce
Julius Caesar
Lewis Carrol
Michelangelo
Napoleon Bonaparte
Niccolo Paganini
Pythagoras
Queen Boadicea
Saint Paul the Apostle
Socrates
Truman Capote
Vincent van Gogh
Winston Churchill

Peter Minuit was conned into buying Manhattan from the wrong Indian tribe.

THE INVASION OF AMERICA

Who was Pancho Villa? Why did he devote himself to killing Americans? And what did the U.S. do about it?

Francisco "Pancho" Villa was the people's hero of the 1911 Mexican revolution, one of the leaders of the guerilla forces that toppled the 45-year rule of dictator Porfiro Diaz. To the Mexican people, he was a latter-day Robin Hood. And why not? The man was a paragon of virtue: a nonsmoker, nondrinker, and nonwomanizer who commanded the utmost respect from his hardened band of men.

THE FATHER OF HIS COUNTRY?
Mexico swarmed with revolutionaries at the time, but Villa's heroic activities so impressed his neighbor Woodrow Wilson that the U.S. president singled him out, dubbing him the "George Washington of the South." However, within a very short time, little "George" would turn on his big brother—with good reason and deadly results.

BETRAYED BY BIG BROTHER
In October 1915, after being defeated by a competing revolutionary force that had been supplied with U.S. arms, Villa was outraged to learn that the United States had just officially recognized another guerilla fighter, Venustiano Carranza, as the legitimate president of Mexico. Just days later, Carranza's men, fully equipped with U.S. weapons, ambushed Villa and his men.

THAT DOES IT!
His disillusionment complete, Villa abandoned the struggle for freedom in his own country and decided to start repaying those backstabbing gringos. From now on, he was going to kill as many Americans as he could find. His first opportunity came in January 1916, when he and his men held up a train carrying 16 American mining engineers. The bandits lined up their victims and, one by one, shot them in the back of the head.

Appetite now whetted for more American blood, Villa made

After the Battle of Little Bighorn, Chief Sitting Bull tried to get sanctuary in Canada.

plans for a full-scale invasion. Or at least as full-scale as he and his small band of 500 "Villistas" could handle.

FULL-SCALE BUT SCALED DOWN
Two months later, Villa and his men invaded the United States. In New Mexico, they took the unlucky 13th U.S. Cavalry by surprise, getting away with more than a hundred horses and a load of machine guns. On their way back to Mexico, the Villistas attacked the sleepy border town of Columbus, New Mexico. The raiders burned down buildings, looted the bank, raped several women, and left 26 people dead.

THAT DID IT!
The people of the United States were outraged. Men from every state volunteered to help hunt down Villa and his men. An expedition that was to cost some $25 million was soon put together, and a staggering 150,000 troops were mobilized to bring the handful of rebels to justice. President Wilson chose living legend General John "Black Jack" Pershing to lead the mission.

TALK ABOUT OVERKILL
The manhunt gave the U.S. the opportunity to try out two new forms of weaponry: tanks, airplanes, and war machinery so new that a lot of the army's casualties were caused by faulty operation of their unfamiliar, high-powered weapons. The 1st Aero Squadron joined the search, making it the only American air unit to fly in combat prior to World War I.

The invasion of Mexico in search of the bandits brought the United States and Mexico to the brink of war. But it didn't result in the capture of Pancho Villa.

UNCLE SAM CRIES UNCLE
Eventually the U.S. gave up on ever finding Villa, and the fever he'd incited died down. He hid out for four years, until he came to a truce with the Mexican government in 1920. On July 20th, 1923, he was driving his car through the town of Parrol, Chihuahua, when three bullets from a high-powered rifle tore through his body. He died instantly. Although Villa's killers were never brought to justice, it's believed that the assassination was orchestrated by one of his many political enemies.

NURSE NIGHTINGALE

Ten things you probably didn't know about Florence Nightingale.

1. Florence Nightingale didn't invent nursing. The female nurses in British hospitals at the time were mostly Roman Catholic nuns or prostitutes. She made it a safe and respectable profession for women.

2. It's true that her father opposed her desire to be a nurse, but he made sure she got an education. Florence and her sister were tutored in Italian, Latin, history, Greek, and mathematics.

3. By 1849, because of her family's opposition to her career and her indecision over a long-standing marriage proposal, Florence suffered a short-lived mental breakdown.

4. Far from rejecting his daughter after she became a nurse, William Nightingale provided an income of 500 pounds a year for her, the equivalent of around $50,000 today.

5. She pioneered the use of graphs for statistical representation. Her work showed, for the first time, that social events could be objectively measured and subjected to mathematical analysis.

6. Among her innovations were hot water piped to all floors, the installation of dumbwaiters to bring patients' food, and bells for the patients to call nurses.

7. After returning from the Crimean War in 1857, Florence was plagued with illness—and posttraumatic stress disorder. She spent most of the rest of her life confined to bed.

8. The small booklet she wrote, *Notes on Nursing*, published in 1861, was a multi-million-copy bestseller.

9. She was a consultant to the Union Army and later helped prepare the medical team for the Union in the U.S. Civil War.

10. She was uninterested in her celebrity status. She refused photographs and interviews, and never appeared at public functions, even those given in her honor. Many people, in fact, thought she was dead long before the actual time of her passing.

Operating out of Sri Lanka, Julia Child worked for a U.S. spy agency during World War II.

HISTORY'S HIT MAKERS

Sex, booze, and symphonies.

What comes to mind when you hear the phrase "rock and roll musician?" For most of us it's probably wild hair, illegal substances, and groupies. Now, think classical composer... okay, wake up; quit that snoring! Behind all that high art and timeless music were some wild and crazy dudes.

JOHANN SEBASTIAN BACH (1685–1750)
BACH BASICS
Bach spent most of his life not far from his birthplace in not-so-fashionable Thuringia, Germany. This gave him time to compose hundreds of musical works and to have 20 children—nine of whom survived. The town of Eisenach in Thuringia is famous as his birthplace. Tourists flock to a house where Bach probably wasn't born, but which was made into a museum anyway. Fortunately for music lovers, Johann's family made melodies instead of sausage. Johann entered the family business early and became one of the greatest composers of all time.

BACH'S ORGAN
Bach had a thing about organs. Yes, including the one you're probably snickering about. At 18, he was a church organist in Arnstadt, where they say he was obsessed with playing the organ. There's a famous story that Bach took four weeks off so he could walk to Lubeck to hear organ music. It's less well known that he stayed away for three months, and his employers suspected that he was making a different type of organ music.

BACH'S OTHER ORGAN
Because Bach wrote most of his music for the church, history often portrays him as holier-than-thou. Actually, church officials caught the young musician sneaking off during the sermons; they discovered that he was fooling around with a maid. This maid was probably Bach's second cousin, Maria Barbara, who later became his wife. After Maria's death, the 36-year-old Bach married a 20-year-old soprano named Anna Magdalena. She adored her husband and bore him 13 children.

BUSINESSMAN BACH

Since a lot of the classical composers were ready to starve for their art, it's refreshing to learn that Bach went after as much money as possible. He turned down one prestigious musical post when his less-prestigious employers in Weimar agreed to double his salary.

In 1717, he began working for Prince Kothen in Leipzig. The prince played a number of instruments, but his mother refused to listen to all that royal noise, so Bach invited the prince to play at his house... then charged him rent! Bach also picked up extra cash playing at funerals.

Not that Bach had it easy. His aristocratic employers often treated the great composer like a servant. At Weimar, when Bach tried to get work with a rival of his employer, Duke Wilhelm Ernst, the duke threw him in prison for a month.

THE BRANDENBURG CONCERTOS

The Brandenburg Concertos were dedicated to Christian Ludwig, the margrave (governor) of Brandenburg because Bach wanted the margrave to hire him as a composer and conductor at his court. Bach's music was too complex for the musicians that played at the margrave's castle, so Bach wasn't hired, and Christian Ludwig never had the concertos performed. The sheet music was put away, forgotten, and later sold for pennies. It wasn't until the 19th century that the concertos were rediscovered. They've remained consistently popular, unlike the forgotten margrave.

WOLFGANG AMADEUS MOZART (1756–1791)
TWINKLE, TWINKLE LITTLE STAR

Born in Salzburg, Austria, his full name was Johannes Chrysosto-mus Wolfgangus Theophilus Mozart. Despite his name, Wolfgang was a fun-loving guy who just wanted to make beautiful music. To this day, people hum his melodies—including his variations on a tune now called "Twinkle, Twinkle Little Star." Speaking of stars, that's exactly what Mozart was as a child. By the age of six he was touring Europe, acclaimed as a composer and a virtuoso. Mozart played for the royals of Europe; he was kissed by Empress Maria Theresa, and petted by Marie Antoinette. The nobility showered him with money and presents. He was his family's primary money-maker—a golden child.

In 1873, Mark Twain was granted a patent for the self-pasting scrapbook.

GROWING UP IS HARD TO DO

Like most child stars, Mozart faced a difficult transition from childhood to adulthood, but in Wolfgang's case his father had the real problems. Leopold Mozart had devoted his life to making his son famous (and collecting quite a packet of change for himself along the way).

When Mozart got older, Leo wanted him to get a well-paying composing job so he could continue to support the family. Whenever he thought Wolfer (that's what his Dad called him) wasn't with the program, the old man laid on the guilt. In one letter Leopold whined, "I look like poor Lazarus. My dressing gown is so shabby that if somebody calls in the morning, I have to make myself scarce." Actually Leopold saved a bundle from Mozart's successful tours, but he kept demanding more and more. He was a classic stage mother who just happened to be a father.

BURNING THE FURNITURE

Mozart had trouble getting cushy composing jobs; life hadn't prepared him for the ups and downs of business and court politics. He wound up working for the archbishop in his hometown of Salzburg. Disgusted, Mozart decided to go freelance. His father warned him that he was headed for ruin. For years biographers claimed that Mozart fell into such terrible straits that he burned the furniture to keep warm. Modern historians think his poverty was exaggerated. People loved his music and paid to hear him play. He ran with a wealthy crowd, lacked money management skills, and had a passion for gambling. In 1782, Mozart married Constanze Weber, the sister of a flame who'd jilted him. There's debate about how much they loved each other, but one thing is certain: Constanze had as much trouble economizing as Mozart.

THE FALLEN LITTLE ANGEL

Mozart, the angelic boy, was not a perfect man. He once described himself as a "scamp" and was famous for being crude. Remember the old flame that jilted him? When she pretended not to know him, Mozart went to the piano and loudly sang a song that included this verse: "the one who doesn't want me can lick my a--." Constanze accused him of playing around when he went on tour, and she was right.

Ben Johnson was buried standing up in Westminster Abbey—he couldn't afford a full plot.

Despite his shortcomings, Mozart worked hard to support his wife and children. He eventually got a position at court, and his determination to go his own way in music led to the creation of some of the most beloved symphonies, concertos, and operas of all time.

THE STORY BEHIND THE HIT REQUIEM MASS

The end of Mozart's life was tragic and mysterious. In July 1791, as the legend goes, a masked stranger asked Mozart to write a requiem mass (a mass for the dead). Though he was only 35, Mozart had a premonition that the work would be his last. In tears, he declared that he had been poisoned, and that he must complete this work as his own requiem before he died. Working frantically, he dictated portions of the requiem from his bed. True to his premonition, Mozart died while completing his work for the mysterious stranger.

Was there really a masked stranger calling Mozart to the grave? It turned out that the man who commissioned the piece was Count von Walsegg-Stuppach, who wanted people to believe that he'd written a great requiem for his wife. The count hid his identity so no one would know he'd actually hired a composer.

And was Mozart poisoned? There is no evidence that anyone did—on purpose. A letter revealed that Mozart ate pork cutlets 44 days before he died. Most of his symptoms sound a lot like trichinosis, which can be contracted by eating undercooked pork! Whatever the cause of his death, Mozart left a legacy of beloved music including his revered Requiem Mass.

LUDWIG VAN BEETHOVEN (1770–1827)
DON'T CALL ME MOZART

Beethoven was born in Bonn, Germany, and for a while at least, things went downhill from there. Young Ludwig's drunken father forced his budding-genius son to practice the piano for hours and beat him when he made mistakes. He wanted Ludwig to be the next Mozart, a child prodigy who could make the family rich and famous. But Ludwig was a late bloomer; he didn't make it to the top until he was in his twenties. In the meantime, his father's beatings may have damaged Beethoven's hearing, which made him too deaf to hear his own music.

Da Vinci could draw with one hand and write with the other—at the same time!

THE MESHUGGA MAESTRO?

As a result, Beethoven developed what they call a "difficult" personality. He was arrogant, rude, and eccentric, but people put up with it for the sake of his kinder side (he had one) as well as his exciting music. His odd behavior (partly due to problems with his increasing deafness) was legendary, and after he died, Beethoven was often portrayed as a lunatic genius. From his first public appearance at 25, Beethoven was a huge success. His music was so grand and passionate that people started to say that he must be the illegitimate son of a king. Since he was a bit of a snob, Beethoven didn't do much to discourage the rumor.

BACHELOR BEETHOVEN

When it came to love, Beethoven had a short attention span. His love for a woman was usually deep—and brief. There's some debate about whether he was successful with the ladies. Historians who say he was a stud usually quote a contemporary who said, "Beethoven was perpetually engrossed in a love affair... he made conquests, which an Adonis (that hunk from Greek myth) would have found impossible." Historians who call him a dud recall the singer Magdalena Wilmann, who apparently refused Beethoven's proposal of marriage because he was "ugly and half-crazy." Most of Beethoven's women were in the hopelessly unattainable category. He fell for aristocratic, wealthy women who couldn't marry the middle-class Beethoven without renouncing their titles and privileges—not to mention their husbands.

THE MYSTERY OF THE IMMORTAL BELOVED

After Beethoven died, a mysterious love letter was found in his desk. It was exquisitely romantic, including passages like: "My thoughts go out to you, my Immortal Beloved...I can live only wholly with you or not at all." Beethoven had signed the letter, but there was no name at the top. Who was the letter meant for? For years biographers have driven themselves crazy trying to solve the mystery. Since Beethoven liked to spread it around, there are a few candidates. The only thing historians agree on was that the Immortal Beloved could never have been Ludwig's sister-in-law, Johanna, who he fought for custody of her son Karl—Beethoven's nephew. The two despised each other. Needless to say, anyone who knew anything about the story was shocked when, in the movie *Immortal Beloved*, they presented Johanna as Beethoven's true love. (For more movie myths, read Uncle John's article "Bad History! Bad!")

THE BELOVEDS BEHIND THE HITS

Three women are strong candidates for Immortal Beloved status; all were close to Beethoven and he dedicated music to all of them. Beethoven fell in love with the Countess Giulietta Guicciardi, and in 1801, when she was 17, he dedicated one of his most lyrical works to her. The poet Ludwig Rellstab named it "Moonlight Sonata" because it was like "moonlight on a lake." Beethoven felt he'd written much better pieces, but it's one of his most popular.

Countess Marie Erdody, a Hungarian aristocrat, was Beethoven's good friend and patron. He moved in with her for a while as a "lodger," though she may have given him more than a place to stay. In 1808, he wrote his D Major Trio for her. The piece was nicknamed, "Ghost," because of mysterious, "ghostly" music in the second movement.

Antonie Brentano is the favorite in the Immortal Beloved name game. She was married and the mother of four children, but she and Ludwig were often together when her husband was away. When Antonie was ill, her greatest comfort was hearing Beethoven play. After his death, two portraits were discovered in Beethoven's desk. One was of Giulietta Guicciardi; the other is thought to be a portrait of Antonie. Perhaps the greatest indication of their love is the beautiful, romantic song, "An die Geliebte" (To the Beloved). Beethoven wrote the piece in 1811, and on one corner of the manuscript, Antonie has written a note, "Requested by me from the author on March 2, 1812." Whoever she was—Giulietta, Marie, or Antonie—Beethoven's music (and the mystery of the Immortal Beloved) has made her immortal. So maybe it's worth it to date a musical genius after all.

*   *   *

"Nothing is capable of being set well to music
that is not nonsense."

Joseph Addison

WOULD IT KILL YOU TO BECOME EMPEROR OF MEXICO?

Like a lot of wives, Charlotte Amélie didn't think her husband,
Maximilian, was living up to his potential. Surely he could do
something to better himself so she wouldn't have to feel
so embarrassed at the opera.

In 1863, Archduke Ferdinand Maximilian Hapsburg was a
happy man. He belonged to one of the most powerful families
in Europe. He lived in the spectacular mansion Miramar overlooking the Adriatic Sea from which he tended the Italian possessions of his brother Emperor Franz Joseph of Austria. He was
married to one of the most prominent women in the European
nobility, the daughter of the king of Belgium. Life was good for
Maximilian until that fateful day when a delegation arrived at
Miramar to offer him the job: emperor of Mexico.

Maximilian was confused. He was Austrian, not Mexican, and
he barely spoke Spanish. Plus, he was under the impression that
Mexico already had a leader, an elected president. Technically yes,
said the delegation, but it seemed that Napoleon III, Emperor of
France, had just invaded Mexico to recover overdue debts…

CINCO DE MAYO

The invasion of Mexico had been a tougher campaign than the
French expected. They'd thought they could just walk into
Puebla, which they considered the key to Mexico City, but they
found a committed Mexican force defending the town. On May 5,
1862, the French attacked. The Mexican army drove them back
and inflicted heavy losses. The victory spawned the celebration we
know as Cinco de Mayo ("fifth of May").

The battle was particularly meaningful because it was the first
time the Mexican army had tested itself against a formidable
international foe since they'd been defeated in the war with the
United States a decade earlier. Unfortunately for the triumphant
Mexicans, Emperor Napoleon III just couldn't get into the spirit of

---

When a Paris mob stormed the Bastille, they missed rescuing the Marquis de Sade by just days.

the holiday, so instead of downing a few brews and maybe dancing a little, he sent another 30,000 troops to Mexico. The following May, the French army finally smashed the resistance at Puebla and took Mexico City.

LOOKING FOR A LEADER

Certain Mexican conservatives were actually thrilled to see the upstart Juarez booted out of office by the invading French army. They begged Napoleon III to find a suitably aristocratic ruler for their nation. Napoleon referred them to Maximilian, so they sent a delegation. The archduke was flattered, but still unsure.

His wife, Charlotte, was not. This was her chance to be an empress. She convinced her hesitant husband that Mexico needed him, and he could do good things for the people there. Seeing it in that optimistic light, the gullible Max agreed. In the spring of 1864, the happy couple boarded a ship and sailed for Mexico as Emperor Maximilian and Empress "Carlotta."

WHO IS THIS GUY?

Not surprisingly, the Mexican people were a little confused. In the first place, no one had told them they were getting a new emperor. In the second place, they didn't understand why their new emperor was Austrian and why the French army was still swarming all over the country. So they didn't exactly greet their new sovereigns with open arms. And things went downhill from there.

Maximilian tried to govern, but he hardly knew anything about the Mexican situation. He waffled on policies, which angered the conservatives who'd supported him, and he never won over Juarez's liberals, who regarded him as a foreign usurper to be driven from Mexican soil.

YOU THINK IT'S EASY BEING AN EMPRESS?

The whole sordid affair wasn't living up to the glamorous dreams that Carlotta had brewed in the gilded ballrooms and opera houses of Europe. She was bitter at the lack of gratitude shown by the Mexican people—after all her sacrifices! The imperial marriage fell apart. Both Carlotta and Maximilian took lovers: she supposedly had an affair with one of her husband's dashing military officers, while Maximilian dallied with the daughter of his gardener.

HENPECKED HUSBAND
In 1866, Napoleon III pulled the plug on his sputtering Mexican adventure and ordered his troops home. As the French soldiers marched to their ships, a depressed Maximilian suggested that he too should abandon the dreary enterprise and return to his cozy life back home. But not Carlotta—oh, no—she didn't want to give up her throne, despite the misery that came with it. She convinced Max to stay. Meanwhile, she went to Europe to talk some sense into Napoleon, promising to return with the military support needed to destroy Juarez and pacify the country.

BEGINNING OF THE END
In Paris, Napoleon was unmoved by Carlotta's entreaty for help. The distraught empress then hurried to Rome to plead for the pope's intercession. The pontiff dismissed her, but she reportedly screamed and clung to his holy robes. It was whispered around Europe that stress was driving the empress insane.

Things weren't going so well back in Mexico, either. Maximilian himself took what was left of his army and led them against Juarez's troops. After a three-month siege, the emperor was arrested. Juarez staged a show trial and the emperor was convicted of treason. On June 19, 1867, Maximilian faced the firing squad with imperial calm.

ALL ABOARD!
With Maximilian dead and Benito Juarez again president of Mexico, the Empress Carlotta was now just plain old Archduchess Charlotte Amélie again. Her family brought her home to Brussels and locked her away in a castle where she lived for another 60 long years. In the spring of every year until her death, she'd walk down to the moat of her castle where a small boat bobbed in the water. She'd climb into the boat and announce, "Today we leave for Mexico."

* * *

"Glory is fleeting, but obscurity is forever."
Napoleon Bonaparte

A New Orleans man hired a pirate ship to rescue Napoleon from St. Helena.

UNMASKING MONA LISA

The Mona Lisa is the best known painting in the world, but who was the mysterious woman in the picture and—more importantly—what was she thinking of when she smiled?

THE WOMAN

She was born Monna Lisa Gherardini in Italy in 1479. In 1495, she married a rich bourgeois chap from Florence by the name of Francesco di Bartolomeo di Zanoli del Giocondo (pronounced "Joe Condo" and hence the painting's nickname "La Gioconda"—that's her). She sat for Leonardo da Vinci in 1506 while in her twenties. She died in 1528.

THE SMILE

The most famous smile in the world, it's been called a combination of elegance and flirtatiousness. In the 16th century, the slight opening of the lips at the corners of the mouth was considered elegant. But what was she pondering? Perhaps Giuliano di Medici filled her thoughts; he was rumored to be her lover.

THE QUIZ

You've seen her dozens of times, but exactly how memorable is she? See if you can answer these questions about the Mona Lisa's appearance. Then check the answers below.

1. Which best describes Mona Lisa's hairdo?
a. parted in the middle
b. parted on the side
c. pulled straight back

2. What's in the background of the painting?
a. A room with windows on a landscape
b. a landscape only
c. drapery panels

3. Which of the following describes her hands?
a. right crossed over left
b. left crossed over right
c. hands clasped tight

4. Which of the following is *not* true?
a. She's showing a little cleavage.
b. She doesn't have any eyebrows.
c. She's wearing a ring.

Answers: 1-a. 2-b. 3-a. 4-c.

France is named for a barbarian tribe called the Franks.

WILL THE REAL SHAKESPEARE PLEASE TAKE A BOW?

*Was William Shakespeare England's greatest author
or the world's greatest imposter? And who was the
real author of all those plays? You decide.*

Modern audiences chow down on popcorn while they watch Leonardo di Caprio play Romeo, or Mel Gibson play Hamlet. But most viewers have no idea that literary historians battle over who wrote the "scripts" for these movies.

WILL'S WILL
Shakespeare's last will and testament lists his every possession, from his silver gilt bowl to his second-best bed. But as Mark Twain wrote, "It was...conspicuously a businessman's will, not a poet's. It mentioned not a single book." Books were a precious commodity in Elizabethan times, much more valuable than gilt bowls or beds. If Shakespeare had books to leave to his heirs, they would have been mentioned. And if he was the greatest writer in the English language, how come the guy didn't own one book?

WHAT WE KNOW OF THE MAN
William Shakespeare was born in Stratford-on-Avon, England, in 1564. It's likely he went to the town's free grammar school, but how much he learned there is in dispute. Traditional historians say that Will received an excellent education, but some scholars believe that the poor kid was barely literate. At 18, he hurriedly married a woman eight years older than himself, and she had a child within six months. The couple had three children by the time our hero headed up to London, leaving his family behind.

ALL THE WORLD'S A STAGE
Once there, Will acted in plays, performed for Queen Elizabeth, and eventually became one of the shareholders of the Globe Theatre. That's nearly all we know about his professional life, except that he became famous as the author of all those "Shake-

---

During France's yearlong Reign of Terror, 17,000 people were beheaded.

spearean" plays. He returned to Stratford a prosperous man, where until his death, he dealt in real estate and other money-making ventures. History portrays him as a tough businessman who never showed any particular love for poetry or drama.

STAGE LEFT, THE EARL OF OXFORD

Since 1785, maverick scholars have been proposing candidates as the "true author" of the Shakespeare plays. The list of usual suspects has included Francis Bacon, Christopher Marlowe, and Ben Jonson, three famous literary contemporaries of the man known as "the Bard." But, more recently, a 20th century skeptic, J. Thomas Looney (whose name doesn't help his case very much), proposed that Shakespeare was really a man most people had never heard of: one Edward de Vere, the 17th earl of Oxford.

CLUES...

- The earl of Oxford established a literary reputation while still in his teens.
- He knew all about royalty and life at court, information that's central to many of the plays.
- Some of Shakespeare's plays were based on sources that hadn't been translated into English. The earl could read in more than a few foreign languages. Shakespeare couldn't.
- Oxford had traveled to some of the locations where the plays took place.
- His personal experiences dovetail neatly with events in the plays. For example, in *Hamlet*, Polonius is the bufoonish father of Ophelia. Literary scholars have long identified a certain real-life Lord Burghley as the model for Polonius, and Burghley's daughter, Anne Cecil, as the model for Ophelia. In the play, Hamlet was unhappily involved with Ophelia. In real life, Oxford was unhappily married to Anne Cecil.
- Another connection with *Hamlet* lies in Oxford's childhood. Hamlet mourned his father's death and berated his mother for remarrying too quickly. The earl was 12 years old when his father died, and it's believed that Oxford's mother remarried within three months. Is *Hamlet* an autobiographical play?
- Oxford was known as a playwright, but not one of his plays has ever been found. And he stopped writing just about the time that William Shakespeare began producing his works.

Apollo 13 was launched at 13:13, military time, and was aborted on Friday, April 13.

- The earl would have written under a pseudonym because show business was a lowly profession, beneath his dignity as a noble. As a member of Queen Elizabeth's court, Oxford might have literally lost his head if the queen felt an insider was publicly satirizing her monarchy.
- At court, Oxford was called "Spear shaker" because of his prowess with a sword. A poet of the time is quoted as saying that Oxford was a man whose "countenance shakes a spear." Shakes-a-spear. Get it?

Did the earl use the actor William Shakespeare as either his front man or collaborator? Is that why William Shakespeare came into a great deal of money and returned to his hometown as a prosperous businessman?

THE LAST LAUGH

Traditional scholars leap to Shakespeare's defense: a lot of Elizabethan playwrights were members of the middle class. Just like the writers of today, they, too, wrote about the rich and powerful. Okay, they admit, William from Stratford was not well traveled or university educated, but he was a genius who could have researched the information he needed. Besides, Will got a practical education through years of work in the theatre. His plays worked because he created great roles for the actors of his day, not because he was a literary scholar. And when he had enough money to retire from the business, he did. And so his backers rest their case.

How much, after all, does it matter? Both William from Stratford-on-Avon and the earl of Oxford would probably agree that "the play's the thing."

*　　*　　*

"The fool doth think himself wise,
but the wise man knows himself to be a fool."

William Shakespeare

"VANDAL-IZED"

A "vandal" is someone who recklessly destroys property. The word originated in the Dark Ages, from the name of a tribe of barbarians that plundered and pillaged their way across the Roman Empire.

Not much is known about the origins of the Germanic tribe known as the Vandals. They're believed to have originated in Denmark and later migrated to the valley of the Oder River on the Baltic Sea, about the fifth century B.C. In A.D. 406, the Huns (a tougher tribe) drove the Vandals from their home by the sea.

LOOK OUT, PIERRE!
The Vandals headed southwest, crossed the Rhine River and invaded Gaul (which is now France). For the next couple of years, they roamed all over Gaul killing, raping, and pillaging—which is just what you'd expect them to do.

Roman troops in Britain heard about what was going on and decided to act. Under their commander, Flavius Constantine, they traveled to Gaul and defeated the Vandals in battle.

LOOK OUT, JOSE!
The Vandals then fled to Spain, laying waste to everything and everyone in their path. The Romans made some attempts to evict them from Spain, but the Vandals defeated every army sent to destroy them. Just when they'd exhausted the riches of Spain, a power-hungry Roman warlord named Bonifatius invited them across the water to help in his campaign to take over North Africa.

LOOK OUT, AHMED, AND EVERYBODY ELSE!
In 428, the largest ever sea-borne movement of a barbarian people took place. About 80,000 Vandals landed near Tangier. They encountered very little opposition from the locals (as you might imagine), and within two years the Vandals controlled nearly all of North Africa. Carthage was next, and by 439, the Vandals controlled a major naval base, which they used to raid all of the cities of the western Mediterranean. In 455, they thoroughly and mercilessly sacked Rome.

Had Queen Mary had any children, England might still be a Catholic country.

THE BYZANTINE EMPIRE STRIKES BACK

In 533 Emperor Justinian sent a huge army to destroy the Vandals. Historians think the once-savage barbarians had gotten too soft to put up a decent fight (that they'd gotten kinda, y'know, laid back, enjoying that warm North African weather, dude). Whatever the reason, the emperor's army captured Gelimer, the last king of the Vandals, and brought him back to Constantinople to be executed. The Vandal's reign of terror finally came to an end. And none too soon for most of the world.

UP WITH VANDALS!

And even though the Vandals left a trail of death and destruction in their wake, they did contribute a couple of nice things that deserve mention (we're serious now, so pay attention): a plow that enabled farmers to plow deeper and straighter furrows, butter, rye, oats, and hops—the latter of which you beer drinkers should appreciate.

So when you're hoisting the next one, don't forget to toast the guys whose name is still synonymous with destruction—the Vandals.

*   *   *

FROM THE MOUTHS OF GENERALS

"We are going to have peace even if we have to fight for it."
General Dwight D. Eisenhower

"We are not retreating… we are advancing in another direction."
General Douglas MacArthur

"We will either find a way or make one [a war, that is]."
General Hannibal

A DIFFERENT POINT OF VIEW

"Mankind must put an end to war,
or war will put an end to mankind."

U.S. President John F. Kennedy

Despite the Shakespearean play, Richard III was not a hunchback.

HERE LIES...

Funny how a turn of phrase like "Here lies" can catch on.
Here lies a bunch of Uncle John's favorite epitaphs.
All real, as far as we know.

Here lies the Body of
Edward Hyde.
We laid him here
because he died.

Here lies old Rastus Sominy
Died a-eating hominy
In 1859 anno domini.

Here lies I, Simon Frye,
Killed by a skyrocket
In my eyesocket.

Here lies a miser who lived for
himself,
who cared for nothing but
gathering wealth.
Now where he is and how he fares;
nobody knows and nobody cares.

Here lies the body
Of Margaret Bent
She kicked up her heels
And away she went.

Here lieth W.W.
Who never more will
Trouble you, trouble you.

Here lies
Johnny Yeast.
Pardon me
For not rising.

Here lies the body
of Jonathan Blake
Stepped on the gas
Instead of the brake.

Here lays Butch,
We planted him raw.
He was quick on the trigger,
But slow on the draw.

Here lies the body of our Anna
Done to death by a banana.
It wasn't the fruit that laid her low
But the skin of the thing that
made her go.

Here lies an Atheist
All dressed up
And no place to go.

Here lies
Lester Moore
four slugs
from a 44
No Less
no more.

Here Lies The Body Of A Man
Who Died
Nobody Mourned—Nobody Cried
How He Lived—How He Fared
Nobody Knows—Nobody Cared

Here lies
Ezekial Aikle
Age 102
The Good Die Young.

Here lie I, Master Elginbrod,
Have mercy on my soul, O God.
As I would have if I were God,
And thou were Master Elginbrod.

In 1813, a British doctor turned some of King Charles I's vertebrae into a saltshaker.

THE STRANGE CONSTITUTION OF STONEWALL JACKSON

Confederate Civil War General Stonewall Jackson had a brilliant military mind—it was a pity about the rest of him. Read about the quirky personal habits of this hero and hopeless hypochondriac.

THE LEGEND IN MORE WAYS THAN ONE

Thomas Jonathan Jackson was Robert E. Lee's most trusted lieutenant. A brilliant leader, he earned the nickname "Stonewall" during the first Battle of Bull Run. Jackson's men faced overwhelming odds, but with their commander at their head, the small band of Confederates held their ground. General Barnard Bee looked across the battlefield and shouted to his men, "Look! There stands Jackson like a stone wall." It was enough to rally the Confederate forces for a counterattack that ended in a rout of the Union forces.

Jackson may also be one of the only Americans to have different parts of his body buried and marked with gravestones in two different places. When the general was accidentally shot in the left arm by his own troops in the Battle of Chancellorsville on May 2, 1863, the arm had to be amputated. It was buried in a graveyard about a mile from the field hospital. Jackson died eight days later, and his body (minus the arm) was sent home to Lexington for burial. A strange turn of events for a man obsessed with his physical health. In fact, by most accounts, Jackson was a bit nutty.

NUT CASE IN POINT

Here are a few of his physical eccentricities:

- Believing his left arm to be heavier than the right, Jackson would often—even in the heat of battle—raise his left arm in the air to allow the blood to flow equally through his body and establish a state of equilibrium.
- He was terribly concerned about his self-diagnosed "dyspepsia," or indigestion, so he maintained a diet that consisted

---

King John managed to lose the crown jewels while riding across an inlet in the North Sea.

almost completely of fruits and vegetables. Whenever his troops overran Union camps, the general grabbed up as much fresh produce as he could.

- Jackson convinced himself that he would perform at his peak only when his bodily organs were stacked properly—in other words, in a bolt upright position. His study in Lexington, Virginia, had no chairs at all. When he did sit down, he never allowed his body to rest against the back of the chair.

- From boyhood, he suffered from poor eyesight for which he devised his own unique "treatment." He would dip his head into a basin of cold water with his eyes wide open, staying there till his breath gave out.

BUT DON'T TAKE OUR WORD FOR IT

The man who was nicknamed "Stonewall" due to his steadfastness in the face of the enemy was remembered by President Ulysses Grant as a "fanatic" who was delusional and who "fancied that an evil spirit has taken possession of him." Colleagues at the Virginia Military Institute, where Jackson was a professor from 1851 until the outbreak of the war, remember him as a strange man who was constantly plagued by illnesses, real or imagined. Unfortunately, Jackson was not a success as an instructor. According to then-superintendent, Francis H. Smith, "He was no teacher and he lacked the required tact to get along with his classes."

SICK, SICK, SICK

By the time Jackson entered the Civil War, his list of ailments included, but was not limited to: rheumatism, dyspepsia, chilblains, poor eyesight, cold feet, nervousness, neuralgia, bad hearing, tonsillitis, biliousness, and spinal distortion.

SO LITTLE TIME

Stonewall Jackson was only 39 when he died. To be killed by friendly fire is a tragedy, but in the general's case it was more than ironic. If only he'd lived to old age: think of all the new ailments he might have contracted. One of them might even have been (gasp) *real*.

Had Edward VIII not abdicated, Elizabeth would not have become queen until 1972.

BURNING WITH GOOD INTENTIONS

Between 16th-century bonfires and the flames of a 20th-century war, records of the Mayan civilization were nearly lost for good.

The Mayan culture reached its height about A.D. 800. In the Yucatan, Mayans built towering pyramids and temples. They developed a calendar and an excellent numerical system. For about two thousand years, they kept records of their achievements using a system of written symbols called glyphs (see below). Our story starts in 1549 when a young Spanish missionary, Diego de Landa, arrived in the New World.

WITH FRIENDS LIKE THESE WHO NEEDS ENEMIES?

Landa found the Yucatec Mayan Indians suffering from starvation, disease, and mistreatment from his Spanish bosses. He came to love the Mayan people and wanted to help them. Horrified by the idea that their history had included human sacrifice, Landa figured that it would be a big help if the Mayans got rid of their pagan past. In Landa's time, there were still many Mayan books stored in the ancient ruins of Mayan cities. He decided to burn them.

SMOKE GETS IN YOUR EYES

Mayan books—called codices—were made of long strips of bark paper, folded like screens. They were written and illustrated in red and black ink with covers made of jaguar skin. The Mayans wrote thousands of codices in glyphs. The books contained prophecies, songs, rituals, genealogies, history, and science. Landa later explained to Spanish authorities that the codices "had nothing in which there was not superstition and lies of the devil"—a pretty nervy assumption, since he couldn't read them. But he sure could destroy them. He told the authorities, "We burned them all."

Well, almost all. To Landa's surprise, he had to kill 157 Mayans who refused to get with the bonfire program. (Talk about human sacrifice!) Some Mayan priests tried to save their books by fleeing into the jungle with them. Although the materials didn't hold up in the wet climate, a few books did survive.

WRONG AGAIN

In 1862, three hundred years after the book burning, an Abbé in Madrid came across a manuscript by Diego de Landa. The manuscript revealed that even though Landa had trashed Mayan books, he had tried to learn the Mayan writing system. Thinking that the glyphs were an alphabet, the missionary pronounced a Spanish letter, then asked an Indian helper to point out the matching glyph. Landa wrote the Spanish letter and sketched the matching glyph above it. Could people now read what the Mayans had written? Well, no. Landa's chart didn't make sense. (Couldn't this guy do anything right?)

FINALLY!

During World War II, books were burning again. A young Russian named Yuri Knorosov was in Berlin with the Red Army when he saw the German National Library on fire. It's believed Knorosov snatched only one book from the flames. That book was a reproduction of three Mayan codices. After the war, Knorosov took the book home. At Moscow University, Knorosov studied ancient languages and tried to crack the Mayan code.

Knorosov tried to imagine what might have gone on between Landa and his Mayan aide. Knorosov hypothesized that the Mayans didn't have an alphabet and wouldn't know what a letter was. Maybe, when Landa spoke the name of a Spanish letter and asked his Indian helper for the Mayan equivalent, his helper pointed to a glyph that contained (perhaps, among other sounds) the sound that he heard when Landa spoke the name of the letter. This would explain why Landa came up with four different glyphs for the letter "A," two for the letter "B," and why his notes weren't much help in reading Mayan.

NO MORE HELP! PLEASE!

In 1952 Knorosov published his ideas, and four hundred years after the books were burned, scholars could finally unravel the Mayan texts. As other linguists worked on the puzzle, it became clear that Knorosov was right. The glyphs stood for syllables, words, and numbers, not letters of the alphabet. Interpretation of the glyphs is still in process, but at least it won't take another 400 years—unless we get help from Landa's ghost.

The Great Pyramid of Giza is found today in a suburb of Cairo.

WHEREWORDS: A QUIZ
(Her Closet)

Come on in. We're in milady's boudoir and we're mentioning
unmentionables.... Where did all this girlie stuff come from?
Choose the explanation you like best, then check it
with the correct answer on the next page.

1. HOSIERY
a. Named for its hoselike shape.
b. From the Latin "hosa," an under-the-toga "leg covering."
c. First sold exclusively in Paris by silk merchant Pierre Hosier.

2. LEOTARD
a. From Latin "leo" for "lion" and "tardus" for "skin."
b. Named for French aerialist, Jules Leotard, who designed it.
c. From a misspelling on an 1877 playbill for the ballet "Leopard Dance."

3. BIKINI
a. The Latin "bi" for "two," and "Kini" after Kini Porter, the first model to wear one.
b. Maori word for "swimsuit."
c. The Bikini Atoll in the Marshall Islands.

4. PURSE
a. The Celtic word "parse" meaning "to count," referring to the coins it carried.
b. From the word "purchase."
c. Greek "byrsa," the leather used to make the first purse.

5. DENIM
a. The shade of blue used to dye the fabric.
b. Meaning "from Nimes" (*de* in French), the French city where it was first made.
c. For Levi Strauss's daughters Dora, Eve, Nancy, Irene, Mary.

6. NEGLIGÉE
a. From Lady Negley, a close "friend" of King Henry VII.
b. The Egyptian word "negli," a kind of silk gauze.
c. From Latin "neglegere," meaning "to neglect" (referring to housework).

7. PUMPS
a. From the sound they make.
b. From their shape—resembling a medieval water pump.
c. They were glued together by pumping machinery.

8. PANTS
a. Meant for women, designed to make men "pant."
b. After Saint Pantaleone, a character in a play.
c. From German "panz," which referred to children's trousers.

It's not true that Napoleon knocked off the Sphinx's nose because he was too African.

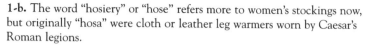

1-b. The word "hosiery" or "hose" refers more to women's stockings now, but originally "hosa" were cloth or leather leg warmers worn by Caesar's Roman legions.

2-b. Jules Leotard packed the audiences in. The ladies were as thrilled with his aerial act as they were with his skintight costume. Eventually it was adopted by dancers and aerobics fans everywhere.

3-c. On July 1, 1946, on the Bikini atoll in the Marshall Islands, the first atomic bomb test took place. At the same time, French designer Louis Reard was putting the finishing touches on his sure-to-be-scandalous two-piece swimsuit. He was looking for a name that would make headlines, and found one in the newspaper. Four days later, his top model walked down the runway and gave new meaning to the word "bikini."

4-c. The first purses were simple drawstring bags made of a leather the Greeks called "byrsa." The Romans called it a "bursa," the French a "bourse." In fact, the stock exchange in Paris is called the Bourse.

5-b. Although no one seems to know for sure, it's commonly believed that denim is short for "serge de Nimes," a twill fabric that dates back to some time before the 17th century.

6-c. Women of certain classes could always sit back and take it easy, but in the 18th century, as women's and men's nightwear started to diverge, a feminine, sometimes lacey, nightie became popular among women (although men liked it, too). It was just as good for relaxing at home as for sleeping, so it came to be named after what a woman did while wearing it—neglecting housework.

7-a. The pump was a German creation that was popular throughout Europe in the mid-1500s. It was a loose slipper with a low heel that made a "pump, pump" sound as the wearer walked across a wooden floor.

8-b. Saint Pantaleone was a fourth century martyr who inexplicably became a clownlike character in Italian folklore. He always appeared in extra-large trousers that came to be named for him (the English called him and his trousers "Pantaloon"). When the character "emigrated" to America in the 18th century, the name was shortened to "pants." And if you're wondering how we came across a pair of pants in a woman's closet, in the U.S., women wear pants, men wear trousers.

* * *

"I have heard with admiring submission the experience of the lady who declared that the sense of being perfectly well-dressed gives a feeling of inward tranquillity which religion is powerless to bestow."
Ralph Waldo Emerson

Mahatma Gandhi used to sleep with naked young women as a way of testing his celibacy.

WHICH WAY DID THEY GO?

We got to wondering what happened to the famous explorers who braved the waters beyond medieval mapmakers' "end of the world." Did they go down with their ships? The answer is bizarre.

HERNANDO DE SOTO

De Soto and crew had been exploring on either side of the Mississippi River, in an area that is now Tennessee, Arkansas, and Louisiana, when he was stricken with a fever and died. The local Indians lived in mud houses, so there was a large hole—the source of the mud—just outside their village. De Soto's men buried his body there, but afterward remembered that their captain had told the Indians that Christians were immortal.

What if the Indians discovered the body? They hadn't been all that friendly to begin with. If they found de Soto's body, they might decide they'd been lied to and do something nasty. The sailors dug up the body, put it in a hollowed-out tree trunk, and sank it in the Mississippi River. So the famous de Soto got a well-deserved burial at sea, but in a decidedly roundabout way.

JAMES COOK

If it's possible to die by coincidence, that's what happened to Captain Cook. He'd been working his way along the Pacific coast of North America looking for a northwest passage to the Atlantic, but as he neared the Arctic Ocean, his way was blocked by ice. So his ships turned south, and he and his crew kept busy through the winter by sailing around Hawaii, charting the islands as they went.

At the same time, the Hawaiians were in the middle of celebrating an annual festival honoring Lono, the god in charge of winter rains, fertility, and the New Year. When our fearless captain came ashore, the Hawaiians welcomed him with great ceremony, thinking he was Lono—or at least his representative. Month after month, the islanders showered him with gifts and anointed him with coconut oil. When Lono's season was over in

---

David Ben-Gurion, who led Israel through two wars, was actually born in Poland.

February, it was time for Cook to tackle the Arctic Ocean again. He and his men sailed away.

A week later, they ran into a storm that damaged one of the ships. They returned to Hawaii for repairs, but this time the Hawaiians saw Cook's presence as sinister. Some suspicious islanders stole one of the ship's longboats and, in an effort to get it back, the sailors tried to take the king hostage. At this point some two or three thousand people got very angry and killed Captain Cook. His crew went on without him, but they never found that elusive northwest passage.

CHRISTOPHER COLUMBUS

After his 1492 voyage, Columbus returned to Spain a celebrity. But by the time he'd completed his fourth voyage, he'd been forgotten. In 1502, he spent the year seeking the Isthmus of Panama; Columbus thought it might prove to be a way to the Pacific (smart boy!). By the end of that year, his four ships were so badly damaged that he was forced to run them aground before they sank. It took him another year to get a ship that would take him home to Spain.

He returned to Spain sick and penniless. Back in 1492, Queen Isabella and King Ferdinand had promised that Columbus would share in the riches he found in the New World. He headed for the Spanish court in Toledo, but only got as far as Seville. He was too ill to go on. Soon after that, Queen Isabella died. Columbus wrote to Ferdinand, but the king didn't reply. So the great explorer struggled out of his sickbed and went to Toledo for some "face time" with the king. Ferdinand refused to deliver on his promises. Columbus died at home in bed in 1506.

Afternote: Columbus' oldest son, Diego, succeeded where his father hadn't. He was eventually appointed Viceroy of the Indies, married one of Ferdinand's nieces, and, from all accounts, lived happily—and financially comfortably—ever after.

FERDINAND MAGELLAN

Although he's known as the first European to circumnavigate the globe, Magellan never intended to go around the world and, in fact, died halfway through the voyage. What killed him? His own fanaticism and a bunch of angry natives. Think fiery televangelist with delusions of grandeur and you've got Magellan. He reached the Philippines in 1521 and started converting the locals to Catholicism. He also told the local chieftain that he would conquer an enemy who lived on a nearby island, a chief named Lapu Lapu. Believing his cause was divinely inspired, Magellan didn't bother with a battle plan. The great captain and his men waded ashore, wringing wet and heavy with armor. When they were far enough inland, the natives surrounded them and cut them to ribbons. Shreds, really, so that even when Lapu Lapu was offered a reward for returning Magellan's body, there was nothing left of el Capitán to be found.

Magellan's crew, under new captain Juan Sebastián del Cano, returned to Spain via the Indian Ocean and around the Cape of Good Hope, thereby completing the first voyage around the world. Del Cano deserves the credit for proving the Earth was round, but Magellan's is the name we remember.

HENRY HUDSON

Hudson sailed closer to the North Pole than any other explorer. That, and his pigheaded determination to find a northwest passage to the Orient, is what really killed him.

Like Columbus, Henry Hudson made a fourth voyage to the New World. But he never came back. On his third voyage, he and his crew navigated what was later to be called the Hudson River. That was when he claimed the Hudson River Valley for Holland. On his next and last voyage, he found the strait (also later named for him) that led to the huge inland sea that is now known as— you guessed it—Hudson Bay. That's where, in November 1610, he found himself stuck in the ice with a near mutiny on his hands.

Their food supply was dwindling, and man, it was cold. But with no place to go, the crew settled in and the expedition made it through the winter. When the ice melted in the spring, most of the crew wanted out. But Hudson, who thought he was in the Pacific Ocean, insisted on sailing westward to the Orient. By June, the crew had had enough. They forced Hudson, his son, and the sailors who were sick and/or loyal into a small boat. The handful of mutineers who made it back home were never punished for the mutiny. And Hudson and the others were never heard from again.

ABE LINCOLN, HARBINGER OF FASHION?

Lincoln gets some campaign advice from an 11-year-old girl and pulls off the Presidency by a whisker.

Abraham Lincoln is remembered as a man ahead of his time. And rightly so. Of the 43 men who've held the office of president of the U.S., he towers above all comers. His intellect, humor, and compassion are legendary. But as a fashion leader? Far from it.

ABE'S LITTLE PEN PAL
When Abe was still a presidential hopeful, he opened his mail one day—October 18, 1860, to be exact—and must have chuckled to himself at the piece of advice being offered by 11-year-old Grace Bedell of Westfield, New York. Give up shaving, she told him, and you've got it in the bag. Wrote Grace:

> You would look a great deal better for your face is so thin … All the ladies like whiskers and they would tease their husbands to vote for you and you would be President.

Abe dashed off this reply:

> As to the whiskers, having never worn any, do you not think people would call it a piece of silly affectation if I were to begin now?

GROWING, GROWING, GROWN
Despite his answer to Grace, the little girl's suggestion must have played on the great one's mind. Lincoln loved to have his picture taken and—fortunately for history—this penchant has left us with an unmistakable chronicle of the rise of the beard:

• November 26, 1860—a thin scraggly line of whiskers appears
• January 26, 1861—more growth, but still straggly
• February 9, 1861—a mature, full growth of facial hair adorns the face of … ta-da! … President Abraham Lincoln.

Until World War II, Winston Churchill was known mostly for disastrous political failures.

SAY HELLO, GRACIE

But before he was inaugurated—and, in fact, on his way from Illinois to Washington to accept the office of president, Lincoln found himself at a whistle stop in Westfield, New York. Remembering the little girl with the uncanny advice, he stopped midway through his prepared speech:

> During my campaign I had a little correspondent from your town. She kindly admonished me to let my whiskers grow, and, since I've taken her advice, I would like to see her. Is she here? Is Grace Bedell here?

A small figure was bustled through the crowd and soon Lincoln was face to face with Grace. As her president bent down to kiss her, the prickly stubble digging into her cheek may well have made Grace wish she'd never suggested the idea in the first place!

THE HEIGHT OF FASHION

Thanks to Grace Bedell, Abraham Lincoln became the first U.S. president to sport facial hair of any kind. He must have started a trend: ten of the next 11 presidents wore beards or sidewhiskers, with or without mustaches.

*　　*　　*

LINCOLNIANA

- Besides being the first president to sport a beard, Lincoln was also the tallest U.S. president at 6 feet 4 inches.

- Lincoln was the first president to pass an income tax— it was three percent on incomes over $600).

- Lincoln once paid $2,600 for a string of pearls and matching earrins at Tiffany's for his beloved wife, Mary.

- Lincoln regarded patent laws as one of the three most important developments in history, right next to the discovery of America and the perfecting of the printing press.

Despite a reputation for vigor, Teddy Roosevelt needed nitroglycerin pills for his heart.

LADIES FIRST

The first woman to sit in the British House of Commons was intelligent, down-to-earth—and an American.

TIMES CHANGE, WINNIE

The usually unflappable Winston Churchill could handle anything; he endured the chaos and terror of World War II without losing his cool. But at least one event in his life had a humbling effect: the day that Lady Nancy Astor became the first woman to sit in the British House of Commons. Here's what Churchill told her ladyship years later:

"When you took your seat, I felt as if a woman had come into my bathroom and I had only the sponge to defend myself."

THE LADY

Nancy Witcher was born in Danville, Virginia, in 1879. She married in her late teens and divorced in her mid-twenties. Three years later, she married Waldorf Astor, whose father and uncle had built the Waldorf-Astoria Hotel in New York. That made young Waldorf a direct descendant of American tycoon John Jacob Astor—and a very nice match for our Nancy.

THE ASTORS

Waldorf's father, William, had moved to England in 1890. After contributing lots of money to the British effort during World War I, William was first made a baron, then a viscount. Waldorf got a seat in the British House of Commons. When Dad died, Waldorf stepped down from the House of Commons to take over the viscountcy. Nancy was elected—by a wide margin—to take her husband's seat while it was still warm. This was in 1919, the same year that American women won the right to vote. Lady Astor was so popular with her constituents that she was reelected by a substantial margin in every election until she stood down in 1945. During her political career she was a staunch supporter of women's rights, temperance, and education.

Charmingly self-effacing, the lady had strong opinions on every subject and, with typical American candor, didn't mind sharing them.

ON HERSELF:

"I refuse to admit that I am more than 52, even if that makes my children illegitimate."

"My vigor, vitality, and cheek repel me. I am the kind of woman I would run from."

ON OTHER PEOPLE:

"The only thing I like about rich people is their money."

"The penalty of success is to be bored by the people who used to snub you."

ON TEMPERANCE:

"One reason I don't drink is because I wish to know when I'm having a good time."

ON MEN & WOMEN:

"We are not asking for superiority for we have always had that; all we ask is equality."

"In passing, also, I would like to say that the first time Adam had a chance, he laid the blame on a woman."

"I married beneath me. All women do."

WINSTON HAS THE LAST WORD...

But in the end, Lady Astor might be most famous for this dinner party conversation with Churchill:

> **Lady Astor:** "Winston, if I were your wife I'd put poison in your coffee."
> **Winston:** "Nancy, if I were your husband I'd drink it."

The exchange took place during one of those country weekends the upper-class British are so famous for. On this particular weekend, Astor and Churchill were staying with Churchill's cousin, the Duke of Marlborough, at Blenheim Palace. By all reports, Nancy and Churchill argued ferociously throughout the weekend.

It must have been fun.

The airfield from which Charles Lindbergh began his famous trip is now a shopping center.

POP WAS A POPE AND I'M A POISONER: WHO AM I?

Lucrezia Borgia lived at the height of the Italian Renaissance.
She was beautiful, smart, and thirsty for power. She and her family
poisoned or otherwise destroyed their rivals during a
reign of terror that lasted nearly 50 years.

During the halcyon days of the Italian high Renaissance (roughly 1450–1550), men were at the centers of art, commerce, and world exploration. Women were expected to keep house, bear children, and remain subservient to men. Even a bright and ambitious woman like Lucrezia Borgia was a victim of Renaissance sexism. But she wasn't about to sit back and be a '50s housewife of any century.

MY PAPA, *IL PAPA*
In the Middle Ages in Italy, the Catholic Church was a choice career path for the male offspring of wealthy landowners and merchants. Conventional "networking" channels such as the Church or craft guilds were open only to men. Fortunately for Lucrezia, she had a unique inside track on the Church: her father happened to be the reigning pope.

THE REIGN IN SPAIN
The wealthy Borgia family had its roots in Spain. But the family's reputation is based largely on the doings of three members of the family after they enlarged their sphere of influence to Renaissance Italy: Don Rodrigo (soon to be Pope Alexander VI), his son Cesare (whose nickname today would have been "Mad Dog" for the number of people he killed during temper tantrums), and the infamous Lucrezia.

HOW MUCH FOR THAT VATICAN?
Rodrigo became a cardinal through pay-offs and purchased the papacy in basically the same way. As pope, he moved his mistresses into apartments near the Vatican, where he could visit them unobserved. It's said that, at one point, Rodrigo and his son

---

Although Charles Lindbergh opposed the U.S.'s entry into World War II, he flew 50 missions.

Cesare shared the same mistress. (Ewwwww!) Dad plotted with his children to insinuate the family name into the blueblood lineages of Italy. Their success depended on the ruthlessness of Cesare (the hit man of the Borgia mob), and the cunning of his sister Lucrezia.

LUCREZIA MacEVIL

Lucrezia was a practical girl: she placed the creation of political power alliances for herself and her family above personal happiness. With a couple of ex-husbands and numerous broken engagements—in several cases caused by the mysterious death of the intended groom—Lucrezia may have been the original "Black Widow." It's likely that Cesare did his bit, too, taking a hand in the murder of at least a few of his sister's fiancés and husbands.

THIS ONE'S A KEEPER

Her last husband was Alfonso d'Este, the powerful Duke of Ferrara. Their son, Ercole, succeeded his father as duke, and another, Ippolito, became a cardinal (as did his Uncle Cesare in 1493). The d'Este kids were known for their love of luxury, and, as such, carried on the Borgia tradition. (Ippolito carried on to such excess that he was already a degenerate when the family bought him his cardinal's post—at 15 years old!)

PRETTY POISON

Lucrezia's favorite—and famous—weapon was a specially designed ring loaded with arsenic. She'd brush it against her intended quarry, make a quick puncture with the sharpened ring and, before they knew it, her victims were singing with the angels.

THE BAD DIE YOUNG

It's a safe bet that Lucrezia went to join a different choir when she died on June 24, 1519 of complications giving birth to her fifth child. She was relatively young—not quite 39 years old. But her reputation as a murderous, power-hungry sociopath has survived more than 500 years.

* * *

"We are not interested in the possibilities of defeat."
—Queen Victoria

The Liberty Bell was nearly sold for scrap metal in 1828.

LISTEN, MY CHILDREN...

*... and you shall hear what really happened on that
midnight ride of Paul Revere...*

The story of Paul Revere's ride is part of American folklore:
the signal lamps in Boston's Old North Church ("One if by
land, and two if by sea,") and then Revere's riding like a
madman, shouting, "The British are coming!" Is that how it really
happened? Well, it's close. Paul Revere was certainly a hero and a
patriot, but the honor of warning the countryside needs to be
shared with a few other riders. Here's what really happened.

A REBEL AND A SPY
In 1775, Paul Revere was a respectable silversmith (by day), and
he was also part of a rebel group that gathered intelligence on
British troop movements (whenever he could). Boston was crawl-
ing with British soldiers, but that wasn't too unusual—after all,
the colonies were considered part of England at the time. But a
revolution was brewing, and tension between the British soldiers
and the Americans was high.

Two days before the fateful ride, Revere and his friends
designed a warning system using lantern signals so they could
communicate in case the British blocked the roads between towns.
They'd need the warning signal sooner than they knew: the
British found out that the rebels had a store of munitions near
Concord and intended to march on the town, and do exactly what
the Americans were afraid of—set up patrols along the roads to
keep messengers from spreading the news.

GET READY TO RIDE
On April 18, 1775, Revere and a compatriot, Dr. Joseph Warren,
heard about the British plan. Dr. Warren called on a secret
informant (rumor has it that the informant was actually the
American wife of British General Gage) and verified that the
British intended to burn up the munitions at Concord and arrest
some of the leaders of the budding revolution. Warren asked
Revere to ride to Lexington to warn the leaders, John Hancock
and Samuel Adams, of the danger.

Knowing that the soldiers might stop Revere, Dr. Warren also

Charles Dickens's son Francis was a Mountie.

sent William Dawes and an unknown man with the same message, by different routes. Revere stopped by the Old North Church on the way, to tell the men there to hang two lanterns in the steeple as a signal: the British were taking the shortcut across Boston Harbor to Cambridge, the quickest way to get to Concord.

Revere crossed the Charles River in a small boat, mounted a speedy horse, and raced off. He was chased by redcoats, but outran them. He arrived at Lexington around midnight and delivered his message to Adams and Hancock; not "The British are coming!" but "The Regulars [i.e., British troops] are coming out!"

THE RIPPLE EFFECT

All along the way from Boston to Lexington, Revere sent other messengers wherever he could find them. They spread the word in every direction, and by early morning, church bells, drums, and guns were sounding the alarm throughout the colony.

But in Lexington the midnight before, right after he'd delivered his message, Revere had no way of knowing how far the word might spread, so he rode on, now aiming straight for Concord— and the British army. He was joined by Dawes and a third man: a young doctor named Prescott who'd been a-courting that night. The three visited every house along the way, knocking on doors, asking the men inside to send riders down other roads to spread the news. And all the time shouting the news to everyone they could reach: the British soldiers were on their way.

SHOT HEARD 'ROUND THE WORLD

Halfway to Concord, some "Regulars" stopped them. The doctor vanished into the night, but Dawes was thrown by his horse and Revere was captured. Revere was something of a patriot celeb, and his captors recognized him. They questioned him—at gunpoint— and he told them the truth, about the British secret mission and the American militia response. The British soldiers rode Revere back to Lexington. As they neared the town, they heard gunfire and realized they'd better warn their commanders about the militia, so they released the prisoners and took off.

Later, Paul Revere was crossing Lexington Common just as the local militia was forming up to meet the British troops. So he was there that day to hear for himself "the shot heard 'round the world"—the first shot of the Revolutionary War.

In 1943, Fred Rose became the only Communist ever elected to the Canadian parliament.

HEAVY METTLE

*How a little old rabbi—in his coffin yet!—overcame
the mighty legions of Rome.*

GETTING THE ROYAL TREATMENT

It had never been easy for Jews living under Roman rule, but in A.D. 65 things had gone from bad to intolerable. To the Jews, Jerusalem was the sacred site of the fabulous temple of Solomon, the heart of the Jewish faith. But the tax-happy Romans were milking the city dry. A group of Jewish dissidents, the zealots, decided to fight back.

WAIT A MINUTE!

A wise old rabbi named Yochanan ben Zakkai counseled the zealots to have patience, but the zealots wanted war, and they truly believed that God would send the Jews a miracle to defeat the Romans. And you know what? By some miracle, the badly outnumbered rebels drove the Roman legions out of Palestine. The zealots were sure that God had performed a miracle for them, but Rabbi ben Zakkai wasn't convinced that the battle was over. He was proven right when, a year or so later, fresh Roman legions battled their way through Palestine and eventually surrounded Jerusalem. Now the Jews needed another miracle.

TAKE ME TO YOUR LEADER

Ben Zakkai knew the zealots couldn't win this time, and he was afraid that Rome would wipe out his people as a lesson to the rest of its empire. So the rabbi decided to match wits with Vespasian, Rome's greatest general. To do that, he had to get to the Roman camp, but the zealots were guarding the city gates, determined that every last Jew in Jerusalem would stand and fight. So the rabbi's followers built a coffin and sealed the rabbi inside. Tearing their clothes in the custom of grief, and wailing in despair, they took the coffin to the city gates, and told the guards that their rabbi had died of a contagious disease. He had to be buried outside.

RAISING THE DEAD

They went straight to Vespasian and laid the coffin before him. When the coffin was opened, out stepped the rabbi. He told

---

Soviet spy Igor Gouzenko had to defect twice in Ottawa before anyone believed him.

Vespasian that he could see into the future, and that the general would soon be the emperor of all Rome. And because the rabbi was bringing the general good news, he would like a small favor when the prophecy came to pass. Would the general allow the rabbi to set up an academy for Jewish learning in Yavneh city?

Vespasian was caught by surprise. Was this some kind of trick? Why hadn't the rabbi—who had risked his life—asked for power or wealth? Intrigued, the mighty general studied the rabbi. He agreed to grant ben Zakkai's request if the prophecy came true.

AND IT CAME TO PASS...

Some people believe that ben Zakkai really foretold the future. Others think that a shrewd man made a calculated guess. Emperor Nero had recently committed suicide. In the chaos that followed, there had been three emperors of Rome in one year alone, and now there was a new vacancy. Like other successful generals before him, Vespasian had an excellent chance of filling the power vacuum. At any rate, the rabbi had established a "relationship," and that might have been his only goal.

It took the Roman legions four years to recapture Jerusalem. In A.D. 70, they leveled the city, carried captives off as slaves, and stayed on to guard the ruins of the temple to make sure no troublemaking Jews came back. For many Jews it seemed like the end. Without the temple, a man couldn't make sacrifices to atone for his sins. The holy city was dead. How could Judaism survive?

THE MIRACLE

Vespasian became emperor. And Rabbi ben Zakkai, at his school in Yavneh, taught that sins could be atoned for with deeds of loving kindness. If the people didn't have the priests of the temple anymore, they still had Jewish scripture to study and the ability to pray. As the Yavneh academy gained influence, Jews took up a religion of prayer, study, and good deeds—a faith that could be practiced anywhere in the world.

WHAT MATTERS IN THE END

Today, ancient Rome is in ruins, and Roman gods are gone, but the Jews and their faith survive. No legend could be as amazing as the historical truth. Yochanan ben Zakkai's humble request led to a miracle. His academy forged a culture that kept the homeless Jews united until—2,000 years later—they returned to Jerusalem.

Romans flavored food with garum, made by leaving fish to rot for several weeks.

THE CRUSADE THAT WASN'T

In 1201, the political and religious leaders of Western Europe were ready to take another shot at saving the Holy Land and Jerusalem from those darn infidels. But what started out as a Holy Crusade ended up more like one of history's greatest muggings.

According to Innocent III—the most powerful of the medieval popes—it was time once again for all good Christians to come to the aid of their brothers in the Holy Land. But this pope was not so innocent that he trusted the leaders of the new Crusade to behave themselves like Christians. So he threatened to excommunicate any crusader who took up arms against a fellow Christian while on a Crusade. As events would later prove, most of the crusaders decided to ignore him.

LET'S MAKE A DEAL
Two men served as the true leaders of the Fourth Crusade. Officially, the supreme commander was Boniface, the Marquis of Montferrat. The other leaders of the Crusade were planning to attack either Cairo or Alexandria, but Boniface had other targets in mind—any target that would stuff his pockets with as much cash as possible.

The arrangement suited the other boss of the Crusade, a man named Enrico Dandolo, known to history as the Doge (chief magistrate) of Venice. The crusaders needed ships to transport them to the East, as well as supplies and additional troops for the campaign. And the Doge was just the man to supply them—for a very steep price. (He charged the crusaders 85,000 marks—not a small sum in those days, even for wealthy nobles and princes.) The Venetians also demanded an equal share in whatever territory or treasure the crusaders succeeded in capturing.

ALMOST A VENETIAN BLIND
Because Venice was an immensely powerful and wealthy player on the European stage—as well as one of the great naval powers of the day—the Doge was automatically one of the most powerful

---

Julius Caesar made history by crossing the Rubicon, but today we don't know where it is.

men in Europe. But he had lost the full use of his eyes in an accident in Constantinople, and after that had a powerful hate for that particular city. As it turned out, the Doge would get his share of revenge (as well as booty).

WILL THE REAL EMPEROR PLEASE STAND UP?

April 1203, the crusaders made a deal with Alexius, the son of the recently deposed Byzantine emperor. If the crusaders would divert their armies to Constantinople, overthrow the current emperor (another Alexius, in fact, Alexius III), and hand the city over to him, they would be well rewarded. Not all the crusaders were wild about the plan, but most eventually agreed.

THE WRONG IMPRESSION

Venetian galleys carried the crusaders to Constantinople in June 1203. The crusaders had been told that Emperor Alexius III was so unpopular that his people would refuse to support him and give up meekly without a fight. They were mistaken. The Greek citizens put up a good fight, but in the end they were no match for a bunch of well-equipped crusaders. On the night of July 16, the terrified emperor scooped up as much treasure as he could carry and fled. Realizing that further resistance was futile, the citizens of Constantinople opened the gates of the city to the crusaders, who placed their Alexius on the throne.

The citizens of Constantinople bitterly resented the arrogant crusaders. On one occasion, a French knight burned down a mosque because it offended his religious sensibilities. The hostility between Greeks and crusaders got so out of hand that the latter were eventually forced to withdraw.

MOON OVER CONSTANTINOPLE

Things came to a head in February 1204. Alexius's political opponents broke into his palace and threw him into prison. The crusaders responded with an attack on the city, but, surprisingly, were beaten back. So elated were the Byzantines at the failure of the assault that they dropped their pants and—in that age-old gesture of scorn—presented their bare buttocks to the crusaders.

Whether it was the mooning or not, the crusaders had apparently had enough, and decided to launch an all-out assault on the city. The Venetian ships parked outside the walls of Constantinople had the latest in "high-tech" weaponry, 13th-century style.

This included "flying bridges" attached to the high masts of the galleys, which could, by a system of tackles and counterbalanced weights, reach up to the top of the high city walls. These flying bridges, up to one hundred feet in length, were sturdily built: three men abreast could walk across them in full armor. Some of the bridges were built to form tunnels, so the attacking crusaders could crawl through them without being hit by arrows. Once the crusaders had crossed over to the city walls, they began setting fire to the city. The people of Constantinople, seeing their city going up in flames, lost heart and stopped fighting.

PROMISES, PROMISES

The crusaders had made a lot of promises before they'd set out. They'd sworn on sacred religious relics that they'd bring all the gold, silver, and other valuables to a central pool, where everything would be divided up fairly between the Venetians and the various leaders of the Crusade. They'd also sworn—maybe even on a stack of bibles—that they wouldn't violate any women (on threat that anyone who did so would be condemned to death). They also had promised to never lay a hand on a monk or priest, and to leave all the churches and monasteries alone.

AND WHAT DO YOU SUPPOSE HAPPENED?

The crusaders broke every promise they made. They ran wild and sacked the city. They subjected their fellow (albeit Greek) Christians to three days of nonstop rape, murder, and pillage. The Crusades had reached an all-time low. It's safe to say that most of the leaders of the Fourth Crusade never had any real intention of heeding Pope Innocent's plea for them to refrain from killing their fellow Christians (in this case, the Byzantine Greeks). Nor did they ever take seriously the holy cause—liberating the Holy Land for Christianity—that had so deeply and fervently motivated the leaders of the previous Crusades. The one thing they did take very seriously was laying their hands on as much loot as possible. In that respect, this gang of crusaders did very well.

* * *

"Avarice and happiness never saw each other,
how then should they become acquainted."
Ben Franklin in *Poor Richard's Almanac*

In 1829, the Duke of Wellington dueled Britain's prime minister in Battersea Park.

WANT FRIES WITH THAT?

Most trivia buffs know that the sandwich was invented by someone called the earl of Sandwich. But who exactly was this genius who made possible the BLT and the pastrami on rye? We wanted to know.

THE SANDWICH CAPITAL OF THE WORLD

Sandwich is a borough in southeast England. Back in 1729, at the tender age of 11, John Montagu became the fourth earl of what was then Sandwich. He grew up to be a member of the House of Lords, served as Britain's first lord of the Admiralty during the American Revolution, and was quite the bon vivant.

A FRIEND TO FOODIES EVERYWHERE

When he wasn't busy with the affairs of government, or with his mistress (with whom he had four children), Montagu loved to spend his time gambling. It was during a 24-hour marathon gambling session that the hunger pangs and the world-changing inspiration hit him. Instead of breaking away to sit at a table with knife and fork, he thought to put some kind of filling between two slices of bread, so he could hold the concoction in one hand and his cards in the other.

WHAT WE DON'T KNOW

History doesn't record the type of bread or the filling, which was probably some kind of salted meat with or without cheese. And we don't know if it was actually eaten at noontime—just that it was consumed sometime during a 24-hour spate of gambling. The sandwich's popularity as a lunchtime treat developed later.

WE, WHO ARE ABOUT TO LUNCH, SALUTE YOU!

Montagu's reputation for gambling is scarcely remembered today, as is little else about his service in the House of Lords, but the fourth earl of Sandwich has left his mark indelibly—or maybe we should say "in-*deli*-bly"?—wherever light lunches are served.

His lunch creation wasn't his only namesake—the state of Hawaii was originally known as the Sandwich Islands. When Captain James Cook landed there, he named them in appreciation of Montagu's naval interests and his promotion of exploration.

Hitler personally saved one Jew from the death camps: Richard Strauss's daughter-in-law.

THE REAL SPARTACUS

The true story of the slave who became the most feared man in the Roman Empire! A noble hero meets a black-hearted villain in battle! A rebel uprising! Romance, adventure, and a cast of thousands!

THRACE IS THE PLACE

As the movie *Spartacus* opens, our hero is sweaty and bedraggled, breaking up rocks. The voice-over tells us that he was the son of a slave, sold into slavery when he was 13.

Not so! The real Spartacus was a tribal warrior from the ancient region of Thrace, which is now part of Greece, Bulgaria, and Turkey. His tribe must have been conquered by the Roman army because the next thing you hear is that he was a Roman soldier. Then he deserted the army, was captured, and was brought to Rome to be sold into slavery. The year was 73 B.C.

GOING, GOING, GONE

Unlike the movie, where Spartacus is a bachelor so he can fall in love with a beautiful slave, the real Spartacus was married. His wife was a priestess and had been captured with him. Legend has it that when they were together in the slave market, a snake coiled itself around Spartacus's face as he slept. His wife interpreted the snake as a lucky sign, an omen that her husband would become powerful. But not just yet, because soon afterward both Mr. and Mrs. Spartacus became the property of a man named Lentulus Batiates. Their new owner ran a gladiator school in Capua, near Mount Vesuvius.

GLADIATOR-IN-TRAINING

Spartacus's fellow students at the imperial gladiator school were mostly prisoners of war from northern Europe like himself. The others were convicted criminals whose lives were saved because they were buff and tough enough to qualify for training. School was really prison, with plenty of time for learning how to kill each other. The men were taught how to handle the gladiatorial weapons: fishing spears, chains, swords, nets, lassos, etc.

Across Italy, gladiatorship was a glamorous profession. Successful fighters were big-name celebrities. Wealthy city folk decorated the walls of their villas with portraits of the greatest gladiators.

The original quisling was Norwegian fascist Vidkun Quisling.

Teeny-boppers swooned over their favorites the way they do over pop stars today. In the ruins of Pompeii, archeologists found love notes to gladiators that young girls had scribbled on public walls.

Back in Capua, Spartacus was one gladiator who couldn't care less. He reportedly told the others, "If we must fight, we might as well fight for freedom." One day they got their chance.

THE FIGHT FOR FREEDOM

Spartacus's words inspired 200 of his fellow gladiators to stage a revolt. Using knives and skewers from the school's kitchen, they fought their way out. Seventy-eight managed to escape, including Spartacus and his wife. Here's where the real story sounds like an unbelievable movie plot: as the gladiators ran through Capua, they found carts filled with gladiatorial weapons. True! The escapees swapped their kitchen tools for the real thing and fled.

Once the rebels made it to the countryside, they selected a leader. Spartacus was the natural choice. His first order of business was to lead his troops against the soldiers who'd followed them. The gladiators defeated their pursuers and traded up in weaponry again. Now they were equipped to handle anything.

In the Roman Empire at that time, slaves accounted for one out of every three people. Most of them had been captured when the Romans defeated their countries, so they came from all corners of the empire: Northern Europe, Africa, and the Middle East. The gladiators headed south toward the now-inactive Mount Vesuvius, plundering farms for food and freeing slaves. Most of the slaves were happy to join the ever-growing rebel band.

SNEAK ATTACK

Back in Capua, the local authorities called in the troops. With 3,000 Roman soldiers bearing down on them, Spartacus and company retreated up a narrow path that was the only access to Vesuvius. The rest of the mountain was too steep and slippery to climb. It looked like the Romans, who waited nonchalantly at the bottom, had them trapped.

At the top of Vesuvius, the rebels improvised rope ladders from vines and climbed down the other side. They had the perfect opportunity to sneak away, but Spartacus couldn't resist catching the Romans with their togas down. The rebels stormed the rear of the Roman camp and captured it easily.

Josef Mengele drowned in Brazil in 1979, where he had been living as Wolfgang Gerhard.

DARN THOSE PESKY SLAVES

Still the Roman senate refused to take Spartacus seriously. And since the best and strongest of Rome's fighting men were out conquering the rest of the world, the next two armies sent from Rome were thrown together piecemeal: a warm body here, a dreg of society there. Spartacus and his men mowed the armies down.

Every victory brought Spartacus more fame—and more slaves to his side. Less than a year after the escape from Capua, the army of slaves totaled a whopping 70,000. The Roman senate became terrified that the rebels were going to head straight for Rome.

This was the last thing Spartacus wanted. He knew only too well the power of Rome and was as frightened of the real, invincible Roman army as the senate was of him. So he started his troops north toward the Alps and out of Italy. But Spartacus had created a monster. His men didn't want to escape. They were having too much fun looting and plundering.

ENTER THE BLACK-HEARTED VILLAIN

Rome enlisted its best troops against Spartacus. The only problem was that the senate couldn't find a general to lead them. It wasn't just the danger of battle: losing to a ragtag bunch of rebels was more indignity than most military men could face.

Up stepped Marcus Crassus, who had been waiting for the right moment to save the day. Crassus was the richest man in Rome, and possibly the most unprincipled—this in a town where a principle was hard to find. He'd made his money in various nefarious ways and is still famous for starting Rome's first fire brigade. In his method of firefighting, though, the property owner had to pay an exorbitant fee before the fire brigade set to work. And the fire itself was usually set by one of Crassus' employees. This is the man who led ten Roman legions against Spartacus.

THAT'LL TEACH YOU A LESSON!

Crassus was smart enough to know that Spartacus wanted to get out of Italy. (But not smart enough to know that the rebels were as greedy as he was and that they weren't going anywhere.)

He sent a lieutenant named Mummius with two legions and strict orders not to fight, but to provoke the rebels into marching north, where he would wait for them. But Mummius led a frontal assault against Spartacus's rebels and got clobbered.

After reading Mummius the riot act, Crassus sentenced the defeated legions to the traditional Roman punishment called "decimation." The soldiers were divided into groups of ten. Each group drew lots to see which of them would die. The unlucky ones-in-ten were killed in agonizing ways in front of the whole army. This inspired the men to try harder next time.

THOSE WHO ARE ABOUT TO DIE...

Crassus and his legions chased the rebels south to the toe of the Italian boot, just across the water from the island of Sicily. The slaves stood with their backs to the sea, facing about 50,000 of the best-trained soldiers in the world. Crassus thought fast. He dug a ditch 37 miles long and 15 feet wide and deep. It cut the rebels off from any escape route but the sea. For extra insurance, the ditch was backed by a wall. The rebels managed to cross the ditch and tried to scale the wall but were beaten back after losing more than 10,000 men. When Spartacus heard that another army was on its way to join Crassus, he led his men in one more desperate charge. This time the plucky rebels made it over the wall and through enemy lines. But as they fled, the new army blocked their way.

DECISIONS, DECISIONS

Spartacus decided to turn and fight. It was a long and bloody battle. Spartacus was killed, and his body was never found among the tens of thousands of dead. His followers fled to the mountains, pursued by Crassus. After one last battle, 6,000 slaves remained. Crassus had them all crucified, their bodies spaced evenly along the road from Capua to Rome. There's no record of the fate of Spartacus's wife.

In the film, Spartacus survives the battle, which leads to a great scene where Crassus promises that he won't crucify the remaining men if someone will identify Spartacus. Of course, the noble Kirk Douglas is about to speak up when the other men, one by one, stand up and shout "I'm Spartacus!" "I'm Spartacus!" Our hero has one last great scene where he dies on his crucifix after having seen his baby son.

*   *   *

According to Kirk Douglas, the slave army's cries of "I am Spartacus" were actually recorded using the crowd at a Michigan State (Spartans) v. Notre Dame football game.

Alexander Hamilton wasn't born in the United States, but on the Caribbean island of Nevis.

GRAVE MATTERS

*If you're dead, you're history. Here are some
not-very-grave epitaphs from around the world.*

Beneath this stone, a lump of clay,
Lies Uncle Peter Dan'els,
Who, early in the month of May,
Took off his winter flannels.

She always said her feet were killing
her, but nobody believed her.

Once I wasn't
Then I was
Now I ain't again.

Looked up the elevator shaft to see if
the car was on the way down. It was.

He valued only what the world held
    cheap
(Refused to work, from laziness and
    pride)
Dreams were his refuge and he
    welcomed sleep
(He failed in business, took to drink
    and died).

"I told you I was sick!"

36-33-01-24-17
Honey you don't know what you did
    for me,
always playing the lottery.
The numbers you picked came in to
    play,
two days after you passed away.
For this, a huge monument I do
    erect,
for now I get a yearly check.
How I wish you were alive,
for now we are worth $8.5.

"Scotty... beam me up!"

On the 22nd of June
Jonathan Fiddle
Went out of tune.

Been here:
Now gone:
Had a good time.

Anna Wallace
The children of Israel wanted bread
And the Lord sent them manna,
Old clerk Wallace wanted a wife,
And the Devil sent him Anna.

I'll thank you not to put your butt on
    my grave.

Under the sod and under the trees
Lies the body of Jonathan Pease.
He is not here, there's only the pod:
Pease shelled out and went to God.

A victim of fast women and slow
    horses

Life is a jest, and all things show it;
I thought so once and now I know it.

Some come to this graveyard
To sit and think,
But I've come here to
Rot and stink.

Owen Moore
Gone away
Owin' more
Than he could pay.

In 1839, Maine and New Brunswick, Canada, fought a bloodless "War of Pork and Beans."

I was somebody.
Who, is no business
Of yours.

Stop, reader, pray and read my gate
What caused my life to terminate
For thieves by night when in my bed
Broke in my house and shot me
    dead.

Charles Thompson, 1891
Shot in the back
by a dirty rat!

Sacred to the memory of
my husband John Barnes
who died January 3, 1803
His comely young widow, aged 23,
    has
many qualifications of a good wife,
    and
yearns to be comforted.

I was not.
I am not.
I grieve not.

In Memory of Beza Wood
Departed this life
Nov. 2, 1837
Aged 45 yrs.
Here lies one Wood
Enclosed in wood
One Wood
Within another.
The outer wood
Is very good:
We cannot praise
The other.

This stone was raised to Sarah Ford,
Not Sarah's virtues to record—
For they're well known to all the
    town—
No Lord; it was raised to keep her
    down.

TOOTHLESS NELL
Killed 1876 in a dance hall brawl
Her last words
"Circumstances led me to this end."

Sacred to the memory of Anthony
    Drake
Who died for peace and quietness
    sake;
His wife was constantly scolding and
    scoffin;
So he sought for repose in a twelve-
    dollar coffin

Weep not for me mother & brothers
    dear
It is God's wish that I am here
At my sweet age I swallowed a bone
That sent me to a happy home.

John Penny's epitaph in the
    Wimborne, England, cemetery:
Reader if cash thou art
In want of any
Dig 4 feet deep
And thou wilt find a Penny.

Enjoy Yourself 'Tis Later Than You
    Think

Reader pass on and ne'er waste your
    time,
On bad biography and bitter rhyme
For what I am this cumb'rous clay
    insures,
And what I was, is no affair of yours.

Ellen Shannon Fatally burned March
21, 1870 by the explosion of a lamp
filled with "R.E. Danforth's Non-
Explosive Burning Fluid"

What is it like after you are dead?
Like it was before you were born and
    for just as long.

Doc Holliday was indeed a doctor, specifically a dentist.

Here lies the body of Thomas Kemp
Who lived by wool and died by
    hemp.

Two things I love most, good
horses and beautiful women, and
when I die I hope they tan this old
hide of mine and make it into a
ladies' riding saddle, so I can rest in
peace between the two things I love
most.

In a cemetery in England:
Remember man, as you walk by,
As you are now, so once was I,
As I am now, so shall you be,
Remember this and follow me.
*To which someone replied by writing on
    the tombstone*
To follow you I'll not consent,
Until I know which way you went.

Storrington Churchyard, England
Little Willy in the best of sashes,
Played with fire and was burnt to
    ashes!
Very soon the room got chilly,
But no one liked to poke poor Willy!

Mary Keith Marshall's epitaph is in a
    graveyard in Kentucky:
She was good but not brilliant;
    Useful but not great."

Somewhere in rural America
Beneath this stone our baby lies,
He neither cries, nor hollers.
He lived but one and twenty days,
And cost us forty dollars.

Location unknown
John Brown, a dentist
Stranger! Approach this spot with
    gravity!
John Brown is filling his last cavity.

He worshipped at the altar of
    Romance
(Tried to seduce a woman half his
    age)
And dared to stake his fortune on a
    chance
(gambled away his children's
    heritage).

At rest beneath this slab of stone
Lies stingy Jimmy Wyatt;
He died one morning just at ten,
And saved a dinner by it.

This one was from a woman who had
    never married:
No hits, no runs, no heirs.

"I've made a lot of good deals in my
    lifetime, but I went in the hole
    on this one"

"Let your wind blow wherever ye be
For holding mine was the death of
    me"

Here lies a poor unfortunate who was
    victim of his own imprudence.

*This epitaph was written for a young
    baby:*
Opened my eyes, took a peep;
Didn't like it, went to sleep.

When I am dead and in my grave
    and all my bones are rotten
While reading this you'll think of me
    when I am long forgotten!

She failed her breathalizer test
now she lays with the best.

WITH A LITTLE HELP FROM BARBARIANS

Barbarians have always gotten a bad rap.
But maybe they weren't such a bad bunch after all.

When the Roman Empire fell in the fifth century, the entire Roman Empire was overrun by barbarians. Now some historians are saying that Rome was on the verge of falling apart anyway, even before the barbarians moved in and spoiled the neighborhood.

WHAT DO YOU MEAN BY BARBARIAN, ANYHOW?
The original Greek word was applied to strangers who didn't speak Greek. The word imitates what the unintelligible foreigners sounded like: "bar-bar-bar" (sorta like "blah, blah, blah"). So, really, every non-Greek civilization is barbarian. Even yours. And the idea that barbarians are more violent than their civilized neighbors is debatable. Take the Romans: they made their reputation sacking cities, beheading enemies, occasionally slaughtering children, and making a public entertainment out of killing Christians, Jews, and slaves in various imaginative ways. Was that nice?

THEY WEREN'T ALL BAD, YOU KNOW
When pagan tribes began to invade the Roman Empire, some of them settled in and became part of the community. They brought fresh ideas, flexibility, tools, and skills with them, and passed them on to the new civilizations that followed. They even introduced some festivities that we still have a lot of fun with today.

BARBARIAN BENEFITS
Here are some of the nice things we got from those barbarians.

- The Germanic tribes were farmers, and in some locations they revolutionized agriculture. They knew how to build a plow that worked better than any local design used in the heavy soil of northern Britain, for example. Land that formerly had to be plowed twice could now be tilled much deeper, and

---

The Battle of the Coral Sea was the first in which opposing ships never saw each other.

much faster. The invaders soon became lords of great estates, making them local VIPs.

- Most people would have trouble staying on a charging horse—much less wielding a weapon—without a saddle or stirrups. Barbarian warriors brought both of those to Europe. In fact, legend has it that invading Goths beat the Roman infantry because Goth horsemen had stirrups.

- Saint Bede the Venerable, an eighth century theologian and historian, wrote that Easter has its roots in the pagan Anglo-Saxon spring equinox festival, around March 20–21. (On the spring and fall equinoxes, day and night are about the same length.) The spring festival was called Eostre after a goddess of spring and of beauty. The barbarian practice of coloring eggs, and their respect for rabbits—both revered as fertility images—were also incorporated into the Christian celebration. (By the way, the Venerable Bede is the one who got everybody started dating events B.C. and A.D.—before and after the year he mistakenly thought Jesus was born.)

- Other barbarian rites of spring survive in May Day celebrations. Cavorting around a gaily decorated maypole was originally intended to encourage fertility in crops and animals.

- Winter solstice—the shortest day of the year—was celebrated by tribal people from December 20–31. Solstice festivals honored vegetation gods, and included decorating with greenery, fir trees, and mistletoe (sound familiar?), which symbolized fertility and long life. Northern tribes also contributed the Yule log, feasts featuring a boar's head (Oh, Mom, boar's head again?) or ham, and even the exchange of gifts. (It's beginning to look a lot like you-know-what.)

- Even today's Santa Claus is partly based on the chief Norse god Odin, who was said to ride all around the world every winter, giving out gifts and punishments (you'd better watch out…). Odin was especially generous to children who put out treats for his eight-legged horse, Slepnir. (Slepnir, the red-nosed…doesn't quite have the same ring, does it?)

THE ADULTERY AWARDS

When it came to philandering, royal spouses stacked up such
astounding achievements that the judging was a tough job.
But somebody had to do it.

We want to thank all the winners for their hard work and dedication. The decision of the judges is final and Uncle John's Historic Adulterer Awards go to:

MOST PROLIFIC: Augustus II of Poland (1670–1733) was nicknamed "The Strong" for such feats as wrestling bears and unbending horseshoes with his bare hands. But that wasn't the only area where he showed great stamina. Augustus is credited with fathering somewhere over 350 illegitimate offspring—so many that he occasionally lost track and ended up having affairs with his own offspring. He only managed to have one legitimate heir, however, as his wife was so disgusted that she left Poland. Among his many, many descendants was the great French writer, feminist, and cross-dresser, George Sand.

BEST DEFENSE: With Caroline of Brunswick, estranged wife of King George IV (1752–1830) of England, the question was always, "Does she or doesn't she?" While Caroline probably only slept with her husband once, she certainly appeared to enjoy herself without him. After the split with George, she maintained a large household where she gave wild parties. Her home was full of children, at least some of whom were rumored to be hers. But Caroline was fat and inclined to go without corsets, so it was hard to tell if and when she was pregnant. In 1814 she moved to Europe, where she occasionally went topless to balls, accompanied by gigolos. Chief among said gigolos was Bartolomeo Pergami. Here again, the question with Caroline and Pergami was, "Do they or don't they?" When George sued Caroline for divorce, the question became a legal issue, and a servant testified that "Her Royal Highness had heard of the enormous size of [Pergami's] machine and sent for him by courier." But Caroline's lawyers claimed Pergami was impotent. Caroline won her case, but died a few months later and was never officially crowned queen.

General George Patton placed fifth in the pentathlon at the 1912 Olympics.

BEST QUOTE: As uncle of the underage Louis XV, Philipe, duc d'Orleans (1640–1701) ruled as Regent of France for nine years. This gave him plenty of scope for his love of drink, entertaining, and women. Even on religious holidays (sacre bleu!), Philipe held dinner parties with prostitutes, engaging in hanky-panky with just about anyone within reach—including, it was rumored, even his own kin. The Regent was a believer in quantity, not quality. When his mother chided him on the ugliness of his girlfriends, he replied, "All cats are gray in the dark."

MOST IRONIC: Charles II (1630–1685) of England fathered at least 20 illegitimate children, prompting a contemporary to quip, "A king is supposed to be the father of his people and Charles certainly was father to a good many of them." The one woman he couldn't manage to get pregnant was his wife. The crown passed to his brother, James II, whose unpopularity led to a revolution.

MOST ORGANIZED: King Louis XV (1710–1774) of France put a lot of thought and effort into his extracurricular activities. In the interests of efficiency, he once went through five sisters in a row. At Versailles he installed an elevator—the first ever—so he could get to his girlfriends more quickly. His wife, Maria, gave up on the job of trying to keep him happy after ten children, pleading that she was always either "in bed or pregnant." Official mistress Madame de Pompadour took up the torch, but her health and enthusiasm eventually flagged. Instead, Louis established a small personal brothel near the palace that was kept well stocked with young girls. (They were told that their wealthy client was a Polish nobleman.) The king did finally close the brothel in 1771, after meeting his last lover, Madame du Barry. If Louis XV had put as much effort into helping his subjects as he put into his love life, things might have turned out better for his son, Louis XVI, and for Madame du Barry, who, in 1793, was hauled out of obscure retirement for a date with the guillotine.

MOST SPEEDY: Honorable mention goes to the son of Charles X, Ferdinand, duc de Beri who was assassinated in 1820. In what looked like a shakedown, a dozen women from the town of Nantes complained to Ferdinand's widow that her late husband had left them pregnant. The duchess was ready to show them the door when one of her staff reminded her that the duke had been in Nantes shortly before his death for a whole week. "Ah, then. In that case it's quite possible," replied the duchess.

MOST FAITHFUL: Sure, Louis XV prayed with his girlfriends, and Philip V of Spain (1683–1746) always confessed afterward (his confessor saw him three times a day). But the piety award goes to John V (1689–1750) of Portugal. When John wasn't constructing elaborate churches, he was religiously attending to the nuns of the Odivelas Convent, who produced at least three illegitimate offspring of the king.

MOST PUBLIC: Peter the Great was an adulterer on a grand and public scale. When he visited Prussia in 1717, he brought along 400 ladies-in-waiting to look after his entourage. During the visit, one of his hosts noticed that about 100 of these women had young children. When questioned about their offspring, the mothers replied happily, "The czar did me the honor." Peter also gets points for keeping the cost of his philandering down. Rather than keep expensive mistresses, he often resorted to professionals and even haggled over the fee.

MOST HENPECKED: Britain's George II (1683–1760) fancied himself a lady-killer, but gave a lot of the credit to his wife, Queen Caroline, who was perhaps not as impressed by George's bedroom skills as he was. She opted to control rather than curtail her husband's extramarital activities. When she found out about her husband's first mistress, Caroline promptly gave her a position at court. From then on she selected all her husband's paramours, making sure that none of them outshone her in the looks department. Even when George toddled off to Hanover, his other kingdom, he wrote regular letters to his wife, discussing his paramours there and seeking her counsel.

MOST MARRYING: The Hanoverian kings of England may have played around, but the most scandalous rumors accused them of bigamy. George III (1738–1820) was widely believed to have married a young Quaker woman and had a son by her. George IV got hitched to a Catholic woman long before he married his official wife, stout Caroline. His brothers William IV and the Duke of

Kent (father of Queen Victoria) were said to be already married to their long-time mistresses when they dumped them in favor of more suitable heir-producers. Three generations later, George V (1865–1936) was accused of having a wife and children in Malta.

MOST MATHMATICAL: Lapetamaka, an 18th-century king of Tonga, took on the awesome burden of deflowering every maiden on his islands, tackling as many as eight cases a day. Not surprisingly, he claimed he never slept with the same woman twice.

MOST FASTIDIOUS: Kublai Khan (1215–1294), emperor of China, turned his dabblings into a 13th-century beauty pageant. Only girls from the Tartar province were eligible, since they were believed to have the nicest complexions in the empire. Hundreds of young women paraded before a panel of judges, who gave them marks for each feature. Those with 20–24 points went on to the capital where the emperor did a second cull, whittling the number of women down to 30 or 40. Those lucky contestants were then given a thorough physical and, if they passed, each was handed over to a lady of the aristocracy for a live-in test. Did they pick their noses, or complain too much about the weather? The ladies even had to sleep with contestants to make sure they didn't snore or kick in their sleep. The winners became part of a companionable workforce. Groups of five women would attend to the emperor's every desire for three days and three nights, then the next shift would take over. The workforce was extremely productive, turning out 47 sons and an unknown quantity of daughters.

MOST HAREM SCARUM: Okay so maybe a harem isn't adultery per se. But rather than exclude some fine competitors, let's hold a side event. Abdul Aziz (1830–1876) stands out for speed and number. He started off his rule as sultan of the Ottoman Empire by immediately ordering an eight-foot bed and increasing his harem to 900. (He also had 5,000 house servants, including one delegated to watch his fingernails and clip them as soon as they got too long.) Mutesa I (1837–1884) was a diplomatic champion of polygamy. When finger-wagging Christian missionaries told the ruler of Buganda (now a part of Uganda) he would have to abandon his 7,000 wives, he told them, "Give me Queen Victoria's daughter for my wife, and I will put away all my wives."

Genghis Khan conquered more land than Alexander the Great, Napoleon, & Hitler combined.

DON'T HOLD THE MAYO!

A couple of egg yolks, some olive oil, lemon juice, and voila!
A gloppy goo that's somehow managed
to nudge its way into our food supply.

Americans love their ketchup, but would they if they knew that it was originally made from fish brine? Enjoy *that* on your fries. These days in America, ketchup refers exclusively to the tomato variety (thus the lame "Isn't 'tomato ketchup' redundant?" crack from your unwashed neighbors), but in the rest of the world, you'll find ketchups made from mushrooms, oysters, and unripened walnuts. Ugh! Ketchup is surely vile, plebeian stuff beside the gentle glow of the estimably refined (emulsified even!) sauce known as mayonnaise.

BORN TO THE NOBILITY

There was a moment, not entirely shrouded in the mists of time, when mayonnaise was a celebrated—even noble—sauce, and not just some glop designed to ease sandwiches down people's gullets. The time was 1756. The place: Mahon, a city on the Spanish island of Minorca. The occasion: the capture of the city by the forces of Louis-François-Armad de Vignerot du Plessis, duc de Richelieu and the expulsion of the hated English from that place (what were the English doing on a Spanish island? Hey, it's Europe). After a hard day fighting the English, Louis decided it was time to celebrate and ordered his chef to whip up a feast.

SAUCE CÉLÈBRE

The chef decided to make a cream sauce for the meats he was making, but then discovered, to his horror, that there was no cream to be found. Sacre bleu! Showing the improvisatory spirit that can only be brought on by sheer panic, the chef grabbed some eggs, some olive oil, and a whisk, and began to pray. The result: Mayonnaise, named for the captured city. Let your palate decide whether God truly answered that prayer. The French love the sauce so much that they've invented over 50 variations on it— from mayonnaise verte (with puréed green herbs) to sauce rémoulade (with anchovies, pickles, and caper).

Vive la mayonnaise!

In 1739, Britain and Spain fought the War of Jenkins' Ear.

THESE BOOTS AREN'T MADE FOR WALKING

When marching through the faux pas of footwear history—
watch where you step.

SOMETHING FISHY

People in the far North made imaginative use of whatever materials were available to them. It seemed logical that fish skins would make good foul-weather boots. They worked fine in the snow, but tended to disintegrate in the rain. These boots were ideal for famines, however, when they could supplement a scanty diet.

SLIPPERS OF DEATH

The Roman emperors were fussy about footwear. Only royalty could wear tzangas, a purple sandal decorated with gold thread and an eagle, while plain purple sandals were allowed for the nobility, and then only on special occasions. Later on the Emperor Aurelian made red the forbidden color. The Emperor Nero, however, took a shine to shoes made from silver, while those of his wife Poppaea were gold. Nero's taste for heavy metal proved unfortunate for Poppaea, however—her husband apparently used his shiny footwear to kick her to death.

SHOES THAT MADE A POINT

Named after the Polish city of Krakow, the crackow (or "poulaine" for Polish in France) started out in the 14th century as a fashion for pointed shoes that soon grew to absurd lengths. The point extended, curled up, and eventually got so long it had to be fastened to the knee, preferably with small silver bells and a thin chain. Of course only the wealthy—i.e., those who didn't have to do any manual labor—could wear these shoes, so every inch of the crackow became a measure of the wearer's status. Even suits of armor sported these long floppy feet. The Pope tried to ban crackows, considering them "lewd," and eventually, Edward III of England felt obliged to set some rules. Noblemen were allowed 24 inches, gentlemen 12 inches, and commoners a mere six inches. (The king of course could wear them as long as he liked.)

In the 1880s, the British used a travel agency to get their troops to Khartoum, Sudan.

MARY'S BROAD BAN

In the 16th century, toes went in the other direction. The trend may have been started, or at least encouraged, by Henry VIII, who had arthritic tootsies and needed the room. But these duckbill shoes eventually got as wide as ten inches across the toes. Queen Mary (or Bloody Mary as she is known to her many non-fans) took time out from burning Protestants to institute a rule that shoes could be no wider than six inches.

SHOES THAT MAKE YOU HIGH

The remaining direction for shoes was up. It started out innocently enough. Turkish women in the 16th century protected the hems of their dresses from muddy, slushy, or dirty streets by wearing chopines, a wooden slab about eight inches high. The temptation to be taller was impossible for women elsewhere to resist. Soon visitors to Venice were complaining that the city seemed to be full of "walking maypoles," accompanied by servants to keep them from toppling over. In France and England chopines reached two feet.

BLAME IT ON THE ITALIANS

When the Italian princess Catherine de Medici (1519–1589) came to France to marry the future Henri II, she brought a more realistic version, with cork wedges under the heels. By being the first to make high-heeled shoes fashionable, Catherine not only confirmed her reputation for cruelty (ask any woman who's stood in high heels for hours), but she necessitated the introduction of separate left and right shoes. Unlike previous shoes, a high-heeled shoe could not be made to fit either foot. (Separate shoes for left and right feet did not appear in the U.S. until 1822, but these "crooked shoes" were not widely accepted for another 40 years.)

LOUIS LIVES THE HIGH LIFE

Louis XIV was sure he had the brains and beauty to be a great king, but not the height. He compensated for his 5 feet, 3 inches with towering wigs and high heels. Louis's dress-up shoes had five-inch heels, painted red or decorated with miniature paintings, launching a fashion that endured for more than a century, until the French Revolution made putting yourself above others a dangerous no-no.

When Hitler won the Iron Cross during World War I, a Jew pinned the medal on him.

THIS POLITICIAN WAS A SHOE-IN
Thomas Jefferson thought he was making a political statement when he wore shoelaces to a public event. He'd picked up the style when he was ambassador to France, where shoelaces were considered more "democratic" than the usual silver buckles. However, the local media missed the point and accused him of being "foppish."

ENGLAND BUCKLES UNDER
Meanwhile, these democratic shoelaces had distinctly ill effects for the masses. In Birmingham, the buckle capital of England, 20,000 buckle makers were laid off. The Prince of Wales, usually a slave to fashion, took a brave stand, continuing to wear buckles, but he was powerless to stem the lace tide.

SOLDIERS GET THE BOOT
The Napoleonic Wars (1792–1815) started a battle in men's footwear. Napoleon fired the first shot by popularizing the Hessian boot, which covered the knee but was cut away in the back for comfortable bending at the knee. The Duke of Wellington countered with the more straightforward Wellington, a tight boot that came to just below the knee. Meanwhile, valets all over Europe acquired a new duty, spending hours polishing their masters' boots with special oils and wax mixtures whose secret ingredients included champagne. (Another common duty for servants at that time was wearing their masters' shoes for the first few months until they became more comfortable.)

SHOES GET HOLY
Women's shoes of the early 19th century were the opposite of these sturdy boots. They were flimsy cloth slippers, which cost 4–5 shillings a pair (about $10-15 U.S.) and might last the equivalent number of weeks. When the Empress Josephine returned a shoe because it had a hole in it, her shoemaker said, "I see your problem. You have walked in them." Fortunately, in 1852 another imperial woman, Queen Victoria, bought a home in the Scottish highlands and needed suitable boots to tramp about in, setting a fashion for more substantial footwear.

A BINDING PASSION
The Chinese passion for tiny feet may have started with a desire
to prevent embarrassment for a princess with deformed feet. Or, it
may have been inspired by the tiny tootsies of court dancers.
Wherever the idea came from, by the 1800s it was de rigueur to
have feet only a few inches long. Girls had to start binding their
feet by the age of seven. A wide bandage ten feet long pressed the
four smaller toes under the sole of the foot, and eventually stopped
the foot from growing at all.

THESE BOOTS AREN'T MADE FOR WALKING
Which also stopped these women from walking. The tiny steps
they were able to take were called the "willow walk," and it made
them trophy wives. A man who could maintain a wife that
couldn't work (or walk) must be prosperous. Tiny feet supposedly
raised a woman's class and beauty; those with unbound, healthy
feet were considered mere peasants. The one thing these women
could do was make elaborate and fragile silk slippers to fit their
little stumps. The practice of binding wasn't completely eradicated
until the Communists shooed it from the country in the 1940s.

MOVE OVER IMELDA
Over 1,500 pairs at Imelda's Malacanang Palace? Ha! Empress
Elizabeth of Russia (1709–1762) had more than 15,000 pairs of
shoes and slippers to match an equal number of dresses. Charles X
of France simply donned a new pair of shoes every day of his reign.
Marie Antoinette was a distant third, with only 500 pairs, but she
had her own servant to look after them. Actress Polly Bergen
discovered a good solution to her shoe obsession. She married the
president of a shoe company, allowing her to add endlessly to her
collection of 300 pairs, some of which she had had for 30 years,
buying half a dozen or more pairs at a time. Catherine Parr, the
last wife of Henry VIII, couldn't compete in quantity, but she
acquired quickly, buying 47 pairs of shoes as soon as she married
the king. (Maybe since she was marrying the notorious wife-killer,
she decided to shop till she dropped.)

FANCY FOOT WORDS
For centuries, wooden clogs provided cheap protection for the feet
of workers. During the Industrial Revolution they found a new
use: French and Belgian workers threw their clogs or "sabots" into

Tamerlane once piled 70,000 heads in a pyramid outside a city he was attacking.

the machinery that was taking away their jobs, creating disarray and a new word—"sabotage."

GIVING BUCCANEERS THE BOOT

Those great, wide boots worn by pirates were handy for carrying contraband, a practice that produced the modern word "bootlegging." (The women of Greenland had a more innocent use for their big boots: they carried their babies inside them.) Fashionable young women of the 1920s wore large galoshes unbuckled, hence the term "flappers."

COPPERS AND GUMSHOES

Policemen are still known by their footwear. The word "cop" comes from the copper tips that reinforce policemen's boots (and their authority), while their gum rubber soles live on in the term "gumshoe," although it's now mainly applied to detectives.

DO YOU HAVE THAT IN RED?

Some of the most famous shoes in legend and literature have been revised over time. Altogether, the costume department made eight pairs of ruby slippers for Judy Garland in the 1939 Wizard of Oz. (One pair sold for $165,000 U.S. at an auction in 1988.) But in L. Frank Baum's original book, Dorothy's famous magical shoes were silver. MGM changed the shade because it wanted to show off a new development—Technicolor film.

BIPPITY BOPPITY BOOT

Cinderella changed her shoes over the millenium. Versions of the fairy tale can be found in many different cultures, dating back at least to a Greek version around 600 B.C. But it wasn't until 1697 that the scullery maid acquired her breakable footwear. Translators, working on Charles Perrault's version of the tale, apparently mistook the French word for fur, "vair," making it "verre," the word for glass.

*   *   *

"You cannot put the same shoe on every foot."
Publius Syrus (42 B.C.)

The world powers outlawed war under the 1928 Kellogg-Briand Pact. It didn't work.

HISTORY'S HANNIBAL LECTER

*He was brilliant with a knife. He mutilated his victims and may
have eaten their vital organs—even if he didn't
wash them down with a nice Chianti.*

His murders were bold, and even though the police called him
insane, he outsmarted them at every turn. This serial killer could
easily have inspired Hannibal Lecter, but he was just Jack—Jack
the Ripper. And he succeeded where Hannibal failed. After more
than one hundred years, his identity has never been determined...

POOR POLLY

On August 31, 1888, in the Whitechapel district of Victorian
London, Police Constable John Neil found a dead woman, her
skirt pulled up to her waist. The constable's lantern light revealed
that the woman's throat had been slashed. In the mortuary,
doctors discovered that her abdomen was mutilated, probably with
a long-bladed knife. The victim was 44-year-old Mary Ann
Nichols, known around the neighborhood as Polly. Polly had a sad
history of alcohol problems, a failed marriage, and terrible poverty.
Experts could find no clues to Polly's brutal killing.

DOCTOR DEATH

Then another body was found on September 8, in a neighborhood
backyard. Annie Chapman, known to her friends as "Dark
Annie," was discovered, like Polly, with her skirts raised. Shocked
doctors guessed that the murderer was a skilled surgeon. How else
could he have removed the victim's pelvic organs so cleanly?

The legend of Jack the Ripper portrays him striking at night
under the cover of London fog. But Annie's murder probably
occurred between 5:30 and 6 in morning—daylight—when a
market was open for business across the street. How had the killer
managed it? The police found the bodies of Elizabeth Stride and
Catherine Eddowes on September 29. And Jack the Ripper
became the terror of London.

The Aztecs sacrificed up to 15,000 people a year to their sun god.

BEAUTY AND THE BEAST

The fifth and final murder usually attributed to Jack (though there may have been as many as eight) took place on November 9. Pretty Mary Kelly, behind in her rent, brought a "john" to her room who turned out to be Jack. A landlord's assistant came to collect the rent the next morning and found the murdered Mary.

JACK THE AUTHOR

The police received two letters, supposedly from Jack. In the first, he promised to send them a pair of ears. (He never did.) The second letter convinced the police that they were dealing with, not Jack, but a journalist looking to set up a story.

A third letter, sent to a Mr. Lusk, who had formed a kind of neighborhood watch, was accompanied by half a human kidney. The doctor who analyzed the kidney said it belonged to someone who had suffered from Bright's disease. It might have belonged to Catherine Eddowes, whose kidney had been taken, and who suffered from the disease. The letter read in part, "I send you half the Kidne I took from one women prasarved it for you tother piece I fried and ate it was very nise." No one knows if the letter was really from Jack the Ripper.

CLUES

Jack's victims were sometime-prostitutes, plying their trade when very broke or very drunk. Police collected eyewitness testimony about a man seen with some of the victims before they died. Most descriptions put the stranger's height at 5'5", and his age at anywhere from 25 to over 40. He dressed "shabby genteel" and was said to be foreign-looking.

Since the murders all took place within a mile of each other, police believed that Jack lived in the East End. They also thought he had a weekday job because he killed on the weekends.

NOT SO CRAZY?

They were searching for a lunatic, but modern pathologists think Jack had a plan. While his victims were busy lifting their skirts, Jack strangled them into unconsciousness, laid them on the ground and killed them so that the blood flowed away from him as he took "trophy organs" with amazing surgical skill. Jack was an insane serial killer, but there was a careful method to his madness.

THE USUAL SUSPECT

No suspect has ever been found who made a comfortable fit with the facts. One who came close was Severin Antoniovich Klosowski, a.k.a. George Chapman, a Polish surgeon who immigrated to England and worked in a Whitechapel barbershop at the time of the murders.

Chapman left England after Mary Kelly's murder and moved to Jersey City, New Jersey, where another prostitute turned up dead and mutilated. (It's possible but not certain that Chapman committed that one.) He had surgical skill and he was a sadist who beat women. Three of his "wives" were poisoned to death, and he eventually died on the gallows. But some profilers don't believe that Jack the Ripper would ever kill with poison.

WILL THE RIPPER BE FOUND?

New theories about Jack-the-Ripper keep sprouting like weeds in a cemetery. The ideas have become more and more far-fetched, such as the *Alice in Wonderland* theory, which posits that anagrams hidden in *Alice in Wonderland* prove that beloved author Lewis Carroll was himself the murderer. As time goes by, it seems even less likely that the murders of the women of Whitechapel will be solved. They lost their lives, and they never found justice. That seems the unkindest cut of all.

* * *

WHITECHAPEL'S OTHER CLAIM TO FAME

Established in 1570 during the reign of Queen Elizabeth I and in continuous business since that date, the Whitechapel Bell Foundry is listed as Britain's oldest manufacturing company in the *Guinness Book of Records*. In fact, the history can be traced back even further to Master Founder Robert Chamberlain, thus tracing an unbroken line of founders in Aldgate and Whitechapel back to the year 1420 (in the reign of Henry V, and 72 years before Columbus sailed for America).

Over the centuries, a great many famous and notable bells have been cast at the Whitechapel Bell Foundry. Among the most famous to Americans is Philadelphia's Liberty Bell. Weighing in at approximately 2,000 pounds, it was cast and shipped across the Atlantic to the colonies in 1752.

Naples is the birthplace of pizza.

WHEREWORDS: A QUIZ
(The Kitchen Table)

Here at the International House of Uncle John's we serve everything. Where did the names of these foods come from? Choose the explanation you like best, then check it with the correct answer on the next page.

1. LOBSTER
a. Hebrew word for "unclean": shellfish was a forbidden food.
b. Lobster Bay, Maine, where the first recorded mention appeared.
c. From "loppestre," the Old English word for "spider" because of the resemblance.

2. CHEDDAR
a. From the Bedouin "cheda," the word for "sour mare's milk."
b. The town in England where it was first made.
c. From the Celtic "chet," describing its yellow color.

3. BISCOTTI
a. From the Spanish word "bisco," for "viscous," which refers to its thick batter.
b. Named for its region of origin, the Bay of Biscay in Turkey.
c. The medieval Latin "bis coctus," meaning "twice cooked."

4. SAUSAGE
a. From German "sosseg" for "cooked," opposite of "rosseg" which means "raw."
b. From Latin "salsus" meaning "salted," for how it's cured.
c. After the Alpine Austrian town Saussedge, where the links originated.

5. ALMOND
a. The French "al" + "monde," which means "in the world."
b. After St. Duane Almond, the monk-horticulturist who first cultivated the tree.
c. The Greek "amugdale" and Latin "amygdala," which means "almond-shaped."

6. PUMPERNICKEL
a. From German "pumpern" for "flatulence," and "nickel" for "goblin."
b. During its preparation, air is pumped inside the dough ball.
c. For its secret ingredient—pumpkin seeds.

7. GRAHAM CRACKER
a. From its natural sweetening ingredient, sorgraham molasses.
b. Each of the original crackers weighed a gram.
c. They were invented by and named for health food activist Sylvester Graham.

8. MAYONNAISE
a. It was named for Mahon, on the island of Minorca, Spain.
b. It was developed by dieticians at the Mayo Clinic.
c. From the Latin "maiorase," for "superiority."

Statistically speaking, the Bermuda Triangle isn't especially dangerous.

1-c. Lobsters have been around long enough to make the Jewish "unclean" list, but the word comes from their resemblance to a spider. Samuel Pepys mentions eating lobster in his diary. In America, the Pilgrims ate fresh-caught lobster, but by 1630 the Massachusetts Bay colonists were sick of them because they were so abundant and "so great, and fat, and luscious." For centuries after, lobster was considered food for the poor.

2-b. In A.D. 1000 commercial cheese was available, by 1500 it was standard fare on Atlantic voyages, and in 1800 Camembert cheese was developed by a priest from Brie, France. The Swiss made the holiest cheese, Limburg the smelliest, and Cheddar comes from a town in England's Somerset County called Cheddar.

3-c. Biscotti are baked twice, first as a bread, then sliced and baked again, just like the zwieback crackers that babies chew on. Like the Latin "bis coctus," "zwieback " means "twice-baked" in German. The word "biscuit" comes from the same source. Biscotti is actually a plural word in Italian: what we know as one biscotti is really a "biscotto."

4-b. The first recorded reference was in Homer's *Odyssey*: "A man beside a great fire has filled a sausage with fat and blood, and turns it this way and that and is eager to get it quickly roasted." Certain things remain unchanged since early man's attempts to preserve his food supply by curing meat with salt.

5-c. Grown in Greece around 2500 B.C., the fruit of *Prunus dulcis* was prized for its sweet-smelling oil used in body emollients and hair treatment. One of only two nuts mentioned in the Bible (pistachio is the other), the almond was named for its shape. "Amygdala" refers to any almond-shaped structure in anatomy, like a tonsil, for instance.

6-a. Egyptians were the first to get a rise out of bread, accidentally allowing a wheat/water gruel to ferment before baking it in 2600 B.C. Three thousand years later, in the Black Forest, the Germans baked a black loaf so hard to digest it was said to make even the devil break wind.

7-c. In 1830s Connecticut—long before it was fashionable—Reverend Sylvester Graham advocated a high-fiber diet for nutritional and spiritual well-being. An early temperance leader, he became a self-styled physician, even going so far as to marry his nurse. He disdained the use of doctors, calling them "pill pushers." He suffered from nervous exhaustion for most of his life. In his 50s he got steadily weaker and died at the age of 57.

8-a. Mayonnaise was most probably invented by a bon vivant, the Duke de Richelieu. He originally called it "mahonnaise," and invented it to celebrate the French siege of the British fort of Mahon, which fell to Richelieu's troops in June, 1756, during the Seven Years' War.

In Egypt the poor bathed by rubbing themselves with castor oil; the upper class used olive oil.

SAINT 'HOOD

*No matter who you are, what you do—or don't do—
for a living, whatever your situation, you've got a
patron saint. Whether you want one or not.*

I t's true. You're a beekeeper? Saint Ambrose. You drive a
gondola? Saint Lucy. A skier? Saint Bernard. See how it works?

FORTUNE-TELLERS
Yes, even those who practice the darkish arts have a saint.

Saint Agabus: Of course, he's not a high-profile saint, but
outside of Greek drama when did fortune-tellers have any pull?
Agabus was a Jewish convert who could see into the future: he
predicted a famine in A.D. 49, the capture of St. Paul, and even
his own martyrdom. Oooh. He could see it coming.

FLIGHT ATTENDANTS
The patron saint of those who frequently fly died in 1207, about
700 years before the airplane was invented. She was assigned to
make the skies even friendlier in 1962 thanks to Pope John XXIII.

Saint Bona: When Bona was three her father left their home
in Pisa, Italy to join the Crusades. When she was seven, she had a
visit from Jesus. After that she started sleeping in a manger with
no blanket. Another three years, this time God appeared and gave
her money for a hair shirt. When she was 13 she went to find her
father. She found him all right, with a wife and three children.
Bona made her way back with the help of St. James the Greater
(saints have to stick together), and because he'd been so nice, she
started organizing pilgrimages to his shrine in Spain. That's why
the connection with the flight attendants. All the traveling, see?

TELEVISION
If you work in television, or even just sit in front of the TV a lot,
here's your girl.

Saint Clare of Assisi: She's the less famous member of the
"of Assisi" family, her brother St. Francis being the really well-
known one—the one who's always shown with all the cute
animals around him and birds on his shoulder.

Anyway, Clare started an order called the Poor Clares, but she wasn't poor to begin with. She had everything: she was pretty and nice, and lively and rich. But her brother converted her. He did such a good job that she swung totally in the other direction: she and her Poor Clares wore no shoes, slept on the ground, and lived in absolute poverty. They had to beg for their food.

So why is she the patron saint of TV? One Christmas in the mid-13th century, when she was old and sick and couldn't make it to the midnight services, Clare heard singing and saw a vision of the nativity scene on her wall. Talk about custom programming!

HANGED MEN

Or probably about-to-be-hanged men, because what do you need with a patron saint after you've swung from the gallows?

Saint Colman: In 1012 Colman was traveling from his native British Isles on a pilgrimage to the Holy Land. He decided to cut through Austria. Big mistake. The Austrians were at war (when weren't they?), this time with Moravia. Colman was arrested as a spy, and because he couldn't speak German, he couldn't defend himself at his trial. Well, you can guess the rest. Except that after he was hanged, his body wouldn't decompose, so the Austrians figured, wow, here was a saintly guy. And guess what, they made him the patron saint of Austria.

THIEVES

Yes, even thieves have patron saints. They probably need them more than the rest of us, anyway.

Saint Dismas: Jesus was crucified between two thieves, Dismas and Gestas. One legend has it that when Jesus was a child, Dismas and Gestas robbed the Holy Family (can you imagine?) while they were traveling in Egypt. On the cross, Dismas repented and went to heaven with Jesus. We don't know what happened to the other guy. Dismas is also the patron saint of undertakers.

JUVENILE DELINQUENTS

Say his name without the "saint" in front of it and it sounds like he was a kid from the old neighborhood and a J.D. himself.

Saint Dominic Savio: He wasn't a delinquent himself—on the contrary, he was a goody-goody, always trying to stop schoolyard fights and confiscating fake hall-passes. You can almost hear

---

Ancient Egypt had at least six known types of beer.

the mothers saying, "Why can't you be more like Dominic?" The sad part is that he died at only 15—he had a lung problem that finally caught up with him. This 19th-century do-gooder was the youngest non-martyr ever to be made a saint. He's also the patron saint of choirboys and boy scouts. A natural.

UNHAPPY HUSBANDS
All you miserable henpecked guys out there, you've got somebody to pray to. Unfortunately, he's got one of the goofiest names.

St. Gomer: Gomer was married to a shrew beyond belief. She was mean to his employees when he was away on business, so he had to perform miracles every time he got back to keep them happy. Added bonus: If you've got a hernia from carrying the wife around all day, you can pray to St. Gomer to cure you.

PRISON GUARDS
Hey, everybody's gotta make a living.

Saint Hippolytus: He started out as a jailer himself, guarding the cell of St. Lawrence (the patron saint of cooks, librarians, and the poor). After Lawrence's grisly martyrdom (roasting over a slow flame), Hippolytus gathered up Lawrence's remains and was himself sentenced to death for it. Since he was dragged by horses until he died, he's also the patron saint of horses.

FALLEN WOMEN
Who else but the most famous fallen woman herself?

Saint Mary Magdalene: She was a serious sinner until she met Jesus. After that, she became his biggest fan. She even went so far as to wash his feet (supposedly with her tears), drying them with her hair. Thus, she's also the patron saint of hairdressers.

HANGOVERS
She's not really the patron saint of hangovers—but she's the one you pray to when you've got one.

Saint Bibiana: She arrived at her patronage by a silly mistake: to the Romans she was "Viviana," "full of life," which the Spanish (who pronounced Vs like Bs) heard as "Bibiana," "full of drink." There's a very old church in Rome dedicated to her; she was martyred in 363.

Miguel Cervantes and William Shakespeare both died on the same day in 1616.

DAMMIT, JIM, I'M A DOCTOR! *AND A* MEDICAL HOBBYIST!

In 1929, he threaded a tube through a vein in his arm all the way to his heart. He then walked two flights of stairs to the radiology department and took his own chest X-ray. If he were alive today, Werner Forssmann would be the darling of HMOs everywhere.

"WHAT IF...?"

Medical breakthroughs usually begin with a visionary who asks, "What if..." and then proceeds to do something reckless enough to land him a write-up in *Ripley's Believe It or Not.* Werner Forssmann was just such a man. It was this 25-year-old German, second-year medical student who first asked the question, "Can I thread a flexible tube all the way to my heart through a vein, and then photograph it for the rest of the guys to see down at the beer hall?"

"BY GOLLY, I'M GONNA DO IT!"

Without waiting for an answer, Forssmann cut an incision into the basilic vein in his upper arm. The plucky student then threaded a urethral catheter—a transparent tube used to help patients who can't urinate—into the vein. Still feeling spunky, Werner walked up two flights of stairs with the tube in his arm. He then calmly walked into the radiology department, sat down on a table, and continued threading the tube toward his heart, using a mirror to watch his progress on a primitive X-ray device known as a fluoroscope. When he threaded the tube all the way into his heart's right atrium, Forssmann X-rayed the event for posterity. At that moment, the diagnostic tool known as angiography was invented.

The experiment created a huge stir in the international medical community. For one thing, other countries began asking why their medical students couldn't be that reckless. (Remember, bungee jumping wouldn't be in vogue for another 60 years!) But

George Washington was named after England's King George.

nothing was done about improving on Forssmann's experiment for a decade... except by Forssmann himself. A year after his initial foray into his own veins, he decided to repeat his magic trick. Only this time, he injected an iodine compound through the hollow catheter and into the right atrium of his own heart for the world to see. So now not only the catheter but the area of the heart injected with iodine could be seen with an X-ray.

A DISCLAIMER

Actually, Forssmann wasn't that crazy, despite what many people thought. He'd read all the required books on anatomy and physiology that a German medical student is supposed to read. One of the first books he must have read was a 17th century tome called *De Motu Cordis* ("Of the motion of the heart") by English physician William Harvey. Harvey proved that the blood circulates through the body and that the heart is the center of circulation.

So, in theory at least, young Werner knew it should be possible to measure the activity of the human heart by determining pressures inside the heart's chambers. If pressures were good, the heart was functioning normally; if low or erratic, the physician could diagnose faulty cardiac function.

"THANKS A LOT, WERNER!"

In 1940, two cardiologists at New York City's Bellevue Hospital, André Cournand and Dick Richards, realized that their patients could benefit from Forssmann's experiment. In collaboration with the Bellevue doctors and other cardiac specialists, Forssmann continued to develop and refine pressure formulas that physicians use in diagnosing human heart function even today.

If it weren't for Forssman, who probably had nothing to do one cold Saturday night in Berlin, the diagnostic tool known as cardiac angiography probably wouldn't have been invented. Not only was it a boon to medicine, it also set the stage for a lot of big fat bills for "diagnostic procedures," warming the hearts (and wallets) of doctors everywhere.

*　　*　　*

"In matters of the heart, nothing is true except the improbable."
Madame de Staël

Mary Queen of Scots ascended to the throne when she was only six days old.

THE REAL CAPTAIN BLIGH

*According to Hollywood, Captain Bligh was the nastiest son of a
sea-cook to ever sail the ocean blue. Well, guess again.
And say hello to Captain Pussycat.*

MUTINY ON THE BOUNTY

In April 28, 1789, a group of British sailors staged a
mutiny against Captain William Bligh of the H.M.S.
Bounty. They forced the captain into a 23-foot open boat in the
middle of the South Pacific, 3,600 miles from land.

The mutineers who later stood trial defended their actions by
testifying that the captain was a sadistic tyrant who flogged his
crew at the drop of a sailor's cap. It's true that Bligh had a terrible
temper. But evidence shows that conditions on the *Bounty* were
no worse than on any other sailing vessel of the time, and that
Bligh's worst crime was that he was perhaps too accommodating.

MOTLEY CREW

The *Bounty* was overcrowded because Bligh couldn't say no to
various acquaintances who wanted jobs for their friends and relatives. Then, in an effort to make life more pleasant for all those
sailors, the captain set up three eight-hour watches instead of the
usual 12-hour marathons. Later in the voyage, the men would use
this extra time to argue among themselves, complain bitterly, and
plot against the captain.

THE LAND OF SUN AND FUN

The ship's mission was simple enough: sail to Tahiti to pick up
breadfruit trees and deliver them to Jamaica. The breadfruit, nicknamed "tropical potato," was a big, starchy fruit that Polynesians
cooked like a vegetable. Captain James Cook saw it on his
voyages, noticed that the crop that took very little labor to raise,
and suggested importing it to Jamaica to feed the slaves, much as
potatoes fed the poor in Ireland. Bligh had served on the crew
during one of Cook's voyages, and now carried out Cook's plan.

But the *Bounty* arrived too early in the season and had to
wait six months before the breadfruit plants could be transported.
So instead of finding chores for the crew to do, their misguided

---

Notre Dame's famous gargoyles were added after its completion.

captain let them hang out in a tropical paradise full of beautiful women where the food grew on trees, and the local (ahem!) mating customs were extremely permissive.

Ooh, that Bligh was such a meanie.

OKAY, TIME'S UP!

Eventually, the breadfruit trees were stowed aboard and it was time to leave. Do you know how hard it is to go back to work after two weeks at Club Med? Well, multiply that by half a year in paradise. Take Fletcher Christian, for instance, Bligh's second-in-command. He'd found himself a beautiful wife and didn't want to leave her. But he and the rest of the crew sighed a deep collective sigh and got back in the boat.

Trouble soon reared its ugly head. The men were cranky, disobedient, and derelict in their duties. Flogging was the punishment of choice in Her Majesty's Service, so the men were flogged, and flogged again. Three weeks after they'd left Tahiti, Mr. Christian and his fellow mutineers said they'd had enough and set Bligh and 18 of his loyal crew adrift. They stocked the little boat with 50 pounds of biscuits, 20 pounds of salted meat, and 120 liters (32 gallons) of water, which Bligh made sure lasted the seven weeks it took to reach land—the island of Timor, 3,600 miles away.

Meanwhile, the *Bounty* sailed back to Tahiti where 16 of the mutineers disembarked. The rest—with wives, girlfriends, and a few Tahitian men—sailed away, looking for a place to hide.

HOW VERY UNBRITISH!

When Bligh got back to England and told his story, the authorities were suitably outraged. They sent a warship to search for the mutineers. Fourteen men were taken into custody on Tahiti. During the trip home, four were killed in an accident when the ship ran aground on the Great Barrier Reef. The rest were brought to trial.

But it was Bligh who was really on trial. The defense implied that he had an "unnatural" attraction to young Mr. Christian and was jealous of Christian's native wife. The prosecution countered that Christian and some of the other mutineers had sailed with Bligh before, more than once in fact, and had signed on to the *Bounty* of their free will. The judges found in favor of Bligh. Seven of the mutineers were exonerated, three were hanged.

The Coliseum, which held 50,000 spectators, is one of the largest buildings in the world.

LIFE IS THE PITS ON PITCAIRN

Meanwhile, the *Bounty* found refuge on Pitcairn, a small, isolated island that hadn't been charted correctly and so, in essence, didn't exist. They stripped the *Bounty* of all contents and then set fire to the ship, fearing retribution if any European vessel were to spot them. Life in the mutineers' new paradise was hardly idyllic. The Tahitian men rebelled against unfair treatment by some of the Englishmen, killing several mutineers. The remaining *Bounty* crew killed the Tahitians. By 1808, when the island was "discovered" by an American sailing ship, all but one of the men were dead by murder or suicide (or in one case, asthma).

MEANWHILE...

Bligh wasn't faring all that well either. He'd served two years as governor of New South Wales when the top officers in the army, citing the same reasons as the *Bounty* mutineers, forcibly removed him from office and sent him back to England. The British Navy would have none of it, of course, and promoted the captain to rear admiral in 1811 and vice admiral in 1814... although records show that he was on half-pay, so these were probably desk jobs that didn't involve actual command.

Bligh died of cancer in London in 1817, and thanks to those darn movies about him, is still remembered as the meanest man to ever command a ship. History just isn't fair!

* * *

IT'S A BREAD, IT'S A FRUIT, IT'S BREADFRUIT!

Captain Bligh did finally make it to Jamaica with a cargo of bread-fruit. Records indicate that 347 breadfruit trees arrived on the H.M.S. *Providence* on the fifth of February, 1793, and were distrib-uted throughout the island. Today, the breadfruit is a staple in the Caribbean. The breadfruit is used as a vegetable when mature but not ripe. Highly starchy, it is paired for good nutrition with leafy green vegetables. Ripe breadfruit is sweeter, and thus used for dessert dishes.

Breadfruit evolved in Indonesia's Sunda Archipelago and became the staple diet for islanders throughout the tropical Pacific islands, where they were spotted by James Cook.

Brasilia, founded in 1960, is one of the newest cities in the world.

ROME AT THE FALL OF THE EMPIRE

What it was like to be in the great city of Rome around A.D. 476, the official date of the fall of the empire.

Talk about a morale crisis: if the foreign invaders or the rampant disease didn't get you, the taxman did. Of course, all these problems didn't surface in 476 exactly. It's just that scholars picked that date as the official date for the fall of the Roman Empire because it was the year the German king, Odoacer, took control of Rome and permanently forced the last western Roman emperor out of office.

HAS-BEEN CITY

For over 800 years, Rome had been the center of the great pagan republic, the home of emperors, and the capital of a vast empire. By the late 400s, though, the capital of the Roman Empire wasn't in Rome any more: Constantinople was the "New Rome." Power had shifted east, and what authority remained in Rome was only bureaucratic. And you know what that's like.

All through the fifth century, barbarians made Rome a regular stop in their sacking and pillaging trips. By the time 476 rolled around, the once-great empire had been gobbled up, divided up, and generally taken over by Vandals, Visigoths, and other invader types. King Odoacer ruled the entire Italian peninsula.

SICK, SICK, SICK

Rome had always depended on imported goods from its provinces, but now there weren't any more provinces, so supplies of virtually everything ran out. Also, the city had been built on the edge of a swamp, and no engineering could fix it. From the time of the fall to the middle of the sixth century, the great aqueducts crumbled, the city's walls were torn down, the drainage backed up, and Rome could have been renamed "Malaria City."

In fact, all diseases associated with dirty water were a threat. Like the plague which, spreading from the east, swept through Rome in the sixth century, taking about half the population.

Machiavelli's *The Prince* may have been based on Pope Alexander I's cruel son, Cesare Borgia.

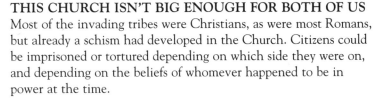

THIS CHURCH ISN'T BIG ENOUGH FOR BOTH OF US

Most of the invading tribes were Christians, as were most Romans, but already a schism had developed in the Church. Citizens could be imprisoned or tortured depending on which side they were on, and depending on the beliefs of whomever happened to be in power at the time.

THE TAXMAN COMETH

Taxes—in cash, or goods (such as food or wood), to support a dwindling army—had become a huge burden to the average Roman. The Roman IRS got hungrier and hungrier, partly because of inflation, and partly because the tax base was shrinking. As invaders carved away chunks of the empire, they were taking away productive farms and estates.

Tax collectors had an added incentive: they had to make up any shortfall in collections themselves.

THE TAXMAN LEAVETH

After a while, Publius Q. Public couldn't pay his taxes any more. So he had to desert his farm and his house. He and a lot of his fellow Romans fled to the estates of the very wealthy, or to villages run by army officers. Once there, they signed away their possessions, labor, even their freedom in return for protection against the tax collector.

In the end, even the tax collectors were running away, leaving the gates wide open for the German chiefs encroaching ever further upon the empire.

* * *

"The rise of a city, which swelled into an Empire, may deserve... the reflection of a philosophic mind. But the decline of Rome was the natural and inevitable effect of immoderate greatness [...] The story of its ruin is simple and obvious; and, instead of inquiring why the Roman empire was destroyed, we should rather be surprised that it had subsisted so long. The victorious legions... acquired the vices of strangers and mercenaries [...] The emperors, anxious for their personal safety and the public peace, were reduced to the base expedient of corrupting the discipline [...]; the vigour of the military government was relaxed, and finally dissolved, by the partial institutions of Constantine; and the Roman world was overwhelmed by a deluge of Barbarians."

Gibbon's *Decline and Fall of the Roman Empire* (1776–1787)

DEATHLESS PROSE

We got to wondering if writers, poets, and other various intellectuals were more creative than the rest of us when it came to those famous last words. What do you think?

Louisa May Alcott
"Is it not meningitis?"

Jane Austern
"Nothing, but death."

Ludwig van Beethoven
"Friends applaud, the comedy is finished."

Dominique Bouhours, French grammarian d. 1702
"I am about to—or I am going to—die: either expression is correct."

Elizabeth Barrett Browning
"Beautiful."

Lord George Byron
"Now I shall go to sleep. Good-night."

Emily Dickinson
"I must go in, the fog is rising."

**O. Henry
(William Sidney Porter)**
"Turn up the lights, I don't want to go home in the dark."

Thomas Hobbes
"I am about to take my last voyage, a great leap in the dark."

Victor Hugo
"I see black light."

James Joyce
"Does nobody understand?"

Walter De La Mare
"Too late for fruit, too soon for flowers."

Eugene O'Neill
"I knew it. I knew it. Born in a hotel room—and God damn it—died in a hotel room."

Edgar Allan Poe
"Lord help my poor soul."

François Rabelais
"I owe much; I have nothing; the rest I leave to the poor."

Dylan Thomas
"I've had eighteen straight whiskies, I think that's the record...."

H. G. Wells
"Go away. I'm all right."

Oscar Wilde
"Either that wallpaper goes, or I do."

SPOONER: THE MAN AND HIS "ISMS"

Nineteenth century Oxford academic Dr. William Spooner muddled his words so often that he unintentionally gave his name to a "tip of the slung" known since the 1890s as a "spoonerism."

Dr. William Archibald Spooner (1844–1930) was an albino. Even when he was a boy his hair was white as skim milk and his skin was translucently colorless because he was missing the right sort of pigments. That explains why his pinkish eyes were very weak. But surely it doesn't also account for the unusual habit he had of mistakenly referring to a "well-boiled icicle" when he meant a "well-oiled bicycle" or saying "cattle ships and bruisers" when he was trying to get his mouth around "battle-ships and cruisers."

IS THE BEAN DIZZY?
Our Spooner went solemnly "up" to Oxford (as they say) as an undergraduate in the 1860s and stayed for 70 years. But his resume would have made impressive reading all the same.

He taught ancient history and classics, but since only clerics made it to the top in Oxford Colleges in the 19th century, Spooner got himself ordained in 1872. It paid off. Four years later he was the busy dean of New College, his pale complexion and verbal gaffes—potentially so hilarious and even risqué that his students no doubt listened attentively to his every word. In 1903 he got the top job of warden, or president. He held the warden's job until he retired at the age of 82.

THESE TICKLE MY BUNNY PHONE
"You have deliberately tasted two worms and hissed all my mystery lectures," Spooner is alleged to have shouted angrily at a lazy student he was trying to dismiss. "You can leave Oxford by the town drain." He toasted Queen Victoria with, "Here's to our queer old dean!" At chapel he prayed, "Our Lord is a shoving leopard." Then there was the occasion when he preached about the poor hopeful camel finding access through the knee of an idol. And

---

After Lindbergh's historic flight, the *Spirit of St. Louis's* first passenger was Henry Ford.

another time when he officiated at a wedding and asked if it was "kisstomary to cuss the bride."

MAY SOD REST HIS GOAL

There's no doubt Reverend Spooner really was given to the speech blunder that's named after him. But sadly, quite a few commentators now think he probably didn't originate most of the priceless ones attributed to him. It is more likely, say those boring debunkers, that Spooner's students—by definition a clever lot— made them up and started rumors that they were Spooner's alone.

Does it matter who said "hush my brat" when he meant "brush my hat" or—still on matters millinery—"pat my hiccup" instead of "pick my hat up" when it blew off in a wind?

Or imagine trying to fight a liar in roaring pain when, say, camping with a scoop of boy trouts. Spooner's uniqueness lives on in countless coinages, historical or newly invented.

*   *   *

SPOONER'S OTHER GAFFES

Remembered chiefly for his nervous tendency to transpose initial letters or half-syllables in speech, Spooner was quite capable of a good many kinds of other verbal blunders as well. A respected classical scholar, he was perhaps the archetypal "absent-minded professor." Check out some of his nonetheless hilarious non-spoonerisms below.

"You will find, as you grow older, that the weight of rages will press harder and harder on the employer."

"I remember your name perfectly, but I just can't think of your face."

"Now let me see. Was it you or your brother who was killed in the war?"

MILK, MICROBES, AND MAD DOGS

Enjoy that milkshake and think of a Parisian named Pasteur who made sure it won't give you TB.

The word "pasteurized" on your milk carton doesn't mean that the cows grazed in a pasture. No, what's been done to the cream in your coffee and the cheese on your burger was to zap the bugs and stop them from giving you all sorts of nasty illnesses—a process invented by a clever chap named Pasteur.

GOOD EVENING, LADIES AND GERMS

Everyone should have a hobby, and Louis Pasteur was no different. Born in 1822, he set to work in his youth studying the chemistry of sugars. He puzzled for a long time about what puts the fizz into fermentation. In 1865, he decided that there must be some sugar-fed organism in wine and beer that was busy reproducing and giving off gas, a micro-organsim so tiny that it was invisible to the naked eye. This came to be known as "germ theory" and it led to Pasteur being dubbed "the father of microbiology."

ATTACK OF THE KILLER BACTERIA

Soon everyone realized that bacteria, although you can't see them, are everywhere and in everything. And they come in battalions, not as single little sneaky guys. You've got a bunch of them right now inside you: without them you can't digest anything because they live, love, and work in your gut. They're also what makes yeast work—and bread, risen by yeast, is the staff of life. Bacteriology was a shiny new science. And in its wake came a number of life-enhancing developments.

BURN, BABY, BURN

Heat, Pasteur knew, kills bacteria, and by experimentation, he found that heating milk or other food to 161.6° F for 15 seconds and then cooling it quickly killed the bacteria. That way, disease-causing bacteria can't be passed from the cow to the human being who drinks the milk.

Jefferson was the first president to institute the handshake instead of the bow.

THE MAN ON THE MILK CARTON
By the time Pasteur kicked the milk bucket in 1895, the old boy's name was everywhere. Almost all the milk sold in the U.S. and most of Europe was being routinely pasteurized. Result? A massive drop in the incidence of typhoid, diphtheria, dysentery, and tuberculosis. Today, worldwide, almost all milk gets the treatment.

A JAB TO THE RIGHT CHEEK
Pasteur was also the man behind immunization. A large number of diseases are caused by an invasion of bad bugs—as opposed to the good guys who make beer. If the body's own army of antibodies can't get rid of them, you're in trouble. "Why not send in reinforcements?" reasoned Pasteur. "Strengthen resistance by making the antibodies multiply. Theoretically, that would prevent diseases from developing." And that is exactly what immunization does.

MAD DOGS AND A DEADLY DISEASE
Pasteur worked on rabies, too. Human beings get it by being bitten—or even licked—by infected animals, mostly dogs, who drool and look mad—not angry, but crazy. The bad news is that no one has ever been known to recover from rabies. Better news is that, thanks to Louis Pasteur, you can prevent it from taking hold.

"I WAS WORKING IN THE LAB LATE ONE NIGHT ..."
Pasteur developed a rabies vaccine, and was so sure it would work that he was ready to deliberately inoculate himself with rabies to demonstrate his discovery. At just about that moment, a nine-year-old boy named Joseph Meister arrived in Pasteur's laboratory. Fortunately for Pasteur, if not for himself—little Joseph had been bitten two days earlier by a rabid dog. So Pasteur had a guinea pig other than himself. The treatment involved a ten-day course of injections. Joseph survived. So did Pasteur's reputation. And medical history took a flying leap forward.

* * *

"There is a wisdom in this beyond the rules of physic.
A man's own observation, what he finds good of and what he finds hurt of, is the best physic to preserve health."
Francis Bacon (1561–1626)

The test bomb dropped on Bikini atoll had a pin-up photo of actress Rita Hayworth on it.

THE ORIGINAL DOGFIGHTS

*You've probably read about flying aces and seen movies about
aerial dogfights. But in the early days of World War I,
it was more like hand-to-hand combat.*

Flying was still in its infancy when the Great War began in
1914. Pilots had their hands full just keeping their wood and
canvas airplanes in the air. (Now we call it World War I, but
back then nobody thought there'd ever be another one.)

THE WRIGHTS GET IT RIGHT
Eleven years earlier, after some aerial hops, skips, and jumps by
various inventors, the Wright brothers had gotten their *Flyer* off
the ground for 59 seconds and a distance of 852 feet. In 1909, a
French pilot made it across the English Channel. By then, the
military had taken an interest in airplanes, and designers in
Europe and America were hard at work on more advanced models.

THE BRASS SITS UP
In 1914, flying machines—mostly double-winged biplanes—were
still rickety, fragile, and hard to control. The pilots loved them,
but, in the early days of the war at least, military leaders thought
they were pretty useless. It was only when the pilots started to
bring in accurate reports of enemy positions and movements that
the honchos started to appreciate the value of planes for observation—although not for much else.

BOMBS AWAY!
The first bombing from a plane took place in 1911, when Italy
and Turkey were at war. An Italian pilot flying a scouting mission
dropped four grenades on Turkish targets.

In the early years of World War I, bombs were usually
dropped from large gas-filled balloons, such as dirigibles or
zeppelins. But airplane pilots wanted to do their bit, too. More
than one flyer held a bomb in his lap and tossed it over the
side at a target. Soon, the pilots were relieved of that particular
responsibility: a few planes were designed specifically for the job of

---

As early as 1676, Nathaniel Bacon led a tax rebellion against the colonial governor of Virginia.

dropping bombs. One of the first was the French Voisin, which carried 130 pounds of small bombs. In the Voisin, the job of dropping bombs fell to the observer riding in the plane's back seat.

Later, the invention of antiaircraft guns forced planes to fly higher. That led to the development of bombsights for more accurate targeting, not to mention more sophisticated methods of releasing bombs than throwing them over the side.

RAT-A-TAT-TAT!
Pilots who were flying observation or bombing missions naturally started figuring out ways to down enemy planes. They tried some ingenious, but primitive, tactics—such as dropping bags of bricks or metal on each other or dangling chains into enemy propellers.

Then they started carrying pistols, rifles, and even shotguns up with them. In two-seaters, backseat observers tried firing machine guns over the side of the plane. And once in a while it actually worked in downing an enemy plane.

The French were the first to mount machine guns directly on airplanes, but with limited success. Pilots really needed guns that could fire straight ahead, so they could get behind an enemy and shoot from there. On all sides, airplane designers were working like mad to pull that off.

OOPS!
The problem, of course, was that shooting straight ahead would take off your own propeller. The British tried putting forward-firing guns on the plane's upper wing, where they could shoot over the propeller. But it was hard for the pilot to know where he was aiming, besides which the guns had a tendency to jam and who was going to go out on the wing to fix it?

The French tried attaching metal deflectors to their propeller blades. Which worked up to a point: their pilots could shoot through the whirling propeller, and at first it didn't seem to matter that a few bullets bounced off the blades. But over time, those bouncing bullets did a lot of damage to the plane.

THE MAN BEHIND THE PLANE
When the war began, a 23-year-old Dutch civilian named Anthony Hermann Gerard Fokker was already designing excellent planes for the Germans. In 1915, the Germans brought him a captured French plane with those metal deflectors attached. They

wanted him to come up with a similar design, but Fokker figured out something completely different—and much better.

BRILLIANT!

The young Fokker quickly realized that the way around the problem was to let the propeller fire the gun. The propeller turned at 1200 rpm, and the gun fired 600 times a minute. He synchronized the two with a system of gears, so the propeller fired the gun on every other turn. Within a few days, Fokker had outfitted a plane so that the pilot could fire a machine gun directly through the propeller blades without ever hitting them.

I'M FROM GERMANY—SHOW ME

The Germans wanted a battlefield demonstration. So they took Fokker to the front, put him in uniform, and sent him up in his own plane. Fokker later described in his autobiography, *The Flying Dutchman*, what happened on that flight. He located a two-seater French scout plane, dived his own armed craft toward it, and then realized he was about to kill two people. The thought made him sick to his stomach, so he pulled up, turned around, and flew back to the field without firing a shot.

IF YOU WANT SOMETHING DONE RIGHT...

The Germans had to get a military pilot to do the test—which worked. It wasn't long before WWI pilots from all countries were flying planes with synchronized machine guns.

Then came Germany's Red Baron, America's Eddie Rickenbacker, and all those other intrepid World War I aces who went down in history as the pedigreed masters of the dogfight.

* * *

DOGFIGHT?

Fokker's innovations were so popular, that already in 1915, aviators had adopted the term "dogfight" to describe a fight between the now much more agile (thus dog-like) warring fighter planes.

As for an actual dogfight, you should never attempt to break one up. Turn a hose on the varmints and call animal control. They'll send out two people: each trained expert will pick up a dog by the back legs and swing the dog through the air away from the other dog. One of the animals must then be immediately kenneled to avoid a resumption of the fight. It's a dangerous job.

Londinium was founded by the Romans in A.D. 60; we know it as London today.

POCAHONTAS: THE NON-DISNEY VERSION

She's the brave Indian maiden who saved
Captain John Smith's life. Right? Not really.

All the legends about Pocahontas cite her extraordinary courage and kindness—the way she intervened between her own. Algonquin tribe and the colonial settlers in general, and how she saved the life of Captain John Smith in particular, when she put her own head down next to his on the execution block.

SORRY TO DISAPPOINT

Unfortunately, there's more trickery than truth to those tales. Although it's possible that Smith and Pocahontas may have crossed paths briefly when Smith skirmished with her father Powhatan in 1607, it's unlikely that the then-12-year-old Indian princess performed any legendary acts of bravery.

ONE SMART COOKIE

She was instead an innocent victim of the colonists, kidnapped as a teenager by British settlers and held hostage in hopes that her father Powhatan would strike a peaceful—and lucrative—settlement. While in captivity a British minister taught her English and tried to "civilize" her.

Pocahontas had an aptitude for both her English lessons and for British culture. By the time she was 19, she was baptized "Rebecca" and had married Englishman-colonist John Rolfe.

THE TOBACCO KING

Rolfe was a planter and cultivator of tobacco and he hoped to make it big in the trade. But his business was suffering under heavy English import taxes. Despite repeated entreaties, King James I (an early anti-smoker) refused to lower tariffs, writing that tobacco was "a customer Lothsome to the eye, hatefull to the Nose, harmefull to the braine, daungerous to the Lungs."

The Mayflower was the size of the average living room—and held 102 people.

POCAHONTAS GOES ON TOUR

Rolfe's solution to this stubbornness? A 1616 promotional tour that used his English-speaking Indian wife as bait while Rolfe introduced tobacco samples. The Virginia Company, which controlled Rolfe's settlement, agreed to pay Pocahontas' travel and clothing expenses to the tune of a then-exorbitant four pounds weekly. Pocahontas was a huge hit with her careful English and her high-necked English dresses, quite a contrast to the traditionally dressed Indians who traveled with her on the tour. Pocahontas was presented at court and exhibited all throughout London to thunderous acclaim.

NOT A DISNEY ENDING

King James I never did lower tobacco duties, despite the efforts of Rolfe and Pocahontas. And her trip to England proved to be her undoing. Like half of the dozen Indians who accompanied her on her tour, Pocahontas was stricken with a European disease: she died of smallpox in 1617, shortly before she was to return to America. She died, only 22 years old, and was buried in England.

AFTER THE FACT

The Smith legend, by the way, appears to be his own publicity-seeking invention. Captain John Smith never even mentioned Pocahontas in his writings until 1624, seven years after Pocahontas had died and decades after he'd landed at Jamestown.

* * *

DISNEY'S POCAHONTAS... NOT QUITE

You don't believe everything you see on TV, so it would stand to reason that you should believe even less things you see in movies, and even less again things you see in *animated* movies. But to set the record straight:

- The Disney-fied looks of Pocahontas and John Smith in the movie don't look anything like reality.

- In the movie, both characters are young adults. In reality, Pocahontas was only a girl of twelve when she met John Smith.

- John Smith probably invented the tale of Pocahontas's rescue, but *even if it were true*, it was likely part of a mock execution ceremony practiced by the Algonquians.

WHEREWORDS: A QUIZ (Miscellaneous)

*Words have a history, too. They all came from somewhere,
be it a grunt from the ancient valley of the Neanderthals
or a brand-new techno-term from the valley of the silicon chips.
Where did the following words come from? Choose the explanation you
like best, then check it with the correct answer on the next page.*

1. BAYONET: A knife blade bolted to the barrel of a gun.
a. It was originally used to hold prisoners "at bay."
b. "Bayon," the Spanish word for "gun barrel."
c. Bayonne, France, where it was first used.

2. TANGERINE: An evergreen citrus tree, or its sweet edible fruit.
a. The 1942 Johnny Mercer hit of the same name.
b. Its "tangy" taste.
c. The Moroccan city of Tangiers.

3. POINSETTIA: The familiar Christmas plant.
a. 19th century Mexican ambassador Dr. J. R. Poinsett who brought it to the U.S.
b. The plant's "pointed" leaves.
c. The Japanese word "posuta," meaning "poison," since eating the berries is fatal.

4. KARAOKE: The audio/video sing-along system.
a. Japan's favorite folk song, about hauling firewood.
b. A contraction of the Japanese words for "empty" and "orchestra."
c. An Asian song style popularized on the island of Okinawa.

5. KAPUT: Destroyed, finished.
a. From Yiddish, it's what happens after you put the "kibosh" on.
b. From Sanskrit, where "tupak" means "rich," but reversed, "poor."
c. From German "kaputt," French "capot," meaning to lose at cards.

6. GARGOYLE: A roof ornament or spout, often in the form of a crouching, grotesque beast.
a. From the Old French "gargole," meaning "throat."
b. Irish architect Hedwig Argoyle, who used them in design.
c. Middle English contraction of "garish" and "guile," designed to both attract and fool evil spirits.

7. GOLF: The outdoor game.
a. The Isle of Goff, near Scotland, where it was first played.
b. From the Old English "gaalf," a shepherd's crook.
c. An acronym for "Gentleman Only, Ladies Forbidden."

8. FORK: The food utensil.
a. The Latin word "furca," a farmer's pitchfork.
b. Medieval slang for "give," as in "fork over."
c. The first French restaurant, *La Petite Fourque* (The Little Bite).

When gold was discovered in California it was still officially Mexican territory.

1-c. In the laste 1600s, as gunpowder replaced catapults and bow-strings, the soldier was particularly vulnerable while reloading, during which time his weapon became little more than a useless stick. The bayonet is named for Bayonne, France, where a dagger was first affixed to a gun.

2-c. The tangerine (or Mandarin orange) takes its name from the African port town where the Vitamin C-filled fruit was taken aboard ships as one of the ways to prevent scurvy in sailors on long voyages.

3-a. For centuries, Mexicans associated what they call "the flower of the blessed night" with Christmas because of its resemblance to the star of Bethlehem. But it wasn't until 1828 when the U.S. ambassador to Mexico, Dr. Joel Roberts Poinsett, brought the plant to the United States, where (in his honor) it got its common English name.

4-b. Unlike a lot of newer Japanese words, like kompyuta (computer), or karar-terebi (color TV), the recently coined (1981) karaoke, comes from a hybrid: the Japanese word "kara" for "empty" and oke, short for the English-derived "okesutora" (orchestra).

5-c. Over a hundred years ago, at the gaming tables on the Riviera, to capot (also capout) was the worst way to lose at a card game called piquet (that is, without winning a single trick, like being "skunked" today). The Germans put the word to work, and since World War I, kaput has come to mean "destroyed."

6-a. The first downspout was created to divert the flow of rain from a roof. By the 13th century, church design had downspouts dispensing blessings as well: sometimes in the shape of an angel, occasionally in the form of an animal, mostly looking like some scary creature, but always shedding water out their mouths. "Gargoyle" comes from the same source as the word "gargle."

7-c. Golf originated in Scotland, where it was played as early as the 15th century, some 500 years before Mark Twain proclaimed it "a good walk spoiled." James I of England (who was also James VI of Scotland) is believed to have introduced golf to London about 1608. But the oldest golfing club is the Company of Gentlemen Golfers where, on the club-house door, gleamed the four gold letters G. O. L. F. (Gentlemen Only Ladies Forbidden).

8-a. The earliest forks go back to the fourth millenium B.C. and were modeled after the tool used for stacking hay, the pitchfork.

*   *   *

"When *I* use a word," Humpty Dumpty said in rather a scornful tone,
"It means just what I choose it to mean—neither more nor less."
Lewis Caroll's *Through the Looking-Glass*

When the FBI was founded in 1908, it had 34 investigators. Today there are over 15,000.

THE GAME

*The Spanish had never seen a rubber ball before,
so when they first saw "the game" played,
they thought it worked by sorcery.*

When the Spanish conquistadors arrived in Mexico in 1519, they found that the country was full of large stone courts for playing a strange ball game. The audiences didn't just watch the game, they bet all they had—gold, slaves, and precious stones—on the outcome.

EXHIBITION GAME: SOCCER WITHOUT THE FEET
The conquistador Cortés was so impressed that he took some Aztec prisoners back to Europe with some of the rubber balls to illustrate the game. No one in Europe had ever seen teamwork in sports before. This became the origin of all modern team games.

In fact, what the Europeans saw was just one version of a game that was played throughout ancient Central America. It had different names—*tlatchli, ulama, pok-a-tok*—and different numbers on the teams, different size courts, but the basic idea was the same. The hard rubber ball had to be kept in the air without using hands—or feet. If it touched the ground, your team lost a point, and if you were very lucky you might be able to score a "goal" by hitting it through a small stone ring set twelve feet up on the wall.

AW, BE A GOOD SPORT!
But the game had a darker side. The ball represented the sun flying through the heavens, and the game represented the game of life and death being played between men and gods. Carvings on the courts suggest that in some versions, the losers would be decapitated. The Mayans used teams of prisoners as guaranteed losers, using the game as a prelude to a mass sacrifice. The Olmecs left sculptures that seem to show their gods dressed in the helmets and padding that were worn to play the game.

Over 1,560 courts at 1,200 locations have been found in Mexico, Guatemala, Belize, and Honduras. Nobody knows how such a peculiar game could have started up in the first place. A version of it is still played in Mexico today, a reminder of this 3,000-year history, but thankfully! the losing team gets to live.

The bride's veil dates to ancient Rome and the head-to-toe cover doubled as a burial shroud.

GREY OWL

He was a pioneer of conservation and ecology.
But he had a secret…

The man known as "Grey Owl" came to the attention of the Canadian Parks service as a result of the groundbreaking articles he'd written, giving a real Native American perspective on the need to preserve the wilderness. They hired Grey Owl as their first official naturalist.

GREY OWL SPEAKS

After writing a best-selling book, Grey Owl was invited on a speaking tour of England. By this time, he was a heavy drinker and he more than once took to the English stage while intoxicated. But when the lights came on, Grey Owl—dressed in full Indian regalia—came alive and delivered his lines without a hitch.

The demanding pace of his lecture tours—up to three engagements a day—left him physically and mentally exhausted. He returned to his home at Beaver Lodge in Prince Albert National Park a spent man. He died of pneumonia in 1938, at the age of 49.

BUT WAIT!

Our story's just beginning. Shortly after his death the world was shocked (and seriously outraged, as the world is wont to be when it's been tricked) by the news that "Grey Owl" was actually an Englishman who'd been christened Archibald Stansfield Belaney.

From early childhood Archie's desire was to escape the confines of his British birthplace and live the life of a free spirit. Not just any free spirit, mind you—no, young Archie wanted to be a Native American—just like the ones he'd seen in Buffalo Bill's Wild West Show.

COWBOYS & INDIANS

Raised by his aunts, Ada and Cara Belaney, in Hastings, Sussex, Archie had to content himself with playing Indian to his schoolmates' cowboy heroes. By the time he was 17 he'd saved enough money from his job as a lumberyard clerk to afford a passage on a ship bound for Canada. His dream was to live in the wilderness with the Indians.

The St. Bernard was named for a medieval monk who built travelers' way stations in the Alps.

BACK TO NATURE
He arrived in Toronto in the middle of 1906 and got a job as a department store clerk. But the job was just a stepping-stone. By early 1907, Archie was in northern Ontario learning to trap, canoe, and survive in the wilderness. It was at this time that Archie first came into contact with real Indians living in the wild. Though a far cry from his romanticized image, these native Americans fascinated the young Englishman. For the next 20 years, Archie lived in the northern Ontario wilds, making his livelihood as a trapper, guide, and forest ranger.

THE WOMAN BEHIND THE MAN
Archie managed to lose his English accent and also started telling everyone he was an Apache Indian. He adopted the name "Grey Owl." He met a woman named Anahero, a half-blood Mohawk, and the two became lovers. She convinced him to give up the "inhumane" work of trapping and refocus his life on conservation. And once he did, his passion grew, fueled in large part by the devastating effects of the timber industry in his adopted neighborhood. That's how it all started. And you already know how it ended.

AT LEAST HE DIDN'T LIVE TO SEE IT
All the articles he'd written, the appearances he'd made, and the importance of the issue that he heralded were all swept aside when he was discovered to be a fraud. Archie was immediately vilified as an imposter, disgraced, and discredited. And things stayed that way for years.

But now, more than half a century later, the rest of the world has discovered the truth behind Archie's words, and Grey Owl's reputation as a pioneer in conservation has been restored.

*   *   *

AFTERNOTE
In 1962, a quarter century after Grey Owl's death, Rachel Carson wrote *Silent Spring*, widely hailed as the "first" environmental work of literature. Not surprisingly, both the book and its author, met with considerable resistance. When excerpts appeared in the *New Yorker*, a chorus of voices immediately accused Carson of being hysterical and an extremist charlatan. Sound familiar?

---

3 countries gave women the vote before the U.S.: New Zealand, Australia, and Finland.

THREE WISE MEN

All three of these men really lived, but there are so many legends about them that it's not always easy to separate truth from myth.

CONFUCIUS
Rules, Rules, Rules

An old joke goes: there are three things the Chinese do better than anyone else—firecrackers, potstickers, and bureaucracy. You think *your* government has accumulated a lot of rules in its mere 200 years? China's been around for over 2,000, and in China, following a complicated system of rules isn't just part of the day's work, it's a religion. The name of that religion is Confucianism.

IT'S SIMPLE
Confucianism doesn't deal with questions of the soul, or God, or life after death. It deals with how we should behave: toward our parents, toward our superiors, and—in the case of government officials—toward the public.

BEST BEHAVIOR
The master rulemaker himself is Confucius, who was born in the province of Lu in 551 B.C. His father died when he was three, and Confucius worked hard after school to support his mother. After leaving school, he gave lessons in his home, charging whatever his pupils could afford. He taught history, poetry, and—his favorite subject—the rules of proper behavior. He only had a few pupils at first, but the word spread, and at the end of his life he boasted that he'd taught 3,000 young men.

THE RELUCTANT CIVIL SERVANT
Now and then Confucius was invited to take a good job in government, but he wouldn't work for any government he disapproved of, so for many years he turned down all the offers. "I don't care that I'm not known," he once said. "I seek to be worthy of being known." An official he disapproved of once asked him for advice on how to rule. Confucius replied that he should learn to govern himself before trying to govern others.

CONFUCIUS SAYS...

Confucius taught his students how to behave through a collection of precepts, all of which were written down by his followers and compiled into a book known as the *Analects*. And yes, many of the anecdotes start with the famous words "Confucius said," or sometimes "The Master said." Here's a sample: "The Master said, 'I guess I should stop hoping. I've yet to meet a man who loved virtue as much as he loved beautiful women.'"

HONESTVILLE

Confucius was nearly 50 when he finally accepted a government position as chief magistrate of Chung-tu, a town in the province of Lu. One legend says that under his rule, the people became so honest that wallets and purses accidentally dropped in the streets would lie untouched until their owners returned to find them.

YOU CAN'T KEEP A GOOD MAN DOWN

Confucius' reputation continued to grow after his death, and in time the *Analects* became the basis of one of China's oldest and strongest religions. Mao Zedong tried to stamp out Confucianism when the Communists took over in 1949, but old habits die hard, and Confucius's principles are still widely practiced, both in government and in private life, to this day.

BUDDHA
From Feasting to Fasting

Buddha was the child of royalty, born in India, near the Himalayas, probably in 563 B.C. His mother died during child-birth, so his doting father took charge of his upbringing.

A LITTLE OVERPROTECTIVE

Fortune-tellers told his father that Buddha would become a great conqueror—but only if he remained interested in worldly things. Forget "my son the doctor"—the old man wanted to boast "my son the world dictator." So he gave the kid everything a growing boy could want, and kept him from knowing that there was any pain or grief in the world.

It was considered in poor taste to show a bed in Victorian advertising.

GOT ENOUGH DANCING GIRLS?

Teenage hormones running wild? No problem: Buddha had 40,000 dancing girls to entertain him. He had the best teachers in the military arts. When he came of age, his dad arranged for 500 women to come around so that he could choose one for his wife. Buddha's pop would have given him a gold-plated Corvette if they'd only been invented.

THERE'S ALWAYS A CATCH

The one catch: every time the kid wanted to go for a walk, his father had to send the guards out first to clear the streets of anyone who wasn't perfectly beautiful and happy. And one day— you guessed it—Buddha decided to go for a walk without telling dad first.

BUDDHA GROWS UP

For the first time in his life, Buddha found out that life wasn't all a bed of roses. He saw poor people, sick people, even dying people. And he was shocked to realize that a big palace and fancy clothes couldn't protect anyone from sickness and death.

THE SEARCH BEGINS

Suddenly he didn't want to grow up to conquer the world anymore. He wanted, more than anything, to *understand* the world—he wanted wisdom—and his wealthy, comfortable life was getting in the way. So Buddha left his wife and went into the wilderness to live as a hermit. He lived a life of self-denial, reducing his meals until he was eating a single grain of rice each day.

NIRVANA

But after six years he saw that this wasn't bringing him wisdom either. Feeling defeated, he sat beneath a shady tree and resolved not to move from that spot until he had achieved enlightenment. He thought about all the causes of human suffering, of sickness, old age, and death. And suddenly he had a vision that showed him how to escape the cycle of life, sorrow, and death, and achieve the state of bliss called "nirvana." He spent the rest of his life teaching what he had learned, and his teachings became the basis of the religion called Buddhism, which is followed by millions of people throughout the East.

MOHAMMED
One Nation Under Allah

In the sixth century A.D., Arabia was a wild and crazy place to live. There were dozens of tribes always fighting and stealing from each other. In between wars, men mostly passed the time with drunken orgies and gambling. And we aren't talking about an occasional weekend in Vegas to blow off steam—it was poker, booze, and broads every night of the week. Everyone was living for pleasure today, because tomorrow you might lose everything, even your life.

THE CAVE DWELLER
Into this unstable world, Mohammed was born in A.D. 569. He was a serious boy, and as he grew up he thought more about spiritual things. As he neared 40, he started to spend several days sitting in a cave near Mecca, fasting, praying, and meditating.

THE VISIT
One night in A.D. 610, while Mohammed was asleep in the cave, the angel Gabriel showed up to tell him that he, Mohammed, was a messenger of Allah (the Arabic word for God). At first Mohammed thought it was just a bad dream. But the vision kept coming back, and always with the same command: to become the prophet of his people, and to bring them a new religion that would end the fighting and bring people together. It was to be called Islam, from the Arabic word for "peace."

THE FAT CATS
So Mohammed started preaching, and slowly made converts, a few at a time. But he also made dangerous enemies, especially among the wealthy upper classes, who didn't like being told that no one was better than anyone else as far as Allah was concerned.

THE YEAR ONE
In A.D. 622, Mohammed was visited by a group of citizens from the troubled city of Medina. They were looking for a strong leader to take charge, and Mohammed accepted their invitation. He moved there with 200 of his followers, and this migration (called the Hijra) is so important in the history of Islam that the Muslim calendar starts numbering from this year.

Early European jesters made balloons out of animal bladders and intestines to entertain.

THE HOMESTEADER

As Mohammed rode into Medina, one family after another begged him to stop and make his home near them. He didn't want to make anyone jealous, so he said he'd leave it up to the camel he was riding. Where the camel stopped, that's where Mohammed dismounted and built his home.

THE DIPLOMAT-SOLDIER

Mohammed often used his talent for diplomacy when dealing with Medina's hostile neighbors. And when that failed, he was equally shrewd in running military campaigns. Over the next ten years, using Medina as his home base, he gained more and more converts to Islam, defeated his enemies, and brought the tribes of Arabia together into a single nation.

THE LADIES' MAN

To the end of his life, Mohammed had a weakness for women—he had scads of wives and concubines. But he was ever the diplomat, and the legends say he eased their jealousy by spending one night at a time with each.

THE BASIC MOHAMMED

But in other matters he remained a modest, down-to-earth man. Even after his victories brought him great power, he lived a simple life. He usually did his own chores, and was often seen mending clothes, milking a goat, or shopping in the marketplace for his family's dinner.

THE GREAT BOOK

Over a period of 23 years, a little at a time, Mohammed wrote the Koran, the holy book of the Muslims. They believe it continues and completes the stories told in the Old and New Testaments. In response to the comments that it was a great miracle that a book like that was produced by a nearly illiterate man, Mohammed said that the book was dictated to him by Gabriel.

Today there are Muslim communities throughout the world, forming the majority population in most of the Middle East and North Africa, and also in southeast Asian nations.

FINALLY, THE LAST CRUSADES

Some people never learn.

After the mugging of Constantinople—also known as the Fourth Crusade—by so-called Christian armies, you'd think there'd be nowhere to go but up for the next round of Crusades. Let's see:

THE FIFTH CRUSADE

By this time the concept of the Crusades—the fire in men's bellies to do battle with the infidel—was starting to get old. Nonetheless, plans were drawn up for a return engagement. By the autumn of 1217 a large army of crusaders (about 15,000 knights and 50,000 foot soldiers) had gathered in Acre on the Palestinian coast. Too many, in fact: a poor harvest year had led to a famine, and there just wasn't enough food to go around.

KEEPING THE CRUSADERS BUSY

Meanwhile, a council-of-war met and decided to invade Egypt. While they waited for additional forces to arrive, the leaders of the Crusade decided to launch a series of small-scale expeditions to keep the enemy—and doubtless the troops in Acre—occupied. One expedition of not more than 500 men was sent to attack Muslim outlaws in the countryside. The whole expedition—which set out just before Christmas—was ambushed and destroyed.

So between the stalemate on the battlefield, the shortage of food, and the presence of the so-called commander of the campaign (an incompetent by the name of Cardinal Pelagius), the Christian army was in a very lousy mood. Knights were continually abandoning the battlefield and returning home to manage their own affairs. Because they were free agents, no one could force them to stay, so they pretty much left when they felt like it.

WHO SAYS THERE'S NO FREE LUNCH?

Finally, in 1221, after a long-awaited showdown with the Muslim forces that produced a smattering of small wins for the crusaders, the cardinal was forced to ask for terms of surrender. The terms

---

The Bank of England was founded by a Scotsman, and the Bank of Scotland by an Englishman.

turned out to be surprisingly lenient: the army would be allowed to go free, and since most of the Christians' supplies were gone, the Muslim commander offered to feed them. So the crusaders left the Holy Land, having accomplished nothing in their long months of fighting, unless you count that free meal, of course.

THE SIXTH CRUSADE

On the very day in July 1215 that he was crowned Emperor of the Holy Roman Empire, Frederick II announced his intention to lead Christendom on a new Crusade to rescue the Holy Land from the infidels. He was a man of great intelligence and imagination, a Renaissance man long before the Renaissance came into existence. But he was also cold, cruel, selfish, and unrelenting in the pursuit of those he regarded as his enemies. Although he claimed to be the viceroy of Christ, charged to bring heaven to Earth, he had very little genuine religious feeling. Just the guy, in other words, to lead the next crusade.

SO WHAT, YOUR HOLINESS

It took him 13 years to carry out his promise. He delayed and tarried until the pope, who was infuriated, accused Frederick— among a lot of other charges—of carrying on secret negotiations with the infidels (which happened to be true). The pope excommunicated Frederick, that is, kicked him out of the Church. The exalted emperor of the Romans couldn't have cared less.

NOT ENOUGH KNIGHTS

At last, on September 3, 1228, Frederick set sail for the Holy Land. The emperor's fleet, 70 ships strong, sailed into Acre on the Palestinian coast, where he put together an army of about 6,000 knights and 8,000 foot soldiers. This was a pathetically small force when compared with the army of al-Kamil, the Sultan of Egypt, with whom Fredrick had been conducting some negotiations.

WHO NEEDS KNIGHTS?

The two leaders signed an agreement in February 1229. It gave Frederick nearly everything he wanted: Jerusalem, Bethlehem, and Nazareth, and a number of key villages were restored to the Christians. There would be a complete exchange of prisoners. And all Frederick had to do was renounce all efforts to conquer Egypt. The truce itself would last for 10 years, 5 months, and 40 days. So

Frederick had managed to do what no other crusading prince or king had managed to do before him: conquer the Holy Land without firing a single shot—er, arrow.

THE SEVENTH AND EIGHTH CRUSADES

King Louis IX of France, leader of both the Seventh (1248–1254) and Eighth (1270) Crusades, was a pious and dignified sovereign. But he also wanted to be remembered as a great warrior and liberator of the rest of the Holy Land. Unfortunately, neither Louis nor his brother Robert, the Count of Artois (who fancied himself the brilliant military strategist of the family), could figure out a decent strategy for reaching their military objectives. Oh, well.

Partly because they didn't have an accurate map of the region they were invading, the brothers had no idea how to find the chief target of the Seventh Crusade: Cairo. And even worse, in their battle plans there was no element of surprise, no feints, no cunning. The army simply marched south through Egypt, while Egyptian spies reported their every movement. And as if Louis didn't have enough problems, there was a bit of an obstacle between his forces and Cairo—the entire Egyptian army.

To reach Cairo, Louis' forces would first have to take the Muslim stronghold of Mansourah, where most of the Egyptians were garrisoned. At Mansourah, Louis was completely outmaneuvered and his army suffered a terrible defeat. Almost 50,000 of his troops were either butchered on the battlefield or died of famine and disease (everything from typhoid and dysentery to scurvy).

AN ANTI-HERO'S WELCOME

Louis went home, but he'd left nearly all his popularity points back in Mansourah. Most of Europe was beginning to think the whole business of the Crusades was senseless and futile. And most of France had developed a strong dislike for their king. But Louis wasn't about to let a little grumbling keep him from launching another Holy War. By early spring of 1270, everything was ready. After a riot among the troops (who probably knew that they were marching to their deaths anyway), the crusaders finally set sail.

SICK OF THE CRUSADES

But instead of heading for the Holy Land, the leaders of the Crusade decided to attack Tunis in North Africa. On the way, Louis' 10,000-man army was incapacitated by an epidemic. Louis

Sir Francis Drake first landed in California on June 17, 1579.

himself caught a serious case of dysentery, so the task of leading the army fell to his son, Philippe le Hardi. Philippe was anything but hardy: he got sick, too. So the task fell to King Louis' younger brother, Charles of Anjou.

CROCODILE TEARS

Charles was a violently ambitious man who had the ability to fake deep religious emotion. After hurrying to the bedside of the now-deceased King Louis, he fell to his knees, prayed, wept, and then started giving orders. His first order was to fake an attack on Carthage, which put him in a nice position to negotiate with the Muslims. They paid Charles 210,000 ounces of gold to call off the siege.

Charles also signed a treaty in October 1270 by which Christians were permitted to live, work, trade, and worship in Tunis. If you can't beat em… don't join em, just cut a deal.

EPILOGUE

The crusades fizzled out over the next two decades. When the year 1291 dawned, only Jerusalem and Acre (and a few minor towns and villages along the Palestinian coast) remained in Christian hands. Muslim forces overran the key stronghold of Acre in May of that year. All the remaining Christian cities and fortresses along the seacoast surrendered without a fight.

Quite a few Christians managed to escape to Cyprus, but a lot more were captured, killed, or sold into slavery. One hundred and ninety-five years after the First Crusade, the dream of a Christian kingdom in the East had evaporated. And good riddance.

* * *

ST. LOUIS IN THE NEW WORLD

Besides leading the Seventh and Eighth Crusades, King Louis IX was well known for protecting the French clergy from secular leaders and for strictly enforcing laws against blasphemy. After going to war against England in 1242, he actually made restitution to the innocent people whose property had been destroyed. He established the Sorbonne University and three monasteries. Pope Boniface VIII canonized him in 1297, and he became the patron saint of France. Little-known fact: he's the Louis in St. Louis, Missouri. That city on the Mississippi was founded by the French.

BEFORE THEY WERE NAZIS

*When Hitler assembled henchmen to help him run the Third
Reich, he picked an assortment of losers and failures who
represented the bottom rungs of German society.*

JOSEF PAUL GOEBBELS Propaganda Master
Although Goebbels' propaganda machine praised the perfect
Nordic physique, Goebbels himself had a physical disability, a
clubfoot so badly twisted that it kept him out of World War I.
Goebbels' Nazi career can be seen as desperate overcompensation
for this physical shortcoming. Yet, in university, Goebbels' favorite
professors were Jews and he was once engaged to a Jewish woman.
After graduating he tried (unsuccessfully) to make a living as a
writer before drifting into the Nazi party's left wing.

HEINRICH HIMMLER Head of Nazi Police
After serving at the tail end of World War I, Himmler got a
diploma in agriculture and tried his hand at chicken farming. He
was a total failure. Chinless and bespectacled, he worked as a
salesman for a fertilizer manufacturer, but it wasn't until he joined
the Nazis that he found his true calling in life as a thug. In 1929,
he became head of Hitler's personal bodyguard, the SS, which he
turned from a 200-man body into a 52,000-strong army by 1933.

ADOLF EICHMANN Chief Executioner
As a boy, Eichmann's complexion earned him the nickname
"Little Jew." Unable to finish his engineering studies, he worked as
an ordinary laborer in a mining company run by his father. He was
later a salesman for an electrical construction company before
becoming a traveling salesman for the Vacuum Oil Company. He
became a Nazi filing clerk, specializing in Freemasons.

HERMANN GOERING Hitler's #2
As a well-bred war hero, Goering was the closest the Nazis came
to respectability. He once even succeeded the Red Baron as leader
of his squadron of flying aces. Nevertheless, his personal life was
marred by scandal; he lured a Swedish baroness to divorce her
husband and marry him instead. And after the Munich Putsch,

The winged hat worn by the Greek god Hermes is called a "pelasos."

Goering was badly injured in "the groin" and became addicted to the morphine he used to relieve the pain. He eventually became monstrously obese, too.

MARTIN BORMANN Hitler's secretary
Bormann has one of the flimsiest resumes of any of the Nazis. A school dropout who worked briefly as a farm laborer, Bormann very briefly served in an artillery regiment during World War I, then went straight into far-right politics. Or, more exactly, far-right violence. He joined a group of disgruntled former soldiers who spent their time attacking Communists. He even helped murder his former elementary school teacher and served a year in prison. Ultimately, though, Bormann was a born master of office politics, scheming his way to the top of the Nazi pile.

RUDOLF HESS Deputy Fuhrer
Born in Alexandria, Egypt, Hess didn't actually live in Germany until he was 14. Whereas most Nazis started their careers as losers and achieved some sort of career satisfaction by successfully wreaking havoc, Hess's career went the other way. His reputation was cemented when he went to prison, voluntarily, to be with his *Führer*. As Hess's largely ceremonial powers began to recede, he hoped to curry favor with a strange peace mission to Scotland that ended with his being locked in the Tower of London.

REINHARD HEYDRICH Final Solutionist
Despite rumors of Jewish ancestry, Heydrich epitomized the blond-and-blue-eyed Nordic ideal. He was also handsome enough to attract a string of sexual partners, for one of whom he seems to have thrown away a naval career. Although he was an award-winning fencer, he was also tall and gangly, and fellow Navy comrades teased him over his high, bleating voice and musical affectations. Heydrich's career came to an abrupt end when he walked into a Czechoslovakian ambush in 1942.

*   *   *

"Evil is unspectacular and always human
And shares our bed and eats at our own table."
W. H. Auden

DEAR DEPARTED: BURIAL CUSTOMS AND CURIOSITIES

Ashes to ashes, dust to dust.
If the coyotes don't get you, the worms must.

—*Anonymous*

From the moment we're born, we begin the journey toward death. With luck, the period in between is long and prosperous. But down through the years, some cultures developed downright odd ways to dispose of the deceased.

NO FRILLS FUNERAL RITES
Burial, along with entombment was, and still is, the most common practice. It costs a bit more than when the Neanderthals painted their dead with red ocher, stuck 'em in the ground, and tossed some flowers and animal bits on top. It was pretty pricey for the Egyptians, if you look at the size of those pyramids. Of course, the catacombs under Rome were gratis; all you had to do was weep, gnash your teeth, and leave the dead in some hole in the wall.

LAYERING THE DEAD TO REST
In more civilized times, multiple burials were allowed in a single or double plot, providing the first occupants were not only kept deep in their loved one's hearts, but very deep in the ground. The next one to be added was often placed a few inches above the first coffin/casket, and the layering continued as long as the last man in was six feet under.

THE GREAT OUTDOORS
Some cultures chose exposure over burial, sometimes by necessity. (It would be hard to dig six feet down into the Artic tundra.) Remains were often left in, or on, trees or platforms. Vultures or other scavenging birds took care of the rest. It was simple, and nobody made any "bones" about the arrangements. Native Americans practiced it, and the Parsis of India still raise their dead on "towers of silence" to avoid contaminating earth, water, or fire.

There are 56 signatures on the Declaration of Independence.

UPS AND DOWNS

The ancient civilization at Catal Huyuk (circa 4,000 B.C.), in what's now southern Turkey, took the practice to new heights... and depths. When only the bones were left, they were buried without exceptional fanfare, a foot deep under the floors of the houses where the dead had lived, accompanied occasionally by a favorite tool or bit of jewelry.

MAKING ASHES OF THEMSELVES

The home fires were burning, quite literally, thousands of years ago. Between 1400 B.C. and A.D. 200, cremation was the preferred method of disposal, with Romans among others.

Depending on the country of "departure," the ashes have been scattered in a river, buried sedately in an urn... or used to fill an hourglass (as one person requested, "So he might still be of some use.").

A variation on the "up in smoke" theme, the Indian practice of "suttee," where wives ritually threw themselves on their hubby's funeral flames, was thankfully abolished by the British in 1829.

SERVING MAN FOR CENTURIES

Less known and least talked about (especially when you're having your mother-in-law for dinner) was the practice of cannibalism, reported as early as Neolithic times, and on into the era of Greek historian Herodotus, and Venetian man of the world, Marco Polo. Sometimes it was disposal of the naturally dead, while at others it was the result of tribal squabbles, whereby the loser was lunch, in the hopes that the victor would then consume... er, *assume* the departed's strengths and powers.

GOING OUT IN STYLE

Although generally credited to the upstart Egyptians, embalming the dead was practiced long before their time. As much as 5,000 years before, the Chinchoros, a fishing tribe from the north coast of Chile, were disassembling corpses, treating internal organs to prevent decay, then reassembling the body, filling it with fiber or feathers, and sometimes using wooden rods to support the spine and limbs. The reconstructed body was then coated in clay on which they painted or carved designs.

TUT, TUT

But the Egyptians really knew how to throw a party for the departed. Anyone who's seen accounts of the opening of King Tut's tomb in 1923, knows that when the boy king died in 1349 B.C. at age 19, he was buried with treasures beyond imagination. All for his use in the afterlife.

Before starting his journey with Anubis, Tut's body underwent the ritual removal of lungs, stomach, liver, and intestines to their own canopic jars, and his body was treated for weeks with a bath of natron, then stuffed with bituminous substances, rubbed with aromatic spices... all in addition to the oils slathered on with each layer of wrappings. The job was so good that an abrasion still showed on the skin of his cheek, and X-rays revealed bone fragments underneath, dispelling the theories of death by tuberculosis and substituting good old murder.

By the time Egyptians discontinued the practice around A.D. 700, it's estimated that over 70 million mummies had been stashed around the deserts and pyramids.

BONE DRY

Desiccation seems to have been the best preserver of all in the East, and a prime example of it are the mystery mummies of the Takla Makan desert in China. In the 1970s and 80s, mummies were found buried throughout the desert. Many of these freeze-dried remains were Caucasian and dated as far back as 4,000 years. But with nothing to say how they got there.

FREEZE-DRIED

The Incas could really chill out. In 1999, Dr. Johan Reinhard found three young sacrificial victims, folded calmly into sitting positions, frozen since their deaths some 500 years before. At 22,000 feet on top of Argentina's Mount Llullaillaco, it was the world's highest archaeological site. Nature did the embalming.

BLUE TATTOOS

Nature also preserved for modern study the Siberian Ice Maiden, discovered in what's called the "Pastures of Heaven" on the High Steppes. Covered in vivid blue tattoos and frozen by extraordinary climatic conditions, the Maiden, six decorated horses, and a last ceremonial meal seem to indicate that women not only got a dinner, but respect, in nomadic societies of 2400 years ago.

In A.D. 700, the largest city in America was Teotihuacan, home to 100,000 people.

LOST AND FOUND

The lost Franklin Expedition of 1852 turned up in the form of sailor-sicles during a 1984 search of the Arctic. John Torrington, dead and decently coffined for 130 years, would yield up pathological evidence of lead poisoning, likely a result of the 8,000 tins of poorly soldered provisions on the ships.

THE ICEMAN SHOWETH UP

Perhaps the most famous iced-over individual is the anonymous "Iceman," discovered along the Austro-Italian border. Middle-aged and dressed spiffily in a cape, fur shoes, and hat, he had dined on grains and bread shortly before laying down for his eternal rest. "Otzi," as he was named, was still making news in 2001. An arrow hole in his chest showed why he hadn't taken a left at the Alps and kept on going.

BOGGED DOWN

Many people get bogged down on their way to glory, but none so neatly as Tollund Man. Fished out of a quagmire in Denmark, his 1950 discovery set the scientific world on their mummified ears. Tollund Man's features are composed and serene, despite his death by hanging (the rope was still around his neck!). Whether they tripped in—or were tipped in—the bog mummies of Northern Europe, were perfectly pickled in the oxygenless peat.

TRADITION!

Modern humans had to invent their own techniques, mostly out of the need to deliver the departed in a decorous state; this would include the fine art of embalming.

Today, in the U.S. at least, traditional embalming and burial is still the favorite (ahem) way to go.

* * *

POTTER WHO?

Potter's field is the name given to burial grounds for the poor and unknown. The name comes from the New Testament in which Judas returns the 30 pieces of silver to the priests. They take the coins, "And bought with them the potter's field, to bury strangers in" (Matthew 27:7). Whether rich or poor, foreigners were not wanted in Jewish graveyards. The potter's field, being excavated for clay, would be of little value, and would sell cheap.

In ancient Rome it was considered a sin to eat the flesh of a woodpecker.

THE BATTLE OF TRAFALGAR

*Ten years before he met his Waterloo, Napoleon suffered a
crushing—and possibly prophetic?—naval defeat at the hands
of the Royal Navy led by Admiral Horatio Nelson.*

BAIT FOR A BIG FISH

In 1805, Napoleon Bonaparte was master of most of Europe. Only
England stood in the way of his complete domination. He had no
respect for the British army, but the navy—especially the fleet
commanded by Vice-Admiral Lord Horatio Nelson—kept him
from crossing the channel. If that darn fleet could be temporarily
removed, Napoleon thought, conquest would be a snap.

SNEAKY, SNEAKY

Hoping to lure Nelson from his post, Napoleon sent a fleet
commanded by Vice-Admiral Pierre de Villeneuve to the
Caribbean. The British thought this was an attack on one of their
colonies and sailed off in pursuit. But Villeneuve started back for
Europe, leaving Nelson hunting for him. By the time the British
realized he was gone, Villeneuve had a long head start. Nelson
and crew scurried off to try to cut the lead to a couple of days.

THE PLOT FOILED

Still ahead of Nelson, Villeneuve reached the coast of Europe.
There, his 20 ships met a British force of 15. In the fight that
ensued the French lost two ships to the enemy; the rest fled to
Cadiz to get Spanish reinforcements.

By the time Nelson caught up with his quarry, they were
bottled up in Cadiz—no longer an invasion threat, but not likely
to come out and be beaten up either. So, leaving a squadron
behind to keep the enemy on their best behavior, Nelson sailed
back to England for a few weeks' rest and relaxation.

AN ALMOST NEW STRATEGY

Nelson returned to his fleet and described his battle plan to his
officers. Instead of attacking with each ship following her leader in
line, he would attack head on in two columns and break the

French-Spanish line. He claimed that this was a new idea and that the enemy would be confused by it. But in fact the British had used a similar tactic in an earlier battle, and Villeneuve was expecting to see something like it. (Which didn't really matter because he had no idea of how to defend against it.)

MEANWHILE, BACK AT HEADQUARTERS

Napoleon gave up on invading England—but he still had a use in mind for his fleet: the conquest of Naples. He ordered Villeneuve to put to sea at the soonest opportunity. That came in mid-October when several of the British ships departed for England, leaving Nelson with only 27 ships to face a combined French and Spanish fleet of 33. Villeneuve liked the odds and set sail. Late one night, he sighted the British off Cape Trafalgar. He ordered his ships into a line and spent all night preparing for battle.

THE VIEW FROM THE OTHER SIDE

Nelson raced to close the distance between himself and the enemy. At daybreak he divided his force into two columns, and with the wind at his back, bore down upon the French-Spanish fleet. But the winds were light, so the attack was too slow to suit the British admiral.

WHAT ENGLAND EXPECTS

While the distance slowly closed, Nelson fretted: he vacillated between predicting the destruction of the enemy and melodramatically foretelling his own death (this is something he did before almost every battle). To pass the time, he decided to send a signal to the fleet. At first he wanted to say, "Nelson confides that every man will do his duty," but his signals officer suggested that "England expects that every man will do his duty," would be easier to make using the cumbersome signal code of the time.

THE BATTLE

At noon, the British fleet broke through the French-Spanish line in two places, and soon the battle became a series of separate actions in which the English held the advantage. Nelson's flagship, the *Victory*, was one of the first to pierce the enemy line. She pulled alongside the *Redoutable*, commanded by one of the best captains in the French navy, who had stationed sharpshooters in his rigging. The two ships fought so fiercely that the *Redoutable*

Of the last 3,500 years, only 230 years saw no major wars.

sank a day later. But she had her revenge. One of the sharpshooters took aim at Nelson—who was easily identified by his glittering medals—and put a musket ball into his spine.

A HERO'S DEATH

Nelson was hustled below to the ship's doctor, but nothing could be done. While the battle raged on, he lingered between life and death, alternately demanding to know how the British were doing and fretting over who would care for his mistress. He stayed alive long enough to learn that the enemy had been crushed. More than half the French-Spanish fleet had been captured; the rest had fled. Gratified by this news, Nelson sighed, "Thank God, I have done my duty," and died.

PICKLED IN RUM

While he was dying, he'd feared that his body would be pitched over the side, but he didn't need to have worried. He was popped into a cask of "spirits" to preserve him for the journey home. To this day, "Nelson's Blood" is a nickname for rum in the Royal Navy. He was given a splendid funeral and laid to rest in St. Paul's Cathedral in London.

NO-TELL HOTEL

Villeneuve didn't survive his opponent by much. He was captured by the British at Trafalgar and freed early in 1806. Within two months of returning to France, he was found dead in a hotel room. Although his death was said to have been a suicide, many believe that Napoleon had him assassinated for his ineptitude.

*   *   *

A RUMMY TALE

"There's nought no doubt so much the spirit calms
as rum and true religion." *Lord Byron*

Long before sailors took to "Nelson's Blood," rum had a long history with the British navy. The Royal Navy issued rum rations as far back as 1655 as a shipboard substitute for water and beer, which went bad within weeks. By 1731, the standard ration was a daily half-pint (8 ounces!), but as a consequence they had problems with men falling out of the rigging while under the influence. The rum was subsequently mixed with an equal amount of water to lessen the effect. Rum rations remained standard until 1969.

Cree Indians used smoking pipes as currency.

FROM ITALY TO LITTLE ITALY, THE MAFIA COMES TO AMERICA

Give me your tired, your poor… your gangsters?
Among the millions of immigrants coming to America
were some notorious "made" men.

A WORD TO REMEMBER

The term *Mafia* muscled its way into dictionaries in the late 1860s. But long before, in Sicily, everybody knew the word. It originated in the tough streets and slums of Palermo. A man who was a *Mafioso*—he was a "man of respect," prepared to take the law into his own hands.

Americans learned the word *Mafia* when it traveled to America along with the flood of immigrants from Italy in the late 19th and early 20th centuries. *Mafia* meant organized crime.

QUESTION AUTHORITY

Located at the crossroads of major Mediterranean trade routes, Sicily had been occupied by a long list of conquerors: the Phoenicians, Arabs, Greeks, Spanish, French, and more. Long oppressed, the Sicilians became wary of outsiders and resentful of legal authorities who'd never done them much good.

Rural bandit chieftains (who secretly pleased peasant neighbors by rustling cattle belonging to nobles of foreign extraction) could be accorded much respect, and some bandit leaders resolved disputes and kept local order. But bandits were feared, too; they could be violent and they charged their countrymen for protection. Eventually Sicily saw secret criminal societies formed, with chieftains, lieutenants, and their followers.

DON' ARGUE WITH A DON

By 1860, as the liberator Giuseppe Garibaldi landed in Sicily to drive out the Spanish and create a united Italy, the Mafia was alive and well. Its chiefs or "dons" were powerful and respected. Don Vito Cascio Ferro (regarded by many as Sicily's first real godfather) brought two big changes to the ways of the Mafia in Sicily. First, he convinced his fellow chieftains that it wasn't good business to bleed their victims dry; it was better to charge moderately for protection so that the business could stay alive and keep generating income for the mob. Legend says he explained it this way: "You have to skim the cream off the milk without breaking the bottle." Don Vito was also the first Sicilian Mafioso to establish ties with leaders in that new land of opportunity for the Mafia, America.

THE NEW AMERICANS
Italy provided the U.S. with some 4.7 million immigrants between 1820 and 1930. By the late 19th century the main source of Italian newcomers to America were the Mezzogiorno, from the southern part of the country, including Sicily.

New York and New Orleans saw Sicilian "Little Italys" spring up, and plenty of the new immigrants brought along their distrust of officials. Crimes like extortion—mostly perpetrated by Italians against Italians—followed the pattern of the Old Country. The Mafia had arrived in the New World.

Italians didn't have a monopoly on organized crime—vicious Irish and Jewish gangs controlled crime territories in New York. But Italian "stand up guys" (often fugitives from Italian justice) had become a force by 1880. By 1890 they shocked the nation.

DEATH IN THE BIG EASY... AND PALERMO
In New Orleans in 1890, the police chief, David Hemmings, who'd been investigating the mob, was fatally gunned down near his home. The crime was bad enough but the trial drove the Big Easy to hysteria. Nineteen Mafia leaders and henchmen were charged with conspiracy to murder the police chief, but all were either acquitted or granted a mistrial. Rumors swirled that the jury had been bought off. Vigilantes stormed the parish jail and 16 (very possibly innocent) Sicilians were lynched.

In 1899, New York City detective Joseph Petrosino, investigating Italy's connection to the mob, was gunned down in an open plaza in Palermo. The hit was said to have been ordered by Don Vito Cascio Ferro himself. But the police responded to Petrosino's murder with a crackdown on the Mafia in New York.

The U.S. first issued paper money in 1862.

THE MOB GOES MOD

Government retaliation to the New Orleans and Palermo killings demonstrated to the up-and-coming "capos" (mob chiefs) that the Mafia had to make changes in order to thrive in the U.S. What the Mafia needed was a charismatic, Americanized don. And they got Charlie "Lucky" Luciano.

As a teenager Salvatore Lucania organized street gangs that terrorized the Lower East Side. He soon took up with some pals or "goombahs." They were Frank Costello, and Jewish tough guys Meyer Lansky and Benny or "Bugsy" Siegel. As these teens grew more sophisticated at crime, a legendary *borgata* (criminal organization) was born.

THE MOB GETS "LUCKY"

Lucania's gang ran bookmaking joints, and put some of their profits into "gifts" for cops and public officials. Lucky wasn't old-school Sicilian, but he was a helluva big earner. When prohibition came, he made millions. Lucania and his multicultural wiseguys became the biggest bootlegging outfit in New York.

Lucania, handsome and charming, became Charlie "Lucky" Luciano, a New York celebrity. Before Lucky went to jail in 1936, he engineered the commission, a confederation of Mafia gangs. Lucky wanted to end internal mob wars that brought unwanted attention from law enforcement and disrupted profit-taking.

CRIMINALS WHO AREN'T POLITICIANS

The Mafia expanded. Bugsy Siegel built the Flamingo Hotel, and began the Las Vegas gambling empire before he was murdered in Beverly Hills in 1947.

Americans got a good look at organized crime when a U.S. Senate investigation of the Mafia led by Tennessee's Estes Kefauver, was televised in 1951. TV viewers watched Frank Costello testify (he wasn't exactly cooperative) for three days. Frank got a five-year sentence for tax evasion, and Americans got an education about the reality of the Mafia in American life.

In the 1960s, President John F. Kennedy had ties to Chicago mob boss Sam Giancana (including a shared mistress), but Kennedy's brother, Attorney General Robert Kennedy, aggressively went after indictments against mobsters. He also championed new laws to prosecute racketeering.

The first English Parliament was called into session on January 20, 1265.

GETTING GOTTI

By the 1980s, prosecutors like U.S. Attorney for New York Rudy Guliani had declared all-out legal war on organized crime. Soon the last big-time Mafia chieftain was on the ropes: John Gotti, the "Teflon Don," the head of the powerful Gambino crime family. Much like Lucky Luciano during the Prohibition days, Gotti was a tabloid celebrity who had friends among "respectable" people. He held court at a social club on Mulberry Street in Manhattan and each year staged a fireworks show for neighborhood residents.

THE POWER OF BULL

In 1992, testimony from turncoat informant Sammy "The Bull" Gravano put his boss John Gotti in prison for life. Law enforcement authorities hoped it would be a fatal blow to traditional organized crime. Gravano had broken the famous Mafia code of silence—a refusal by members to "rat" on each other regardless of pressures or threats.

NOSTALGIA AIN'T WHAT IT USED TO BE

The mystique surrounding the Mafia is as old as the organization itself. Back in Palermo, two wildly popular plays about prison life, *The Mafia* and *The Mafioso of Vicaria*, packed Palermo theaters in 1860 and 1863. In Hollywood in 1972, the film *The Godfather*, based on the best-selling novel by Mario Puzo, packed American movie houses. *The Godfather* won the Oscar for Best Picture and spawned a sequel, *The Godfather Part II*, which also was named Best Picture by the motion picture academy. Puzo's book became one of the best-selling novels of all time, now at 22 million copies sold and counting.

MOVE OVER I LOVE LUCY

The Sopranos, a TV series, follows the trials and tribulations of contemporary mobster Tony Soprano and his families—the one in the mob world, and the one at home. If the success of *The Sopranos* is any indication, the Mafia is alive and well—even if mostly in our imaginations. It may not be as powerful as it once was, but the Mafia holds a special, dark, place in both Italian and American history and culture.

Queen Liliuokalani of the Hawaiian Islands was America's first and only queen.

GOODBYE, CRUEL WORLD

*What some famous people had to say just as they
were about to enter death's door.*

John Adams, U.S. president
"Thomas Jefferson… still survives…" (He didn't know that Jefferson had died earlier the same day.)

Ethan Allen, American Revolutionary War general
In response to an attending doctor who attempted to comfort him by saying, "General, I fear the angels are waiting for you."
"Waiting are they? Waiting are they? Well, let 'em wait."

Lady Nancy Astor, English politician and society dame
When she woke briefly during her last illness and found all her family around her bedside: "Am I dying or is this my birthday?"

P. T. Barnum, entrepreneur
"How were the receipts today at Madison Square Garden?"

John Barrymore, actor
"Die? I should say not, dear fellow. No Barrymore would allow such a conventional thing to happen to him."

Napoleon Bonaparte
"Josephine… "

Winston Churchill, British Prime Minister
"I'm bored with it all."

Charles Darwin, scientist
"I am not the least afraid to die."

Amelia Earheart, aviator
In a letter to her husband before her last flight: "Please know that I am quite aware of the hazards. women must try to do things as men have tried." Final radio communication before her disappearance: "KHAQQ calling Itasca. We must be on you, but cannot see you. Gas is running low."

Thomas Alva Edison, inventor extraordinaire
"It is very beautiful over there."

Elizabeth I, Queen of England
"All my possessions for a moment of time."

Benjamin Franklin, American statesman and inventor
"A dying man can do nothing easy."

There is no record of Patrick Henry actually saying, "Give me liberty or give me death."

Ernesto "Che" Guevara, revolutionary
To his executioner: "I know you have come to kill me. Shoot coward, you are only going to kill a man."

Heinrich Heine, poet
"God will pardon me, that's his line of work."

Henry VIII, King of England
"All is lost. Monks, monks, monks!"

Andrew Jackson, U.S. President
"Oh, do not cry—be good children and we will all meet in heaven."

Thomas "Stonewall" Jackson, U.S. Confederate General
"Let us cross over the river and sit in the shade of the trees."

Thomas Jefferson, U.S. president, died July 4, 1826
"Is it the Fourth?"

Louis XIV, King of France
"Why do you weep? Did you think I was immortal?"

Louis XVIII, King of France
"A king should die standing."

Louise, Queen of Prussia
"I am a queen, but I have not the power to move my arms."

Malcolm X, African-American civil rights activist
To the men who shot him: "Let's cool it, brothers… "

Karl Marx, revolutionary
"Go on, get out. Last words are for fools who haven't said enough."

Benito Mussolini, Italian dictator
"Shoot me in the chest and don't make a mess of it!"

Eugene O'Neill, dramatist
"I knew it. Born in a hotel room—and God damn it—died in a hotel room."

Anna Pavlova, ballerina
"Get my swan costume ready."

Pablo Picasso, painter
"Drink to me!"

Pancho Villa, Mexican revolutionary
"Don't let it end like this. Tell them I said something."

Leonardo da Vinci, artist, inventor, Renaissance man
"I have offended God and mankind because my work didn't reach the quality it should have."

Florenz Ziegfeld, showman
"Curtain! Fast music! Light! Ready for the last finale! Great! The show looks good!"

Uncle John's
Bathroom Reader series
—— Order Info ——

Uncle John's **All-Purpose Extra Strength** *Bathroom Reader,*
Copyright © 2000. $16.95

Uncle John's **Absolutely Absorbing** *Bathroom Reader,*
Copyright © 1999. $16.95

Uncle John's **Great Big** *Bathroom Reader,*
Copyright © 1998. $16.95

Uncle John's **Giant 10th Anniversary** *Bathroom Reader,*
Copyright © 1997. $16.95

Uncle John's **Ultimate** *Bathroom Reader (#8),*
Copyright © 1996. $12.95

The **Best of** *Uncle John's Bathroom Reader,*
Our favorites from BRs #1 – #7.
Copyright © 1995. $16.95

Uncle John's **Legendary Lost** *Bathroom Reader,*
BRs #5, #6, & #7 (See page 500)
Copyright © 1999. $18.95

* NOTE: The first four *Bathroom Readers* are published by
St. Martin's Press, New York.

For U.S. bulk orders, wholesale prices, and credit card orders,
dial (800) 284-3580 or fax (800) 499-3822, or go to our website:
www.bathroomreader.com. Or just send a check
or money order (including S & H) to the address below:

U.S. Shipping & Handling rates:
• 1 book (book rate): add $3.50
• 2 – 3 books: add $4.50 • 4 – 5 books: add $5.50
• 5 – 9 books: add $1.00 per book

Bathroom Readers' Press
P.O. Box 1117, Ashland, Oregon 97520
Phone: (541) 488-4642 Fax: (541) 482-6159

If you like reading our books...
try

VISITING THE
BATHROOM
READERS'
INSTITUTE
WEBSITE!

www.unclejohn.com
or
www.bathroomreader.com

- Visit "The Throne Room"—a great place to read!
- Receive our irregular newsletters via email.
- Submit your favorite articles and facts.
- Suggest ideas for future editions.
- Order additional BRI books.
- Become a BRI member.

Go with the Flow!

HYSTERICAL SCHOLARS

Our contributors. Proud members of the
Bathroom Readers' Hysterical Institute.
We couldn't have done it without them.

Christine Ammer

Lee Bienkowski

Allison Bocksruker

Michael Cala

Jennifer Carlisle

Steve Cecil

M. Christian

Wim Coleman

Kent Duryee

Susan Elkin

Diane Forrest

Clay Griffith

Kathryn Grogman

Shelley Johnson

Vickey Kalambakal

Mark Lardas

Jennifer Lee

Christopher Lord

Dennis Love

Cynthia MacGregor

David Scott Marley

Elizabeth McNulty

Art Montague

Tia Nevitt

JoAnn Padgett

Ken Padgett

Paul Paquet

Pat Perrin

Jessica Pierce

John Michael Scalzi, II

Frederick Sherwood

Joyce Slaton

Betty Sleep

Stuart Smoller

Stephanie Spadaccini

Alan Spencer

Susan Steiner

Johanna Stewart

Steve Theunissen

Diana Moes VandeHoef

THE LAST PAGE

FRIENDS, BATHROOM READERS, AND COUNTRYMEN:

We at the Bathroom Readers' Hysterical Society do not take your quest for good and plentiful bathroom reading lightly. We sit firmly and believe that it is your inalienable right to have quality reading material.

So we invite you to take the plunge. Sit down and be counted by joining the Bathroom Readers' Institute. Send a self-addressed, stamped envelope to: BRI, P.O. Box 1117, Ashland, Oregon 97520. Or contact us through our website at: www.bathroomreader.com. You'll receive your attractive free membership card and a copy of the BRI newsletter (sent out irregularly via email), receive discounts when ordering directly through the BRI, and earn a permanent spot on the BRI honor roll!

UNCLE JOHN'S NEXT BATHROOM READERS ARE ALREADY IN THE WORKS! INCLUDING:

Uncle John's #15, **The Biggest & Best Ever**

Uncle John's #15 **Limited Edition (we hope)**,
a special project for members & friends

Uncle John's **Book of Extremely Useful Information**

Uncle John's **Page-a-Day Calendar**

Uncle John's **Mini Book**

Uncle John's **First Australian Edition**

Uncle John's **First U.K. Edition**

The **Little John Series for Young Adults**

Well, we're out of space, and when you've gotta go, you've gotta go. We hope you've enjoyed this book as much as we have. And never forget:

Go with the flow!